Proceedings of the
Ninth International Congress on
Mathematical Education

Proceedings of the
Ninth International Congress on
Mathematical Education

2000 Makuhari Japan

Editors:

Hiroshi Fujita

Yoshihiko Hashimoto

Bernard R. Hodgson

Peng Yee Lee

Stephen Lerman

Toshio Sawada

Distributors for North, Central and South America:
Kluwer Academic Publishers
101 Philip Drive
Assinippi Park
Norwell, Massachusetts 02061 USA
Telephone (781) 871-6600
Fax (781) 681-9045
E-Mail: kluwer@wkap.com

Distributors for all other countries:
Kluwer Academic Publishers Group
Post Office Box 322
3300 AH Dordrecht, THE NETHERLANDS
Telephone 31 786 576 000
Fax 31 786 576 254
E-Mail: services@wkap.nl

 Electronic Services < http://www.wkap.nl>

Library of Congress Cataloging-in-Publication Data

Title: Proceedings of the Ninth International Congress on Mathematical Education
Co-Editors: Hiroshi Fujita, Yoshihiko Hashimoto, Bernard R. Hodgson, Peng Yee Lee,
         Stephen Lerman, Toshio Sawada
ISBN HB: 1-4020-8093-X
ISBN PB: 1-4020-7902-8
ISBN E-book: 1-4020-7910-9

A C.I.P. Catalogue record for this book is available
from the Library of Congress.

Printed on acid-free paper.

Printed in the United States of America.

Contents

Preface

With the attached CD, this book constitutes the Proceedings of the 9th International Congress on Mathematical Education (ICME 9), which was held in Tokyo/Makuhari, Japan, from July 31 to August 6, 2000. There were 2,012 registered participants from 70 countries, who were joined by 239 accompanying persons.

The previous sequence of these quadrennial ICMEs had taken place in Lyon (France), Exeter (United Kingdom), Karlsruhe (Germany), Berkeley (United States of America), Adelaide (Australia), Budapest (Hungary), Quebec (Canada) and Seville (Spain). Thus ICME 9 is the first ICME that was hosted by an Asian country.

The ICMEs are held under the auspices of the International Commission on Mathematical Instruction (ICMI), and on the occasion of ICME 9 the official hosts were Science Council of Japan and Japan Society of Mathematical Education. To execute actual jobs of organization, the official sponsors set up a National Organizing Committee (NOC) for ICME 9 in cooperation with Mathematics Education Society and Association of Mathematical Instruction, and with scientific assistance rendered by Mathematical Society of Japan, Japan Society for Industrial and Applied Mathematics, and other academic societies related with mathematics education. During the four years of preparation, members of the NOC and those of its subcommittees worked with devotion and feeling of honor to be involved in organization of this exceptional event in mathematical education, ICME 9.

As on previous ICMEs, the Executive Committee of ICMI set up an International Program Committee (IPC) for ICME 9 who was responsible for making the major scientific planning of the Congress. In positive appreciation of the main trends and achievements of recent ICMEs, the IPC decided that the general pattern used at Seville would be followed, while some innovative amendments and new measures were to be introduced, as mentioned by the IPC Chair in his greeting at the opening ceremony. For instance, Working Groups and Topic Groups kept their important positions in the program, while they were re-defined and re-named as Working Groups for Action and Topic Study Groups. There were 13 WGA and 23 TSG. As in recent ICMEs, the International Round Table was a plenary activity but at this time it was realized with distance speakers.

The IPC also invited four distinguished plenary speakers, fifty-two speakers to present regular lectures of 45-minutes on a large range of issues and matters, four national presentations (France, Italy, Japan, Malaysia) and reports from current ICMI studies, and from ICMI Affiliated Study Groups (PME, HPM, IOWME, WFNMC). As for organization of each of WGA or TSG, a Chief Organizer (CO: in many cases, two equivalent Co-COs), two or three Associated Organizers (AO) and a Local Assistant Organizer (LAO) were invited to form the Organizing Team of the group. Among the invited special meetings, there was Forum of All Chinese Math Educators to celebrate the first coming of ICME to Asia.

As a whole, the IPC structured a rich and extensive scientific program to keep traditional value of meeting in face-to-face groups and of exchanging through individual contacts, and thus intended to encourage presentation as well as learning over various aspects of mathematics education: its researches, experiences, materials, information, etc. with special emphasis on achievements and trends that arose in mathematics education during the years 1996-2000 and that would contribute much to mathematics education in the new century. A number of components of the program were designed hopefully to link the scientific spirit and human wisdom for harmony on the cultural backgrounds from the East and the West, and from the North and the South,

Furthermore, all participants were invited to submit proposals for short presentation in the form of a poster, videotape or sample software. Qualified short presentations, 368 in number, were accepted and displayed. A booklet of their abstracts was distributed to all participants and visits to displays to hear the authors' comments were arranged. Non-commercial and commercial exhibitions attracted participants by including a selection of curriculum development projects, and materials from academic institutions, and also advanced products from companies.

The participants literally relaxed in Happy Hours, which included Bon-dancing, and enjoyed the Congress Tour Day, some courses of which included Japanese school visits and some others included sightseeing in famous places as Nikko, Mt. Fuji etc.

The activities of ICME 9 took place in Nippon Convention Center (NCC) , which is an international convention complex located in the core of Makuhari, and in Chiba Institute of Technology (CIT) neighboring Makuhari.

The book part of these Proceedings of ICME 9 includes, in its main body ,the address by the ICMI President and remarks by the ICMI Secretary, a record of International Round Table, the 4 Plenary Lectures, abstracts of the 52 Regular Lectures, and a summary report on each of Working Groups for Action and of Topic Study Groups. Brief reports on the ICMI Studies, the ICMI Affiliated Study Groups and the Chinese Forum are also included. On the other hand, the CD part of these Proceedings contains, in addition to files for the whole content of the book part, vivid scenes of the ceremonies and the IRT, full texts of regular lectures if available, and some scientific animation etc.

The editors wish that these Proceedings reflect the activities and atmosphere of the Congress, and can give an overview of the whole Congress, even to those who participated actively in some sections of the program, while many important sessions of their interest took place in parallel.

Lastly but not least, the editors want to thank all the people who provided reports for these Proceedings and would like to thank once more to all participants of ICME 9 who contributed to the success on the Congress, and hope that in spite of a delay of publication these Proceedings should be still useful and inspiring to the participants of ICME 9 and other people who are concerned with Mathematics Education in the 21st century.

Hiroshi Fujita

May 2003

On behalf of Editors:
Hiroshi Fujita
Yoshihiko Hashimoto
Bernard Hodgson
Peng Yee Lee
Stephaen Lerman
Toshio Sawada

Local Editors:
Toshiakira Fujii
Nobuhiko Nohda
Izumi Nishitani
Katsuhiko Shimizu
Yoshinori Shimizu

Presidential Address at the Opening Ceremony of ICME

Hyman Bass
University of Michigan, USA
President of ICMI

President Yoshikawa,
President Sugiyama,
Chairman Fujita,
Secretary Sawada,
Guests and Participants of the Ninth International Congress on Mathematical Education.

As the incoming President of the International Commission on Mathematical Instruction, it is my honor and privilege to welcome you to this important Congress, and to express the appreciation of all participants for the generous efforts of our Japanese hosts. Particular thanks are due to the International Program Committee, chaired by Professor Fujita, and the National Organizing Committee, chaired by Professor Sugiyama together with its Secretary, Professor Sawada, for their major organizational work, and to the Science Council of Japan, led by Rector Yoshikawa, for its generous support of the Congress.

This Congress represents two important and underdeveloped kinds of linkage. They are symbolized in the very name of the Congress. One is the strong connection between mathematics education on the one hand, and mathematics as a discipline on the other. The other is the international character of the Congress, which creates opportunities for building cross-cultural linkages among people concerned with educational practice and scholarship.

Mathematics as a discipline has a long history, emerging from many cultures. It is truly international, even universal, in character. Mathematicians throughout the world have a fundamentally common understanding of the nature of mathematics and of its central problems and methods. Research mathematicians working on a mathematical problem, be they in Africa, Asia, Australia, Europe, or the Americas, are part of a cohesive intellectual community that communicates fluently. Though mathematics is an enabling discipline for the other sciences, it has a theoretical core whose interest does not reside solely in these applications.

Mathematics education, in contrast, has a variable and culturally based character. This is certainly true of educational organization and practice. Education is conditioned by social goals and educational organization that vary widely in different countries. Educational research is both an applied social science and a multidisciplinary domain of theoretical scholarship. And it too is culturally influenced. So the international assemblage of educational practitioners and researchers at this congress is much more extraordinary and significant than the corresponding gatherings of mathematicians at the International Congresses of Mathematics.

Among organizations devoted to mathematics education, the International Commission on Mathematical Instruction (ICMI), the sponsoring organization of this Congress, is distinctive because of its close organizational and structural ties to the mathematics research community. One expression of this is that ICMI has historically been presided over by research mathematicians, including such figures as Felix Klein, Hans Freudenthal, and Marshall Stone. As strong and fruitful as this tie has been, it does not imply an automatically healthy and symbiotic relationship between the mathematics and mathematics education professional communities. Indeed, the great challenges now facing mathematics education around the world demand a much deeper and more sensitive involvement of disciplinary mathematicians than we now have, both in the work of educational improvement and in research on the nature of teaching and learning. There are many things that have impeded such boundary crossing and collaboration, such as the need to reconcile language, epistemology, norms of evidence, and, in general, all of the intellectual and attitudinal challenges that face multidisciplinary research and development. ICME 9 brings together people who know and understand different things, to learn from each other, and hopefully to foster collaboration.

Let me conclude with some observations about the central place of mathematics in the school curriculum. Along with language, mathematics has always been at the core of education in all civilized societies. Today the study of mathematics occupies many students for the entire twelve years or more of their public schooling. This preeminent place of mathematical study is being seriously questioned in some quarters. It places hard and exacting demands on students. Other subjects, in the social as well as natural sciences, are making claims for a larger share of the curricular territory. Much of the skill traditionally conveyed by the study of mathematics is now considered by some people to be made obsolete because of the presence of modern computational technology.

Most people I know in mathematics and in mathematics education, myself included, feel deeply that this is a misguided and retrograde tendency. Yet we are challenged to articulate a compelling case for maintaining, and even strengthening, the study of mathematics in the schools. The traditional rationale has been a mixture of pragmatic, economic, social, intellectual, and cultural reasons. Pragmatic to learn the basic skills of arithmetic and of measurement, and the rudimentary geometric concepts and figures. Economic because of the quantitative literacy demanded by the rapidly evolving technological workplace. Social to provide the resources for responsible citizenship in a modern democracy. Intellectual since mathematics is the enabling discipline for all of science, and it offers fundamental tools of analysis, quantitative expression, and disciplined reasoning. Cultural because mathematics exposes students to some of the most subtle and sublime achievements of the human spirit.

Yet people can still question whether these arguments suffice to justify so many years of mathematical study. Who today will be doing significant arithmetic without a calculator? How many people will ever have occasion as adults to solve a quadratic equation? Even engineers have no need to prove that their mathematical methods work. Why are our cultural arguments for the study of mathematics so different from those advocating the study of ancient languages and history?

I believe that these questions have compelling answers. But the answers must be framed in new ways, and grounded in new conceptions of what a contemporary mathematics curriculum and learning goals must look like. Articulating that new rationale for the study of mathematics in the schools, and a correspondingly new conceptualization of what such study should look like, is an important challenge to all of us. Perhaps the participants at this congress can give some thought to this question.

With that, it is now my privilege, on behalf of the International Commission on Mathematical Instruction, to join with Secretary Sawada in declaring open this Ninth International Congress on Mathematical Education.

TIME-TABLE OF ICME-9

As of June 23, 2000

	July 30 (Sun)	July 31 (Mon)	August 1 (Tue)	August 2 (Wed)	August 3 (Thu)	August 4 (Fri)	August 5 (Sat)	August 6 (Sun)
8:30								
9:00		Registration	RL (1)	RL (3)		RL (5)	PL (3)	Reports on WGAs
10:00		Opening Ceremony				10:00		10:10
11:00	REGISTRATION		RL (2)	RL (4)		10:30 Short Presentations (1)	10:45 RL (6)	10:40 PL (4)
12:00		IRT			CONGRESS TOURS	11:30	11:45	11:40 / 11:50 Closing Ceremony
13:00			Break	Break		Break	Break	
		Break						
14:00						14:00 Short Presentations (2)		
15:00		PL (1)	WGA (1)	WGA (2)		15:00	WGA (3)	
16:00						15:30 ICMI Studies (1) ICMI A.S.G.		
		PL (2)				16:30	WGA (EX)	
17:00			TSG (1)	TSG (2)		17:00 ICMI Studies (2) ICMI A.S.G.		
18:00		Attraction				18:00 ICMI GA		
19:00			ICMI A.S.G.	ICMI A.S.G.				
		Welcome Cocktail				19:30		
20:00			Happy Hour	Happy Hour		Happy Hour	Happy Hour	

ICME 9

International Round Table: The Role of Mathematics in General Education for the 21st Century.

Abstract.

This is a record of the proceedings of International Round Table at ICME 9. Issues like technology, preparation of teachers, and others were discussed, and views given. The speakers identified some current issues of great concern. Furthermore, they offered their views on future trends.

1. Introduction

The twenty first century is often designated as the century of technology. The idea of having an online International Round Table (IRT) with distance speakers was mooted many years ago. It was realized only at the Ninth International Congress on Mathematical Education (ICME 9) in Tokyo. The event, as the first programme on the first day of the Congress, was to create public awareness and to draw attention to the latest happenings in mathematics education. It was also a display of what technology is capable of. The event took place simultaneously on three different sites, namely, Tokyo in Japan, Washington in the United States, and Singapore, via a teleconference system.

The three distance speakers were Dr Akito Arima of Japan, Dr Bruce Alberts of the United States, and Mr Wee Heng Tin of Singapore. They are all prominent members of the society, heavily involved in shaping educational policy in their respective countries, and also the implementation of such policy. In addition, there were three panel members at the Makuhari conference site. They were Akihiro Nozaki of Japan, Gilah Leder of Australia, and Hyman Bass of the United States. They are academics from the institutes of higher learning of their respective countries. The IRT was chaired by Lee Peng Yee of Singapore.

First, the distance speakers were invited to share their views, vision, and wisdom on education in their own countries. After the distance speakers had set the scene, the panel members at the conference site were asked to react to a series of questions posed by the chair. At the end of the discussion, distance speakers came back to give their responses. Then the IRT was concluded by a final remark given by one of the panel members. The proceedings lasted for one and a half hours.

In the following sections, we shall give the details of the presentation of distance speakers, their responses, and the discussion session of the panel members. The details will be presented in the order as they were delivered. In a few lines here we describe some of the background leading to the selection of the topics to be discussed at the IRT.

The teaching of Euclidean geometry lasted for more than two thousand years. Calculus was often regarded as the next milestone in mathematics education in the west after Euclidean geometry. It was taught in universities and later in schools in many countries for over two hundred years. However an active use of information technology in mathematics education is barely twenty years. Such is the time scale of change. In the new century, we see the globalization of commerce. We see the growth of service industry. We see the advances of information technology. Consequently, our society becomes more and more knowledge-based. Education is not only to gain knowledge but also to acquire applications of such knowledge. We train our students for workplace. We make demand on standards of syllabuses. We ask for paradigm shift in teacher preparation. Against such background we ask the question: what can we or should we do in mathematics education in order to meet the challenge of the new century?

2. Presentation of Distance Speakers

Three distance speakers gave their views on what happened concerning education and in particular mathematics education in their respective countries. They identified issues of great concern in their countries, looking at them from the speakers' perspective. Dr Akito Arima was not able to be present in person. His presentation was given in video.

2.1. Uniformity versus Diversity.

Dr Akito Arima was formerly the Minister for Education and the President of the University of Tokyo, Japan. He would like to see greater diversity in educating the young in Japan while preserving the uniformity. He began his presentation by emphasizing the importance of mathematics in education. Then he carried on to say:

"Japanese students have been ranked very high in the first International Mathematics and Science Study, the second study (in 1981), the third study (in 1995), and the third-repeat study (in 1999). Furthermore, I learned that the score for the 1999 test was almost the same as that in the 1995 test. Similar questions were used in these two tests. I would like to comment on the International Mathematics and Science Study, and I hope that the study will continue in future." An interesting observation is that many highly ranked countries (or regions) like Chinese Taipei, Singapore, Korea, Japan, and Hong Kong SAR are those which only recently became developed countries (or regions) after many years being developing countries (or regions). On the other hand, many developed countries such as the

3

United States, United Kingdom, France and Germany are ranked average. I believe this fact reflects the need for diversity of education in schools in the countries of the first group, where education and schools in these countries have much in common. On the other hand, in the advanced countries, school education has greater diversity and individuality. They probably need slightly more uniformity. The question is where Japanese mathematics education should be directed. Uniformity or diversity? I myself want to see the high average level being maintained and at the same time want to encourage more individuality, especially creativity, among the students in Japan."

"The role of mathematics teachers is extremely important in all countries in the world. I hope that you (the participants of the Congress) will find better ways in training mathematics teachers. Many children dislike mathematics and science in Japan, Korea, and Chinese Taipei, although they are highly ranked in the international study mentioned above. I do ask you to find ways to attract students to mathematics by using modern techniques of teaching. I hope that this congress succeeds in the exchange of ideas and produces fruitful results."

2.2. Thinking Schools Learning Nation

Mr Wee Heng Tin is the Director-General of Education, Ministry of Education, Singapore. He elaborated on the new initiatives introduced into schools by his ministry under the banner of Thinking Schools Learning Nation. He started by stating his belief that "education must embrace change". Then he observed that the 21st century celebrates "the  triumph of the individual", and went on to explain the change that took place. He said:

"Back in the early 1980s, we embarked on a move to stream our students based on their abilities. It was a hotly debated issue then, and it still is. However, results have shown that this has worked for us. More students are getting into institutions of higher learning, more are staying longer in school and more are achieving better academic results. For those not academically inclined, streaming has helped them to acquire basic literacy and numeracy skills learned at their own pace. They are adequately prepared to take advantage of vocational courses offered at post-secondary institutions. We are pleased that the practice of streaming has reduced educational wastage. Streaming, as we do it, is a crude form of mass customization."

"But we certainly can do more to fine-tune our system. Within the broad categories of streams, there are students who exhibit exceptional talents and abilities in certain areas. It is the responsibility of the school and teacher to help each child

4

discover that ability and develop it to the maximum. We call this the ability-driven paradigm for education. We want each child to excel according to his own talents and abilities. And to excel does not mean to outdo everyone else. To excel is to be the best that one can be, and to do the best that one can do."

"How do we achieve this? How do we get our schools, our teachers to do this? For a start, we must recognize the uniqueness of each school and each student. While the Ministry may set broad directions and goals, it must allow schools enough flexibility in the implementation. While the Ministry can produce a common national curriculum, it must allow schools to teach it in accordance with their respective needs. And while the Ministry sets high expectations, it does not demand uniform attainment. The Ministry will continue to define the desired outcomes and boundaries that should be observed. Schools, however, will use their best judgement to formulate strategies to cater to their own needs. Schools have been given a great deal of autonomy over the past few years to make decisions on key issues such as programme implementation and deployment of resources. While we have one vision, we allow and encourage different approaches."

Then Mr Wee talked about "riding the technological wave". He said:

"The fast pace of change in technology and its impact on society is a new development that we cannot ignore. It is not only fast, it is also pervasive. Many homes now have access to the internet. In Singapore, the latest survey shows that 40% of all households have internet access, and this is set to increase. The internet is a great equalizer. It allows small companies with limited resources to provide services without incurring high costs. It allows organizations in remote places to have a world audience as long as they are able to establish an internet presence and market their products well. However, the internet technology can also be a great divider, widening the gap between the haves and have-nots and creating what is now commonly called the digital divide."

"We recognize the importance of the information revolution. It will change the way services are provided, including education. Our comprehensive IT master plan for education launched 3 years ago, aims to prepare our students for a future dominated by high-speed cross-border communication and a high demand for IT literacy. From teacher-training in the use of IT for teaching and learning to the provision of hardware and software; from assisting teachers to own computers to ensuring that there are enough computers in every school, we have equipped all our schools to embrace IT. Every school is now networked and connected to the internet. We want to make sure that every child leaves school with the advantage of having learned how to use information technology for learning and for work."

Finally, he gave "a notion of life-long learners". He said:

"Technology has quickened the pace of change. While we are still learning to cope with the information revolution, the recent development in life science has already taken the world by storm. What we learn and consider as strategic importance today may not be as important and relevant tomorrow. There will never be any shortage of ideas as to what more we can teach in our school curriculum. The real challenge for us is to be selective and not overload our curriculum with too much content knowledge, but to teach our students how to acquire knowledge, think critically and creatively. The thinking programme we introduced shifted the focus of learning from concentrating on the product to placing greater emphasis on the process. Education and learning can take place any time anywhere and should continue through life."

"The school environment is important for the cultivation of such habits. If we want students to think critically and creatively, take risks and cultivate a habit of life-long learning and improvement, then the very institution must be seen to embrace this ideal. We encourage our schools to constantly look for ways to improve and innovate, and reward them for being innovative. Our vision of "Thinking Schools, Learning Nation" captures our desire to promote this culture not only in our schools but also as a nation. We are beginning to see schools develop their own unique identities and niche areas."

"To round off, let me add that we have a quality teaching force. The initiatives would have remained on the drawing board if not for the committed school leaders and teachers who understand the rationale of the initiatives and translate them into school programmes and activities."

2.3. National Standards et al.

Dr Bruce Alberts is the President of the National Academy of Science, USA. He highlighted the recent publication of National Education Standards and said that it could be a starting point for raising the level of achievement for students in US. His presentation follows.

"As President Clinton (US) and Prime Minister Mori (Japan) have indicated, mathematics and science are becoming increasingly important in our world, a world that changes daily through advances in technology. This importance will only grow in this new century.

All of these advances depend on people who understand, and can use, both the quantitative thinking and the language skills provided by a sound education in mathematics and science. These are global issues, and the ICME 9 plays a very important role in bringing together educators from across the world to share their knowledge."

"The United States is a large and diverse country with a tradition of local community responsibility for education. It is nevertheless important for us to articulate a national vision of the type and level of mathematics and science education that the students in our schools should be offered. The US National Council of Teachers of Mathematics launched this attempt to create a national vision in 1989 when it published its National Standards for Mathematics Education. The second edition of these Standards, called Principles and Standards for School Mathematics, was just released a few months ago."

"The counterpart in science is the National Science Education Standards, a 250-page report produced by the National Academy of Sciences in 1996. These are voluntary standards. Both documents represent massive efforts, in which thousands of people were involved. The Science Standards took us four years and involved 18,000 people. I believe that this was the most difficult report that our organization has ever tried to produce."

"Both sets of US Standards share a vision of mathematics and science as exciting and empowering subjects, which are connected to children's lives. Both promote a teaching practice that conveys those qualities? hands-on problem solving and inquiry-based learning, taking advantage of children's natural curiosity about the world. The focus is on teaching young people how to learn on their own, and on giving them the tools and the self-confidence they need to succeed."

"All of this means that we must do a much better job of supporting and educating teachers. Teachers need to be prepared to use the best research-based knowledge about how children learn, and to engage all of their students in challenging and meaningful mathematics and science lessons. In fact, one of the most active areas of the current effort in the US is a major rethinking of how we prepare our teachers: it is increasingly clear that all of these efforts require that teachers be much more effectively educated and supported for the crucial work that they do."

"Our standards documents are a good starting point for discussion about public education in the US. It is clear that there is much that we in the US need to learn from other countries. The results of TIMSS exams were a shock to our nation. The analyses that were part of TIMSS have already given us valuable insights from the successful practices of others. And we hope to learn more from meetings such as this Congress."

"Finally, our effort to improve mathematics and science education will succeed only if those of us in universities change the traditional notion that the education of young people is somebody else's business! Instead, we need to involve everyone in the work ahead? mathematicians and scientists, those who use mathematics and science at all levels ? from kindergarten to graduate schools."

"As an example, I was a university science professor for most of my professional career, carrying out teaching and research over the course of 30 years. In my own teaching, I was setting the example of what science education should be like. If I only lectured about the facts, and did not challenge my own students through inquiry-based lessons and laboratories, how could I expect those teaching at lower levels to change the way that they define science teaching? If I paid no attention to the science teachers in the lower schools in my city, who else would provide them with the connections they need to real science to inspire their children to learn?"

"In conclusion, a high priority for the US is to raise the level of achievement for all of the students in our nation through an intensified focus on getting education right. Thank you for your help in making this happen."

The link between Tokyo and the US was temporarily disconnected when Dr Bruce Alberts was about to speak. While the chair was trying to amend the mishap, the connection was resumed though with sound only at times. It was perfect afterwards. It showed that technology however advanced has its hazardous aspect.

3. Panel Discussion

Distance speakers touched on the general issues. Panel members addressed the particulars. Six issues were raised and discussed. The discussion will be presented in the dialogue form that follows.

3.1. Technology

Chair: "How has the introduction of technology affected instruction and curriculum? What are we doing and what should we be doing?"

Akihiro Nozaki: "I like to mention the negative side of information technology in education. In my view, one strong point of the modern technology is the power of visualization. It can draw pupils' attention easily and strongly, much more than books and calculators can do. However, there are some dangerous aspects of this power. For instance, I saw some students who were satisfied with operating computers and getting outputs, without understanding the meaning of the outputs. Some were happy just by downloading a lot of junk information, without understanding the contents. Sometimes I wonder whether these students understand the meaning of the word to understand. On the other hand, the power of visualization when applied to game-playing software is far more interesting than ordinary educational software. When we discuss technology in education, we should keep these points in mind."

Gilah Leder: "I too am somewhat ambivalent about the role of technology. It allows us to explore inside the classroom different problems and issues in meaningful and exciting ways. It is both an equalizer and a contributor to the digital divide? a divide which can be seen within a country and across countries. Technology inside the classroom can result in a shift in power balance, with students being more knowledgeable and more comfortable with this medium than their teachers. Professional development for teachers is often insufficient. If we are to embrace technology optimally, we must make sure that teachers inside the classroom have the same opportunity to play, to learn and to get excited about technology as our students."

Hyman Bass: "In many ways as in all environments, technology has given opportunity for networking with people in remote places, and access to almost limitless sources of information. Within mathematical instruction calculators and computers have made available enormous rapid computational capacity, both numerical and symbolic, and powerful tools for geometric representation and visualization of mathematical structures. But this capacity is not automatically accompanied by intelligent or judicious use. Technology affords tools of great power and potential. But their appropriate use must be based on understanding and judgement, things requiring much more than an instruction manual. In some ways the proper use of technology requires deeper understanding of the underlying mathematical structure."

3.2. The Third International Mathematics and Science Study (TIMSS)

Chair: "What is the impact of TIMSS? How do we look at it?"

Akihiro Nozaki: "First, it is a good benchmark, which supplied us a lot of information. For instance, we learned from TIMSS that Japanese pupils were very strong in calculation, but rather poor in reasoning. So we Japanese teachers have to emphasize conceptual understanding and logical mind, instead of dry memorization of mathematical formulas and mechanical skill of computation. I think this is what Dr Arima is actually trying to realize. Secondly, TIMSS is not a sole measure. We know that USA is very strong in the research level mathematics, although their TIMSS score is not very high. The measurement of mathematics in higher education could be another interesting topic."

Gilah Leder: "I want to concentrate on aspects other than student achievement. This aspect of the TIMSS study has dominated debate. There is a lot of other useful information that is given far less

9

attention. For example, we can compare the amount of time spent on mathematics in different countries, and possibly use these data to advantage to argue for a solid time allocation to mathematics in our own school curriculum; we can compare different conventions, for example, whether elementary school students should be exposed to different teachers each year, or whether the teacher should move up to the next grade with her students, so that she works with the same group of students for a number of years. (Another example is the video tape study, which offered brief glimpses of the way mathematics is taught in three different countries.) The video tape study provided a wealth of information about strategies used inside the classroom, what mathematics is covered and how, issues about class organization, and much more. This study also raised important issues about the conduct of such research."

Hyman Bass: "The main value of TIMSS is that it presents much more than comparative performance of students. It provides massive data and analyses that give us insights into the nature of the educational systems? school organization, curriculum, instructional practice, and student performance? in many countries. This helps each country better understand its own educational system, and how one might try to improve it. For example, in the US TIMSS revealed the so-called "mile wide, inch deep" nature of our curriculum."

3.3. Workplace

Chair: "A current trend is that education should train students for the workplace. Are we doing a good job? What is the role of mathematics? What are the issues involved?"

Gilah Leder: "Arguing for a link between school mathematics and vocational needs is not a new idea. But it depends on how we look at the workplace. Today, more than ever, it is difficult to predict what the workplace is going to look like x years from now. Yes, we must be responsive to the needs of the workplace, but these are not the only criteria (or challenges) for selecting curriculum or instructional strategies. We must also consider mathematics for future living, and for those not able to find employment. We must accept that we live in an era of rapid change and unpredictability. We need to encourage flexibility, problem solving skills? including persistence and a recognition that many problems require more than the 40 minutes or so allocated to one lesson to solve. We need to recognize that jobs are no longer for life; that many will have a number of different positions during their working life. Therefore we should emphasize continuing education. Mathematical knowledge is empowering? within and beyond the workplace."

Hyman Bass: "In the US our schools are not doing a very good job of preparation for the workplace. Many large corporations find that they must invest large sums in remedial education to repair deficiencies in what their new employees bring from their schooling. On the other hand, the rapidly changing nature of the workplace calls for an education that emphasizes thinking, problem solving, and life long learning more than acquisition of a fixed and narrow set of technical skills. This suggests that perhaps there should not be a significant difference in the curriculum of preparation for the workplace, and that for general students."

Akihiro Nozaki: "According to a graduate of the faculty of engineering, his knowledge taught in university became obsolete in three years. We should give students not only the latest knowledge, but also the ability to understand new knowledge and attitude to challenge a new situation, without asking for prescriptions or manual about it."

3.4. Preparation of Primary Teachers

Chair: "How much mathematics should a primary school teacher know? Is there a minimum requirement?"

Hyman Bass: "It is now widely recognized in countries seeking major educational improvement that the primary and most difficult challenge is not the design of new curricula or assessment, but rather the improvement of teachers and teaching. The curriculum is changing, embracing new subject areas and adapting to the influences of technology. Pedagogy has become more sophisticated as we better understand student thinking and learning. All of these things place new demands of understanding and skills on teachers. They must acquire an integrated knowledge of subject matter and of student thinking, and hold this knowledge in ways that are directly useful in practice. In the US we are still experimenting to develop a curriculum for teacher education and development that will give teachers this capacity."

Gilah Leder: "How teachers think about, and approach mathematics, is as important as what they know. They are important models for the students they teach. Do they convey a sense of curiosity? A willingness to learn from their mistakes? A willingness to explore, to find out if they don't know? To recognize when group work might be appropriate, when individual effort is needed?"

"What is missing all too often is this emphasis on how mathematics is approached. Knowing a lot of mathematics without being able to convey the richness and excitement of mathematics does not do our students justice. I would like to add to the cognitive aspect the importance that our primary teachers feel whole-heartedly about mathematics, have a passion for the subject, and we are able to model that to our students."

Akihiro Nozaki: "In my view, we do not need to require primary school teachers to know deep knowledge of mathematics. How to convince pupils the usefulness of mathematics and the reasons to study mathematics is much more important than technical details of higher mathematics."

3.5. Real Life Applications

Chair: "Is it realistic to talk about real life applications at the school level?"

Hyman Bass: "This is a good idea that is often misinterpreted and implemented naively and in counter productive ways. The sound principle is that learning should build on prior knowledge and experience, in particular on real world experience. At the same time, credible real world contexts, if not presented in a kind of caricature, are typically complex, and have many significant features that are unrelated to the learning goals for which one might use them. So the  productive use of real world contexts requires a judicious balance of respect for actual features of the context while not losing focus on the primary learning goals of the lesson."

Gilah Leder: "Whose real life applications do we mean here? Do we pay sufficient attention to, for example, cultural differences within a class, a school, a country? This topic is attracting a lot of attention and will be explored and debated at some length during the ICME conference."

Akihiro Nozaki: "The word "real life application" is quite ambiguous, but it should not be limited to numerical problems, and should cover logical problems. We must teach students how to overcome prejudices and assertions without basis."

3.6. Future

Chair: "What do you think about the future? What are your wishes?"

Gilah Leder: "Children spend much time at school? so this time should be productive, rich and enjoyable. Teachers play an important role in students development (since so much time is spent at school). We need to recognize their central contribution to children's development. I would like to see that teachers be passionate about mathematics and convey this passion to their students."

"The attainment of equity in mathematics is another important goal? far too many students still miss out in many different ways. Technology is able 'to open' many new windows, yet it is likely to exacerbate rather than diminish equity issues. The IRT has offered a unique opportunity for interactions with and between those at vastly different geographic locations. These discussions have highlighted a number of common issues, but generally issues of concern to developed rather than developing countries. We must ensure that the latter group are equal partners as we strive to improve mathematics learning and teaching."

Hyman Bass: "I think of this question in terms of where I see the most need rather than what I most wish for. One of basic needs is a better recognition that the improvement of education and mathematics education requires the development of a larger and serious knowledge base. As far as I can see, much of what we do now is essentially ad hoc experiment. There is a great deal of knowledge that has been gained. But there is much more we have to know than what we now do know."

"The commitment of public resources to improve education often makes a large and impulsive gesture with little knowledge how it is going to work. It meets with predictable failure, and with poor monitoring of why it failed. We go into a cycle of disappointment and often adverse reaction from other communities."

"The discourse surrounding the effort to improve education, it seems to me, lacks sufficient knowledge base to give the rationality that is needed. I would like to see the development of a larger effort in research and in particular the better deployment of intellectual resources needed to support that work. That would involve the commitment of mathematicians and scientists and people from other disciplines. This is going to require re-configuration of the way we organize our universities to address some of these questions."

Akihiro Nozaki: "Now a big change is taking place on education policy in Japan. I really wish its success in embracing the change until ICME 10 in Denmark."

4. Reponses of Distance Speakers

Distance speakers were invited to give their responses to the discussion that took place at the conference site.

4.1. Response from Dr Bruce Alberts

Dr Bruce Alberts re-iterated the support we must give to teachers, and reminded us of the negative and positive aspects of technology. He said:

"Everything we said about teachers and learning implies that we must encourage the very best of our students to become

13

teachers. This is not something we have done traditionally in the US. Teaching is a highly skilled occupation; it is crucially important, but greatly undervalued in the US today."

"How to change this situation is a harder question. One thing we can do rather quickly is to connect mathematics and science teachers to our colleagues--the scientists, mathematicians, and engineers in universities and industry--in partnerships that treat teachers with great respect, support them and listen to their needs, and create a dynamic that is healthy for both sides. In the US today, scientists and engineers are respected and we can use some of our prestige to give teachers high visibility, more support, and more respect. In the long run, we have to change the salary structure. Teaching is a critical endeavor for the future of our society. We simply must do something to value it more at all levels."

"Technology could be a great disaster. It offers many distractions. There is a lot more competition for young people's attention now that they are connected to the Internet. The Internet is not all positive by any means. There is a lot of material on the Web that is useless, wrong, misleading and counterproductive to education. At the same time, the new technology is challenging us to do a better job of exploiting this tool in ways that will attract students back to learning."

"My own feeling is that the easy access to information on the Worldwide Web is a major resource we can use for teaching young people how to search through all the knowledge and learn how to learn on their own. The idea of memorizing masses of information seems ridiculous to me as a scientist. We can go to the Web today and find out quickly information of any kind. The problem is that all of us need to be able to discriminate between what is true and what is false. The ability to do that is something students must learn in schools. I envisage an educational system that recognizes that students 11 years old are already very sophisticated people compared to myself when I was at that age. They are connected with the adult world much more than I ever was. We need to re-invent education so as to make it really relevant to these students. That means fully exploiting what technology can do for schools and preparing teachers to teach using this resource, because it is going to be challenging to teachers and make their jobs even more demanding."

"We have a great deal to learn still about what works and why in education. How we can use technology to make education more meaningful and effective for all children? We need a new kind of scholarship. We need to engage our best minds in this endeavor. The problems are the same in all countries. We can work together round the globe to make this a continuous learning process, based on evidence, through which education becomes a real science."

4.2. Response from Mr Wee Heng Tin

Mr Wee responded on the importance of teachers, the power of technology, and the gems contained in the database of TIMSS. He said:

"The three speakers on the panel represent three different school systems. Having heard all three of them, my sense is that we have more agreement than disagreement about mathematics teaching in schools. We all agree that mathematics must be retained in the school curriculum."

"We also agree that teachers are very important. Whether we have good mathematics teaching hinges on the quality of the teachers, their competence, and enthusiasm about mathematics. Whatever we do in introducing new initiatives, the first person we look at is the teacher. How we can help him or her to implement the initiatives well. It is not just at the point when a teacher joins a teacher training institute that we help him or her. It is the responsibility of the authority and the employer to make sure that the teacher is helped throughout his or her career."

"Another point is about technology. Again we agree that technology will have a part to play in education and, in particular, in mathematics and science education. The issue is whether there will be enough opportunity to make use of technology, and whether there will be access to the technology. Hopefully, the part on equality will be addressed. On technology, I think it is probably value free. Whether we are able to harness the power of technology is really our own doing. Obviously, we need to help our teachers and all of us in education to master the use of technology."

"Notwithstanding that Singapore has done well in TIMSS, I think the point mentioned by Professor Gilah Leder is worth noting. We seem to be so obsessive at the result of TIMSS. In the course of it, we fail to pick up the gems contained in the huge database of TIMSS. We should look more into the database to pick up those important pieces of information to help us to improve teaching of mathematics in schools."

"This huge gathering is a reflection of the important role that mathematicians and mathematics educators play in the development of our society. It is also an affirmation by the world mathematics community of its commitment to provide quality mathematics education for the benefit of mankind."

4.3. A Final Remark

Gilah Leder summed up the feeling of the IRT. She said:

"Making the IRT panel a reality represents a concrete example of international

15

cooperation (there was much done behind the scenes) and showcases technology now available to make it possible. The panel was an ambitious undertaking and showed what real-time, meaningful dialogue at multiple sites could achieve. Many of us have had experience with distance teaching? but not at this ambitious scale. Can? and should? schools of the future have such links? What would we gain and what would we lose?"

"The panel dialogue has revealed the similarity of aims and concerns in the educational systems in developed countries, and in particular with respect to the impact of technology. We have had a taste of uniformity versus diversity within mathematics education. The central role of mathematics teachers has been acknowledged and emphasized. However, the voice of developing countries has been less obvious. So the digital divide has also been reinforced by this exercise."

"The IRT venue raised many issues which warrant debate at greater depth than possible in this setting. Significantly, more questions were raised than answers given. ICME congresses are an excellent venue for further exploration of these and topics not addressed at all by the panel."

5. Conclusion

There are so many issues in mathematics education and we have so little time at the IRT to talk about them. Hence we could only select a few topics of general interest. Also we could not deal with them in depth. However we have at least identified some important issues, and we have expressed some views on what might happen and what we would like to see happen in future.

The issues raised at the IRT are:

* What are the major changes in education and in mathematics education?
* How does technology affect instruction and curriculum?
* What is the impact of TIMSS?
* How should education train students for workplace?
* How much mathematics is sufficient for primary teachers?
* How real could real life applications be?
* What do we look forward to in the 21st century?

The responses are:

* Technology is powerful, and if not used properly is a distraction. Internet is an equalizer and also a divide.
* TIMSS provides rich database which we could use profitably to improve the classroom teaching in mathematics and science.
* In this new age, students should learn beyond immediate need.
* There should be more mathematics thinking for teacher preparation and more working with mathematics for students.
* Education is not just schooling but a life-long learning.

Indeed, there were more questions asked than answered at the International Round Table. Surprisingly or perhaps not so surprisingly, there were more agreements than differences. All speakers saw great potential in the use of technology. All agreed that mathematics education should not be teaching and learning of mathematics alone and that it should also be teaching and learning of mathematical thinking. One message came through clearly at the IRT, that is, we must give continued support to teachers, not just during their initial preparation but also throughout their career. As Mr Wee Heng Tin said aptly, "teachers are the heart and soul of everything we do in education". To end the report let us quote a remark from Gilah Leder that "our often incomplete answers to issues raised, and not raised, (at the IRT) will act as a catalyst for richer and deeper discussion at the conference (ICME 9) and beyond."

Acknowledgement: Thanks are due to Temasek Polytechnic (Singapore), National Academy of Science (USA), and specially NEC (Japan) for their kind assistance in providing the teleconference facilities. Thanks are also due to the teams of technical persons at three different sites, particularly the team in Tokyo led by Ryo Nagaoka.

Plenary Lectures

Goals of Mathematical Education and Methodology of Applied Mathematics

Hiroshi Fujita
Tokai University, Japan

1 Introduction and Summary

The purpose of this paper is to reflect on the nature and methodology of modern applied mathematics in order to associate the result with our efforts for improvement of mathematics education. The view presented here is an outcome of the author's activities (study and experience) in his dual specialty for many years: 45 years of research in functional analysis and its application and 35 years of mathematics education.

1.1 Motivation of the Present Paper

Needless to say, the mathematics education at every school-level should be beneficial to the learners' future for their life and work. The intellectual activities of humankind in the 21st century require mathematical backgrounds than in any century before. Indeed, the level might depend, but every intellectual citizen will need appropriate quantitative literacy, of which mathematical literacy is a core component, because of the accelerated progress of science and technology and because of the IT-driven paradigm change of intellectual and practical activities, which is taking place in many sectors of the society.

As for the motivation to study (or to do) mathematics, the mathematicians and the others are different. Mathematicians do it for its own sake, and any successful mathematics research is self-rewarding. It is no wonder if some mathematicians are indifferent to applications of their result, while philosophical longing and/or aesthetic emotion and/or academic ambition dominantly motivate their study. We wish that the society supports these researches in pure mathematics as a glorious component of human culture, although we believe that recovery of strong ties between mathematics and the outer world will be the key to revive the creativity of mathematics research beyond its apparent stagnation caused by being inward-oriented and by excess ramification.

In contract, most learners who do not make mathematicians study mathematics for its utility and merits. Therefore, when it comes to mathematics education, the purpose of learning mathematics is different from that for potential mathematicians. Obviously, the number of those students who could make good mathematicians is very limited. Years ago, I heard that Dr. Heisuke Hironaka, a famous Japanese mathematician, who was awarded a Fields Prize and is currently working as President of Yamaguchi University, expressed his estimate of the relative frequency of these mathematically gifted students among Japanese senior high-school students as 0.0002 - 0.0003 %. Incidentally, the enrollment ratio to the senior high school in Japan for one age cohort was already 94% when Dr. Hironaka expressed the estimate above. Although these extremely gifted students are treasures of the humankind, they should be located and brought up exceptionally from the view point of education.

Thus almost all students learn mathematics because learning of mathematics will be useful for their further education and for their future career. In other words, usefulness of mathematics for the learners should be a leading criterion in designing and implementing mathematics education, particularly, in the secondary education as well as in the university/college education, graduate programs in pure mathematics being exceptions. Hence we claim that the first target of mathematics education is to let the students acquire capabilities to make use of mathematics and to foster their intellectual power through learning mathematics in order to meet real problems in their life, workplace, and profession.

From this point of view, it is worthwhile to review the nature and methodology of applied mathematics, which is directly or indirectly intended for use of mathematics to solve real problems and to understand the mathematical phenomena in the outer world. Moreover, the role of mathematics in the society and the way to use mathematics are time-dependent. Thus, if we wish that mathematics taught to students is really useful in their future, we must be concerned about this evolution of usage of mathematics and must have a far-reaching vision over applicable mathematics in order to encourage students for learning mathematics. In this connection, all of us have to recognize the overwhelming influence of computers (IT), while we think over mathematics education in our era. From this view-point also, it deserves again to examine the recent trends of applied mathematics, where the impact by relevant progress of computers and other IT devices is evident.

1.2 Plan of the Present Paper

Now let us describe the plan of this paper. In Section 2, the author's cherished assertion, which claims, as the targets of mathematics education, cultivation of mathematical intelligence with double foci on *mathematical literacy* (ML) and *mathematical thinking* ability (MT), will be revisited in the context of our reflection. Section 3 is devoted to review of the nature and methodology of recent applied mathematics, in terms of the three key words: *concepts, methods, objects*. Also we shall mention the desired competence for researchers to do good jobs in applied mathematics, which could offer a helpful hint to design the application-oriented mathematics education. This section also includes a subsection where the role of

20

computers is elaborated for current mathematics, with particular reference to the newly developing field of mathematical sciences, i.e. the field of SEC (Scientific and Engineering Computation). In Section 4 we move to a viewpoint of history of mathematics and observe that the new giant peak of mathematics is arising in the historical scale. It is the peak of *Mathematical Sciences* which follows the three preceding peaks: *Euclidean Geometry, Calculus, Modern Axiomatic Mathematics.* The nature of the new peak will be discussed in comparison with other peaks. Finally, in Section 5, we sketch a recent work of the author's collaborators, which illustrates the methodology mentioned before. The work is concerned with simulation and visualization for nonlinear problems arising from certain pollution phenomena in a sea beach by oil spilled on and driven by seawater, and certain phenomena of a related ecological system which involves a biological purification process by bacteria in the sand layers. The CD-version of this paper include animation to show the result of simulation visually.

1.3   A Remark

We believe in application-oriented strategy for mathematics education, which is beneficial to the learners. It should be materialized in mathematics curricula for science and technology students in universities, and in those for high school students in a properly reduced form. To proceed in this direction, however, the sense of usefulness of mathematical should not be restricted too narrow or too shortsighted as we discuss in some detail in Sections 2 and 3. Moreover, we have a reservation against introduction of real raw problems into classrooms. We sincerely hope that the curriculum designers and school teachers have a reliable knowledge and sound view concerning the trend and methodology of applied mathematics, while topics and problems to be adopted for actual teaching must be cooked with a full educational care in accordance with the students' mathematical and mental preparation. In this connection we quote a saying of the late Professor Kenichi Fukui who was a Nobel Prize winner in chemistry and served as a former President of Council for Educational Curricula of Japanese schools:

The most important subject for those students in the secondary education who intend to become scientists, is definitely Mathematics, and, in particular, Euclidean Geometry. Through the concentrated thinking to search a logically successful path to solve challenging problems in Euclidean Geometry, the youth's "brain" experiences sparks and is enhanced in its power and scale.

2   Objectives of Mathematical Education

In the preceding section, we have asserted that mathematics taught in school must be useful for each learner's future in his/her life, work, profession, and culture. Here we discuss what competence mathematics education should foster in learners, from our viewpoint with an emphasis on the application-oriented strategy for the 21st century. In this connection, let us revisit the author's cherished opinion since around mid-80s, concerning the objectives of mathematics education, which introduces some terminology used in later sections.

Namely, we assert that in the coming information and high-tech society, the purpose of mathematics education is to cultivate the mathematical intelligence of the learners. And the efforts to cultivate the mathematical intelligence of the learners should be pursued with foci on the following mutually non-exclusive components: *fostering mathematical literary* and *enhancing ability of mathematical thinking*.

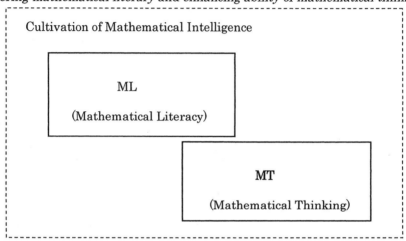

This assertion appears to apply most properly to the secondary education as a philosophical principle and significantly well to the university education in various departments except for mathematics. On the other hand, in the primary education level, the bifurcation between mathematical literacy and mathematical thinking capability in children does not take place yet and the traditional notion of numeracy can be maintained as the target of mathematics education there. Before elaborating on the notions of mathematical literacy and mathematical thinking ability, let us state remarks on their balance and their order in actual teaching and learning.

During recent decades, as the secondary education is expanded, the diversity of students' level in a mathematics class is increased in many countries. In these countries a strong polarization of students into two streams is observed: one stream is the group of students who desire to make high-level preparation in mathematics for their further education and professional career, while the other stream is the group of students (the majority in number) who are bound for specialties or jobs which need less mathematics. In order to meet this diversity of students in class as well as in school, we ought to try to organize and implement mathematics curricula in an appropriate balance which is compatible with the state of students. Skillful teachers of mathematics could make it even with proper adjustment to individual students.

One and the same topic can be dealt with often in either way: for ML or for MT. For example, at the secondary education, descriptive statistics and elementary probability can be dealt with as a part of mathematical literacy, while mathematical thinking may be the focus when analysis of random variables and probability distributions is taught.

Let us note the effect of appropriate ordering of acquisition of ML and MT in a certain iterative manner. Even if a student dislikes systematic or deductive learning of a topic of mathematics, he/she may make a good progress and get interested in the topic via teaching/learning with the focus on mathematical literacy and could eventually acquire a deep understanding by his/her second-round learning toward mathematical thinking. As a matter of fact, it is just traditional to encourage learning certain topics twice. Euclidean geometry is an example (J. Perry [12]): firstly, experiential comprehension by intuition, and then systematic understanding through proof. Another example is calculus: firstly, formal operations and simple applications, then theoretical understanding of theorems and sophisticated applications.

Furthermore, enhanced thinking ability is an important basis for higher mathematical literacy required by further study. Actually, Prof. Fukui's saying quoted in Section 1 can be regarded as a recommendation of enhancing thinking power by intensified learning of geometry at the secondary education, which leads to reliable mathematical preparation, i.e., mathematical literacy for able scientists.

2.1　More on Mathematical Literacy (ML)

The notion of ML as the target of mathematics education was new when the author first proposed it early in 1980s regarding the re-organization of Japanese mathematics curricula, but now the community of mathematics education has accepted the notion internationally. Let us, however, review the meaning here.

Firstly, we do not limit the notion of ML to its narrow sense such that it only refers to an ability to use mathematics as a language in necessary situations. Instead, we will define it as an ability of intelligent use of mathematics with emphasis on concepts, on communication with mathematical certainty and in mathematical terms, on awareness of mathematical facts, and on a global feeling of rigorous mathematical reasoning. Symbolically, it can be described as the user's mathematics to be applied with wisdom by intelligent citizens to be with self-reliance.

Actually, there is some parallelism in the usage of the word literacy between 'computer literacy' and 'mathematical literacy', as computer literacy usually means combination of both fundamental ability to operate computers and awareness of usage and function of computers. On the other hand, mathematical literacy is one of main components of quantitative literacy, which includes science literacy and computer literacy and is a popular notion now.

The actual content of ML to foster in school depends on the level of education. If a senior high school student is going to terminate his/her learning of mathematics at graduation, then what the student should acquire as ML is mathematical competence of intellectual citizens, reasonable clues to lifelong learning of mathematics being included. On the other hand, if it is for university students of science and technology, ML that she/he needs will be useful mathematics required by each specialty. For instance, if the student intends to go into physics or computer science, he/she should master some high level mathematical literacy with concepts and methods that are selected from the whole advanced mathematics in a similar level to the one required for students with mathematics major. Furthermore, ML for students bound for civil engineering and architecture should be reliable but could be more practical and computational.

Concerning approaches toward ML in general, we assert that students can acquire ML through more experiential and inductive understanding; namely, its path is not limited to the traditional pattern of definition, theorem and proof. Particularly, under convenient environments and with conscious instructors, this could be achieved effectively by active use of computers and calculators. Furthermore, as mentioned above, it depends on the aptitude and aspiration of students, but the students who have grasped ML through experiential understanding can then climb in a self-motivated way up to the level of systematic and abstract understanding with rigor, which is a quite natural way to enhance MT for them.

2.2   More on Mathematical Thinking Ability (MT)

MT has been traditionally emphasized as an important objective of mathematics education. However, in order to contrast it to ML, we like to describe the notion of MT, particularly, for the secondary education, as

MT = ability to think mathematics deeply in order to acquire understanding of systematic knowledge and in order to strengthen heuristic insights in challenging problems.

In view of the rapid innovation of methodologies in various fields of science and technology, we assert that enhancing MT at the secondary education should not aim at a wide range of knowledge and technical proficiency in mathematics; instead we stress developing a fundamental ability that has potential expansion in students' further study or professional career. By analogy of gymnastics, training of MT in the secondary education is similar to foster basic physical power and fundamental athletic ability rather than trying to attain new records and master specific high-level skills.

Concerning MT at the university level, we could describe it as the thinking power in mathematics toward creative works in each specialty, and practically, an ability to amend or improve or invent mathematical methods when it is required.

3   Methodology of Applied Mathematics

In recent decades, we observed the birth and growth of new fields of applied mathematics brought about by computers. Actually, the development of scientific and engineering computation (SEC in abbr.) has made possible for scientists and engineers to solve various complicated nonlinear problems of large scale and even to create new fields of applied sciences. Actually, some fields of SEC are already flourishing: e.g., simulations for theoretical or manufacturing purposes, mathematical approaches to the material design, mathematical modeling and processing for finance, and mathematical approaches to global problems in climatology, oceanography, and ecological and environmental problems. Some applied mathematicians are now excited to organize mathematics for life science as well as for imaging technology. With these impacts, the whole mathematics appears to be moving toward a new realm of mathematical sciences.

In order to perceive these trends of applied mathematics in a bird-eye view, let us propose to introduce three key words below, regarding the structure of methodology of applied mathematics, which would be suggestive also in our designing of application-oriented mathematics curricula:

Concepts,　　　Methods,　　　Objects.

Actually, when we meet phenomena to study in the light of mathematics or problems to solve with the aid of mathematics concerning certain objects, we start with mathematical modeling of the matter. There, proper concepts must be called for and we formulate the problem into a mathematical model. In carrying out this process, it can happen that some concepts are taken from the outside of mathematics, and that the model is formed with the aid of laws or formulas in the related fields of science. In these cases, a good model is an outcome of the researcher's multi-disciplinary scholarship or his/her tight cooperation with experts of relevant fields. In contrast, formulation of some models in physics and other exact sciences employ concepts from highly advanced mathematics, which reminds us that mathematics is the language of physics and other exact sciences.

The mathematical model thus obtained is analyzed or solved by means of mathematical methods which are chosen by the researcher, sometimes in consideration of computing facilities and cost. The necessary mathematical calculation or computation is carried out, very often with the aid of computers. The choice of suitable methods depends on researchers' scholarship, experience and wisdom. We hear from engineers that in dealing with practical problems for industrial applications, a clever combination of (mathematically) simple methods can yield a good result. This means that a good engineer should have a mastery of mathematical literacy concerning their possible tools. On the other hand, particularly in scientific research, analysis of some new types of models can be possible provided that a new method is introduced by improving exiting methods or by inventing a proper method anew. The mathematical thinking ability of the researcher is called for in these cases.

In this way, analysis by the method is accomplished. The outcome may be a satisfactory success in solution of the problem or may be a failure. In the latter case, we feed the outcome back to the objects and try to improve the model or the method. Thus progress is sometimes advancing and sometimes iterative.

3.1 Preparation for Applied Mathematics

In accordance with the key words introduced above, we can give a structure of mathematical preparations for applied mathematicians in general or for science-technology students who will need high-level mathematical literacy. Here we exemplify this viewpoint, by mentioning the titles of booklets of recent lecture series on applied mathematics published by Iwanami Shoten, Tokyo, for which the author sat in the editorial committee.

Let us begin with *Concepts*. As mentioned above, researchers would have to adopt concepts specific to the problem they are facing, sometimes, on a multi-disciplinary knowledge. As for the fundamental concepts, however, the researchers should have a good mathematical literacy with sound understanding, e.g., concerning the following basic topics:

linear algebra, basic analysis, complex function theory, differential equations (ODE&PDE), functional analysis, vector analysis and manifolds, basic algebra, groups and their representation, algebraic geometry, various geometry, logic and computation, discrete mathematics, probability and stochastic processes, (13 topics).

Secondly, we regard that important *Methods*, which are traditional or innovated, are built on the topics below:

basis of numerical computation, linear computation, numerical solution of differential equations, Fourier-Laplace analysis, asymptotic analysis, inverse problems, optimization, discrete optimization and algorithm, computational algebra and computational geometry, stochastic methods and simulation, statistical methods, (11 topics).

How do individual *Objects* come up, it depends. Here we just pick up some objects in the large, for each of which remarkable progresses have been made in recent decades from the view point of applied mathematics and theoretical sciences:

mathematics of classical physics, mathematics of quantum physics, mathematics of statistical physics, mathematics of solitons, nonlinear mechanics, methods of computational sciences, mathematics of fractals, mathematics of life science, mathematical methods in social sciences, mathematics of systems and control, mathematics of information and coding, methods of information geometry.

Finally, we wish to present another set of key words which symbolize the competence required for successful applied mathematician, and toward which university students of science-technology and high-school students bound for these fields are encouraged to attain: They are

Motivation, Discipline, Wisdom.

Strong motivations are the starting point to do a good work in applied mathematics as well as in all valuable activities of the humankind. Serious disciplines are necessary to be prepared for doing trusted applied mathematics. Wisdom to link the scientific research with real world phenomena, and to choose a method optimally fitted to the purpose, to judge the outcome, and to find next targets must be the highest and most crucial function of the researcher. It is our belief that this competence can be best cultivated in students via a good chain of well-prepared teaching/learning with synthetic problem solving in due stages.

3.2 The Role of Computers for Mathematics

As already mentioned, the influence of computers is prevailing over many sectors of intellectual human activities; it is direct and extensive on applied mathematics. In fact, computers are indispensable means for SEC, which will be exemplified by our use of numerical algorithms and visualization techniques for nonlinear partial differential equations to be presented in the last section.

Generally for this type of problems, the scientific computing through numerical (algorithmic) methods yield the result, while the visualization of the result can convince us of the validity of the result and can inspire our better understanding of the mathematical reality in the objects. In other words, the role of computers is nowadays beyond mere means of solution of problems, and actually it inspires researchers' scientific insight and thus induces further challenges. In this connection, the role of computers in applied mathematics can be fully compared with the role of experiments, say, in physics. In fact, we observe that various kinds of computer simulation are revealing unknown mathematical phenomena, which could give such a crucial push to the progress of mathematics itself just as telescopes gave to astronomy or just as microscopes gave to biology.

In this way, computers and other related IT devices will assist us to recover a link between mathematics and the outer world. Namely, with the aid of these, we, the humankind can recognize new mathematical realities around us and can see the so-far hidden harmony of mathematical structures: those existing in natural phenomena, in human activities and in the challenging global and environmental problems. For mathematics itself, this will be a source of progress and will give birth to rich new fields in this century. Hopefully, by pursuing this way we shall be able to get to a new paradigm of mathematics where the Western scientific spirit and the Oriental wisdom for harmony are well unified.

3.3 Computers and Math Education at University Level

However powerful they may be, computers are tools for human intelligence. Hence, a clever use of computers in mathematics can be realized only with the researcher's profound knowledge and over-all wisdom. This fact must be reminded of, whenever we consider the use of computers and calculators for mathematics education.

The author has his own teaching experience which has convinced him that a proper and timely use of computers is effective for fostering students specialized in analysis at the university level.

It was concerned with the initial-boundary value problems of fundamental partial differential equations. A study via simple simulation by means of computers, which the students carried out in a group of several members, 1) made them more motivated and 2) made them happier by being conscious of their own problems. Moreover, most of the students were able to 3) recover their aspiration toward theoretical study, when they see that the concepts and theories are useful in their actual pursuit of solutions by computers.

4 A Historical View-Point

With intention to project the result on our efforts to design mathematics education in the 21st century, we examine the current trends of mathematics from the historical viewpoint.

It is well known that ancient mathematicians in Arabic counties, China, India and other parts of the world made great contributions. We could, however, count the following three as giant peaks in the history of mathematics, as far as the direct influences on modern mathematics are concerned.

1st peak: Birth of Euclidean Geometry in about 300B.C.
2nd peak: Discovery and Development of Calculus in 17th and 18th centuries.
3rd peak: Rise and Development of Modern Axiomatic Mathematics in 20th century.

It was the late Professor Yukiyosi Kawada who proposed around 1970 that each of these great achievements should be included as a main topic in mathematics curricula for the Japanese secondary education, in some form to match the learners' level, when the wave of New Math movement reached Japan. In fact, Prof.

Kawada's proposal had been realized to a significant extent in the Japanese national mathematics curricula until the curricula were mutilated decades later under the pressure of the nearly saturating enrollment ratio to senior high schools which was coupled with the social tendency inclined exceedingly to the equality/uniformity principle.

Coming back to reflections in the historical scale, and as a main point of this section, we claim that a new peak is now showing up. It is the computer-driven advance of mathematical sciences. In its wide range and its potential depth, the new peak deserves the title of *the fourth giant peak* in the history of mathematics, although it might be better to use the word "a *chain of giant peaks*" instead of the word "a giant peak". In this direction, we believe, mathematics will find its promising way with its own vivid creativity and with recovered links between mathematics and the real world. At this point, however, we note that as to mathematics, the rise of a new big peak does not mean that the former peaks are wiped out, which the very history of mathematics shows. As for mathematics, such a big change takes place, so to say, as sublation (Aufheben) rather than a drastic paradigm shift observed in some fields. The heritages of modern mathematics remain important and will be respected even in the era of mathematical sciences, although its stagnation caused by excess ramification inside and by unconcerned isolation outside must be cured. In this connection let us quote a writing by H. Poincaré[11]:

If I may be allowed to continue my comparison with the fine arts, the pure mathematician who should forget the existence of the exterior world would be like a painter who knew how to harmoniously combine colors and forms, but who lacked models. His creative power would soon be exhausted.

The second point we want to emphasize here in this section is that this new peak, the fourth peak, shares basic features with the second one in the sense that both are characterized by 1) realistic concepts, 2) powerful methods for rich and far-reaching applications, and 3) tight linkages with outer fields and objects. In short, the fourth peak of unified mathematical sciences is outgoing in its character just as the second peak of calculus was. Incidentally, we could point out that the third peak of axiomatic modern mathematics has much in common with the first peak of Euclidean geometry. These observations would give a helpful hint when we wish to have prospects of mathematics and mathematics education in the 21st century.

4.1 Desired Movement for Reform

In consideration of the recent trends of mathematics mentioned above, and also from our belief in the importance of the application-oriented mathematics education, we appeal that an extensive research and movement to build up mathematics education in the 21st century is necessary. We know that various works and serious efforts toward this goal have been already made in many countries, for instance, as reported in the IRT of this congress, especially by the distant speakers, Dr. B.

Alberts from U.S.A and Mr. H. T. Wee from Singapore. We appreciate these works and efforts, but still we want a more coherent movement on a firm philosophical basis for reform/improvement of mathematics education that can be regarded as a counterpart of the Perry Movement around a century ago. In terms of the great peaks in the history of mathematics, we can say that John Perry wanted to innovate mathematics education at that time on his appreciation of the second peak, Calculus, and from his strong emphasis upon the merits and utility of learning mathematics (J. Perry [12], K. Itakura [7], H. Komatsu [9], O. Kota [10]). By the way, J. Perry came to Japan in 1875 at the age of 25 and spent 4 years in Japan to found the initial body of the Faculty of Engineering of the University of Tokyo. It would be natural to recall his assertion at this congress held in Makuhari, Japan.

To be more logical, we recognize a strong similarity between the second peak and the fourth peak which is now arising. Thus we have a reason to call for a counterpart of the Perry Movement, which is duly updated to match the trend of the fourth peak, the mathematical sciences in the 21st century. The movement should aim at the usefulness of mathematics for the learners in the same way as the Perry Movement, which could be attained by means of the double foci strategy of ML and MT, even if there exits a polarization of students' aptitude toward mathematics as mentioned above.

Incidentally, the New Math Movement aimed to innovate mathematics education in the spirit of (mathematicians') appreciation of modern mathematics, i.e., the third peak, although it was boosted by the Sputnik shock. We do not deny that the New Math Movement yielded some positive effects, but it should give the place to the movement intended for the fourth peak, i.e., for mathematical sciences.

5 An Example of Simulation in Applied Analysis

The last part of this paper is devoted to a brief presentation of a typical work of applied analysis, which is carried out along the methodology described in Section 3.

Actually, the study is concerned with pollution caused by oil spilled over the sea surface and driven by sea waves to the sand beach. The movement of the oil patch floating on the sea surface is the first target of our study. Before that, we have to analyze the movement of the seawater which laps the shore and then circulates, partly through the sand layer, back to the sea.

Then at the interface between the liquid and the sand, the adhesion and penetration of oil must be treated mathematically by means of certain interface/boundary conditions, which we call the conditions of friction type. Furthermore, the movement of oil itself must be considered as a non-Newtonian fluid, i.e. as a Bingham fluid, while the movement of the seawater as well as the movement of the air above the sea surface follows the Navier-Stokes equation for

Newtonian fluids. Thus the equations of motion of the related liquids are highly non-linear. Moreover, the sand layer under the beach is a porous media, where its tiny holes are filled with air when the sand is dry, but are filled with water when the sand is wet. When the sand is polluted by oil, the tiny holes are blocked by oil. This nonlinear multi-phase problem involving air-water-oil-sand will be denoted by Oil-Pollution Problem (OP Problem). Then we consider another problem related with the oil pollution, which we call Purification-by-Bacteria Problem (PbyB Problem). There is an interesting observation that certain *bacteria living in sand* are known to *decompose the oil* into water and other harmless chemicals which can be washed away by water. A mathematical analysis of this decomposition process by the bacteria is our second target.

The mathematical model of OP Problem is formed by virtue of the following:

Concepts and laws from physics Flow velocity, pressure, density, phases, laws of fluid motion (Newtonian, Non-Newtonian), laws for flow in a porous media.

Interface conditions Free surface condition, boundary and interface conditions of friction type.

As for PbyB Problem, we have to employ, furthermore, some concepts and empirical laws from biology. The plenary lecture of the congress and hence this paper are not appropriate occasions where we go into the mathematical details of the involved partial differential equations and boundary/interface conditions, which are never trivial theoretically. However, let us show the equations here which form the mathematical model of OP Problem without much explanation.

Conservation of mass

$$\frac{\partial \rho}{\partial t} + \frac{\partial}{\partial x_j}(\rho u_j) = 0, \quad \text{in } \Omega, \ t > 0 \tag{1}$$

Conservation of momentum

$$\rho\left(\frac{\partial u_i}{\partial t} + u_j \frac{\partial u_i}{\partial x_j}\right) + c(\chi_{ws} + \chi_{fs})u_i = -\frac{\partial p}{\partial x_i} + \rho\chi_s g_n \frac{u_j n_j^{(fl)} + k_f \chi^{(b)}}{\sqrt{\left(u_j n_j^{(fl)} + k_f \chi^{(b)}\right)^2 + \varepsilon_g^2}}(\nabla \chi_{fl})_i$$

$$+ \rho\chi_s \frac{g_T}{\sqrt{2}} \frac{u_j(\Sigma\chi_{fl})_j}{\sqrt{\left(u_j(Z\chi_{fl})_j\right)^2 + \varepsilon_g^2}}(\Sigma\chi_{fl})_i + \rho\chi_s \frac{g_T}{\sqrt{2}} \frac{u_j(T\chi_{fl})_j}{\sqrt{\left(u_j(T\chi_{fl})_j\right)^2 + \varepsilon_g^2}}(T\chi_{fl})_i$$

$$+ \frac{\partial}{\partial x_j}\left\{\left[\mu_{air}\chi_{air} + \mu_{wt}\chi_{wt} + \left(\mu_f + \frac{\eta}{\sqrt{4D_\pi + \varepsilon_b^2}}\right)\chi_{fl}\right]\left(\frac{\partial u_i}{\partial x_j} + \frac{\partial u_j}{\partial x_i}\right)\right\} + \rho K_i$$

$$- (k_f + k_w)\chi^{(b)}\triangle\chi_{fs} \cdot n_i^{(fs)} \qquad \text{in } \Omega, \ t > 0, \tag{2}$$

Free surface of air

$$\frac{\partial \chi^{(wf)}}{\partial t} + u_j \frac{\partial \chi^{(wf)}}{\partial x_j} = 0 \quad \text{in } \Omega, \ t > 0. \tag{3}$$

Free surface of oil

$$\frac{\partial \chi^{(fl)}}{\partial t} + u_j^{(fs)} \frac{\partial \chi^{(fl)}}{\partial x_j} = k_f \cdot \left|\nabla \chi^{(fs)}\right| \chi^{(b)} \quad \text{in } \Omega, \ t > 0, \tag{4}$$

···, ···,   and so on.

By a glance of these equations, one is convinced that solution is only possible by means of numerical methods with the aid of computers. Moreover, in order to recognize the result of the time-evolution of the system, with some feeling of reality and intuition, it is necessary to visualize it.

In fact, near the end of delivery of this plenary lecture, we showed some typical parts of result through a video animation (silent with the duration about 10 minutes). The animation was not so spectacular and did not cover the entire problem in the full scale. Still it served to convince the audience about the effect of the methodology of modern applied mathematics. Some of the essential parts of the

32

video animation is now included with a slight modification in this CD version of the present paper, as is explained in the following subsection.

5.1 The Result in Animation

The video animation is concerned with OP Problem as well as with PbyB. At this point, we note that the scientific computation and visualization of this study has been done mostly by my colleagues, Prof. H. Kawarada of Chiba University and his assistant, Dr. H. Suito ([8]), while I joined them to establish the theoretical basis of the study in regard to the boundary/interface conditions of friction type ([6]).

Concerning OP Problem, the files for animation which visualizes the result of simulation of the time-dependent phenomena are the following two written on the CD: Oil_Amoving.mpg and Oil_Bmoving.mpg. And the file for PbyB Problem is Decomp_moving.mpg.

The spatial domain of analysis for OP Problem is divided into time-dependent sub-domains as shown by the image-picture below:

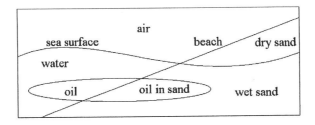

In the animation, these sub-domains are colored as follows.

Ω_a :   filled by air and colored in gray,

Ω_w :   filled by sea water and colored in blue,

Ω_f :   filled by oil and colored in black,

Ω_{as} :   filled by dry sand and colored in orange,

Ω_{ws} : filled by wet sand and colored in brown,

Ω_{fs} : filled by oil penetrating into sand

again colored in black.

This subdivision is illustrated here by a few frames of the animation.

Figure 1 : OPP frame 1

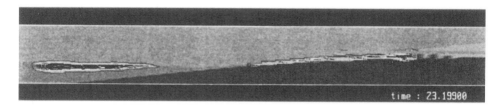

Figure 2 : OPP frame 2

The peripheral zone of the oil patches which is colored in green stands for the viscous zone regarding the Bingham model for oil.

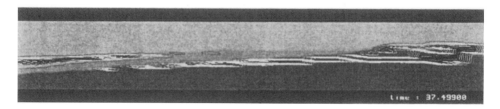

Figure 3 : OPP frame 3

The animation Oil_Bmoving is a zooming up with focus near the beach of the animation Oil_Amoving.

The spatial domain of analysis for PbyB is divided into three Sub-domains: air-filled domain in light blue, oil-filled domain in dark vermilion, and water-filled domain in dark blue.

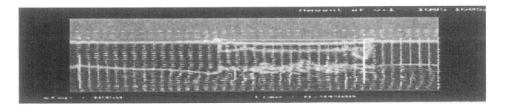

Figure 4:PbyBP frame

The bacteria are assumed to live around the narrow patch of the oil shown in the frame above and their function of purification decomposes oil into water and thus make the oil patch shrink more.

We wish you to find the animation suggestive and enjoyable, and conclude this paper.

References
[1] H. Fujita: The present state and a proposed reform of mathematical education at senior secondary level in Japan, *J. Sci. Educ. Japan*, vol.9 (1985), pp. 39-52.
[2] H. Fujita: The present state and current problems of mathematics education at the senior secondary level in Japan, *Development in School Mathematics Education around the World*, vol.1, NCTM and UCSMP, 1987, pp. 191-224.
[3] H. Fujita, T. Miwa and J. Becker: The reform of mathematics education at the upper secondary school (USS) level in Japan, *Development in School Mathematics Education around the World*, vol.2, NCTM and UCSMP, 1991, pp. 31-52.
[4] H. Fujita: Principles in organizing the university mathematics curriculum for scientists and engineers, *Proc. SEACME-6*, 1993, Surabaya, Indonesia, pp. 1-11.
[5] H. Fujita: High Lights and Shadows of Current Japanese National Curriculum of Mathematics for Secondary Schools, *8th International Congress on Mathematical Education. Selected Lectures*, S.A.E.M. Thales, 1998, pp. 181-193.
[6] H. Fujita: Non-stationary Stokes flows under leak boundary conditions of friction type, *J. Computing Math.*, vol.19 (2001), pp. 1-8.
[7] The Life of John Perry (1) -- (4) (in Japanese), *Pleasure of Mathematics* (Sugaku no tanoshimi, Nihonhyoronsha), No.20 (2000) pp.111-119, No. 21 (2000) pp. 90-108, No.22 (2000) pp. 110-119, No.23 (2001) pp. 91-101.

[8] H. Kawarada, H. Fuita, H. Suito: Wave motion breaking upon the shore, *Recent Developments in Domain Decomposition Methods and Flow Problems*, Gakuto International Series, Mathematical Sciences and Applications, 1998 vol.11, pp. 145-159.

[9] H. Komatsu: Why is Mathematics at the Center of Education? (in Japanese) *Mathematical Education, Science University of Tokyo*, vol. 43 (2001) No.1, pp. 176-203.

[10] Kota: John Perry and Mathematics Education in Japan (in Japanese), *RIMS Kokyuroku, Kyoto University*, No. 1195 (2001), pp. 191 - 206.

[11] H. Poincaré: *La Valeur de la Science*, Flammarion, 1905, English Translation by G. B. Halsted: The Value of Science in *The Foundations of Science*, Science Press, 1929.

[12] J. Perry: *The Teaching of Mathematics*, Mcmillan, 1902.

Key Issues and Trends in Research on Mathematical Education

Mogens Niss
Roskilde University, Denmark

. Introduction

Mathematics education as a research field is no longer in what Geoffrey Howson in he proceedings of ICME-2 (Howson, 1973) called 'the formative years', i.e. a 'child' r a 'teenager', but a 'young adult' whose development, character and achievements an now be considered and discussed. However, even though our field has reached a irst stage of maturity, it is definitely not marked by coherence and unity, let alone uniformity, but by considerable complexity and diversification in perspectives and aradigms. Against this background it is not a trivial matter for a single individual o set out to identify and discuss key issues and trends in research on mathematical ducation. In fact, the more I indulged in preparing this talk, the more I have been orced to realise how impossible the task is. First of all, any attempt to deal with *the* ssues and trends, in an exhaustive way, rather than with *some* issues and trends, is leemed to failure. Therefore, focal points have to be determined, choices have to be nade, constraints have to be faced, all of which will, inevitably, reflect the imitations, tastes and biases of the person who is silly enough to embark on such a launting endeavour. In other words, the deliberations I am going to submit to the reader's consideration will be of a fairly personal nature. However, it is not my orimary intention to act as a critic, rather as a cartographer or an anthropologist. I shall, however, at the end of this paper, express some personal views of the future levelopment in of our field.

A final remark before take off. In line with other researchers (e.g. Cronbach & Suppes, 1969, and Kilpatrick, 1992, and others), I adopt, here, a fairly inclusive and oragmatic definition of the term 'research' by taking it to mean *disciplined enquiry*, .e.,questions are asked and answers are sought by means of some methodology, the specific nature if which is not predetermined. Below, different types of disciplined enquiry concerning mathematical education are identified.

I. Focal questions and approaches

In attempting to identify, describe and discuss issues and trends in research on mathematical education, a number of different foci appear to be relevant to the analysis. The following **focal questions**, among others, lend themselves to such an analysis.

*What are the prevalent general **issues** and the specific **questions** that are posed and studied in research?

*What are the **objects** and the **phenomena** which are typically subjected to investigation?

*What are the predominant **research methods** adopted by researchers to deal with the questions they pose? What can be said about to the foundations, ranges, strengths, and weaknesses of these methods?

*What kinds of **results** are obtained in research, and what sorts of scope do they typically have?

*What are the current and emerging **problems** and **challenges** regarding research on mathematical education that we have to face?

All of these focal questions can be considered from a *static*, a *kinematic* or a *dynamic* perspective. A static perspective attempts to look at the state of affairs at a given point in time in order to produce a snapshot of this state. In contrast, a kinematic perspective tries to provide a description of how the state of affairs has changed over a certain period of time, whereas a dynamic perspective endeavours to uncover the forces and mechanisms that are responsible for the changes detected.

Furthermore, the issues can be viewed from either a descriptive perspective ("what *is* (the case?)") or a normative perspective ("what *ought* to be (the case)?") (Niss, 1999). It is worth emphasising that both perspectives can be pursued in an analytic manner.

The approach I have adopted to deal with aspects of the first four foci combines a dynamic and a descriptive perspective, whereas the last focus automatically implies some form of a normative perspective. The analysis will be based on sample observations obtained from probing into research journals, ICME proceedings and other research publications from the last third of the 20th century and, of course, on my general knowledge and perceptions of our field.

III. General issues and research questions, objects and phenoma of study

An overarching characteristic of the development of mathematical education as a research domain is the gradual widening of its field of vision to encompass more and more educational levels. In the beginning, the objects and phenomena of study primarily referred to school mathematics (primary school throughout the 20th century, secondary school since the 60's) but soon aspects of post-secondary education were addressed as well. Teacher education and pre-school education gained momentum in the 70's and 80's, as did tertiary education in general (in the 80's and 90's). Today, undergraduate education for mathematics majors is a growing item on the research agendas all over the world. To my knowledge higher graduate education has not yet been included but that might well happen in a not too distant future. Non-tertiary mathematical education for adults returning to education, e.g. early school leavers, has been an expanding area of interest during the 90's. This widening of the scope of research to encompass virtually all kinds of mathematical education is, above all, a reflection of the fact that mathematical education at any level is being provided to a steadily increasing group of recipients. 'Mathematics for all' could be a slogan for this development.

When it comes to the objects and phenomena studied in research, mathematics educators in the 1960's and 70's were predominantly preoccupied with the mathematical **curriculum** and with ways of **teaching** it (for a similar observation, see Kilpatrick, 1992, p. 22). This was in continuation of the prevalent preoccupation in the first part of the century. Traditionally, the underlying, often implicit, issues were to identify, structure, sequence and organise 'the right content' and to devise and implement 'the right mode of presentation': What topics should be included, on what conceptual basis, and in what order? What should the teacher do, and when? What tasks and activities for students should be orchestrated? What properties should textbooks have? And what is the role of technical aids for teaching? Questions such as these, though seldom formulately explicitly in the publications, can often without too much difficulty be detected as the ones which actually drove the deliberations. Until the mid-70's, in many publications the term 'curriculum' was given a fairly narrow meaning, namely that of 'syllabus', in which only the issue of mathematical content is on the agenda. During the 70's, 'curriculum' gradually gained a much wider meaning, encompassing also aims, teaching approaches and assessment modes.

One manifestation of the preoccupation with curriculum issues in general is the series *New trends in mathematics teaching* that was prepared under the auspices of ICMI and published by UNESCO. These publications attempted to identify and describe curriculum trends throughout the world. For instance, Vol. III, which appeared in 1973 (UNESCO, 1973, edited by Howard Fehr and Maurice Glaymann), looked at the situation in primary school mathematics as a whole, whereas, for post-primary education, the focus was on mathematical topics, such as algebra, geometry, probability and statistics, analysis, logic, and applications of mathematics. Besides, there were chapters on 'trends in methods and media', on 'evaluation', and on 'research'. Also Vol. IV (UNESCO, 1979, edited by Bent Christiansen and Hans-Georg Steiner) spent the first five chapters on depicting curriculum trends at all educational levels. In addition to international trends, national or local trends were described in hosts of papers outlining the situation in a given country or in particular schools, most certainly meant to simply serve as a source of factual information and inspiration for people in other places. Papers on national and international trends are particularly plentiful in times of worldwide reform movements such as the emergence and dissemination of the 'New (or Modern) Mathematics'. Thus the first volume (UNESCO, 1980) in UNESCO's series *Studies in mathematics education* (established by Edward Jacobsen as the editor-in-chief, while Robert Morris edited the individual volumes) was devoted to national presentations of the situation in Hungary, Indonesia, Japan, The Philippines, The Soviet Union, and Tanzania, and more were published in the second volume (UNESCO, 1981) on the Arab States and the USA. It should be stressed that although the interest in curriculum issues and trends was particularly manifest in the 60's and 70's, this interest has never really vanished. This can be seen in the ICMEs, this one included, which have always had well-attended sessions dealing with curriculum issues at various levels, in response to the continued widespread interest amongst participants in learning about new developments and exchanging experiences and views.

Every so often mathematics educators have cultivated a deep interest in the 'sub-curriculum' of a specific mathematical topic. This can be seen, for instance, in the papers from the 'Conference on the Teaching of Geometry', Carbondale, Ill, USA, March 1970, published in *Educational Studies in Mathematics* in Volumes 3 and 4 (1971). Papers include 'n-Gons' (Bachmann, 1971), 'Geometrical Activities for Upper Elementary School' (Engel, 1971), 'The Teaching of Geometry - Present Problems and Future Aims' (Fletcher, 1971), 'Topology in the High School' (Hilton, 1971), 'Geometric Algebra for the High School Programme' (Levi, 1971), 'The Geometry Relevant to Modern Education' (Menger, 1971), 'The Introduction of Metric by the Use of Conics' (Pickert, 1971), 'The Position of Geometry in Mathematical Education' (Revuz, 1971), 'The Geometry and Algebra of Reflections (and 2x2 Matrices)' (Room, 1971), 'A Foundation of Euclidean Geometry by Means of Congruence Mappings' (Steiner, 1971), 'Learning and Teaching Axiomatic Geometry' (Stone, 1971), 'A Logical Approach to the Teaching of Geometry at the Secondary Level' (Villa, 1971). It appears already from the titles of these papers that discussions were centrered around the role and position of geometry in the curriculum, the choice of basic approach and of which content to present to students, and the way to structure it once it has been chosen. Quite a few of the papers can actually be seen as (potential) textbook sections under the motto 'look how this can be done!'. It is characteristic of all the papers mentioned that the focus is on mathematical subject matter and that the deliberations, if any, offered with regard to teaching are predominantly of a theoretical nature, only empirical to the extent that they draw on authors' general observations and experiences with students and teaching. Besides, some of the approaches proposed had been used (successfully, we are told) by the author in his own teaching. So, the predominant objects of study in these papers are of a mathematical nature and are situated in the realm of (potential) teaching. A few papers from the conference took slightly different perspectives, however. Robert Davis in 'The Problem of Relating Mathematics to the Possibilities and Needs of Schools and Children' (Davis, 1971), insisted on the importance of real schools and real children, in addition to mathematics (geometry), and discussed issues of teaching and cognition while illustrating his points by interview episodes with young children. And Hans Freudenthal, in 'Geometry Between the Devil and the Deep See' (Freudenthal, 1971), offered an essay on the nature of geometry and on how mathematics is (not) learned.

Interests in fundamental particular topics gain momentum and fade away, gain momentum again, and so forth in waves. Geometry is a topic that enters the agenda every now and then. Thus a recent ICMI Study, 'Perspectives on the Teaching of Geometry for the 21st Century', was published in 1998 (Mammana & Villani, 1998). That study, however, was certainly not confined to considering curriculum issues only.

As soon as discussions on matters pertaining to curricula become non-technical and non-rhetorical they will inevitably involve issues of the goals and aims that should guide the selection of subject matter and the organisation of teaching, and the more specific objectives to be pursued. So, in the 70's and early 80's **goals**, **aims** and **objectives** became objects of debate and investigation: What should they be? And why? And what are their interrelations? Clearly, these questions touch upon the ultimate ends and the very purposes, roles and functions of mathematical education for different groups of recipients and hence implicate value-laden perceptions of society and culture. It follows that research in this category tends to include strong normative components. In *New trends...III* (UNESCO, 1973), for instance, goals were briefly touched upon from a combination of descriptive and normative perspectives, in terms of objectives to be pursued in the teaching of various topics, e.g. geometry, probability and statistics, logic etc. The common pattern is that these topics should be studied for three reasons: Their significance to the application of mathematics in other subjects and fields of practice, their role in relation to the world at large, and their position and function in a unified mathematics curriculum. Overarching goals were discussed in the chapters on 'applications in mathematics' and, in greater depth, in the chapter on 'trends in methods and media used in teaching mathematics'. The emphasis given to identifying and discussing goals of mathematical education was increased during the 70's. Thus a chapter on 'overall goals and objectives' (D'Ambrosio, 1979) was included in *New trends ...IV* (UNESCO, 1979), in addition to being paid attention to in the other chapters of that publication, and the second volume (1981) in the UNESCO's *Studies in mathematics education* series was mainly devoted to considering goals of mathematical education from a variety of perspectives. A few years ago, I attempted to provide a conceptual and historical analysis of aspects of goals of mathematics teaching (Niss, 1996).

One thing is to write papers for journals and books and to hold scholarly meetings to consider what the goals, content and organisation of mathematics curricula are, and perhaps reach agreement on what they ought to be. It is quite another thing to implement such ideas in the reality of the classroom. This often requires change that is not so easy to bring about because of obstacles present in various places in the educational system, e.g. with curriculum authorities, with teachers, or with society's stakeholders in education like, for instance, employers and parents. This fact gave rise to an interest, since the mid 70's, in **mathematics curriculum** development, as such, which in turn implied consideration of a spectrum of societal and institutional matters. A major chapter in *New Trends...IV* (Howson, 1979), 'A critical analysis of curriculum development in mathematical education' was devoted to examining these questions in quite a detail, by considering the meaning of curriculum development (including the forces that can initiate such development), identifying agencies, strategies, and difficulties for curriculum development, and by examing the role of the teacher (and of in-service education) and the transfer of materials and know-how.

The agencies and agents of curriculum development are different in different countries at different times. In some countries teachers are protagonists in the design and development of the mathematics curriculum, sometimes even as what Clarke et al. (1996) call 'the curriculum maker'. In any country, however, the teacher plays a key role in the acceptance and implementation of the curriculum, whether or not that role is of an official and formal nature. If we remember that many mathematics educators are involved in pre- or in-service teacher education, it is only natural that issues related to the education and profession of **mathematics teachers** have been included in research agendas since the 70's.

It goes without saying that the luggage teachers are (to be) equipped with in order to exert their profession has always been a major issue in teacher training. In the past this issue was seen as boiling down to the issue of the pre-service - and in times of reform also in-service - *curricula*. In that way the discussion was parallel to the one concerning students' curricula. What knowledge should the teacher of mathematics have, and how should it be organised and sequenced? How to strike a balance between pre-service and in-service training? (see, e.g. Scandura, 1971) During the 70's it became clear, however, that matters other than the mathematics the teacher knows and the methods courses (s)he has taken are no less important to his or her functioning as a teacher. Not only was it no longer possible to pack the teacher's mathematical suitcase once and for all, whence it was necessary to prepare the teacher for acquiring new knowledge, the role of the teacher in the classroom changed dramatically from one of transmitting a well-defined syllabus in well-established ways, to one requiring the teacher to orchestrate a variety of activities for the class as a whole and for students individually or in small groups, so as to allow for independent student work to explore situations, make discoveries, deal with problem solving and much more. The more multi-faceted the teacher's job becomes, the greater is the impact of that job on the mathematical education of the students, in particular when the teacher is required to not just deliver a message but also to look into and after the learning of his/her students. These matters were studied already by the two groups which at ICME-2 (1972, see Howson, 1973) considered 'the initial training of primary school teachers' and of 'secondary school teachers', respectively.

Piling up demands on the teacher is not much of a research task in itself, but systematic reflection on the nature and conditions of the profession of mathematics teacher is. It seeems that Ed Begle's paper 'Teacher Knowledge and Student Achievements in Algebra' (Begle, 1972) inaugurated the study of such issues. At ICME-3, the section on the theme of teacher education agreed on recommending to the Executive Committee of ICMI that 'the education and professional life of mathematics teachers' should be accorded a permanent place in all future ICMEs. A paper of exactly this title, written by Michael Otte and collaborators, in *New trends ...IV* (Otte, 1979) was one of the first to offer a framework for the conceptualisation and study of this theme. Since then this theme has indeed been on the agenda of all ICMEs - which was already markedly visible at ICME-4 - and in many other places. Two volumes in *Studies in mathematics education* were devoted to 'the mathematical education of primary school teachers' (Vol. 3) (UNESCO, 1984) and 'the education of secondary school teachers of mathematics' (Vol. 4) (UNESCO, 1985).

A fairly early paper to study teachers' conceptions of mathematics and mathematics teaching was published by Alba Thompson in *Educational Studies in Mathematics* (Thompson, 1984) (a previous seminal dissertation by G.B. Shirk, 1972, remained unpublished). The generic question raised in this paper and in several subsequent studies could be phrased as follows 'what is the impact of teachers' perceptions of mathematics and its teaching on their actual teaching and ultimately on their students' learning?' For such questions to be answered it is a primary (and non-trivial) task to uncover teachers' actual perceptions and beliefs, to study their classroom practices, and to look into the possible outcomes of both for the students. From the mid-80's perspectives widened to encompass also studies of the profession of mathematics teacher, and the teacher as researcher. Today, matters pertinent to all aspects of the education, profession and belief systems of mathematics teachers constitute a vigorous and flourishing area of research (as is reflected in several chapters in *Handbook of Research on Mathematics Teaching and Learning* (Grouws, 1992) and in *International Handbook of Mathematics Education* (Bishop et al., 1996)). The National Council of Teachers of Mathematics, in the USA, devoted its 1994 Yearbook to the professional development of mathematics teachers (Aichele, 1994).

As outlined above, the field of mathematics education originated in an interest in curriculum design and teaching methods. Although research on mathematical education really gained momentum in the 70's, throughout the 20th century there has always been some amount of research, primarily in the USA, that was preoccupied with studying the teaching of arithmetic. As a consequence of the curriculum changes in the 60's and onwards and of the broadening of the spectrum of recipients of mathematical education, it became increasingly important to examine the effects and outcomes of the new curricula and new approaches to teaching. Thus studies in which an innovative curriculum or teaching approach was compared with a 'traditional' one became commonplace in the 70's, and have remained so ever since even if the meaning of 'innovative' and 'traditional' as well as the basis for comparison have changed over time. For instance, the use of teaching aids, ranging from concrete materials and audio-visual media in the 60's and 70's, through handheld calculators and educational software such as LOGO in the 70's and 80's, to computerbased high-powered information and communication technology in the 80's and 90's, became immediate objects of interest as soon as they were available. The overarching question guiding all such studies are (and remain): 'What are the effects, and what can be achieved in terms of desirable learning outcomes, of adopting such and such an approach?'. The May 2000 issue (Vol. 31, No. 3) of *Journal for Research in Mathematics Education* contains two papers (Fuson et al., 2000, and Huntley et al., 2000) that compare students' outcomes of two so-called Standards-based curricula (and textbooks) with the outcomes of 'traditional' curricula.

Now, the classical way of trying to answer questions regarding the effects of mathematics teaching and learning is to study student achievement on tasks. During the 70's this led to a rapidly growing interest in students' reponses to tasks, in the patterns of *errors* displayed in the responses and the underlying *misconceptions*, and in the problems researchers had in fully understanding and interpreting these patterns. If errors are not haphazard but occur in patterns that stem from misconceptions, what do these misconceptions consist in and, more importantly, what are their origins and geneses? Classical papers along this line were published by Erlwanger (Erlwanger, 1975 a & b). As mathematical education was provided to new and growing groups in society it became important to cater for categories of students that, in the past, were mostly neglected or dismissed. However, it soon became clear that despite the development and implementation of new curricula and new approaches to teaching, large groups of students seemed to continually experience severe problems at learning and benefitting from the mathematics taught to them. Apparently, improving the delivery of mathematics was not sufficient for progress. Similarly, at higher educational levels, experiences showed that students had substantial difficulties in grasping fundamental ideas and conceptions in mathematics, like, for instance, understanding not only the methods of *proof and proving* but also the very notion of a proof - why was that? The interest in looking into such questions consituted one line of development leading to today's formidable interest in *students' learning* of mathematics, a line which can be seen as a continuation of the classical huge body of research on errors and misconceptions in the learning of arithmetic. Carried a little further this interest soon removed the prefix 'mis-' and arrived at a general interest in students' conceptions, formation of concepts, and beliefs and the backgrounds to these.

Another line of development leading to that interest came from the emphasis on new curricular goals and aims that gave priority to *understanding* over reproduction of facts and procedures and focused on *problem solving*, pure and applied, as the incarnation of what mathematical competence is all about. Here, students' conceptualisation of problems, and the strategies they employ to solve them, were the main objects of attention. This began in the late 70's, had its heydays in the 80's, but never left the agenda ever since.

Finally, as mathematics education in the 60's and 70's was much influenced by cognitive and educational psychology as represented by the Genève school (Piaget, and his collaborators), the Harvard school (Bruner, Dienès), and the Soviet school of psychology (Krutetskii, Vygotsky), all of which focused on the individual or social conditions for learning, that influence, which also gave rise to the establishement of the PME after ICMEs 2 and 3, was a third, and rather permanent, factor behind the growing interest in the learning of mathematics.

The result was a whole new field of research into students' actual **cognition** and learning processes, and the products thereof, at any educational level. Gaining serious momentum in the 80's, research on the learning of mathematics soon expanded its scope of interest to encompass all aspects of mathematical concept formation, problem solving behaviours and strategies, cognitive schemata, sense making, affective and attitudinal characteristics, and so forth with students. The generic question is: 'What happens/can happen in, to and with the individual student in his/her attempt to learn and to do mathematics, and what are the underlying causes?'. Since the 80's it has become increasingly clear that one important determinant for students' learning processes is the context in which the mathematics is embedded. Very different types of learning result if 'the same' mathematics is activated in different contexts (e.g. of application) or situations (Boaler, 1993 & 1998, Verschaffel & De Corte, 1997, Verschaffel, De Corte & Vierstrate, 1999). In the 90's, research on students' notions and beliefs with respect to mathematics, and factors that influence them were added to the agenda (see e.g. Pehkonen & Torner, 1996). One such factor, already encountered above, is the notions and beliefs that teachers hold towards mathematics as a subject and towards its teaching and learning. Today, research on cognition and learning of mathematics is undoubtedly the predominant type of research in the discipline of mathematics education, so much so that different schools of tought have emerged that hold different theories of the constituents of mathematical learning.

Studies of learning and its conditions did not stop at the level of the individual student. The teaching of mathematics usually takes place in classrooms, and involves activities on the part of the teacher and the students, interaction between the teacher and some or all of the students, and intra-class interaction amongst students themselves. Hence studies of the **mathematics classroom**, in particular as regards its communication and sociology, became prevalent since the 80's. A seminal paper in this direction is Bauersfeld's 'Hidden Dimensions in the So-Called Reality of a Mathematics Classoom' (Bauersfeld, 1980), in which he identifies four such dimensions said to 'represent weak areas of research': Teaching and learning of mathematics are realised and receive meaning through human interaction, take place in institutions, exert influence on a distinctive part of the student's life including the development of his/her personality, and is characterised by an immense complexity that needs to be substantially reduced yet paid due respect to. Since the 80's Brousseau has studied what he calls 'didactical situations' and 'the didactical contract' (Brousseau, 1990) in the classroom and Voigt and others have investigated the micro-sociology of the classroom. So, classroom studies have flourished in the 80's and 90's and still new aspects were given emphasis, in particular language and communication, as reflected in Pimm's *Speaking Mathematically: Communication in Mathematics Classrooms* (Pimm, 1987) and in a recent book coming out of ICME-7, *Language and Communication in the Mathematics Classroom* (Steinbring et al., 1998).

But why stop research into factors that influence learning at the level of the classroom or the institution? After all, students (and teachers) live in societies with socio-economic, technological, political and cultural characteristics, they belong to gender, social and perhaps ethnic subgroups, they speak languages, they are subject to habits, traditions, etc., all of which act as boundary conditions, or preconditions, for their encounter with mathematical education. This, too, then has given rise to a growing and rich body of research, intiated in the late 70's and early 80's, on the **gender, social, cultural** and linguistic influences on the teaching and learning of mathematics. Pioneering work in these domains has been done by (amongst several others) Fennema and Leder (on gender) since the late 70's, by Damerow, Howson, Keitel, Mellin-Olsen, and Skovsmose (on social and societal issues) since the mid-70's, by D'Ambrosio, Ascher and Ascher, Bishop, and Gerdes (on aspects of culture), by Clements, Ellerton, Cocking & Mestre and Secada (on language) in the 80's and 90's, The so-called *ethno-mathematics* has its origin in such issues. Another aspect is *cross-cultural* studies that compare, say, students' achievement, problem solving strategies, or mathematics anxiety across a number of countries, e.g. Asian countries and the USA, or Germany and the UK, and try to uncover culture specific mechanisms that can explain possible differences. The research components of the huge international *comparison projects* undertaken by IEA (TIMSS) and OECD (PISA) represent extensions of this interest. A forthcoming ICMI study will investigate the differences and similarities between the East Asian and the Western perspectives and traditions of mathematical education.

However, not all mathematical experiences are gained from the school or from the classroom. Some are gained from and embedded in people's everyday lives in society and culture, mostly without carrying any label with explicit reference to mathematics. The sorts of learning of mathematics which are shaped in such environments have become subject of increasing research interest during the last

46

couple decades, sometimes under the heading of **everyday mathematics**, situated learning etc. This research, inaugurated by researchers such as Carraher, Lave, Nunes, Saxe, and Schliemann in the mid-80's, has shown that there is no general isomorphism, let alone identity, between learning generated as part of formal education and learning originating in everyday life.

One particular factor which resides at several places in the educational system at the same time, from the individual learner to society at large, and has a formidable impact on teaching and learning is assessment. While **assessment** did not attract much research interest with mathematics educators a couple of decades ago (but did so amongst psychometricians), this situation changed in the late 80's when mathematics educators began to study assessment in mathematics education inside and outside of the classroom. The generic questions here are 'how do established assessment modes influence the teaching and learning of mathematics', which is mostly descriptive, and 'how can we devise and implement assessment modes that correspond to the goals we want mathematics education to pursue?', which evidently invokes strong normative perspectives.

Nearly all the research issues and objects mentioned above have been of a general nature, pertaining to mathematics at large. Needless to say, each of them can be specialised in numerous ways to particular mathematical features, competencies or topics, such as symbolism and formalism, problem solving, applications and modeling, proof and proving, algebra, geometry, calculus and analysis, probability and statistic, and so forth, as well as to specific educational levels. However, as such specialisation goes far beyond the scope of this paper I shall abstain from pursuing it any further.

It appears from this outline that most of the current research issues and questions, objects and phenomena of study had, in large part, actually been identified and posed already by the end of the 70's. Although our field has certainly moved since then, by reclaiming new land and by further cultivating old ones, were are, I would submit, pretty much in a steady state situation as far as the issues and phenomena considered in research are concerned. The questions posed today and the objects and phenomena they address are of the same kinds as the ones considered a quarter of a century ago. In the next section we shall examine whether the same holds for research methods and results.

IV. Research methods and types of results

The **results** obtained in mathematics education research are of varying types as are the **methods** employed to obtain them.

Some research consists in the **raising of concerns or issues**, founded on reasoning, and the outcomes of such research are the points made in order to attract the attention of the research community, and the reasoning underpinning these points. Generally speaking, results of this type are arrived at by combining impressions and observations originating in experience, for instance from practice, with controlled reflection on them. It is worth mentioning that parts of the experience referred to may very well concern existing literature in the field. This method, which we might call **controlled experiential reflection**, involves a continual, intricate, and adaptive ping-pong (with several balls in play simultaneously!) between looking at the section of mathematical education with which one is familiar and thinking about it. As long as mathematics education research has been with us this sort of research has been prevalent. In fact, a considerable body of research in our field is of this type (for example, the aforementioned paper by Bauersfeld (1980) falls under this category). It was the predominant form of research thirty years ago, but many mathematics educators do not accept it as research, because it does not comply with the standards of classical empirical research. From the 80's and onwards it has had a pretty 'bad press', and labels like 'anecdotal evidence' and 'impressionistic opinionating' have been used to characterise it. The adolescence of mathematics education as a research discipline has largely been associated with getting rid of this type of work. Yet, if you'll allow me a normative remark here, such work is the salt of our field. The raising of issues and concerns obtained by controlled experiential reflection constitutes the main feeding source and stimulus for all significant research in our field. It is from such work that the intriguing research questions are derived, and it is by considering how well we are able to deal with important concerns and issues that we should gauge the progress we are making.

Other research leads to analysing or putting forward notions, **distinctions**, or **terms**, sometimes amalgamated into **concepts**, or further to the establishing of entire hierarchical networks of concepts, **conceptual theories**. Vinner and Hershkowitz (1980), at PME-4, introduced the distinction between 'concept definition' and 'concept image' thus coining the terms that are used to date. A seminal paper by Balacheff (Balacheff, 1980) offers several distinctions and terms of significance to understanding and classifying students' work on proofs. The work by Douady (1991), Dubinsky (1991), Sfard (1991) and Sfard & Linchevski (1994), and Tall (1991), and others, have introduced the notion of process-object duality of mathematical concepts, and proposed terms to grasp aspects of this duality (tool-object, encapsulation, procept, reification). An example of a conceptual theory is Chevallard's theory of 'didactical transposition' in which he puts forward a conceptual formalisation of the relationship between mathematics as a discipline and mathematics as an educational subject (Chevallard, 1985). Again, the basis of the methodology - which we might name **conceptual analysis** - for this type of research is controlled experiential reflection, but a strong component of systematic logico-philosophical analysis is added. Sometimes such analysis is purely theoretical, sometimes it is employed to organise empirical observations.

A major body of research leads to **empirical findings** of objects, phenomena properties, relationships, and classifications. By definition empirical findings result from seeking empirical answers to questions, except that the questions need not always be explicitly formulated.

Empricial research ranges over a very broad spectrum. Some research consists in finding facts, i.e., *collecting data* by immediate (not to confuse with 'easy') 'tapping' from reality, as is the case, for example, with surveys of the position of mathemics in educational systems, or of curricula, or assessment procedures in different countries, or with educational statistics on, say, enrolment, retention, and graduation rates. Some empirical research consists in **organising and reporting experiences** from one's own or others' real practice, be it everyday or experimental, on the basis of observations and impressions, without the involvement of anything like a controlled experiment. These types of empirical research were rather commonplace in the 60's and 70's. In fact they still are, but nowadays reports about them, because of their often impressionistic and narrative nature, tend not to find their way into prestigious international journals or books. Instead they are published in local or national journals or magazines.

The classical paradigm for empirical research is systematic observation and controlled experimentation. In an often quoted passage from his address at ICME-1, Ed Begle described the role of **systematic observation** in mathematics education research as he saw it: "We need to follow the procedures used by our colleagues in physics, chemistry, biology, etc. in order to build up a theory of mathematics education [...] We need to start with extensive, careful, empirical observations of mathematics teaching and mathematics learning. Any regularities noted in these observations will lead to the formulation of hypotheses. These hypotheses can again be checked against further observations, and refined and sharpened, and so on. To slight either the empirical observations or the theory building would be folly. They must be intertwined at all times." (Begle, 1969, p 242). This quote may well serve to describe the position held by many researchers in our field then and today. Lots of mathematics education research has been carried out according to this paradigm at all times. This is true whether the systematic observation considers 'undisturbed' everyday situations and circumstances not shaped by the researcher, or situations in which some element of organised intervention by the researcher has been introduced, like for instance new teaching materials or approaches, orchestration of particular student activities, administration of tasks, etc., whether the observation focuses on the individual student or teacher, the classroom or subgroups of it, an institution, the educational system in a country, or the educational systems of several countries, or whether it studies student achievements on tasks, classroom communication, student or teacher behaviour at work, and so forth. If we take a random issue of a research journal, e.g. *Journal for Research in Mathematics Education* No. 5 of Vol. 27, November 1996 (published just after ICME-8), three of the five articles (on middle school students' problem posing (Silver & Cai, 1996); elementary students' notion and use of measurement units in an area setting

(Reynolds & Wheatley, 1996); a teacher's cognitions and actions with respect to implementing a function approach to algebra (Haimes, 1996)) ontain major components of reporting the outcomes of systematic observation.

The ultimate epitomization of empirical research, however, is the **controlled experiment**. Here, the archetypical model is the 'clinical experiment' in which a group of patients are given a certain medical treatment, the possible effects of which are examined by comparing certain probe results from the experimental group with corresponding results from a similar group, the control group, which is given a neutral treatment or none at all. By making any effort to ensure the similarity of the two groups prior to the experiment it is hoped that possible differences in the probe results can be ascribed to the different treatments administered to the two groups. Elaborate research designs of this category typically include statistical procedures to eliminate random but insignificant fluctuations and to determine the conclusions. Hence such studies contain a strong quantitative component. The larger the scale of the experiment (in terms of participating patients), the better and more reliable the outcome is considered to be.

The controlled experiment transferred to mathematics education (where the patients are replaced by students and the treatment consists in some novel curriculum, teaching material, teaching approach, student activity, assessment mode and suchlike), was undoubtedly the major means by which, in many mathematics education researchers' opinion, the field should mature into a proper research discipline. Only by demonstrating, in a convincing manner as provided by the controlled experiment, that new ideas really *work*, could they be justified to the outside world. Although this is no longer a predominant position amongst mathematics educators - primarily because there are so many crucial interrelated factors in mathematics education, which can hardly be accounted for in such a research design, that a valid and reliable interpretation of the outcomes of controlled experiments can be extremely difficult - a large but varying proportion of research in our field has been of this type throughout the last three decades. It flourished in the 70's, lost some steam in the 80's and early 90's, but gained momentum again in the late 90's. The two papers (Fuson et al., 2000) and (Huntley et al. 2000) already referred to belong to this category.

But there are other ways to conduct empirical research in mathematics education. Because of the problems already mentioned in validly interpreting the observations resulting from systematic observation and controlled experiments in the immensely complex domain of mathematical education, in particular when studies are done primarily by means of quantitative instruments put to use on large data sets, researchers in the 80's began to develop and cultivate in-depth empirical **case studies** of teaching, learning and cognition phenomena and processes in contexts of a very limited number of a participants, sometimes just one or two individuals, as in the famous study by Erlwanger (Erlwanger, 1975a) who was one of those who inaugurated the use of case studies in mathematics education. By their very nature case studies are of a *qualitative* rather than a quantitative nature and hence call for a different methodology. Much inspiration for such a methodology has been received from psychology, anthropology, and sociology. Thus different modes of observation, including participant observation, field notes, interviews, questionnaires, questioning of students at work on tasks, all carefully (audio- or video-) recorded and transcribed, have been added to the traditional equipment of a classical empirical researcher. The outcome of a case study does not in itself allow for generalisation. Nor is it meant to. Instead, if convincingly conducted, it provides an *existence proof* that such and such phenomena or processes can in fact occur (because it did so in this case), and perhaps an uncovering of possible causes responsible for the phenomena or processes detected. So, often the result of a case study is the construction of **interpretations** and **models** of mechanisms and causal relationships meant to explain what was observed. Since the introduction of case studies into mathematics education, such studies have come to constitute what is, today, a prototypical form of investigation in our field. If you pick a paper at random from current research literature there is a high probability that it is entirely, or to a great extent, a qualitative case study of the learning processes, cognition and beliefs of a small groups of students or teachers. A paradigmatic example is Lithner's recent study of beginning university students' reasoning in dealing with non-routine calculus tasks (Lithner, 2000).

Sometimes a set of interpretations is organised and assembled into a network, a system which we might call an **interpretative theory**. This can be of a mainly theoretical nature as is the case with the so-called APOS (action-process-object-schema) theory developed by Dubinsky and others (Dubinsky, 1991) as a general theory of (mathematical) learning in continuation of Piaget's work on reflective abstractions. Or, if several case studies of the same kind are carried out with other subjects and objects of study and give rise to similar findings, there is a case for potential empirical generalisation resulting in the establishment of certain patterns. Brousseau's theory of 'the didactical contract' is an example of an interpretative theory of one fundamental constituent of classroom dynamics (Brousseau, 1990). Since the mid-80's even **intepretative meta-theories** and schools of thought of a general and transcendental nature, such as constructivism, activity theory, habitus theory, inspired by psychologists, philosophers, or sociologists such as Piaget, Vygotsky, von Glasersfeld, and Bourdieu, have found their way into mathematics education research as overarching methodologies guiding research or researchers.

The final types of outcome of research on mathematical education are **designs** and, if eventually implemented in practice, **constructions**, of curricula, teaching approaches and materials, instructional sequences, assessment modes, and so forth. Not all designs or constructions fall under a research umbrella. For that to be the case, the design has to be based on an *a priori* theoretical or empirical *analysis*, at least in the form of reasoned opinions, ideas and proposals, and the construction has to be confronted with some form of *a posteriori empirical examination* as outlined above. In both cases the methods applied will bring the research conducted in line with the sorts of research already discussed, but the results of the research are the designs or constructions themselves.

In summary, current mathematics education research makes use of a large spectrum of research methods and yields a wide variety of types of findings. Many studies use several of the methods discussed above in combination. While I concluded the previous section by stating that the issues and questions of research were more or less in place by the end of the 70's the same is not true with regard to research methods and results. The 80's brought a considerable extension of both the spectrum of methods and the spectrum of types of results. Since then our field has not witnessed any major new developments as far as methods and types of results are concerned. In other words, methodologically speaking the current situation can be described as a steady state situation.

V. Problems and challenges

The deliberations in this section differ from the ones in the previous section by being of a more personal nature.

The conclusion of the previous sections was that mathematics education research of today, i.e., since the late 80's, is pretty much in a steady state situation, both in terms of the issues and questions dealt with and in terms of the methodologies employed and the types of results obtained. This may give the impression that our field has now reached a stable stage with a set of more or less established paradigms. However, I do not think that this is the case. In what follows I shall share some of my reasons with you.

In the 70's and 80's it became essential to more and more researchers in mathematics education to make sure that no factor which might exert significant influence on the teaching and learning of mathematics be excluded from theoretical or empirical consideration. This conviction, which was often formulated as the necessity of avoiding unjustified reduction of complexity, led to a virtual explosion of studies that went into considerable detail in order to come to grips with all sorts of aspects of teaching, learning, cognition, affect, and communication, in mathematics. Much of this research is to be considered as fundamental research conducted in order to secure a foundation for future effective mathematics teaching which, to a fair degree of certainty, may lead to desirable, or at least satisfactory, learning and mastering of mathematics (Niss, 1999).

In my opinion, too, it is indeed a matter of crucial importance to our field, as in any field of research, to avoid unjustifed reduction of complexity. There is so much we don't know or understand in mathematical education that there is every reason to continue to observe this principle. However, we should also not forget that the ultimate goal of any scientific endeavour is to achieve *justified reduction* of complexity. I would like to submit that while major parts of research in mathematics education in the past three decades have paid due and necessary attention to the former demand, we may soon be in a position to pay more attention to the latter. As I see it, there is such a huge body of highly valuable outcomes of excellent research that need to be surveyed, structured, brought together and synthesized. It appears to be one of the weaknesses of our profession that many of us, myself included, tend to write and speak too much and read and contemplate too little. I would conjecture that if more systematic revisiting and synthesizing of research were carried out we would realise that 'we know more than we know that we know'. One aspect of this is that we have focused on understanding what happens in case studies of a limited number of participants, and insisted on validity as a necessary prerequisite to any further work, again for very good reasons. I am wondering whether we are not approaching a situation where it is possible to look for reliable generalisation and transfer of our particular findings, while always keeping in mind that reliability is worth very little if validity is missing.

However, I am certainly not suggesting that the only thing that is needed is systematisation and rearrangements of existing research. As long as we cannot produce considerably more justified reduction of complexity than we are currently able to offer, we haven't reached a stage with a stable set of research paradigms. It seems that we need to break new ways to accomplish that. As long as we haven't reached a stage of stable research paradigms it is extremely important that we don't fool ourselves into believing that we have. It is dangerous to our field, therefore, to stick to too narrow and rigid an interpretation of what counts as acceptable research. We have to be very open-minded with respect to the formats of research we accept, but very demanding in our requirements to quality, while recognising that quality comes in many different forms. We have to maintain that reflective raising of concerns and issues is the source of life for mathematics education. So, although we want to pose more difficult questions than we have the tools to answer, a major challenge for mathematics education research in the new millenium, as I see it, is to achieve justified reduction of complexity so as to allow for substantial improvement in mathematics education for all. There is still a long way for us to go.

There is another challenge related to the one just mentioned. One observation that a mathematics educator can hardly avoid to make is that there is a widening gap between researchers and practitioners in mathematics education. The very existence of such a gap is neither surprising nor worrying in itself. The cause for concern lies in the fact that it is widening. There are very good explanations for this fact, but for the health and welfare of our field we have to do our utmost to find ways to reduce the gap as much as possible. For the time being we are not in a position to reduce the *epistemological gap* by requesting research to offer well-defined recipies or prescriptions which are guaranteed to succeed if properly implemented. For we know of no royal road to success. Instead, what we can do is to reduce the *sociological gap* between teachers and researchers. This can be done by creating meeting points and fora for concrete collaboration between teachers and researchers, by making the demarcation lines between the two professions less rigid, by giving teachers opportunities to take part in research from time to time, and by having researchers never be completely out touch with the practice of teaching mathematics. If we are unsuccessful in all this, research on mathematical education runs the risk of becoming barren, inconsequential dry swimming, while the practice of teaching runs the risk of becoming more prejudiced, narrow-minded, and inefficient than necessary and desirable. Present and future generations of students, as well as society and culture at large, deserve a better service from us than that.

References

Aichele, Douglas, B. (ed.): 1994, P*rofessional Development for Teachers of Mathematics* - NCTM 1994 Yearbook. Reston (VA): NCTM.

D'Ambrosio, Ubiratan: 1979, 'Overall goals and objectives for mathematical education', in UNESCO: *New trends in mathematics teaching, Volume IV*, Paris: Unesco, pp. 180-198

Bachmann, Friedrich: 1971, 'n-Gons', *Educational Studies in Mathematics* 3, pp. 288-309

Balacheff, Nicolas: 1980, 'Une étude, a l'aide des graphes, de démonstrations mathématiques formulées par des élèves', *Educational Studies in Mathematics* 11, pp.91-111

Bauersfeld, Heinrich: 1980, 'Hidden Dimensions in the So-Called Reality of a Mathematics Classoom', *Educational Studies in Mathematics* 11, pp.23-41

Begle, Edward: 1969, 'The role of research in the improvement of mathematics education', *Educational Studies in Mathematics* 3, pp. 232-244

Begle, Edward: 1972, *Teacher Knowledge ans Student Achievement in Algebra* (SMSG Reports, No. 9). Palo Alto (CA): School Mathematics Study Group.

Bishop, Alan & Clements, Ken & Keitel, Christine & Kilpatrick, Jeremy & Laborde, Colette (eds.): 1996, *International Handbook of Mathematics Education*, Vols. 1-2. Dordrecht: Kluwer Academic Publishers.

Boaler, Jo: 1993, 'Encouraging the Transfer of 'School' Mathematics to the 'Real World' Through the Integration of Process and Content, Context and Culture', *Educational Studies in Mathematics* 25(4), pp. 341-373

Boaler, Jo: 1998, 'Open and Closed Mathematics: Student Experiences and Understandings', *Journal for Research in Mathematics Education* 29(1), pp. 41-62

Brousseau, Guy: 1990, 'Le contrat didacttique: le milieu', *Recherches en didactique des mathématiques* 9 (3), pp. 309-36

Chevallard, Yves: 1985, La Transposition Didactique. Grenoble, La Pensee Sauvage

Clarke, Barbara & Clarke, Doug & Sullivan, Peter: 1996 'The Mathematics Teacher and Curriculum Development', in Bishop et al. (eds.), *International Handbook of Mathematics Education*, Vol. 2 (Chapter 33), pp. 1207-33

Cocking, R.R. & Mestre, J.P.: 1988, *Linguistic and Cultural Influences on Learning Mathematics*. Hillsdale (NJ): Lawrence Erlbaum.

Cronbach, L. J., & Suppes, P. (eds.): 1969, *Research for tomorrow's schools: Disciplined inquiry for education*. New York: Macmillan.

Davis, Robert B.: 1971, The Problem of Relating Mathematics to the Possibilities and Needs of Schools and Children', *Educational Studies in Mathematics* 3, pp. 322-36

Douady, Regine: 1991 'Tool, Object, Setting, Window', in Bishop, Alan & Mellin-Olsen, Stieg and Dormolen, Joop van (eds.), *Mathematical Knowledge: Its Growth Through Teaching*. Dordrecht: Kluwer Academic Publishers.

Dubinsky, Edward: 1991, 'Reflective abstraction in advanced mathematical thinking', in D. Tall (ed.), *Advanced Mathematical Thinking*. Dordrecht: Kluwer Academic Publishers, pp. 95-123

Engel, Arthur: 1971, 'Geometrical Activities for Upper Elementary School', *Educational Studies in Mathematics* 3, pp. 353-394

Erlwanger, Stanley H.: 1975a 'Benny's conceptions of rules and answers in IPI mathematics', *The Journal of Mathematical Behavior* 1 (2), pp. 7-25

Erlwanger, Stanley H.: 1975b 'Case studies of children's perceptions of mathematics', *The Journal of Mathematical Behavior* 1 (3), pp. 157-281

Fletcher, Trevor J.: 1971, 'The Teaching of Geometry - Present Problems and Future Aims', *Educational Studies in Mathematics* 3, pp. 395-412

Freudenthal, Hans: 1971, 'Geometry between the Devil and the Deep Sea', *Educational Studies in Mathematics* 3, pp. 413-35

Fuson, Karen C., & Carroll, William M, & Drueck, Jane V.: 2000, 'Achievemen Results for Second and Third Graders Using the *Standards*-Based Curriculum Everyday Mathematics, *Journal for Research in Mathematics Education* 31(3), May, pp. 277-295

Grouws, Douglas A. (ed.): 1992, *Handbook of Research on Mathematics Teaching and Learning*. New York: Macmillan.

Haimes, David H.: 1996, 'The Implementation of a "Function" Approach to Introductory Algebra: A Case Study of Teacher Cognitions, Teacher Actions, and the Intended Curriculum', *Journal for Research in Mathematics Education* 27(5), pp. 582-602

Hilton, Peter: 1971, 'Topology in the High School', *Educational Studies in Mathematics* 3, pp. 436-53

Howson, A. Geoffrey (ed.): 1973, *Developments in Mathematical Education - Proceedings of the Second International Congress on Mathematical Education*. Cambridge: Cambridge University Press.

Howson, A. Geoffrey: 1979, 'A critical analysis of curriculum development in mathematics education', in UNESCO: *New trends in mathematics teaching, Volume IV*, Paris: Unesco, pp. 134-161.

Huntley, Mary Ann & Rasmussen, Chris L. & Villarubi, Robertso S. & Sangtong, Jaruwan & Fey, James T.: 2000, 'Effects of *Standards*-Based Mathematics Education: A Study of the Core-Plus Mathematics Project Algebra and Functions

Strand', pp. 328-61

Kilpatrick, Jeremy: 1992, 'A History of Research in Mathematics Education', in Grouws, D.A. (ed.), *Handbook of Research on Mathematics Teaching and Learning.* New York: Macmillan, pp. 3-38

Levi, Howard: 1971: 'Geometric Algebra for the High School Programme', *Educational Studies in Mathematics* 3,pp. 490-500

Lithner, Johan: 2000, 'Mathematical Reasoning in Task Solving', *Educational Studies in Mathematics* 41 (2), pp. 165-90

Mammana, Carmelo, and Villani, Vinicio (eds.): 1998, *Perspectives on the Teaching of Geometry for the 21st Century,* New ICMI Study Series, Vol. 5. Dordrecht: Kluwer Academic Publishers.

Menger, Karl: 1971, 'The Geometry Relevant to Modern Education', *Educational Studies in Mathematics* 4, pp. 1-17

Niss, Mogens: 1996, 'Goals of Mathematics Teaching', in Bishop et al. (eds.), *International Handbook of Mathematics Education,* 1996, Vol. 1 (Chapter 1). Dordrecht: Kluwer Academic Publishers. pp. 11-47.

Niss, Mogens: 1999, 'Aspects of the nature and state of research in mathematics education', *Educational Studies in Mathematics* 40 (1), pp. 1-24.

Otte, Michael: 1979, 'The education and professional life of mathematics teachers', in UNESCO: *New trends in mathematics teaching, Volume IV,* Paris: Unesco, pp. 107-33

Pehkonen, Erkki & Törner, Günther: 1996, 'Mathematical beliefs and different aspects of their meaning', *Zentralblatt für Didaktik der Mathematik* 28(4), pp. 101-08

Pickert, Gunther: 1971, 'The Introduction of Metric by the Use of Conics', *Educational Studies in Mathematics* 4, pp. 31-47

Pimm, David: 1987 *Speaking Mathematically: Communication in Mathematics Classrooms.* New York (NY): Routledge and Kegan, Paul

Revuz, Andre: 1971' The Position of Geometry in Mathematical Education', *Educational Studies in Mathematics* 4, pp. 48-52

Reynolds, Anne, and Wheatley, Grason H.: 1996, 'Elementary Students' Construction and Coordination of Units in an Area Setting', *Journal for Research in Mathematics Education* 27(5), pp. 564-81

Room, Thomas G.: 1971, 'The Geometry and Algebra of Reflections (and 2x2 Matrices)', *Educational Studies in Mathematics* 4, pp. 53-75

Scandura, Joseph M.: 1971, 'A Research Basis for Teacher Education', *Educational Studies in Mathematics* 3, pp. 229-243

Sfard, Anna: 1991, 'On the dual nature of mathematical conceptions: reflections on processes and objects as different sides of the same coin', *Educational Studies in Mathematics* 22(1), pp. 1-36

Sfard, Anna & Linchevski, Liora: 1994, 'The gains and pitfalls of reification - the case of algebra', *Educational Studies in Mathematics* 26(3), pp. 191-228

Silver, Edward A., and Cai Jinfa: 1996, 'An Analysis of Arithmetic Problem Posing by Middle School Students', *Journal for Research in Mathematics Education* 27(5)

pp. 521-39

Steinbring, Heinz & Bartolini Bussi, Mariolina G. & Sierpinska, Anna (eds): 1998, *Language and Communication in Mathematics Classrooms: Developing Approaches to a Research Domain*. Reston (VA): National Council of Teachers of Mathematics.

Steiner, Hans-Georg: 1971, 'A Foundation of Euclidean Geometry by Means of Congruence Mappings', *Educational Studies in Mathematics* 4, pp. 87-90

Stone, Marshall: 1971, 'Learning and Teaching Axiomatic Geometry', *Educational Studies in Mathematics* 4, pp. 91-103

Tall, David (ed.): 1991, *Advanced Mathematical Thinking*. Dordrecht: Kluwer Academic Publishers, Chapter 15

UNESCO: 1973, *New trends in mathematics teaching Vol III*. Paris: UNESCO

UNESCO: 1979, *New trends in mathematics teaching Vol IV*. Paris: UNESCO

UNESCO: 1980, *Studies in mathematics education* (Morris, Robert, ed.), volume 1

UNESCO: 1981, *Studies in mathematics education* (Morris, Robert, ed.), volume 2

UNESCO: 1984, *Studies in mathematics education* (Morris, Robert, ed.), volume 3

UNESCO: 1985, *Studies in mathematics education* (Morris, Robert, ed.), volume 4

Verschaffel, Lieven & De Corte, Erik: 1997, 'Teaching Realistic Mathematical Modeling in the Elementary School: A Teaching Experiment With Fifth Graders', *Journal for Research in Mathematics Education* 28(5), pp. 577-601

Verschaffel, Lieven & De Corte, Erik, & Vierstrate, H.: 1999, 'Upper Elementary School Pupils' Difficulties in Modeling and Solving Nonstandard Additice Words Problems Invlving Ordinal Numbers', *Journal for Research in Mathematics Education* 30(3), pp. 265-85

Villa, Mario: 1971, 'A Logical Approach to the Teaching of Geometry at the Secondary Level', *Educational Studies in Mathematics* 4, pp. 111-134

Vinner, Shlomo, and Hershkowitz, Rina: 1980, 'Concept images and common cognitive paths in the development of some simple geometrical concepts', in *Proceedings of the Fourth International Conference for the Psychology of Mathematics Education*. Berkeley, CA, pp. 177-184

How Mathematics Teaching Develops Pupils' Reasoning Systems

Terezinha Nunes
Oxford Brookes University, England

Recent theoretical discussions have pinned constructivism and social constructivism against each other. In this paper, I argue that Piagetian constructivism and Vygotsky's social constructivism are coherent and complementary. If we can reach a synthesis of these two theories, we will have a more encompassing approach to analysing how pupils learn mathematics and how mathematics teaching develops their minds. I suggest that the theories are consistent because they are based on the same metaphor of the mind and that they are complementary because they explain different aspects of the development of reasoning. Together they can help us understand the developments in pupils' reasoning systems that result from changes in the thinker (Piaget's contribution) and in the thinker's activity when using different thinking tools (Vygotsky's contribution). In order to develop these ideas, I will first discuss the concept of thinking systems. I will then work with a simple example in mathematics education, multiplicative reasoning. I will first consider the origin of multiplicative reasoning - i.e., the development of the thinker and then discuss how mathematics teaching can affect pupils' reasoning systems in this domain. To conclude the discussion, I will consider a research agenda for mathematics education based on the conception of thinking systems.

Reasoning systems

Systems theory was applied to reasoning by Piaget and the Russian developmental psychologists in the first half of the twentieth century. Piaget and the Russian developmental psychologists were attempting to solve the same problem and envisaged systems theory as the solution. The problem they were trying to solve was the mind-body problem. The problem is posed by the contrast between biological and higher mental functions.

Biological functions are typically carried out by specialised organs. For example, digestion is carried out by the digestive system; breathing by the respiratory system. Biological functions involve a constant task performed by the same mechanisms leading to an invariant result. If we consider breathing as an example, the task is to bring oxygen to the cells in the body. This is accomplished by an invariant mechanism: oxygen is received by the blood cells and transported to all the cells in the body. The invariant result is that the cells receive oxygen.

58

In contrast, higher mental functions are not carried out by a specialised organ but through the co-ordination of different actions. They are carried out by functional systems. According to Luria's definition, in functional systems "a constant task [is] performed by variable mechanisms bringing the process to a constant result" (Luria, 1973, p.28). I will take two of Luria's examples to make this point. The first one is 'remembering'. It is easy to be misled into thinking that we have a specialised organ for remembering: the brain. But Luria points out that remembering involves functional systems rather than a single biological unit. Imagine it is your partner's birthday and you want to remember to buy some flowers before going home. Your task is to remember to buy flowers. You can accomplish this through a variety of means. You can simply repeat this to yourself many times until you think it is now impossible for you to forget. You may tie a knot around your finger: as you don't normally have a string around your finger, this will remind you to buy the flowers. You might write it down to help you remember - on your palm, where it will be very visible. Or on a yellow sticker, for example, and paste it on your wallet. Or you may type it into your electronic diary and set an alarm to go off just before you leave your office. These variable mechanisms can be used with the same end: to recover the information. No single biological unit can account for all the different mechanisms you may call upon.

A second example used by Luria is locomotion. Walking involves the same organs: it is a biological function. But locomotion can be accomplished by variable mechanisms: it involves a functional system. If your aim is to go from A to B, you may walk, swim, ride your bike, drive, or fly. The end result will be to get to B. One of the mechanisms will be chosen for practical reasons. Although it could be argued that all of these mechanisms are under the control of some brain centre that helps us make connections between different places, this is evidently not so. If I fly from London to Tokyo, I might not have the faintest idea of how London and Tokyo relate to each other. When I take a taxi from the airport to the hotel, I do not need to know anything about the spatial relations between the airport and the hotel. Locomotion is not a biological function and many of our target destinations could not be achieved if all we could do was walk.

Higher mental systems are open systems: they allow for the incorporation of tools that become an integral part of the system. When we take notes in order to remember something, writing becomes an essential part of remembering. When we fly from London to Tokyo, the aeroplane becomes an essential part of our locomotion. Vygotsky suggested that what is most human about humans is this principle of construction of functional systems that allow activities to be mediated by tools. He termed this 'the extra-cortical organisation of complex mental functions' to stress that these functional systems cannot be reduced to the brain.

Even the most elementary mathematical activities are carried out by functional systems. Solving the simplest addition problem, for example, involves a functional system. Paraphrasing Luria: we have no specialised organ for addition. If asked to solve the problem 'Mary had five sweets and her Grandmother gave her three more; how many does she have now?', a pupil can find the answer through a variety of mechanisms. The pupil can put out five fingers, then another three, and count them all. The pupil can put out just three fingers and count on from five. The pupil can recall an addition fact, 5+3, and use no fingers. In this were a large number, the pupil might decide to use a calculator. These are variable mechanisms that bring the invariant result of finding the answer to addition problems.

For educators, one of the most significant features of higher mental functions is that they are open systems: the variable mechanisms - which are often created through the incorporation of tools - can be replaced by taking into the system something new from the environment. When a mechanism is replaced with something new, the system changes. Children first solve addition problems using their fingers to represent the objects in the problem. The principle used by the pupils' reasoning system in this representation is one-to-one correspondence: one finger represents one sweet; one counting word is tagged to one finger; the last counting word indicates the number of sweets. When pupils replace the use of five fingers with the word 'five' by itself, the system changes: instead of one finger for each sweet, one word represents all five sweets at the same time. This small change has a huge impact on the reasoning system: whereas the pupil has a limited number of fingers, number words continue indefinitely on. A system with fixed limits becomes much more powerful because its limits are removed by a change in tools.

This change - from using fingers to using words - is not simple because it requires refinements of the principles that organise the reasoning system. Fingers represent sweets through one-to-one correspondence but this principle is not sufficient for pupils to understand numeration systems with a base. It has been widely documented that pupils need to understand additive composition of numbers in order to be able to use number systems efficiently. Vygotsky (1978) himself pointed out that forming complex mental systems mediated by tools involves a complex and prolonged process subject to all the basic laws of psychological evolution. Sign using activity by pupils - such as the activity of using numeration systems to quantify answers to problems - is neither simply invented by children nor passed down by adults. Children's own activities and the signs they know are initially not connected. When they become connected, a major development is accomplished.

To sum up: The points of convergence between Piaget's and Vygotsky's theory reside in the use of the same metaphor of mind, the search for a solution to the same problem, the acknowledgement of variations and invariants in thinking systems, and the acknowledgement of qualitative developmental processes that precede the possibility of mediated action. On its own, each theory is incomplete. Piaget had a theory for the development of children's reasoning schemas but did not have a theory about the consequences of acquiring conventional systems of signs. Vygotsky did not have a theory for the developmental processes that precede mediated action but stressed the increased power that conventional systems of signs bring to our reasoning.

The consequences of these gaps are that Piaget's child can understand number but cannot solve numerical problems. To solve numerical problems, we need numeration systems. Vygotsky's child can count but may not know when and how to use counting to solve problems. As mathematics educators, we must bring these two together: we must understand how children organise their actions and help them incorporate new tools into their thinking systems.

The description of simple problems, like the addition problem mentioned earlier on, only gives a glimpse at how this process of co-ordinating pupils' own activities with conventional signs works. Because the problem is so simple, the example conveys the false idea that a reasoning system will inevitably change - and change for the better -when a new mechanism is incorporated into it. Unfortunately, as mathematics educators know only too well, there isn't necessarily a happy end to all stories. An analysis of multiplicative reasoning will illustrate this point.

Multiplicative reasoning

Piaget's (1965) hypothesis was that reasoning about multiplicative situations starts with pupils' use of one-to-many correspondence as an organising principle. One-to-many correspondence encapsulates the concept of ratio or a fixed relation between two variables, which are at the core of multiplicative reasoning. Starting from the Piagetian work, I will argue that mulplicative reasoning cannot be reduced to repeated addition and that successful teaching about multiplicative reasoning should attempt to promote the incorporation of systems of signs into the correspondence reasoning. This is the contribution from Piagetian theory to mathematics education: the identification of a schema of action that forms the basis of multiplicative reasoning. From this starting point, we might ask which systems of signs used in mathematics should be coordinated with this reasoning and what is the best route to accomplish this in the mathematics classroom. The discussion that follows will be based on research as far as possible. But there are many points where only hypothetical answers are possible presently: we do not have the research to answer many of the questions raised here.

One to many correspondence and multiplicative reasoning

Piaget's initial investigations on correspondence can be illustrated quite simply. The interviews with children started with the well-known method of asking the children to take one red flower for each vase. The red flowers are then put aside in a bundle and the child is asked to take one yellow flower for each vase. The vases are then taken away and the child is asked whether there are as many red and yellow flowers on the table. Piaget suggested that this problem is not too difficult for children at about age 5. They can understand that if the number of red flowers is the same as the number of vases, and the number of vases is the same as the number of yellow flowers, then there are as many red as yellow flowers. This is an example of the famous transitive inferences studied by Piaget: if A = B and B = C, then A = C.

Piaget continued this interview by putting all the vases back on the table and asking the children how many flowers would be in each vase if all the flowers were distributed evenly in the vases. Children who succeeded in the preceding question also knew that there would be two flowers per vase. Piaget's final test of children's understanding of correspondence was then to put the flowers away, leaving only the vases on the table, and ask the children to pick up the correct number of drinking straws so that each flower would be placed in one straw. The children could see the vases but not the flowers. In order to solve this problem, the children would have to think: there are two flowers per vase. To take the same number of tubes, I need to take two tubes per vase. Piaget suggested that children at ages 5 and 6 show a good degree of success in these problems.

In the last few years our research team investigated pupils' use of one-to-many correspondence reasoning to solve a variety of multiplicative reasoning problems. Kornilaki and I examined pupils' solutions of multiplicative reasoning problems in action; with Bryant, Watanabe and van den Heuvel-Panhuizen, I investigated solutions to written problems, and with Park I investigated the teaching of multiplication to young children.

Kornilaki (1999) asked young pupils in English schools to solve the following problem: In each of three hutches there are four rabbits; all the rabbits will eat together in a big house; the child's task was to place on the big house the exact number of food pellets so that each rabbit had one pellet. In front of the child was a row of three hutches but no rabbits. Kornilaki observed that 67% of the 5-year-olds and all of the 6- and 7-year olds were able to pick up the exact number of pellets needed to feed the rabbits. The 5- and 6-year-olds had two ways of solving the problems. One route to solution was by establishing a correspondence between the pellets and the hutches, placing three pellets in correspondence with each hutch. The second solution involved counting: the children first determined the number of rabbits by pointing four times to each hutch as they counted, and then took that number of pellets. The 7-year-olds could either use these correspondence solutions or solve the problem through arithmetic, because they had learned multiplication tables. It is significant that the lack of knowledge of multiplication tables did not disadvantage the 6-year-olds in comparison with the 7-year-olds: all the children in both groups were successful. Thus the principle of correspondence was used by the younger children to solve multiplication problems before they learned about multiplication in school; the older children could use a new mechanism, multiplication tables.

In another study, Kornilaki (1999) gave children a slightly more difficult problem: I bought three boxes of chocolate; in each box, there are four chocolates. How many chocolates do I have? What makes this problem more difficult is not that it requires a different reasoning schema nor that the problem is about boxes of chocolate: it is that there was no starting point for the children. In the previous problem, Kornilaki gave the children a starting point: she set out in front of the children a row of cut-out paper hutches. The representation of one of the variables facilitates the use of the correspondence schema because the child only needs to create a representation for the second variable. In this problem, the children had no such initial representation of one variable. The problem involves the same numbers, so there is no extra difficulty in terms of counting. But the children have to come up with a representation for both variables on their own. This representational difficulty significantly changes levels of success: 37% of 5-year-olds, 70% of 6-year-olds, 87% of 7-year-olds and all of the 8-year-olds succeed in this more difficult problem. Because the schema of correspondence is still the solution chosen by the majority of 5- to 7- year olds, the comparison between the results of this experiment and the previous one shows that representing both variables is a considerable step in children's progress. It also suggests a course of action for teachers. It is quite likely that young children can profit from solving problems presented along with the representation for one variable and that they will, in time, come to co-ordinate this activity with the representation of both variables on their own. This would help them progress in their ability to solve multiplication problems as a result from new co-ordinations between reasoning and representations.

Young pupils can also solve such problems when they are presented through drawings because drawings facilitate the use of correspondence. We have presented the following problem to approximately 1,000 children in England: In each house in this street (the drawing shows 4 houses) live 3 dogs. Write down the number of dogs that live in this street. The percentage of correct responses for 6-year-olds in this problem is approximately 60%. Although it is not as high as the level of success when the children have cut-out paper hutches in front of them, it is remarkable that 6-year-olds, who did not receive instruction on multiplication, can show such high level of success. Figure 1 shows children's productions in a problem where they are asked to draw the number of carrot biscuits necessary to feed all the rabbits inside all the houses: in these productions, the children left no doubt about the mechanisms they used to solve the problem.

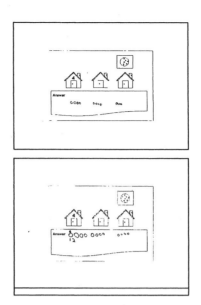

Figure 1

Reasoning by correspondences is not restricted to solving multiplication problems. It is also used to solve multiplication problems where information on a factor is missing. There are two ways in which the information about the factors could be missing; we will consider each one in turn.

The first missing-factor multiplication problem would be: 'I had a party; each child that came brought me three flowers; I got 12 flowers; how many children came?' In this case, the children know the correspondence - 1 to 3; if they repeat this until the total of flowers is 12, they will know how many children came to the party. This problem, known in the mathematics education literature as 'quotitive' or 'measure' division problem, is in my view actually an inverse multiplication problem. This is not simply a matter of terminology: if we think about it as an inverse multiplication problem, we have a theory about how the child will solve the problem. In the same way that missing-addend problems are initially solved by children through addition strategies - the child figures out how many to add to one set to arrive at the total - quotitive division problems should be solved by children initially through correspondence. This analysis also allows for some predictions regarding children's success. Children should show a higher level of success in direct multiplication problems than in the inverse ones. Note that this is not a prediction about division problems in general because sharing division problems are as easy for children as the direct multiplication ones.

A second possibility would be to say: 'I had a party. Three children came. Each child brought me the same number of flowers. I got 15 flowers. How many children came to the party?' This problem has the same structure as the problems described earlier on in the sense that it involves a fixed ratio. However, because the ratio is no described, the children will find it very difficult to use the correspondence schema. Thus this is an inverse multiplication problem where we expect much less success.

Kornilaki did find that direct problems were easier than both types of inverse problems and that inverse problems of the type traditionally described as quotitive division were significantly easier than this second type of inverse multiplication question. The rates of success in quotitive division problems were 30%, 50%, 80% and 83%, respectively, for 5-, 6-, 7-, and 8 year-olds whereas in the second type of inverse multiplication problem they were 10%, 30%, 56%, and 80% for the same age levels.

An analysis of children's strategies showed that in the first type of inverse multiplication problem, where the children knew the ratio, the vast majority of the children who solved the problem correctly (83%) did so through correspondence reasoning, either creating an explicit representation of both variables or creating an explicit representation of the groups of flowers while counting the children in correspondence with each group. In the second type of division problem, where the ratio was not known, a correspondence solution could only be implemented by trial-and-error. Only 21% of the children successfully used the correspondence solution whereas about 50% seemed to be able to understand the inverse relation between multiplication and division and actually shared out the total number of flowers into three groups.

Reasoning by correspondences can also be documented amongst young children solving simple proportion problems before they have been taught about proportions in school. The example in Figure 2 shows a problem adapted from van den Heuvel-Panhuizen. It was given to approximately 1,000 pupils in England. Because these were given to whole classes of pupils, it is not possible to describe their strategy. Only some of the children make marks on the booklets, giving us a clue to their solution process. However, the similarity between the percentage of children solving the missing-factor multiplication problems and these simple proportion problems is suggestive of the use of similar approaches to the solution of the two problems.

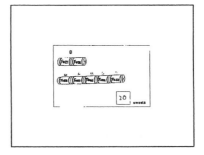

Figure 2

These analyses of children's solutions to multiplicative reasoning problems suggest that mathematics teaching can develop pupils' reasoning system by helping them co-ordinate their correspondence reasoning with counting. As indicated by Vygotsky, a very significant moment in children's development is that when children co-ordinate their actions with systems of signs. The hypothesis about the development of the concept of multiplication is made more specific by Piaget's theory, which suggests that the schema of correspondence is the crucial action in the case of multiplication.

The hypothesis is by no means trivial: the teaching of multiplication in many countries is based on repeated addition, not on correspondence reasoning. It is noteworthy that the mathematics education literature contains arguments in favour and against the use of repeated addition as the basis for multiplicative reasoning. Whereas Yamanoshita and Matsushita (1996) argued that repeated addition is only a means to solve multiplication problems but does not represent its meaning, Fishbein, Deri, Nello, and Marino (1985) and Steffe (1994) appear to suggest the opposite. Our hypothesis is based on the analysis of reasoning systems developed here: if the child's multiplicative reasoning is based on correspondences, not on addition, the best way to develop the child's reasoning system is to promote its co-ordination with new systems of signs. It leads to a very specific prediction: that children taught about multiplication through correspondence reasoning will make more progress in solving multiplicative reasoning problems than children taught about multiplication through repeated addition.

We (Park & Nunes, 2001) tested this prediction in an experimental study with 42 children attending two schools in London. The children's mean age was 6 years and 7 months and they had received no instruction on multiplication in school, according to their teachers. The children were randomly assigned to one of two instruction groups: repeated addition or correspondence. The children were pre- and post-tested on a set of mixed additive and multiplicative reasoning problems. We use the phrases 'additive' and 'multiplicative' reasoning problems, rather than addition and multiplication, because the problems included both direct and inverse (i.e., missing addend and missing factor) problems. During the teaching phase, the children in both groups solved a total of 16 problems, which could be represented by the same arithmetic sentences. For the repeated addition group, the problem was phrased as a sum of two identical sets; for the correspondence group, the problem was phrased as a question where two variables were in a fixed ratio to each other. For example, for the arithmetic sentence 2 x 3, the repeated addition group solved the question: 'Tom has three toy cars. Ann has three dolls. How many toys do they have altogether?' The same arithmetic sentence was exemplified in the correspondence group by the question: 'Amy's Mum is making 2 pots of tomato soup. She wants to put 3 tomatoes in each pot of soup. How many tomatoes does she need altogether?'

Consistently with our theoretical framework, we expected the children to make different levels of progress in the multiplicative reasoning problems from pre- to post-test: we expected the children in the correspondence group to make significantly more progress in multiplicative reasoning problems than the repeated addition group. This prediction was supported by our results. Although the groups did not differ at pre-test, their post-test performance was significantly different at post-test, with the correspondence group performing better than the repeated addition group in multiplicative reasoning problems. This difference could not be explained by a similarity in the grammatical structure of the problems because the verbal description of problems in the pre- and post-test was varied and did not simply follow the description of a ratio situation. For example, in three problems much of the information was visually presented (see two examples in Figure 3).

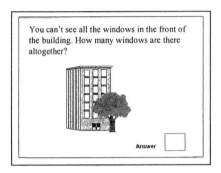

Figure 3

In conclusion, evidence seems to support the idea that children's reasoning schema for multiplicative situations is based on setting correspondences between variables. In order to develop their reasoning systems, mathematics teaching should lead the children to use a variety of mathematical tools in connections with this reasoning schema.

Reasoning by correspondences can create powerful systems for solving multiplicative reasoning problems. Relevant evidence comes from a variety of situations where people solve problems outside school: children selling products in the streets, foremen working out the size of walls from scale drawings, fishermen calculating the amount of processed sea-food from the amount fished (Nunes, Schliemann, & Carraher, 1993), and peasants calculating volume (Soto Cornejo, 1992), all reason mainly by correspondences. They all have replaced the overt actions of a correspondence schema with a new system of signs: instead of setting objects in correspondence, they use number words followed by the quantities indicated. Although they may occasionally make computational errors, they hardly ever make errors in their reasoning.

Three examples are presented here as illustration. The first one comes from the work on street mathematics (Nunes, Schliemann, & Carraher, 1993). A girl was selling lemons, which cost 5 cruzeiros (the Brazilian currency at the time) each. Posing as customers, we asked for 12 lemons. She calculated the price by separating out 2 lemons at a time, as she said: 10, 20, 30, 40, 50, 60. She replicated the ratio 2-10 until she reached 12 lemons. Note the similarity in the activity of correspondence, which was carried out in a more powerful way because the 1-5 correspondence was changed into 2-10.

Another illustrative example comes from our work with fishermen. The fishermen we interviewed in Brazil sold the fresh fish they caught to middlemen. The middlemen salted and dried the fish to be sold far from the ocean. In order to know more about their own commercial activities, the fishermen must understand that the quantity they sell to the middleman is not the same quantity sold by the middleman to the customer. When the fish is salted and dried in the sun, there is a loss of weight. The quantity of processed fish is proportional to the quantity of unprocessed fish. The same is true, for example, for the connection between quantity of unprocessed and shelled fish.

A fisherman was told that there is elsewhere a kind of shrimp that yields 3 kilos of shelled shrimp for every 18 kilos that you catch; if a customer wants to buy 2 kilos of shelled shrimp, how much do you have to fish for him? The fisherman calculates: One and a half kilos [processed] would be nine [unprocessed], it has to be nine because half of eighteen is nine and half of three is one and a half. And a half-kilo [processed] is three kilos [unprocessed]. Then it'd be nine plus three is twelve [unprocessed]; the twelve kilos would give you two kilos [processed] (Nunes, Schliemann, & Carraher, 1993, p.112). His use of correspondence is quite clear: for each quantity of unprocessed food, he names the corresponding amount of processed food. This is accomplished by performing the same operation on each variable: if one is halved, the other is also halved. This type of solution is known in mathematics education as 'scalar' reasoning, in contrast to 'functional' solutions. In functional solutions, an operator is identified, which can be applied to one quantity to calculate the value of the other one. Functional solutions have not been reported in unschooled adults and are less common than one would expect even in British adolescents (see Nunes & Bryant, 1996, for an analysis).

The third example I take from Soto Cornejo, who interviewed rural workers in the North of Chile. The workers sold wood for processing into vegetable coal by volume. It has been documented often that students have difficulty with the concept of volume and make many mistakes in calculating volume, particularly if there is a decimal point involved in the calculation. Soto Cornejo drew a lorry showing the dimensions 5 meters by 2 meters by one and a half meters, and asked the worker to calculate the volume of its trailer. An illiterate worker reasoned like this: 'First I make a layer one meter high and always five meters long. That will give you five cubic meters. (Note that the layer is an imagined object that he sets into correspondence with the measures of volume) And that two times (the width of the trailer is two meters), that makes ten cubic meters. Now I've got 5 (*sic*) centimetres two times. We will take 5 centimetres (*sic*), this makes five times five, twenty five, that is two and a half cubic meters. The total is ten plus five, fifteen cubic meters'. Once again we see the use of correspondence reasoning: to each layer corresponds a volume, and the layers are simple (1 x 1 x 5) so that the correspondence is easily established. This is in a most imaginative way to solve a problem that students find difficult after 7 or 8 years of school.

Multiplicative reasoning out of school is abundant with examples of scalar reasoning; functional reasoning is almost completely absent. My conclusion is that outside school people form powerful reasoning systems for the solution of multiplicative problems by using new symbolic tools from arithmetic instead of manipulatives. But they do not appear to refine the reasoning principles involved in the system to generate functional solutions easily.

What happens in school? Can mathematics teaching develop pupils' reasoning system?

Piaget considered Vygotsky's position optimistic with respect to didactic intervention: 'One must guard against an excessive bio-social optimism into which Vygotsky sometimes seems to fall' (Piaget, 1962). According to Piaget, teaching will have a positive influence if it is coherent with the pupils' reasoning; otherwise, teaching might actually be ineffective or even lead the pupils astray.

The teaching of multiplication in many countries may not take pupils' multiplicative reasoning into account. In many countries pupils are taught that multiplication is the same thing as repeated addition. And in many countries pupils seem to develop misconceptions about multiplication and have difficulty with proportional reasoning (see, for example, Hart, 1988). This analysis of multiplicative reasoning using systems theory offers hypotheses about what could be changed in the teaching of multiplication in order to promote the development of pupils' multiplicative reasoning. Many of these ideas will already be used in different places by different teachers. They are not necessarily new ideas in this sense. What is a new outcome from this analysis is a framework that can provide coherence and help choose - and test - effective ideas.

The first one is related to the representation of multiplicative reasoning problems in the classroom. Earlier on I suggested that is appropriate for teachers of young children to promote the co-ordination of the correspondence schema of action with counting. But what next? How can this schema be translated into paper and pencil representation?

I would hypothesise that the first translation might be into tables that show the correspondences, rather than into arithmetic operations. Figure 4 shows two examples of problems used in the classroom to support primary school pupils aged 7·8 years in developing their multiplicative reasoning. A mixture of figurative and numerical representations was used to strengthen the connection between the schema of action and paper and pencil representation.

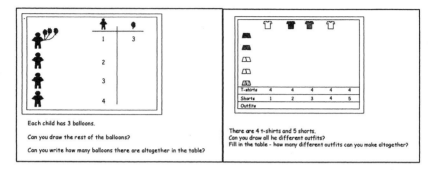

Each child has 3 balloons.

Can you draw the rest of the balloons?

Can you write how many balloons there are altogether in the table?

There are 4 t-shirts and 5 shorts.
Can you draw all he different outfits?
Fill in the table - how many different outfits can you make altogether?

Figure 4

A second co·ordination with symbolic systems may be to represent the problems through graphs. Figure 5 shows examples of graphs used with the same group of primary school pupils after they had worked with tables for a few lessons. The teacher was initially sceptical about the possibility of working with graphs with such young children. After the sessions, he was enthusiastic. A small scale, pilot study in the school showed that the children participating from this programme made significantly more progress than the control children from pre· to post-test, although the intervention only lasted a few weeks. A more detailed study is still needed.

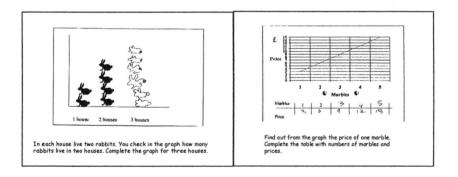

In each house live two rabbits. You check in the graph how many rabbits live in two houses. Complete the graph for three houses.

Find out from the graph the price of one marble.
Complete the table with numbers of marbles and prices.

Figure 5

The consequences of introducing the idea of graphs in close connection to the solution of multiplication problems can only be speculated about. The difficulties that pupils have in establishing connections between graphs and functions may be much less important if they learn about graphs in the manner suggested here. Algebraic representation of graphs and tables could be the third type of

70

representation used in this context, which could be introduced perhaps through the explicit representation of the constant ratio in graphs and tables. But our explorations have not gone that far yet.

Conclusion

I conclude with a research agenda, rather than a solution. The use of systems theory helps us understand how reasoning systems become more powerful through mathematics teaching. But we know that progress is not an automatic result. In order to be certain that we are building more powerful reasoning systems in the classroom, we must investigate which principles are essential for the system to work well, the variable mechanisms or tools that teachers can insert into the reasoning system, and what type of changes we expect to accomplish. I suggest that in many cases we should not be satisfied with the simplest changes, where the same principles are used without the refinements that can result from the incorporation of new tools. If we are able to understand the principles used by pupils in the organisation of their reasoning, we should also be able to examine which refinements they need, and investigate ways of promoting these refinements in the classroom.

References

Hart, K. (1988). Ratio and proportion. in Hiebert & M Behr (Eds), *Number concepts and operations in middle grades.* New York: Macmillan.

Hoyles, C., Noss, R., & Sutherland, R. (1991) *The ratio and proportion microworld.* Final report of the Microworlds Project. Institute of Education, University of London.

Kornilaki, K. (1999). *Young children's understanding of multiplication: A psychological approach.* PhD thesis, Institute of Education, University of London.

Luria, A. (1973). *The working brain.* Wandsworth (UK): Penguin.

Nunes, T. & Bryant, P. (1996). *Children doing mathematics.* Oxford: Blackwell.

Nunes, T., Schliemann, A. & Carraher, D. (1993) S*treet mathematics, school mathematics.* New York: Cambridge University Press.

Park, J. & Nunes, T. (2001). The development of the concept of multiplication. *Cognitive Development* 13, pp. 1-11.

Piaget, J, (1965). *The child's conception of number.* New York: Norton.

Piaget, J. (1962). Comments on Vygotsky's critical remarks concerning The Language and Thought of the Child and Judgement and Reasoning in the Child. in L. Vygostky, *Thought and language.* Cambridge MA: MIT Press.

Soto Cornejo, I. (1992). *Mathématiques dans la vie quotidienne des paysans chiliens.* Faculté de Psychologie et des Sciences de l'Education, Louvain-la-Neuve, Belgium.

Vygotsky, L. S. (1978). Mind in society. in M. Cole, V. John-Steiner, S. Scribner & E. Souberman (Eds.). *The development of higher psychological processes.* Cambridge MA: Harvard University Press.

Watanabe, A., Nunes, T., Bryant, P., & van den Heuvel-Panhuizen, M. (2000). Assessing young children's multiplicative reasoning. *Newsletter of the Developmental Psychology Section the British Psychological Society* 55, pp. 7-15.

Yamonoshita, T. & Matsushita, K. (1996). Classroom models for young children's mathematical ideas. in H. M. Mansfield, N. A. Pateman, & N. Descamps-Bednarz (Eds.), *Mathematics for tomorrow's young children: International Perspectives on curriculum*. Dordrecht: KIuwer Academic.

Developing Mathematics Education in a Systemic Process[1]

Erich Ch. Wittmann

University of Dortmund, Germany

The aim of this paper is to make a concrete proposal for bridging the gap between theory and practice in mathematics education and for establishing a systemic relationship between researchers and teachers as well as to explain the background and the implications of this proposal.

1. Bridging the gap between theory and practice: The role of substantial learning environments

You cannot fail if you follow the advice the genius of human reason whispers in the ear of each new-born child, namely to test thinking by doing and doing by thinking.

J. W. von Goethe

In Brousseau 1997 the scene is set with a teaching example, the "race to 20", which is based on a game of strategy. In a somewhat modified version this game can be described as follows: A line of circles is numbered from 1 to 20. The first player starts by putting 1 or 2 counters on the first circle or the first two circles, the second player follows by putting 1 or 2 counters on the next circles similarly. Continuing in this way the players take turns until one of them arrives at 20 and in doing so wins the game.

The "race to 20" helps to corroborate basic arithmetical ideas (relationships of numbers on the number line, addition, repeated addition). It is also a rich context for general objectives of mathematics education (exploring, reasoning and communicating) and a typical example of the fundamental principle of "learning by inquiry". If children analyse the moves backwards they recognise that the positions 17, 14, 11, 8, 5 and 2 are winning positions. So the first player has a winning strategy: In the first move she puts down two counters and then responds to a

---

[1]The paper was prepared during a sabbatical leave at the University College Chichester/UK. The author is indebted to Afzal Ahmed, Brian Griffiths, Honor Williams and Heinz Steinbring for critical comments. The author also would like to express his gratitude to Jerry P. Becker who was one of the very first Western mathematics educators to recognise the impact of research conducted by Asian mathematics educators. Since the seventies Jerry Becker has been providing first hand information about the Japanese approach to mathematics education which has greatly influenced the author's research.

2-counters move of the second player with a 1-counter move and to a 1-counter move with a 2-counters move. In this way the first player jumps from one winning position to the next one and finally arrives at 20.

There are many variations of this game: Any natural number can be chosen as the target, and the maximal number of counters to be put down on every move can be increased. In fact we have a whole class of games of strategy before us which require a continuous adaptation of the strategies used. The basic ideas of analysing these games can be generalised to the wider class of finite deterministic games of strategy for two persons with full information which cannot end in a draw: by means of the game tree and the marking algorithm one can prove that for each of these games there exists a winning strategy either for the first or the second player.

As mentioned in Brousseau 1997 the "race to 20" was reproduced 60(!) times under observation and each of its phases was the object of experimentation and clinical study. Based on a variety of other examples Brousseau developed his theory of didactical situations. In the research context "aspects of proving" Galbraith (1981) studied students' processes in their attempts to uncover the structure of the "race to 25".

The "race to 20" and its variations represents what has been called a substantial learning environment, an SLE, that is a teaching/learning unit with the following properties (Wittmann, 1995, pp. 365-366):

(1) It represents central objectives, contents and principles of teaching mathematics at a certain level.
*(2) It is related to significant mathematical contents, processes and procedures **beyond** this level, and is a rich source of mathematical activities.*
(3) It is flexible and can be adapted to the special conditions of a classroom.
(4) It integrates mathematical, psychological and pedagogical aspects of teaching mathematics, and so it forms a rich field for empirical research.

The concept of an SLE is a very powerful one. It can be used to tackle successfully one of the big issues of mathematics education which has become more and more urgent and which is of crucial importance for the future of mathematics education as a discipline: the issue of theory and practice. Fortunately, for some years now this issue has been more and more recognised and addressed by mathematics educators. Referring to the ICMI Study "Mathematics Education as a Research Domain" (Sierpinska & Kilpatrick 1998) Ruthven stated that there is a wide gap between the scholarly knowledge of researchers on the one hand and the craft knowledge of teachers on the other hand, and argued in favour of a re-orientation of mathematics education (Ruthven, 2001): *„While most of the contributors identify the development of knowledge and resources capable of supporting the teaching and learning of mathematics as an important goal for the field, there is disappointment* *with what has been demonstrated on this score."*

A claim similar to Ruthven's was made by Clements and Ellerton for the South East Asian and by Stigler and Hiebert for the American context:

"From our perspective, at the present time mathematics education needs less theory-driven research, and more reflective, more culture-sensitive, and more practice-orientated research which will assist in the generation of more domain-specific theory." (Clements&Ellerton 1996, p184).

"Perhaps what teachers are told by researchers to do makes little sense in the context of an actual classroom. Researchers might be very smart. But they do not have access to the same information that teachers have as they confront real students in the context of real lessons with real learning goals ... It is clear that we need a research-and-development system for the steady, continuous improvement; such a system does not exist today." (Stigler&Hiebert 1999, pp. 126-127).

This criticism can be extended: for teachers' decision-making the logical and episte-nological structure of the subject matter is at least as important as are psychological, social or more general aspects of learning and teaching. However, in the mainstream of current research in mathematics education this very structure has not received the attention it deserves. Therefore the gap between theory and practice is also due to a gap between mathematics on one side and mathematics education on the other side. This gap is particularly obstructive to progress in reforming mathematical education as the epistemological structure of the subject matter contains psychological and social aspects at least implicitly while the converse does not hold.

Of course the issue of relating theory and practice to one another is not specific for mathematics education. In all fields of society we have as one extreme mere "doers" who act in a pragmatic manner, who don't see any point in worrying about theory and who even think of theory as a threat to practice. At the other extreme are mere "thinkers" who develop analyses and theories with no grounding in practice and without caring for practical implications and applications.

In tackling the issue of theory and practice a superficial re-arrangement of the field is not sufficient. If we seriously want to establish links between theory and practice a fundamental change is needed. For systemic reasons it is highly unlikely that theories developed independently of practice can be applied afterwards: *"The developing theory of mathematical learning and teaching must be a refinement, an extension and a deepening of practitioner knowledge, not a separate growth."* (Bell, 1984). Therefore in order to organise a strong and lasting systemic interaction between theorists and practitioners we have to look for some common core in which theory and practice as well as mathematics and mathematics education inseparably permeate one another. Substantial learning environments can serve this purpose quite naturally (cf. Wittmann,1984 and 1995/1998). Accordingly, the main proposal of this paper is as follows (see Fig. 2 which is an extension of a diagram presented in Ruthven,2000):

The design of substantial learning environments around long-term curricular strands should be placed at the very centre of mathematics education. Research, development and teacher education should be consciously related to them in a systematic way.

Fig. 2

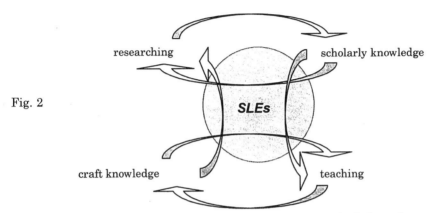

This proposal is supported by encouraging experiences which have been made in various projects around the world. Prominent examples are the work of the British Association of Teachers of Mathematics in the sixties (cf. Fletcher, 1965 and Wheeler, 1967), the prolific Dutch *Wiskobas* project and its follow-up projects conducted at the Freudenthal Institute, and the systematic work of Japanese mathematics educators (cf., Shimada&Becker, 1996). These projects show what an important role SLEs can play for both researchers and practitioners: as common points of reference, as knots in the collective memory, and as stimuli for action.

The proposal reflects a certain understanding of the particular nature of the system of education which will be examined in the next section.

2. (Burst) Dreams

Variety can only be absorbed by variety.
Ross Ashby

It is not by chance that development projects based on SLEs have been successful in changing mathematics teaching as well as in changing teachers' attitudes: in these projects fundamental systemic conditions have been taken into account. This will be explained in more detail by referring to three dreams that were dreamt by a prominent philosopher, a prominent mathematician and a prominent educator. These dreams have been selected because they capture the non-systemic tradition of teaching and learning which must be fully recognised in order to be overcome.

2.1 Descartes' Dream

In 1619 the young René Descartes (1596-1650) had a vision of the "foundations of a marvellous science", which later on he elaborated in several writings, particularly in his *"Discourse on the method of properly guiding the reason in the search of truth in the sciences"* (Descartes, 1637). Basically this method consisted of a few rules by which the mind can arrive at more and more complete descriptions of reality. In modern words the method was a totalitarian programme for mathematising reality. By separating the thinking mind, the *res cogitans*, from the world outside, the *res extensa*, Descartes established a sharp split between man and his environment which later on became a fundamental ideology of Western thinking. Already before Descartes Francis Bacon (1561-1626) had formulated the inductive method of science and summarised its technological use in the slogan "Knowledge is Power". So from the very beginning Descartes' dream of arriving at a complete description of the environment was accompanied by the dream of controlling and making use of it. The "Cartesian system" of philosophy has paved the way for an unrestrained mathematisation, control and also exploitation of more and more parts of our natural and social environment. In our time the availability of computers has accelerated this process (cf. Davis&Hersh, 1988). "Benchmarking", "controlling", "evaluation", and "assessment" have become key notions in the management hierarchies of economics and administration.

2.2 Hilbert's Dream

At the turn to the 20th century the very science to which Descartes wanted to ground truth, mathematics, was fundamentally shaken by the discovery of inconsistencies within Cantor's set theory. Among those mathematicians who were particularly alarmed was David Hilbert. In order to defend "the paradise" which Cantor had created in his eyes he started the so called "finitistic programme" by which he hoped to prove the consistency and infallibility of mathematical theories once and for all (Hilbert, 1926). Although Hilbert's dream burst already in 1930 when Gödel proved his incompleteness theorem, the formalistic setting of Hilbert's programme has survived and turned into an implicit theory of teaching and learning. Interestingly, the Bourbaki movement which set formal standards in mathematics up to the seventies started in the mid-thirties from a discussion about how to teach analysis. Also in this day and age the belief in formal precision as a necessary if not sufficient means to get hold of teaching/learning processes is still widespread among mathematicians and non-mathematicians. The *Mathematically Correct* movement, at present one of the most aggressive pressure groups in the U.S., is a horrifying example.

2.3 Comenius' dream

Johann Amos Comenius (1592 - 1670) is well-known as one of the founding fathers of didactics. His famous book "Great Didactic" published in 1657 was the first comprehensive work on teaching and learning. In many respects Comenius was far ahead of his time. For example, he was among the first to project a plan of universal education and to see the significance of education as an agency of international understanding. In one respect, however, he was a child of his time. Deeply impressed by Bacon's visions of a technological age and by the efficiency of newly invented machines, he was obsessed by the idea of transposing the functioning of machines to the functioning of teaching. In the chapters 13 and 32 of the "Great Didactic" he states (Comenius 1910, pp. 96-97,p289):

"The art of teaching, therefore, demands nothing more than the skilful arrangement of time, of the subjects taught, and of method. As soon as we have succeeded in finding the proper method it will be no harder to teach school-boys, in any number desired, than with the help of the printing-press to cover a thousand sheets daily with the neatest writing ...The whole process will be as free from friction as is the movement of a clock whose motive power is supplied by the weights. It will be as pleasant to see education carried out on my plan as to look at an automatic machine of this kind, and the process will be as free from failure as are these mechanical contrivances, when skilfully made ... Knowledge can be impressed on the mind, in the same way that its concrete form can be printed on paper."

Comenius' dream has been dreamt over the centuries in ever new forms and is still present in some corners of cognitive science and education, including mathematics education, as various forms of "direct teaching" and "hard science"-like methods of research demonstrate (cf. for example, Begle,1979).

Also a certain tendency within the research community to consider teachers as mere recipients of research results is clearly related to Comenius' dream: *"I suspect that if teachers are mainly channels of reception and transmission, the conclusions of research will be badly deflected and distorted before they get into the mind of pupils. I am inclined to believe that this state of affairs is a chief cause for the tendency ... to convert scientific findings into recipes to be followed. The human desire to be an 'authority' and to control the action of others does not, alas, disappear when a man becomes a researcher."* (Dewey,1929/1988, p24)

2.4 The "systemic-evolutionary" vs. the "mechanistic-technomorph" approach to the management of complexity

It may seem as too far-fetched to look at Descartes, Hilbert and Comenius from the point of view of modern systems and management theory. However, there is a good reason to do so, for the three dreams, as different as they may appear, share a common feature: They reflect the self-concept of individuals who perceive themselves as standing on a higher level and as equipped with the capacity to gather complete information about some field and to use this information for bringing this field under control. The Swiss management theorist Malik has called this attitude the "mechanistic-technomorph approach to the management of complexity" and described it as follows (Malik, 1986, p36 ff., transl. E.Ch.W.): *"The paradigm [underlying this approach] is the machine in the sense of classical mechanics. Basically, a machine is constructed according to a given purpose and to a given plan, and its function, reliability and efficiency depend on the functions and the properties of its elementary components ... The technological success which has been achieved by following this paradigm is overwhelming, and gave rise to the belief in its unlimited applicability far beyond the engineering disciplines. ... The paradigm includes the firm conviction that no order whatsoever which corresponds to human purposes can be brought about without following this paradigm."*

During the past decades another paradigm has been taking ground which is based on the fact that biological and social organisms are far too complex in order to allow for a "mechanistic-technomorph" description and control from outside. In order to achieve certain goals with living systems a fundamentally different approach is appropriate (Malik, 1986, p38 ff. transl. E.Ch.W.):*"The systemic-evolutionary approach [to the management of complexity] starts from quite different assumptions. Its basic paradigm is the spontaneous, self-generating ordering exemplified best by the living organism. Organisms are not constructed, they develop. Spontaneous orderings develop also in the social domain. They arise by means of and as the result of human actions, but they do not necessarily correspond to preconceived intentions, plans or goals. Nevertheless they can be highly rational."*

According to the systemic-evolutionary paradigm the only reasonable and feasible way of influencing and guiding a social system is to interact sensibly with the self-organising powers inside the system. Recommendations and instructions from outside which do not fit into the internal processes of the system are at best useless. If in addition a minute control is exerted from outside the development of spontaneous powers inside the system is suppressed, and this undermines its efficiency. A system without a proper infrastructure is not able to interact adequately with a complex environment: variety can only be absorbed by variety.

The systemic-evolutionary approach to the management of complexity has been developing in Western philosophy only during the last decades. So it is even more astounding that it has emerged in Asia more than 2000 years earlier when Lao Tzu and Chuang Tzu founded taoism. Their basic maxim for leaders is "wu wei". This means: leaders should not interfere with the natural powers and inclinations of their clients, but should instead build upon self-organisation and offer help for self-help. It is the present author's hope that the Asian societies will succeed in preserving the systemic-evolutionary thinking as a precious heritage from their past while it is spreading only slowly and with great difficulties in Western societies which are still in the claws of deeply rooted mechanistic-technomorph patterns of thinking and action.

3. Consequences for mathematics education

A little child needs no famous teacher to learn to speak. He or she learns to speak spontaneously in the company of people who can speak.

Chuang Tzu

Individual students, individual teachers, classrooms, staffs, school districts, states, countries: all are living organisms and therefore highly complex systems. *Beyond any political or educational ideologies* the following systemic conclusions can be drawn just from the natural law of the inherent complexity of these systems:

1. Learning unfolds best if the spontaneous powers of all involved are brought to bear and encouraged, and if autonomy and self-responsibility are developed.

The inevitable results of - possibly well-intended - strait jacket schemes of teaching, assessment and accountability are *"over-standardisation, oversimplification, over-reliance on statistics, student boredom, increased numbers of dropouts, a sacrifice of personal understanding and, probably, a diminution of diversity in intellectual development."* (Stake, 1995, p213).

2. The traditional borderline between the researcher on one side and the teacher on the other side has to be abandoned. Research has to build upon the spontaneous powers of teachers in the same way as teaching has to build upon the spontaneous powers of students.

Donald Schön described this new relationship between theorists and practitioners very convincingly in his book *The Reflective Practitioner* (Schön, 1983, p323):

"In the kinds of reflective research I have outlined, researchers and practitioners enter into modes of collaboration very different from the forms of exchange envisaged under the model of applied science. The practitioner does not function here as a mere user of the researcher's product. He reveals to the reflective researcher the ways of thinking that he brings to his practice, and draws on reflective research as an aid to his own reflection-in-action."

3. At all levels the traditional hierarchies have to be transformed into networks of co-operation and mutual support.

A good account of what this means in different contexts is given in Burton 1999.

Although the "mechanistic-technomorph" paradigm of management is still dominating in all fields of society around the world the awareness of the systemic nature of teaching and learning is steadily growing. As far as research and development in mathematics education are concerned there are already innovative research programmes which follow the new paradigm with remarkable success, for example *developmental research* (Freudenthal 1991, Gravemeijer 1994), Guy Brousseau's *theory of didactical situations* (Brousseau, 1997), the Japanese *lesson studies* (Stigler&Hiebert, 1999, chapter7), and *action research* (cf. Ahmed&Williams, 1992, Clements&Ellerton, 1996, chapter 5).

The impact of these research programmes on practice rests on the fact that they are systematically focused on the design and empirical research of SLEs. In this way a firm basis for a systemic researcher-teacher-interaction, for "SLE studies", is provided as the following examples illustrate.

Example 1. In German primary schools the traditional approach to arithmetic in grade 1 has been to introduce the number space 1 to 20 step by step: The first quarter of the school year is restricted to the numbers 1 to 6, the second quarter to the numbers 1 to 10. The third quarter is open to numbers 1 to 20, however, tasks like 7+5, in which the 10 has to be bridged, are postponed to the last quarter of the school year. Also children are expected to follow the arithmetic procedures given by the teacher.

In the project "mathe 2000" this traditional approach was challenged and replaced by a holistic approach: The open number space 1 to 20 is introduced fairly quickly as one whole, the children are encouraged to start from their own strategies and are not restricted to just one procedure. This new approach was formulated and published as a connected series of SLEs in a handbook for practising skills (Wittmann&Müller, 1990, Grade 1: chapters 1-3). It was based on a systematic epistemological analysis of arithmetic, on inspirations from the developmental research conducted at the Freudenthal Institute (cf. Treffers et al. 1989/1990, van den Heuvel-Panhuizen, 1996) and on the intuitions of the designers. It was not based on empirical research conducted by professional researchers. Empirical studies which confirmed the holistic approach came only later (cf. Selter, 1995, Hengartner 1999). So it was teachers who first tried it out and found that it works better than the traditional approach. Through the existing networks of teachers this new approach has spread widely in a remarkably short period of time. Now an innovative textbook is available (Wittmann&Müller, 2000) which is based on the holistic approach, and its wide acceptance by teachers has forced authors of traditional textbooks to modify their approach. From the systemic viewpoint the success of this innovation is no surprise (Bell, 1984): *"One might ask the general question whether, in the present state of our knowledge about mathematical education, we should progress faster by collecting 'hard' data on small questions, or 'soft' data on major questions. It seems to me that only results related to fairly important practitioner questions are likely to become part of an intelligent scheme of knowledge ... Specific results unrelated to major themes do not become part of communal knowledge. On the other hand, 'soft' results on major themes, if they seem interesting and provocative to practitioners, get tested in the myriad of tiny experiments which teachers perform every day when they 'try something and see if it works'."*

Example 2. The second example is an SLE from the Japanese "open-ended approach". This unit was thoroughly researched before it was published (Hashimoto, 1986, Hashimoto&Becker, 1999). Its guiding problem is the so-called "matchstick problem": Children are shown a linear arrangement of squares (Fig. 3) and asked to find out how many matchsticks are needed to build 5,6,7 or more squares.

Fig. 3

There is a great variety of counting strategies to solve this problem. After having discussed the various solutions the children determine the number of matchsticks needed for other numbers of square, and try to find a general formula. In a similar way arrangements of matchsticks with more rows can be studied. Based on these concrete examples fundamental counting principles can be extracted, for example the addition principle and the principle of multiple counting (cf. Schrage, 1994).

Systematic lesson studies of the matchstick problem provided exactly the professional knowledge teachers need in order to teach this unit successfully. The matchstick problem has been included in a textbook, too (Seki et al.1997, pp.117-118).

Stigler/Hiebert (1999, p163) comment on the impact of lesson studies as follows: *"The knowledge contained in this reports ... is not made up of principles devoid of specific examples or examples without principles. It is theories linked with examples. This knowledge is notable in several respects. First, theoretical insights are always linked with specific referents in the classroom. When a lesson-study group reports, for example, that one of its hypotheses has been supported, it is never outside the context of a specific lesson with specific goals, materials, students, and so on, all of which would be described in the report."*

Example 3. A third example is provided by Heinz Steinbring's empirical research on the interplay between the epistemological structure of the subject matter and psychological and social factors (cf. for example, Steinbring, 1997). Though highly theoretical his research is strongly related to SLEs which are part of the current teaching practice. So the applicability of the research results is guaranteed from the very outset.

4. Substantial learning environments for practising skills

What counts is not memorising, but understanding, not watching, but searching,
not receiving, but seizing, not learning, but practising.
A. Diesterweg

Focusing mathematics education on substantial learning environments involves a danger that must be clearly recognised in order to be avoided: substantial mathematics is fundamentally related to mathematical processes such as mathematising, exploring, reasoning and communicating. These are *higher order thinking skills*. Emphasising them can easily lead to neglecting *basic skills*, in particular at a time when efficient calculators and computers are available. Basic skills also tend to be neglected for another reason: to a large extent traditional ways of teaching consisted of prescribed procedures and their stereotyped practice. In their eagerness to get rid of "teach them and drill them" routines in favour of "constructivist" ways of learning and teaching reformers easily get trapped: they tend to identify practice with stereotyped practice, and by abolishing stereotypes they are likely to do away with the practice of skills at all.

As the mastery of basic skills is an indispensable element of mathematical competence we have to find ways how to integrate the practice of skills into substantial mathematical activities. This is not an easy task as stated, for example, by Ross (1998):

"... drills of important algorithms that enable students to master a topic, while at the same time learning the reasoning behind them, can be used to great advantage by a knowledgeable teacher. Creative examples that probe students' understanding are difficult to develop but are essential."

The following example of an SLE (cf. Wittmann&Müller, 1990, grade 2, chapter 3.3) illustrates how the practice of a basic skills and the development of higher order skills can be combined. The example refers to an area of arithmetic which is notorious for drill and practice: the multiplication table.

The epistemological structure of the unit is unfolded in a heuristic manner as this is the best way to capture the potential of an SLE for both teaching and research (see also section 5.1).

The rule on which the unit is based is very simple: With two arbitrarily chosen pairs of consecutive numbers two calculations are performed: one „top down", the other one "crosswise" (Fig. 4).

3   4 $3 \cdot 6 + 4 \cdot 7 = 18 + 28 = 46$ 4   5 $4 \cdot 8 + 5 \cdot 9 = 32 + 45 = 77$

$|\!\times\!|$ $|\!\times\!|$

6   7 $3 \cdot 7 + 4 \cdot 6 = 21 + 24 = 45$ 8   9 $4 \cdot 9 + 5 \cdot 8 = 36 + 40 = 76$

Fig. 4

After sufficiently many calculations with numbers chosen by the children themselves a pattern is recognised: The result obtained „top down" seems always 1 bigger than the result obtained "crosswise". Children who have found pairs for which this relationship does not hold will spot some mistake in their calculations.

In trying to explain the pattern children have to go back to the meaning of multiplication: 3·6 means 6+6+6, 4·7 means 7+7+7+7, etc. So 3·6 + 4·7 contains one 7 more and one 6 less than 3·7 + 4·6 which gives it an advantage of 1 (Fig. 5).

$3 \cdot 6 + 4 \cdot 7 = 6 + 6 + 6 + 7 + 7 + 7$ $+ 7 = 18 + 21$ $+ 7$

$3 \cdot 7 + 4 \cdot 6 = 7 + 7 + 7 + 6 + 6 + 6$ $+ 6 = 21 + 18$ $+ 6$

Fig. 5

Of course the standard proof of this relationship is an algebraic one employing variables which are not available in grade 2. But variables are not needed at this level, the argument used above is absolutely appropriate.

As a next step the distributive law can be made more explicit. For example, 3·6 + 4·7 can be written as 3·6 + 3·7 + 7 and compared with 3·7 + 4·6 written as 3·7 + 3·6 + 6. This pre-algebraic form is an excellent preparation for algebra in higher grades.

As typical for substantial learning environments the activity can be extended: Instead of pairs of consecutive numbers pairs of numbers which differ by 2, 3 or any other number can be chosen. In Fig. 6 the differences are 2. The differences can also be mixed (Fig. 7).

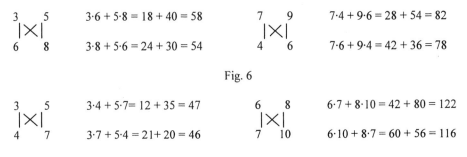

3   5 $3 \cdot 6 + 5 \cdot 8 = 18 + 40 = 58$ 7   9 $7 \cdot 4 + 9 \cdot 6 = 28 + 54 = 82$

$|\!\times\!|$ $|\!\times\!|$

6   8 $3 \cdot 8 + 5 \cdot 6 = 24 + 30 = 54$ 4   6 $7 \cdot 6 + 9 \cdot 4 = 42 + 36 = 78$

Fig. 6

3   5 $3 \cdot 4 + 5 \cdot 7 = 12 + 35 = 47$ 6   8 $6 \cdot 7 + 8 \cdot 10 = 42 + 80 = 122$

$|\!\times\!|$ $|\!\times\!|$

4   7 $3 \cdot 7 + 5 \cdot 4 = 21 + 20 = 46$ 7   10 $6 \cdot 10 + 8 \cdot 7 = 60 + 56 = 116$

Fig. 7

From these examples a general pattern is emerging: the difference of the results of the two calculations is the product of the differences of the given numbers. It is not difficult to generalise the above proof for the introductory case. All one has to do is to decompose the second product in both calculations according to the distributive law. Furthermore: beyond pairs of numbers triples of consecutive numbers (Fig. 8) and triples with fixed differences can be considered. In this case the "top down" result can be compared with two other results: one obtained by multiplying cyclically "from left to right", the third one obtained by multiplying cyclically from "right to left". In this case each triple involves nine multiplications.

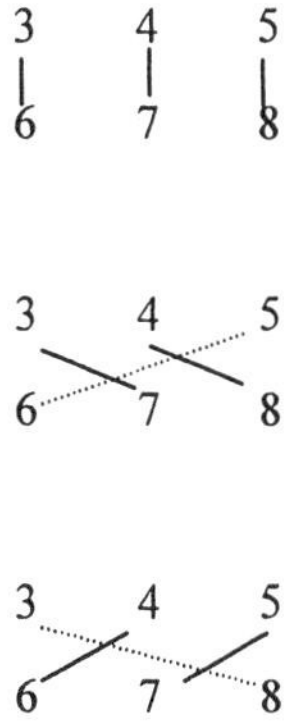

$$3 \cdot 6 + 4 \cdot 7 + 5 \cdot 8 = 18 + 28 + 40 = 86$$

$$3 \cdot 7 + 4 \cdot 8 + 5 \cdot 6 = 21 + 32 + 30 = 83$$

$$3 \cdot 8 + 4 \cdot 6 + 5 \cdot 7 = 24 + 24 + 35 = 83$$

Fig 8

Of course also triples with higher differences can be studied, and triples with different differences can be mixed as well. Furthermore: Pairs and triples can be generalised to n-tuples. Also more advanced mathematics can be employed as the expressions are scalar products of vectors ...

In grade 2 or 3 only a tiny section of this very substantial learning environment can be explored. However, this does not reduce its importance for mathematics education as will be shown in the final section.

5. Substantial learning environments in teacher education

I never force a piece of wood into a salad bowl. It's a raw material, living and
talking.
P. Peeters, Belgian wood artist

Efforts to establish a systemic relationship between theory and practice must include teacher education as it is in this field that the foundations for being able to act as a reflective practitioner are laid. SLEs, if properly used, can play a fundamental role here, too. It is appropriate to discuss didactical and mathematical courses separately as their positions in teacher education are different.

5.1 Didactical courses

The use of substantial learning environments is obvious for the didactical education of student teachers, that is for methods courses. By their very design SLEs offer unique possibilities for linking theoretical principles to concrete examples. If student teachers leave the university with the intimate knowledge of theory-based learning environments they have at their disposal a professional background that will help them immensely to act as reflective practitioners. As convincingly explained in chapter 6 of Stigler&Hiebert (1999, p85 ff.) teaching is a cultural activity that can only be understood by becoming active in this culture. For this reason the best way for student teachers to capture the spirit of a substantial learning environment is to explore its epistemological structure, to reflect it in terms of didactical principles and to test their anticipations in the light of practical experiences. John Dewey gave a wonderful account of this "laboratory point of view" in his fundamental paper *The Relation of Theory and Practice in Education* first published almost 100 years ago (Dewey, 1976).

In the last few years enormous progress has been made in applying the new technological possibilities of Multimedia to teacher education (cf. Lampert&Ball, 1998). Here SLEs can be of great help in order to identify teaching episodes that are substantial, mathematically and didactically, theoretically and practically, and to establish a well-structured and manageable information system that reflects the contents, objectives and principles of teaching mathematics at the corresponding level.

5.2 Mathematical courses

It is a simple matter of fact that around the world mathematical courses or even whole programmes often make only little or no sense for student teachers, for various reasons: Either the relevant subject matter is not covered at all, or the mathematical substance is stifled by a formalistic style of presentation or, even worse, there is no substance: mathematics is reduced to conceptual or procedural skeletons. Nevertheless, it would be wrong to conclude from meaningless courses that mathematical courses proper are of no use for student teachers in principle and that the necessary mathematics should be better integrated into courses in mathematics education. On the contrary, a specific understanding of subject matter is of paramount importance for teachers as was convincingly explained, for example, by John Dewey in the paper mentioned above (Dewey, 1976). Dewey's arguments are based on a genetic perspective. He saw scientific enquiry as a social process and knowledge as the result of it.

From this perspective Dewey's emphasis on teachers' subject matter knowledge must not be taken as an unconditional support for mathematical courses of any kind but for courses which meet specific criteria. Courses in the context of specialised mathematics are perhaps appropriate for prospective mathematicians in industry or in research. However, from the point of view of mathematics education, it is counterproductive to take such courses as a model for teacher education. To consider specialised mathematics as something absolute and as a yardstick for the mathematical training in any other professional context would be a fundamental mistake. It is a fact well established in the psychology of learning that knowledge cannot be acquired as a formal structure independently of the context in which it is to be used. So what is needed for teacher education is an idea of *mathematics in the educational context* as formulated, for example, by Freudenthal (1986, transl. E.Ch.W.):

"The idea of transposing academic mathematics (savoir savant) down to school mathematics (savoir enseigné) is wrong at its very outset, because the thinking behind this idea is directed top down and not bottom up. The mathematics to be learned at school by the big majority of our prospective citizens does not correspond at all to any theories of academic mathematics from which it could be watered down (didactically or not); at best it corresponds to the mathematics of scholars who lived centuries ago. The vast majority of our young people must be prepared to a technological know how (at various levels), not to the special knowledge of experts. The role of academic mathematics within this technological culture is much more modest than it has been claimed since a quarter of a century."....

To postulate a specific conception of mathematics in the educational context has implications for both contents and methods. Elementary topics which are closely related to the curriculum are far more important for teachers than advanced topics, and above all student teachers must experience mathematics as an *activity* (Freudenthal, 1973, Wittmann, 2001). It is only in this way that they can learn to deal with elementary mathematics in a productive way and to play their role as reflective practitioners also with respect to contents: SLE studies presuppose a flexible mastery of the content.

In order to make mathematical courses meaningful for teacher education they should be systematically related to SLEs. By their very definition SLEs are based on substantial mathematics **beyond** the school level. Therefore every SLE offers mathematical activities for student teachers on a higher level. However, disconnected pieces of mathematical islands attached to scattered SLEs do not serve the purpose. What is needed in teacher education are systematic and coherent courses of elementary mathematics which cover the mathematical background of a variety of SLEs. To develop such courses is a challenging problem for the next decade. Within the project "mathe 2000" a special series *Mathematics as a Process* has been started which is an attempt in this direction (cf. Müller/ Steinbring/

Wittmann, 2002).

Focusing the mathematical education of student teachers to substantial learning environments can serve another purpose. At a time when education in general is in danger of being subordinated to economic purposes and to methods of mass production, when, as a consequence, mathematics at school is in danger of being reduced to a toolkit for applications, and teaching is in danger of preparing students just for passing tests, the following point is crucially important: Student teachers of all levels must experience the aesthetics of a genuine mathematical activity leading to the creation of structural wholes. The presence of SLEs in the mathematical studies can contribute to making student teachers aware that mathematics is not a homogeneous mass that can be cut into arbitrary pieces and forced into instructional schemes. Mathematical structures are living organisms, and learning processes must follow their inherent dynamics if learning mathematics is to make a deeper sense.

References
Ahmed, A.& Williams, H.I.M., 1992: *Raising Achievement in Mathematics.* London: WSIHE/Department of Education and Science

Beglé, E.G., 1979: *Critical Variables in Mathematics Education.* Washington, D.C.: NCTM

Becker, J.&Shimada, Sh. (eds.), 1997: *The open-ended approach. A new proposal for teaching mathematics.* Reston, Va.: NCTM

Bell, A.W., 1984: Book review of Lesh, R. & Landau, M., Acquisition of mathematical concepts and processes, New York 1983. *Educational Studies in Mathematics* **15**, pp. 103-110

Brousseau, G., 1997: *Theory of Didactical Situations in Mathematics.* Dordrecht: Kluwer

Burton, L., 1999: *Learning Mathematics - From Hierarchies to Networks.* London: Falmer Press

Clements, M.A. ("Ken") & Ellerton, N., 1996: *Mathematics Education Research: Past, Present and Future.* Bangkok: UNESCO

Comenius, J.A., 1967: *The Great Didactic,* transl. and ed. by M.W. Keatinge. New York:

Davis, Ph.&Hersh, R., 1988: *Descartes' Dream.* London: Penguin Books

Descartes, R., 1637: *Discours de la méthode.* Leiden

Dewey, J., 1976: The Relation of Theory to Practice in Education. in: Dewey, J., *The Middle Works 1899-1924, vol.3*, ed. by Jo Ann Boydston, Carbondale/Ill.: SIU Press, pp. 249-272

Fletcher, T.J., 1965: *Some Lessons in Mathematics*, London: CUP

Freudenthal, H., 1973: *Mathematics as an Educational Task.* Dordrecht: Reidel

Freudenthal, H. 1986: Review of Yves Chevallard, La transposition didactique du savoir savant au savoir enseigné. *Educational Studies in Mathematics* **17**, pp. 323-327

Freudenthal, H., 1991: *Revisiting Mathematics Education*. Dordrecht: Kluwer

Galbraith, P., 1981: Aspects of Proving: A Clinical Investigation of Process. *Educational Studies in Mathematics* 12, pp. 1-28

Gravemeijer, K., 1994: *Developing Realistic Mathematics Education*. Utrecht: CD-β Press

Hashimoto, Y. 1986: Classroom practice of problem solving in Japanese elementary schools. In Becker, J. and Miwa, T. (eds.), *Proceedings of the U.S. - Japan Seminar on Mathematical Problem Solving,* Carbondale, Ill.: Southern Illinois University, Dept. of Curriculum & Instruction, pp. 94-112

Hashimoto, Y.& Becker, J., 1999: The open approach to teaching mathematics - creating a culture of mathematics in the classroom. In L.J. Sheffield (ed.) *Developing Mathematically Promising Students*, Reston, Va.: NCTM, pp. 101-119

Hengartner, E., 1999: *Mit Kindern lernen.* Zug (CH): Klett & Balmer

Hilbert, D.,1926: Über das Unendliche.*Mathematische Annalen* 95, pp. 161-90

Lampert, M.& Ball, D., 1998: *Teaching, Multimedia, and Mathematics.* New York

Malik, F., 1986: Strategie des Managements komplexer Systeme, Bern: Haupt

Müller, G.N., Steinbring, H.& Wittmann, E.Ch., 2002: *Arithmetik als Prozess.* Leipzig und Stuttgart: Klett (to appear)

Ross, K., 1998: Doing and Proving: The Place of Algorithms and Proofs in School Mathematics. *Amer. Math. Monthly, March 1998*, pp. 252-255

Ruthven, K., 2000: Linking Research with Practice: Towards synergy of scholarly and craft knowledge. To appear in English, L. (ed.), *Handbook of International Research in Mathematics Education*, Mahwah NJ: Lawrence Erlbaum Ass.

Schön, D., 1983, *The Reflective Practitioner.* New York: Basic Books

Schrage, G., 1994, Analyzing Subject Matter: Fundamental Ideas of Combinatorics. In Cooney, Th.J. et al., *Mathematics, Pedagogy, and Secondary Teacher Education.* Portsmouth, NH: Heinemann, pp. 167-220

Selter, Ch., 1995: *Eigenproduktionen im Mathematikunterricht der Primarstufe.* Braunschweig/Wiesbaden: Deutscher Universitätsverlag

Stake, R., 1995: The invalidity of standardized testing for measuring mathematics achievement. In T. Romberg (ed.), *Reform in school mathematics and authentic assessment,* New York: SUNY, pp. 173-235

Seki, S. et al. 1997: *Eighth Grade Mathematics*. Dainippon-Tosho Corporation (in Japanese)

Sierpinska, A. & Kilpatrick, J. 1998: *Mathematics Education as a Research Domain. A search for Identity.* An ICMI Study. Books 1 and 2. Dordrecht, Boston and London: Kluwer

Steinbring, H., 1997: Epistemological investigation of classroom interaction in elementary mathematics teaching. *Educational Studies in Mathematics* 32, pp. 49-72 Stigler, J & Hiebert, J., 1999: *The Teaching Gap.* New York: Free Press

Treffers,A., de Moor, E. & Feijs, E., 1989/1990: *Proeve van een nationaal programma voor het reken-wiskundeonderwijs op te basisschool.* Deel 1: Overzicht einddoelen, Deel 2: Basisvaardigheden en cijferen. Tilburg: Zwijsen

Van den Heuvel-Panhuizen, M., 1996: *Assessment and Realistic Mathematics*

*Education.*Utrecht: CD-β Press

Wheeler, D.H. 1967:*Notes on Mathematics in Primary Schools.* London:CUP

Wittmann, E.Ch., 1984: Teaching Units as the Integrating Core of Mathematics Education. *Educational Studies in Mathematics* **15**, pp. 25-36

Wittmann, E.Ch., 1989: The Mathematical Training of Teachers form the Point of View of Education. Survey Lecture ICME 6 Budapest 1988. *Journal für Mathematik-Didaktik* **10**, pp. 291-308

Wittmann, E. Ch, 1995: Mathematics Education as a "Design Science". *Educational Studies in Mathematics* **29**, pp. 355-374 (reprinted in Sierpinska, A. & Kilpatrick, J.1998, pp. 87 - 106)

Wittmann, E.Ch., 2001: The Alpha and Omega of Teacher Education: Stimulating Mathematical Activities. To appear in: T*eaching Mathematics at the University Level.* An ICMI Study, ed. by D. Holton

Wittmann, E.Ch.& Müller,G.N., 1990/92: *Handbuch produktiver Rechenübungen.* Vols. 1&2, Düsseldorf und Stuttgart: Klett

Wittmann, E.Ch. & Müller, G.N. et al. 2000: *Das Zahlenbuch [The Book of Numbers]* vols. 1-4, Leipzig: Klett

Regular Lectures

Widening the lens - changing the focus: Researching and describing language practices in multilingual classrooms in South Africa.

Jill Adler
University of the Witwatersrand, South Africa

One of the defining features of the current South African context is the breath-taking extent and pace of social, political and economic transformation desired by the country in this early post apartheid period. Rapid change produces both extreme and often contradictory conditions that in turn throw a spotlight onto complex social practices. What might otherwise remain hidden or taken for granted in 'normalised' day to day practices elsewhere can be seen in a new light and in new ways. Teaching and learning mathematics - curriculum in use - in multilingual settings is one such practice under the spotlight in post apartheid South Africa. The South African context offers the field a dynamic site for exploring classroom communication. This lecture draws on two research studies of languages practices in multilingual mathematics classrooms in South Africa.

I will begin the lecture with a description of changing curriculum and language-in-education policy and practice in post apartheid South Africa, and locate these within the wider context of diversity, inequality and poverty. The extent of diversity, inequality and poverty in the country presents its people with enormous challenges - challenges that easily overwhelm. At the same time, each day, each step forward reinforces possibilities of a more humane and democratic future, and within this, a qualitatively better education for all South Africa's children. I paint the South African landscape to bring to life pictures of different multilingual mathematics classrooms that form focal points of the lecture. I locate research on the dynamics of teaching and learning mathematics in multilingual classrooms firmly within the South African context, in order to localize the research, and so enrich its story. At the same time, rich contextualisation provides the means for take-up and recontextualisation elsewhere. Placing educational research done in South Africa clearly within its socio-economic and political context is what enables others elsewhere to make sense of the conclusions drawn for their own practices in their different contexts. It is always in the interaction between theory and practice, and between policy and on the ground realities that the issues embedded in the teaching and learning of mathematics in multilingual classrooms need to be understood.

Indeed, I have a concern that dominant mathematics education research on language and communication in the classroom does not draw on, nor relate to, the insights gained from research in bi-/multilingual mathematics classroom settings. There are probably many reasons for this, including ignorance (in the sense of not knowing) and exoticism. Perhaps one reason is that in more homogeneous language settings, where the language of learning and teaching is the primary language of both the teachers and all the learners in the classroom, communicative competence is taken for granted, and like the air we breathe, not easily 'seen'.

I believe that the insights into mathematical learning in contexts where communication between all participants cannot be taken for granted has much to offer. In particular, I don't believe there is any classroom where linguistic capital is equitably distributed. In consequence, what might appear as extremely 'different' settings that do not speak to mainstream practice, in fact are illuminating of communication issues in all classrooms.

In this presentation I will draw particular attention to the contradictory position of mathematics teachers and learners in South Africa. They understand the pedagogical benefits of exploratory talk in learners' primary languages, but such practice is constantly undermined by a context where English is the language of power, government and commerce. I will discuss a recent study of teachers' knowledge of their practices in multilingual classrooms. I have argued that the multilingual mathematics classroom is a dilemma-filled terrain. The classroom contexts that informed that research were all urban, and located in 'African' townships or city-suburban schools. I approached the study through teachers' knowledge and experience and from a social practice perspective. Here, knowing is tied to being. I worked from the theoretical stand point that what teachers know, how they select what they share, what they focus on when they talk within and about their practice will reflect their identity. Their knowledge will reflect what it means for them to teach, to teach mathematics, and to teach mathematics in a particular multilingual setting. I will describe three inter-related dilemmas that were constitutive of and constituted through classroom practices observed in the study to reinforce the argument that the dilemmas of code-switching, mediation and transparency capture the challenges and tensions that teachers in multilingual secondary mathematics classrooms in South Africa face as they go about their work. As that research has shown, dilemmas are not either-ors, but rather a way of coming to understand, name and work on inherent tensions that need to be managed in moments of practice. How teachers go about their work and manage dilemmas in their practice, is a combination of both their personal histories, and the contexts in which they find themselves.

My current research resides in the intersecting fields of mathematics teacher education and resources, including language, in use in classroom practice. I have been working with colleagues in mathematics, science and English language teacher education to investigate changing language practices in and across primary and secondary classrooms, different subjects, and classrooms in urban and non-urban areas in South Africa. I will show how the study above has been an impetus for, and influence on, a language focus in this current teacher education research. This research forms the heart of the lecture. I will describe how in order to interpret our research across sites, particularly urban and non-urban, we have come to distinguish between what we are call 'foreign' and 'additional' English Language Learning Environments. These environments place different linguistic demands on teachers and learners. They have particular consequences for the ways in which mathematics teachers get things done in day to day classroom practice.

In widening the lens and changing its focus, we have come to understand better the complex journey required as teachers and learners navigate between exploratory talk, typically in learners' main language, and discourse-specific, i.e. mathematical, talk and writing in English.

In the lecture I will provide illustrations from the research to support our claim that, by and Large, in the complex conditions in which teachers in South Africa find themselves, this journey remains incomplete.

I will discuss further our conscious attempts to move away from deficit discourses, both in terms of how bi-and multilingual learners are described (their languages are resources rather than problems), and in terms of how teachers and school classrooms are constructed (as complex sites of practice with complex demands on teachers and teaching in contrast to teachers somehow always not being good enough). This does not mean that the story is romantic, devoid of any difficulties and challenges. On the contrary, there are numerous difficulties and challenges, both compounded by the complex politics of access in a world where dominance is increasingly technological and English-speaking. It is crucial to capture and name these challenges in ways that feeds and promotes, and does not unintentionally undermine, professional practice. There are interesting research and development possibilities, particularly in teacher education, that emerge from these studies and I will conclude by pointing to some of these.

Gaudi's Ideas for Your Classroom: Geometry for Three-Dimensional Citizens

Claudi Alsina

Universitat Politecnica de Catalunya. Spain

How Johnny became a flatlander

The talk will start with the sad story of Johnny, a boy who was born in place with three dimensions but became, in a few short years, a pure flatlander.

On Gaudi's legacy

Antoni Gaudi (1852-1926) was an exceptional architect who succeeded in combining imagination, ingenuity and creativity in all his masterpieces. His celebrated old buildings, show how he managed to combine the geometry of shapes with stable structural design and great originality. We will describe some of the Gaudi's findings concerning 3D-Geometry. For all of us Gaudi's ideas can guide us today as we face the challenges of educating three-dimensional citizens.

Space is the answer; what is the question?

Teachers are not confident about dealing with three-dimensional geometry, there is a lack of good three-dimensional models in the teaching resource catalogues and most children end compulsory schooling without spatial literacy. We have developed some ideas and projects for improving spatial literacy.

Towards a spatial culture

Below there are 2^3 principles that could guide us, as mathematics educators, in providing our students with a spatial culture.

1. Visual thinking in three dimensions, which is a key point in spatial culture, must not be confined to early grades and can be stimulated at all levels. Visual thinking is not just an appetiser for the main course of abstraction. Clearly, at different levels one is restricted to some spatial items but there are opportunities to offer a broader spatial culture at all ages.

2. Spatial common sense must be cultivated and developed since it is not necessarily an innate capacity. If spatial common sense is not properly cultivated and worked on in maths activities, then students may have difficulties in problem solving when facing 3D objects or transformations.

3. Spatial culture requires: a break with the traditional educational ordering of dimensions (line-plane-space) and a reordering of some technical difficulties. By finding "appropriate descriptions" one can explore space without using technical difficulties as a criteria for selection. Intuition may allow one to face realities that the majority of citizens would never be able to see if advanced mathematical knowledge was required.

4. **Spatial culture can be based upon the reality of our world, exploring its many interesting faces and solving real world problems.** Real things constitute the 1:1 models for exploration, representation and transformation.

5. **Spatial culture may be enriched by means of appropriate use of different languages, technologies and mathematical models.** By combining different languages and different geometrical mechanisms it is possible to improve spatial culture.

6. **Spatial culture can include artistic dimensions, and is therefore an ideal area for interdisciplinary links.** While our main interest is to focus on the geometrical understanding of space, it is also true that an exploration of space provides good opportunities to show links to other topics.

7. **Spatial culture provides opportunities to promote the research spirit in mathematics classrooms.** Space offers intriguing open-ended questions that can be best faced in a spirit of research.

8. **Spatial culture can provide future citizens with tools for developing basic spatial skills and can open a window to creativity.** On completion of compulsory education, students should be able to successfully face basic spatial tasks in their daily lives as citizens, but it would be marvellous if they could also be imaginative, and creative in their jobs and lives.

Time for action. On one occasion, Gaudi showed one of his visitors a range of geometrical models and he remarked, with excitement in his eyes:

"Wouldn't it be beautiful to learn geometry in this way?"

This is our challenge.

Cognitive Processes in Algebraic Thinking and Implications for Teaching

Luciana Bazzini
University of Padua, Italy

Suggestions for a better achievement of the ideas and potential of algebra as well as a productive use of the algebraic code have been given by many researchers from different perspectives. Observing students' behaviour has also induced a reflection on the nature of algebraic thinking and of its underlying dynamics. Algebraic thinking is analysed here in a semiotic perspective: the question "What does a sign represent?" is at the center of the problem between the signifier and the signified. We assume a triadic model, in which the relationship between the object and the subject is mediated by a third entity. Only by means of a semiotic act (which has an essentially triadic nature) one can really grasp the meaning of mathematical objects, but it is also by means of a semiotic act that the subject can evolve his personal senses towards a scientific and socially shared knowledge (in the sense of Vigostsky). This approach seems to be adequate for our purposes, since it is able to integrate these different standpoints into a holistic framework.

The semiotic perspective outlined above allows to identify some basic cognitive processes which we noticed during the observation of students' behavior in solving algebraic problems. Existing literature has shown the possibility of taking 'instant pictures' of students' difficulties, but it is not equally easy to find the way to analyze the cognitive processes involved for longer periods of time and from more a global point of view and, consequently, getting suitable suggestions for teaching.

Firstly I will focus on the very start of algebraic thinking (cognitive genesis and the naming process), secondly on the processes which constitute the central core (activation of senses, anticipation and transformation) and finally on the processes which are the outcome of the solving procedure (condensation and evaporation).

As a premise, it should be noted that students' cognitive processes develop within mental spaces, i.e., the fictitious world, that students create to do experiments. A mental space has spatial, temporal and logical features, not all necessarily are present in the same subject. Its reality depends on the situation (namely, the problem, the pupils, the negotiation in the class, and so on). The way in which students use signs and endow them with meaning has been studied by Radford (1999) with reference to tasks related to the algebraic generalization of patterns. His approach is grounded in the claim that the learning of algebra and the emergence of students' algebraic thinking (cognitive genesis) appears not as an a-cultural process of abstraction in the intellectual development of the students, but as an instance of a social and individual enterprise of acquiring a historical and culturally developed sign system which, in our culture, has proven very useful in carrying out certain tasks. We agree with his claim that the students' reflections and their understanding and production of signs are embedded in discursive schemes.

The process of naming (Arzarello, Bazzini and Chiappini, 1994) consists in assigning names to the elements of a problem in order to make possible incorporating and clarifying the sense of a problem into the system of algebraic representation. The choice of names to designate objects is strictly linked to the control of the variables introduced.

In this process, one main difficulty, especially for novices, derives from the

impossibility of sustaining the stream of thought using natural language.

The activation of senses as a cognitive process has been discussed by Arzarello,Bazzini and Chiappini (1993, 1995) in terms of a theoretical model based on the distinction between sense and denotation of an algebraic expression. It has been observed that algebraic reasoning is like a trip, whose destination and outcome are not known in advance.

Thus the transformation function is performed through a dialectic relationship between standard patterns of transformation, deriving from instruction and practice, which produce the transformations, and anticipations which suggest a suitable "shape" for the formula to be processed and the direction of transformations (Boero, 1994).

Furthermore, pupils must work in mental spaces where objects lose their extra-mathematical and procedural tracks and they must translate them into symbolic expressions, which are highly synthetic, ideographic and relational. To do that, a student is required to write concisely and expressively the amount of information of a term, whose complexity and generality cannot easily be measured with the language of arithmetic. In one sense, the stream of thought which sustains her/his computations and arguments contracts and condenses its temporal, spatial and logical features into an act of thought, which grasps the global situation as a whole (process of condensation).

At the opposite side of condensation we find a typical process of poor algebraic performers, that we call evaporation. While condensation entails a strong semantic control, on the contrary, evaporation concerns the dramatic loss of the meaning of symbols met by most pupils when losing semantic control in algebraic problem solving.

Typically, it happens when they can no longer express the meaning of mathematical objects and relationships in ordinary language when referring to the subject's actions, to the very processes of their construction and generation and to any other extra mathematical information about them. In such cases, they can no longer use algebraic language as a stenography of their thinking processes, possibly mediating with the natural language. As such, evaporation is one of the main obstacles in developing an algebraic way of thinking and a non-empty use of the algebraic code.

References

Arzarello F., L.Bazzini, Chiappini G. P.: 1993, Cognitive processes in algebraic thinking, *Proceedings of the 17th International Conference for the Psychology of Mathematics Education*, Vol. I ,pp.138-145, Tsukuba, Japan.

Arzarello F., L.Bazzini, Chiappini G.P.: 1994, The process or naming in algebraic thinking, in J.P. da Ponte and J.F. Matos (Eds.), *Proceedings of the 18th International Conference for the Psychology of Mathematics Education*, Vol.1,pp.40-47, Lisbon,Portugal:PME Program Committee.

Arzarello F., L.Bazzini, Chiappini G.P.: 1995. The construction of algebraic knowledge: towards a socio-cultural theory and practice in L.Meira (Ed.) *Proceedings of the 19th International Conference for the Psychology of Mathematics Education*, Vol.1,pp.119-134, Recife, Brazil.

Boelo, P .:1994, About the role of algebraic language in Mathematics and related difficulties, *Rendiconti del Seminario Matematico, Universita di Torino*, **52**,(2), 161-194

Radford. L.: 1999. The rethoric of generalization, in O. Zaslavsky, *Proceedings of the 23th International Conference for the Psychology of Mathematics Education*, Vol.4, pp.89-96, Haifa, Israel.

A Perspective for Teaching Elementary School Mathematics based on the Research Literature

Jerry P. Becke
Southern Illinois University Carbondale, US.

It is well known that elementary school mathematics teaching is undergoing refor
in many countries of the world. In most cases, reform work in mathematic
education is determined by well-researched recommendations included in th
individual country's national documents. For example, in the United State
Principles and Standards for School Mathematics (April, 2000) appeared in just th
last few months and, as with its predecessors [the Curriculum Standards (1989
Teaching Standards (1991) and Assessment Standards (1995)], it will have a
important influence on work to improve mathematics curricula, teaching an
assessment.

A common thread runs through the national documents which considers that the ol
paradigm of "teaching as a treatment and learning as an effect" has given way to
new paradigm of students as active constructors of knowledge in mathematics.
great deal of research has been carried out in several countries analyzing this ne
view.

This research provides some direction for the teaching of mathematics consisten
with the constructional viewpoint at the elementary level. While a key element i
this viewpoint is the active role of students, this idea has existed in education for
very long time; however, it is expected that this idea will play a more prominent rol
in schooling in the future.

The focus of this paper will be on examining the direction that research suggests fo
teaching elementary school mathematics. There are four types of learnin
discussed: active learning, individual learning, cooperative learning, and learnin
in strands and contexts.

Attention will be given to ways of organizing teaching, assessment, and teache
education as well as ideas for future research.

Attention will also be given to the consideration of the reality of most elementar
classroom teachers   (con'))

The literature in mathematics education also shows a renewed emphasis o
communication in mathematics. When communication in mathematics is combine

with the open-ended teaching processes of the constructive paradigm, language factors in teaching and learning need to be considered. How communication and language development can be achieved in the classroom will be demonstrated through a description of classroom interaction in the Japanese open approach to teaching mathematics. The open approach provides a vehicle for working towards language development in the classroom, while also tying in closely with the theme of children as active learners.

Overcoming Obstacles to the Democratisation of Mathematics Education

Alan J. Bishop
Monash University, Australia

Modern society is demanding much greater mathematical knowledge of its citizens than ever before and the essential challenge for mathematics educators concerned with issues of democracy is how to provide an adequate mathematics education for the greatest number of citizens. In this paper I will talk from the perspective of research, because I believe that research in mathematics education is fundamental to the development of our field, and that it provides our principal intellectual protection against the narrow-minded and populist demands of our current educational politicians.

The focus of this paper is on the idea of democratising mathematics education for three main reasons. Firstly the whole process of education should be a democratising one. I see the main goal of universal education to be one of democratising knowledge and making it available to as many learners as possible, including mathematics. This has been a theme of several important UNESCO publications as well as others.

Secondly mathematics seems to be an easy subject in which to develop elites. This is mainly due to the way that mathematics has been used, and is still being used, to select students for higher education study, and therefore for more prestigious positions in society .

Thirdly the future of the world depends on the quality of the education we give to all our children. The fight against ignorance is one of the biggest challenges of our times, and in our field the task is the democratising of mathematical knowledge, without which a large majority of our young people are being impoverished and disenfranchised. Sadly mathematics is a subject that most of them still believe they fail at or that they have little interest in.

To my mind the fault lies not with the subject, nor with the learners. It lies with the curricula, and with the way they are required to be taught. It lies with political processes that deny adequate resources to needy educational systems. It lies with media images that imply that it is "non-cool" to study hard and to become an effective learner of subjects like mathematics. More generally it lies with the way many people in powerful positions continue to support the myth that it is an elitist subject, often unknowingly, and thereby promote curricula and methods that are basically anti-democratic.

Education reflects on the knowledge from the past, from the perspective of the present, but with a vision of the future. Without the knowledge from the past there is nothing with which to educate the present generation - there is merely the sharing of ignorance. Without a vision for the future there is no goal towards which the education of the present learners should be directed - there is merely training. Genuine education requires both. Mathematics education certainly relies on the knowledge from the past. Mathematics has a long history and mathematics curricula are locked into that history. But to what extent do our mathematics curricula offer a vision for the future? What is needed is a mathematics education that is democratising, in the fullest sense -empowering, informative, action-oriented, locally-based but globally aware, reflective, critical, creative, and responsible.

Considering the mathematics curricula what are some of the democratising trends we can see from the research? The main trend we can see is that the research interest is overcoming the conceptual obstacle of content by considering context instead. Local mathematical knowledge should also help to shape the local school mathematics curriculum, because there are often great differences between situations, knowledge, languages, and customs in different parts of many countries. There is also an increasing interest in numeracy, reflecting both a concern that Mathematics teaching is not succeeding, and also a desire to have a more relevant and context-related mathematics curriculum in the schools. Developing numeracy, or 'matheracy' as D'Ambrosio prefers to call it (meaning mathematical literacy), is clearly a democratising goal that should be supported by all.

One of the favourite constructs from Mathematics education in common use is also one of its most anti-democratic - the idea of 'mathematical ability'. The problem is that it is associated with a description of learners as if it had no relation to any other variable. It takes no heed of the context in which the learner is learning. Yet modern research has shown the importance of the idea of 'situated cognition' which describes the fact that when you learn anything you learn it in a certain situation. Also what researchers are far more interested in these days is the idea of 'mathematical abilities' or 'multiple intelligences' as Howard Gardner (1993) calls them. Democratic teaching recognises and celebrates difference and diversity.

Awareness of other mathematical practices enables teachers to create problems and tasks in class that can allow the students to demonstrate the knowledge that they have acquired elsewhere. It helps teachers to democratise their teaching. Democratising mathematics education means among other things, from a teacher's point of view, understanding a richer picture of mathematics learners,

not making unwarranted assumptions about mythical levels of ability,

being aware of the learner's social situation and how that is affecting the quality of their learning,

recognising the limits of situated learning,

giving the learners more control over their own learning.

However teachers are not autonomous and therefore it is important that those of us who are in a position to influence the anti-democratic constraints surrounding mathematics teaching at present accept our share of the responsibility. This means that if mathematics education is to become more democratised then this must happen in all aspects of the work including the research process itself.

We have a responsibility to the future generations, who will inherit this complicated and mixed-up world, to overcome the ignorance, fear and failure that is currently present in mathematics education. We must all strive to overcome the obstacles to democratisation in our own ideas and our own practices. The ideas and the possibilities exist, so all we need is the professional and political will-power.

What Research Evidence Tells Us About Effective Mathematics Teaching for Children aged 6-13

Margaret Brown
King's College,University of London, UK

Research Paradigms

In examining research on effective teaching it becomes clear that the ideal empirical study should combine iteratively both quantitative and qualitative methods. Small-scale mainly qualitative studies lead to insights which can be tested on a wider scale; patterns in large-scale quantitative data suggest associations which can be explored and better understood by case-studies, and so on. Quantitative studies offer the evidence for evidence-based practice that politicians are now seeking; qualitative analysis can provide the understanding of the processes involved.

The research includes both monitoring studies, which focus on the description, interpretation and evaluation of current practice, and intervention, studies which aim to explore the effects of deliberate changes in practice.

Effective Teaching: International Studies

The main TIMSS (Third International Mathematics and Science Study) analysis of performance is a large-scale quantitative monitoring study of performance with accompanying data on a variety of other variables (Beaton et al., 1996; Mullis et al., 1997)). However like the two previous IEA studies (Husen,1967; Burstein,1992), there are no consistent findings about what features characterise effective teaching.

The TIMSS video study (e.g. Stigler & Hiebert, 1997) is in contrast an interesting example of a monitoring study which combines qualitative and quantitative approaches and leads to some promising conclusions about the effectiveness of the Japanese model of well-crafted and challenging lessons which aim at depth of thinking and discussion, in contrast to lessons focusing on undemanding exercises requiring repetition of teacher-demonstrated procedures. However there are some doubts about generalisability.

There is also some evidence from evaluations of NCTM Standards-based programmes in the United States that conceptual and discussion-led teaching has positive effects (U.S.Dept. Ed., 1999). Such intervention studies, however, can be less convincing than monitoring studies because of the difficulty in controlling for teacher development input.

Effective Teaching: Work at King's College London

We have been engaged in a number of studies of effective teaching at King's which adds to the knowledge gained in the international studies:

Experiencing School Mathematics

This study of secondary teaching by Jo Boaler (1997), now at Stanford, is again a combination of a qualitative and quantitative monitoring study. This study is now being followed up by an investigation of the interaction between school context, ways of allocating students to classes, types of pedagogy and student attitudes in six schools (Boaler et al., 2000).

Cognitive Acceleration in Mathematics Education (CAME)

This is an intervention study, with a mainly quantitative evaluation, in the early years of the secondary school (Grades 6 and 7). It uses two-weekly 'thinking maths' lessons (Adhami et al., 1998), designed according to both Piagetian and Vygotskian theory (Cobb & Bauersfeld, 1995) and putting a considerable investment into professional development and support of teachers. The work has now been extended into primary schools, where more qualitative data is also being gathered on teacher development

Effective Teachers of Numeracy

This study of primary teachers (K-Grade 5) was a short monitoring study which employed qualitative and quantitative data to find the characteristics of teachers whose classes made very high gains in numeracy (Askew et al., 1997).

The Leverhulme Numeracy Research Programme

This is a major 5-year programme which is composed of six projects, one mainly quantitative (a longitudinal study of two cohorts, each of 1500 children in 40 primary schools). There is also a mainly qualitative case-study of the progress of a sub-sample of 30 pupils in each cohort, and four other mainly qualitative studies focus on different aspects of primary numeracy. Most are monitoring studies but two involve intervention.

Conclusions from the King's Studies

Our findings so far confirm those of studies referred to earlier. They are demonstrating that the teachers whose children have the lowest learning gains are those who use transmission teaching which aims at standard techniques, and those who use discovery styles of teaching which emphasise, readiness and manipulatives. The most successful teachers have a commitment to making connections, both between different mathematical ideas, and between the mathematical ideas and children's current states of understanding.

To achieve this they encourage social participation and sensitive assessment.

Although some Successful teachers are exceptions to this trend, easily measurable factors related to pedagogy or to teacher attributes seem to be unimportant in explaining effectiveness. These findings are being used in new curriculum developments in the UK such as CAME. And the new Interact series (SMP, 2000) at secondary level.

References

Adhami, M.,Johnson,D. & Shayer, M. (1998) *Thinking Maths: Accelerated learning in mathematics.* Oxford, Heinemann.

Askew, M.,Brown, M., Rhodes, V., Wiliam, D. and Johnson, D. (1997a) *Effective Teachers of Numeracy.* London: King's College Lonclon.

Beaton, A E, Mullis, I V S, Martin, M O, Gonzalces, E J. Kelly, D L and Smith, T A (1996) *Mathematics Achievement in the Middle School Years: IEA's Third Mathematics and Science Study.* Chestnut Hill, Massachusetts: Boston College.

Boaler,J. (1997) *Experiencing School Mathematics: Teaching styles, sex and setting.* Buckingham: Open University Press.

Boaler, J., Wiliam, D. & Brown. M. (2000) Students' experience of ability grouping - disaffection, polarisation and experience of failure. *British Educational Research Journal,*27(4).

Burstein, L (1992) *The IEA Study of Mathematics III: student growth and classroom processes.* Oxford: Pergamon Press.

Cobb,P. & Bauersfeld H. (1995) *The Emergence of Mathematical Meaning.* Hillsdale, N.J: Lawrence Erlbaum Associates.

Husen, T (1967a,b) *International Study of Achievement in Mathematics,* Vols. I & II. Stockholm/New York: Almquist & Wiksell/Wiley.

Mullls, I. V. S, Martin, M. O., Beaton, A. E., Gonzalez, E. J., Kelly, D. L. & Smith. T. A. (1997) *Mathematics Achievement in the Primary School Years: IEA's Third Mathematics and Science Study.* Chestnut Hill, Massachusetts: Boston College.

Stigler, J. W. & Hiebert, J. (1997) Understanding and improving classroom mathematics Instruction. *Phi Delta Kappan,* September 1997, pp. 14-21 .

School Mathematics Project (SMP) (2000 -) *SMP Interact Cambrigde* : Cambridge University Press.

United States Department of Education, Mathcmatics and Science Expert Panel (1999) *Exemplary Prmising Mathematics Programs.* Washington: US Department of Education.

A Sociocultural Approach to Infinitesimal Calculus

Ricardo Contoral, Rosa Maria Farfan,
Cinvestav IPN, Mexico

Science and science education are not disunited from social practices wherein these are able to develop. However, mathematics, for example, as is well known, have developed under the premise that they deal with abstract objects, so therefore prior to social practice and consequently external to the individual. This Platonist vision of knowledge equally impregnates the didactic activity of our days; a professor communicates preexisting truths to his pupils by means of a speech; the form, then, assumes this vision, will at some early moment uncover the meaning of the abstract objects among the alumni.

In this lecture we will sustain the thesis that mathematical knowledge, even those we consider advanced, have an origin and a social function associated with the set of socially established, human practices. This affirmation should not be understood in the sense that every mathematical knowledge obeys a practical need of nature because it is been sufficiently documented that mathematical notions do not necessarily come from successive abstractions and generalization of empirics. As a matter of fact, our thesis has a sociologic orientation, since it establishes an affiliation between the nature of knowledge as produced by human beings with their activities by means and as a consequence of which said knowledge is produced. In this sense, we sustain the existence of dialectics between the use and the symbol or, said in other words, between activity and object.

We have followed a systemic approach, which we call socioepistemology, which allows for dealing in an articulate manner with the four fundamental components of the social construction of knowledge: its epistemological nature, the sociocultural dimension, the levels of cognitive matter and the modes of transmission through teaching (Cantoral, 1999).

By social construction of advanced mathematical knowledge, we understand the set of explicit or implicit interactions, established between the relative poles to the advanced processes of thought, the epistemology of advanced mathematics and the highly specialized human practices. In the exposition, we will discuss some examples such as the one relative to the formation of Newton's binomial and we will analyze the role acquired by the notion of prediction in the sociocultural vision of the era.

This notion of prediction is socially built from daily experiences of individuals. That means that in certain situations we need to know the value that will take a specific magnitude in the course of time. Then it will be required to determine the value taken by the depending variable before the independent one passes from stage one to stage two. But as a result of our impossibility to advance the time at will, we must predict. In such a case, we will not count with reasons to believe that the true value sought is distant from the expectations that in the beginning will generate for us the values of the form where to they change and change their changes, and so on.

For example, the binomial mathematical object of Newton present itself in that case as an entity that progressively emerges from the system of socially shared practices, linked to the resolution of a type of situations that will be in need of prediction, from which it will fare up to taking the abstract shape of the concept of analytical function.

Originally, the binomial of Newton is written as $(P + PQ)^{m/n}$ and not, as is usual in contemporary textbooks, by means of the expression $(a + b)^n$. We sustain that this obeys to an alternative conception sustained upon an epistemology that differs from that we nowadays teach in our classrooms, and which is addressed to a program in the field of science by which we seek to predict the behavior of the phenomena of change. A program of mathematization of modellable phenomena by means of the metaphor of water flow equally applied to the evolution of other magnitudes (Cantoral, R. & Farfan, R.-M., 1998).

Newton publishes his famous theorem of the binomial in 1696 as a generalization of previous some works on infinite series and wherein he anticipates the prediction idea. He proposes a sophisticated interpretation of Pascal's triangle to solve the squaring of the hyperbole, wherein he construes the arrangements {1}, {1, 1}, {1,2,1}, {1,3,3,1}, etc., as a collection of successive powers from 11 ; i.e., $1=11^0$, $11=11^1$, $121=11^2$, etc.

The theorem establishes, for the rational m/n, the following equality:
$(P + PQ)^{m/n} = P^{m/n} + m/n\ AQ + (m \cdot n)/2n\ BQ + (m\text{-}2n)/3n\ CQ +$ etc.
Wherein A P B m AQ C m2nn BQ, etc.
$A=P^{m/n}$, $B=m/n\ AQ$, $C=(m\text{-}n)/2n\ BQ$, etc.

The question we want to deal with, refers to the meaning of the expression P + PQ. The era wherein the binomial theorem is published, is characterized by the pretension of scientists to model, mathematically and logically, the evolution of things that flow, let's say, they are interested in predicting. Let us imagine that P represents some physical magnitude, for example temperature or position. If the magnitude Q is smaller that the unit, $0 < Q < 1$, then $0 < PQ < P$. Consequently, the magnitude P + PQ represents the next state of P; whereas the term PQ represents a small portion of P. Due to the fact that in that period the expression $y = x^{m/n}$, represents the most general possible function, the expression in question, $(P + PQ)^{m/n}$ represents the state which the expression $P^{m/n}$ shall have some time thereafter. In this manner, the aim is to determine the value that the expression $(P + PQ)^{m/n}$ will have to assume in terms of the beginning values. This vision was extensively developed during the whole eighteenth century and was consolidated as a socially valid paradigm. So science sought to predict the evolution of the phenomena of continuous flow basing itself on the water flow metaphor.

References

Cantoral, R. (1999). Approccio socioepistemologico a la ricerca in matematica educativa. *La matematica e la sua didattica*, Vol.3, pp. 258 - 273.

Cantoral, R. & Farfan, R.-M. (1998). Pensamiento y lenguaje variacional en la introduccion al analisis. *Epsilon* **42**, Vol, 14(3), pp. 353 - 369.

Cultural Cross-Purposes and Expectation as Barriers to Success in Mathematics

Megan Clark
Victoria University of Wellington, New Zealand

In New Zealand, Maori and Pacific Islands students participate and perform in mathematics at a much lower level than the population at large as is the case with indigenous and migrant groups in many other countries. The teaching of mathematics to Maori and Pacific Islands students is characterised by practices that do not enhance the earning experiences of these students. Practices such as: holding back an extra year in junior school, competitive activities, the use of worksheets and solitary study, a lack of culturally appropriate contexts for problems, and low expectations all have a negative impact on the mathematics learning of both groups of students. The lack of examples and activities that are set in meaningful contexts that relate to the cultures of these students has long been decried, but efforts to remedy this are usually superficial and have little effect. The unsociable nature of many mathematics classrooms, especially at secondary school is a substantial hindrance to many Maori and Pacific Islands students who much prefer to talk about mathematics rather than write about it. The lack of talking in the mathematics classroom is felt by many students to be uncomfortable and unpleasant.

With Pacific Islands students, a lack of teacher understanding of their cultures, especially with regard to the role of questions and questioning in the classroom, and their attitude to authority cause many misunderstandings and difficulties. Such students may enter school having experienced a strong transmission model of education provided by the home and church, and find it very difficult to understand and adjust to the child-centred, social constructivist model of leaning which largely prevails in the junior school. Many parents of these first or second generation migrant children, like those in migrant groups elsewhere, have a very strong desire for their children to succeed, but frequently do not know how to assist the school to achieve this. Teachers often have little knowledge of the wider family responsibilities that such students (especially young women) may have, while parents may be unaware of the importance that the school places upon homework.

Consequences of these gaps in understanding can be significant for the student. A failure to complete homework on a regular basis, or an inability to regularly attend school may lead eventually to dropping out, unless the school and teacher make particular efforts to understand the child's circumstances and work out a strategy to

111

enable the child to achieve their potential. Another source of difficulties can be the " English is Intelligence" mentality of some teachers.

Both groups are subject to low expectations (including inappropriate praise for trivial tasks), the 'shaming' effects of remedial programmes and public questioning, and insufficient oral assessment, which might help to better discover their real level of ability.

Those Maori and Pacific Islands students that do succeed in the mathematics classroom often succeed by adopting strategies which lead to success in primary and the lower secondary school but which hinder later success, especially at the tertiary level. Teachers need to be on the alert to ensure that the habits of learning a student is acquiring are ones that will be effective for all of a student's academic career.

Some suggestions will be given as to how to improve matters in such a way that a pupil's culture is enhanced and not damaged by mathematics teaching, and that pupils continue to participate in mathematics learning.

Histrical Trends in Mathematics Education: Developing International Perspective

McKenzie A. Clements
Universiti Brunei Darussalam, Brunei Darussalam

This lecture an outline of the history of mathematics education in Southeast Asian nations and Oceania in the 19th and 20th centuries will be presented. Australia, New Zealand, and all Southeast Asian nations except Thailand, have a colonial heritage which has played a major part in the evolution of their 19th and 20th century school mathematics curricula and practices. Consequently, many of these countries share mathematics education models that closely resemble those of the colonising countries. Thus, for example, the history of mathematics education in Australia reflects major movements within mathematics education in the United Kingdom. Indeed, throughout the 20th century, school mathematics education in Australia, Brunei Darussalam, Hong Kong, Malaysia, New Zealand, and Singapore had much in common with school mathematics in the United Kingdom.

Given the forces of colonialism, it was not surprising that many of the transitions in the mathematics curriculum of Southeast Asian nations resembled the transitions within the United Kingdom, the United States of America, Russia, France, and Australia.

The acceptance of overseas models for school mathematics was supported by international agencies, such as the World Bank, the Asian Development Bank, and UNESCO. Selected persons were sent overseas for higher degree studies, and on their return "home" became part of the "educated" elite who developed education policies They tended to want to replicate in their own nations, what they had learned abroad. Furthermore, consultants from "advanced" nations were introduced, and these naturally recommended the kinds of approaches that were occurring in their nations.

Often the funds made available by aid agencies for such developments came in the form of loans, and therefore important cost-benefit analyses were carried out. However, these analyses were almost always done by those who were responsible for the policies (i.e., the aid agencies, or the governments that sought aid). From that point of view, were less neutral than has often been supposed.

There is nothing inherently wrong with educators in one nation learning from the experiences of the organisation of schools, curricula, assessment, and articulation practices. There is something wrong, however, if one nation merely follows the education practices and ideas of another nation as a matter of course (or because of perceived future economic and social advantages), when cultural and social factors would suggest that something different is what is needed. It will be argued in this presentation that educated elites in many Southeast Asian nations decided that certain forms of school and university mathematics were needed, when local conditions suggested that the paths they chose were unsuitable, and indeed, unwise.

Conflicting pressures on mathematics education programs, arising from the classical mathematics heritage, the advent of mass primary and secondary education, the new math(s), and mastery-learning all contributed to the development of mathematics curricula as they are now defined and interpreted in classrooms and school systems in the various nations. Although, there are many structural differences, there are also many similarities.

In the presentation there will a focus on similarities and differences in school mathematics in four nations: Australia, Brunei Darussalam, Singapore and the United Kingdom. It will be argued that although, at the beginning of the 21st century, the intended and implemented mathematics curricula in schools in the four nations, are similar, the approaches adopted are more suitable for Australia, Singapore and the United Kingdom than they are for Brunei Darussalam. Indeed, Singapore and Brunei Darussalam have almost identical intended mathematics curricula; they use the same textbooks, and prepare their students for the same upper-secondary examinations (administered by the University of Cambridge Local Examination Syndicate). However, examination results in the two nations are very different, raising the possibility that existing practices suit one of the nations (Singapore) but no the other (Brunei Darussalam). This caveat is used as the basis for arguing that local cultural forces should be the most important consideration in the design of mathematics education programs. It is also argued that principle should apply to programs at all levels.

The Dilemmas of Preparing Teachers to Teach Mathematics within a Constructivist Framework

Beatriz S. D'Ambrosio,
IUPUI- School of Education, USA

Teaching future elementary teachers to teach mathematics requires making choices and taking positions from among the multiple pressures placed upon mathematics teacher educators. As part of a broader teacher education faculty, mathematics teacher educators find themselves negotiating the positions of the mathematics education community and the larger community of teacher educators. Furthermore, pressures from licensure agencies, accreditation institutions, and the positions of practicing teachers-- collaborators in the teacher education process, add further complexity to the frameworks within which teachers are prepared to teach mathematics.

From the realm of the mathematics education community, reform in mathematics teaching requires that teachers take a new stance on their role in the classroom. Shifter (1996) suggests that classrooms that promote understanding of mathematical ideas are those in which the teachers take on the role of monitor of student learning, making sense of their students' sense-making. In these classrooms teachers take a stance as researchers of student understanding. In these classrooms, the pedagogy enacted by the teacher, the approach to knowledge as constructed by the learner, and the culture of the classroom represent a setting never experienced by most future teachers.

New practices in teacher education also aim to prepare teachers as agents of social change. These practices are grounded in the belief that teachers should orchestrate the classroom environment in ways that promote equity and social justice, and that teachers should model democratic education.

The current climate of teacher education includes preparation of new teachers for the "new social realities of teaching" (Lieberman & Miller, 2000). According to Lieberman and Miller, these new social realities of teaching represent major shifts in both dispositions and practice (p.51). Some of the new positions assumed in teacher education programs include commitments to developing the following dispositions and practices in future teachers: viewing learning as the construction of knowledge, enacting teaching through inquiry, viewing inquiry as a major component of the life of a teacher, valuing a strong content knowledge base, understanding one's role as a collaborator within a community of practice, viewing reflection as the basis of life-long learning and continuous renewal.

Within this web of differing views and foci regarding teacher preparation how can education programs define themselves in ways that prepare teachers to teach in the 21st century? In this talk I will describe the position assumed by a teacher education program that has accepted the challenge of supporting future teachers to embrace a constructivist perspective on teaching all subjects, including mathematics. In the description of the program, and the process we have undergone to implement the program I will analyze the difficulties we have encountered as we move towards a program that is inquiry-based, student-centered, field-based, and participatory.

I base my work with future teachers on the notion of constructivist teaching in which a constructivist teacher is one who studies the knowledge constructions of students and who interacts with students in a learning space whose design is based, at least in part, on a working knowledge of students' understanding of concepts and ideas (Steffe & D'Ambrosio, 1995). In this sense I enact constructivist teaching with my university students and with children in the field. Together future teachers and I explore the many facets of teaching that embrace a constructivist perspective. The focus of our work together lies in the construction of models of children's understanding of mathematical ideas. At the same time my personal inquiry lies in my own construction of models of future teachers' understanding of mathematical ideas.

I will describe the activities in which we involve our future teachers and analyze their performance as to what strides they make towards understanding children's knowledge of mathematics. Future teachers in our program are asked to respond to performance assessment tasks. These responses are analyzed by the teacher education faculty and inform the experiences designed throughout the program. As a program we have narrowed the scope of experiences for future teachers to a focus on learning to listen to children. The performance assessment tasks are designed to assess the effectiveness of the program in shaping future teachers' skill in accessing student knowledge and building a model of student understanding.

In this presentation I will draw on data from these performance assessment tasks and analyze future teachers' performance raising questions about the experiences that are needed in order to shape their growth in becoming effective mathematics teachers. The analysis of the data is framed on Brent Davis's (1996) perspectives on three types of classroom listening (evaluative listening, interpretive listening, and hermeneutic listening). The data is also looked at through the lens of Belenky, Clinchy, Goldberger, Tarule's (1986) conception of silent, received, connected, separate, and constructed knowers.

The difficulties of embracing a constructivist perspective towards teaching mathematics are evident when we analyze future teachers' difficulties in building models of children's understanding. Our understanding of these difficulties can be further shaped by considering characteristics of future teachers as to their own approaches to learning mathematics and their perceptions of the nature of mathematical knowledge and mathematical learning.

References

Belenky, Clinchy, Goldberger, Tarule (1986). *Women's Ways of Knowing : The Development of Self, Voice, and Mind.* Basic Books.

Davis, B. (1996). *Teaching Mathematics : Toward a Sound Alternative.* Garland.

Shifter, D. (1996). *What's Happening in Math Class?* New York: Teachers' College Press.

Steffe, L. & D'Ambrosio, B. (1995). Toward a working model of constructivist teaching: A reaction to Simon. *Journal for Research in Mathematics Education,* **26**, pp. 146-159.

Liebermann, A. & Miller, L. (2000). Teaching and Tacher Development: A New Synthesis for a New Century. In R.S. Brandt, *Education in a New Era*, pp. 47-66. ASCD Yearbook.

Geometry in Russian Schools: Traditions of Past and State in Present

Nikolai Dolbilin

Steklov Mathematical Institute, Moscow, Russia

The role of geometry in education and life is enormous. Plato regarded geometry as the first essential in the training of the mind. 'Let no one destitute of geometry enter my doors' said the inscription over the door of his school. V. Arnold says that anyone who never studied art of proving cannot a distinguish correct reasoning from a wrong one. Learning solid geometry is important for its applications in physics, crystallography, chemistry etc. Geometric shapes by themselves very often are real works of art and the visual perception of ornaments, polyhedra, their symmetries delights the eye and the underlying structure stimulates the mind. Therefore, in particular, geometry is a powerful tool to attract students to mathematics.

Nevertheless, in many countries mathematics curriculums ignore geometry and try to "save" class time on geometry in favor of other parts of mathematics. Needless to say, that school geometry is about dying there, though no notable success in teaching other mathematics subjects is attained either. It is likely that the following sad correlation is true: if there is no good school geometry there is no good school mathematics education in the whole. In contrast to this, Russian school, regardless severe economics conditions and well-known political tension in the past decade, is still keeping relatively high standards in teaching geometry, as well as in teaching the rest of mathematics.

A point of peculiar interest is that by the late 1980's all schools across the former Soviet Union had one national curriculum of mathematics as well as one and the same textbook. Fortunately, the only textbook on geometry which had been functioning in Russian school for over 50 years up to the 1960's was a beautiful "Elementary Geometry" written back in the 1890's by outstanding pedagogue A.P.Kiselev. The textbook of Kiselev was designed for teaching geometry in grades 6--10 (for students between the ages of 12 and 17). Although this textbook starts with introductory pages on which the very first geometric concepts and statements are exposed informally as obvious ones requiring no proof, the Kiselev textbook is a deductive Euclidean-type course. Really, already on the first pages Kiselev tactfully introduces elements of reasoning and proving. After an intuitive definition of congruent triangles (through their juxtapositions) and non-rigorous proving the three basic theorems on congruent triangles the course becomes deductive and rather rigorous. Thus, Russia has a successful longstanding experience of teaching a deductive course of geometry in mass school. One can surely say that by 1970's graduates attained a high standard of geometric knowledge.

Here one should mention that by 1960's the soviet compulsory school numbered only 7 grades but everyone could freely get complete 10-year education. In fact, about a half of pupils got complete education, what, to some degree, meant a natural selection of high school pupils. Post-World-War II changes in the country impacted on the whole school system and curriculum development. Compulsory school and free high school got numbered 9 and 11 years, respectively. As a result of reforming the public school in the 1960's.

-- a number of mathematics classes decreased from 7 to 5 hours a week;
-- curriculum has been all revised from the set theory viewpoint;
-- calculus has entered the curriculum 10-11;
-- school geometry has been supplemented with vectors and Cartesian co-ordinates.

The new curriculum and textbooks prepared under guidance of Andrei Kolmogorov (one of the best Russian mathematicians in XX century) were promptly put into action. In the beginning a week opposition to the reform looked like a conflict between conservators and reformators. In 1977, the first post-reform graduates took entrance exams in universities. Selection committees of universities found out obvious decrease in the rate of mathematical knowledge and skills of new students in comparison with pre-reform graduates. After that "the critical mood has immediately matured into a powerful counter-reforming movement'". In this counter-reformation a traditionalist view of school mathematics took over.

Among reasons of the failure of reforming mathematics education in 1960's
-- besides needless abstractization -- I mention the following:
-- neglecting a role of word problems in arithmetic;
-- significant increasing curriculum with simultaneous decreasing class time;
-- underestimating effect of 9-year (instead 7-year) compulsory education;
--insufficient readiness of teachers to teach "new" mathematics.

During the 1980 counter-reformation some textbooks of the previous reform have been revised. A geometry textbook was replaced by a book of the outstanding geometer A.Pogorelov. This very short textbook starts with ten so-called 'basic properties'. Playing a role of axioms they are explicitly formulated. All the rest geometric content is derived from them in a deductive way. One should mention that the set of the axioms in the textbook is given as simple and as transparent as possible. On the other side the style of the book is very concise and rather dry, the geometrical content and an attached set of problems are strictly limited by curriculum.

Since the mid 1980's school actively uses a parallel textbook by L.Atanasyan et al. This Euclidean-type textbook won the first prize at the All-Union competition of geometrical textbooks in 1988.

I must name also a new geometrical textbook by I.Sharygin which has recently entered the Federal set of textbooks. The author emphasizes that the value of learning geometry is not only in training the mind or in its practical utility. Geometry should be studied since it is an antique, beautiful, and very essential part of the human culture. The textbook contains a nice collection of original problems. What is very important, Sharygin also created a pre-formal course of visual geometry designed for grades 5-6. Material in this pre-formal course is attractive and able to rouse real interest of pupils to geometry. The set of Sharygin's textbooks seems to be very promising because it gives a chance to make learning geometry both mathematically interesting and fun.

Towards A Theory of Learning Advanced Mathematical Concepts

Ed Dubinsky
USA

In this talk I will consider the role of theories in collegiate mathematics education research. I will propose characteristics that a theory might have, describe one particular example of a theory and consider the extent to which it possesses these characteristics. I will also describe how this theory has been used by its developers and others throughout the world to increase our understanding of the learning process and enhance student learning of post-secondary level mathematical concepts in Calculus, Discrete Mathematics, and Abstract Algebra. Finally, I will give specific examples of the use of this theory in helping students learn certain concepts in abstract algebra.

Theories in Mathematics Education. In my view, the role of theories in mathematics education is to provide tools for increasing our understanding of how mathematics can be learned and how educational experiences can help. For example, a theory of how a particular mathematical concept can be learned might propose specific pedagogical strategies to help students learn these concepts and point to questions that can be asked of data on the effectiveness of these strategies. One consequence of this view is that the question of whether or not a theory is true may not be relevant. Rather, we should judge a theory in terms of how well it performs its role as a tool. One way of doing this is to establish general characteristics of a theory and to consider how a particular theory measures up in terms of these properties.

General characteristics of a theory. I suggest that the following characteristics are important for a theory in mathematics education: it should support prediction of learning outcomes, possess explanatory power; be applicable to a broad range of phenomena, help organize thinking about learning phenomena; serve as a tool for analyzing data, and provide a language for communication about learning.

APOS Theory. In addition to the characteristics mentioned in the previous paragraph, I also feel that in each specific study, one should focus on a single theory rather than try to use several at the same time. In particular, it is useful to choose this theory at the outset of an investigation.

In most of my own research, I have chosen to use what has come to be known as APOS Theory. This is a constructivist theory based on the idea that an individual constructs her or his mathematical knowledge in a social context as a means of dealing with mathematical problem situations. APOS Theory provides a framework for analyzing these mental concepts in terms of what are called actions, processes, objects, and schemas. In the talk, I will explain what these terms mean and give examples in the context of cosets of a subgroup and quotient groups in abstract algebra.

Use of APOS Theory. A typical study of learning a mathematical concept using this theory begins with an APOS analysis of the concept. This analysis is a description of the specific actions, processes, objects and schemas that an individual might construct in trying to learn the concept. Pedagogy is then designed to help students make these constructions and use them to develop an understanding of the concept. Tools for doing this may involve having students work in groups on tasks assigned by the teacher, write computer programs that implement various actions, processes and objects, and reflect on the work they are doing through discussion in groups and individual contemplation. Data is then gathered and analyzed. The analysis tries to determine the extent to which the students made the proposed mental constructions; how well the theoretical analysis appears to describe the students' thinking, both in success and failure to understand; and the level of learning the concept in question that the students appeared to achieve.

Initially, the theoretical analysis is based on the general theory and the researchers' understanding of the mathematical concept. After the activities just described, the researchers may decide to revise their analysis and the process can be repeated. This is done as often as necessary to obtain the desired level of student learning.

Characteristics of APOS Theory. The basic prediction in the use of APOS Theory is that if the mental constructions proposed in the theoretical analysis of a concept are made by a student, then he or she is likely to learn this concept. The accuracy of these predictions can be evaluated by looking at the various research papers that have been published describing studies that were made based on APOS Theory. Some of these papers are listed on the web site at http://www.cs.gsu.edu/~rumec/ index.htm, and others can be found in the literature. In using APOS Theory as a tool in the analysis of data, the differences of levels of understanding displayed by students are explained in terms of making or failing to make specific mental constructions. The explanatory power of APOS Theory and its value in helping to organize thinking about learning phenomena lie in its effectiveness in analyzing these differences. The papers reporting on the use of APOS theory that can be found at the above web site and elsewhere in the literature show that this theory can be and has been applied to a vast array of mathematical concepts, mainly but not exclusively, at the post secondary level. A partial list of concepts that have been treated would include functions, binary operations, groups, subgroups, cosets, normality, quotient groups, induction, permutations, symmetries, existential and universal quantifiers, limits, chain rule, derivatives, infinite sequences, mean, standard deviation, central limit theorem, place value, base conversion and fractions. Finally, it seems that terms like action, process, object, schema, interiorization and encapsulation are now part of the language of mathematics education.

Example of using APOS Theory. In the talk, I will give some details on using APOS Theory in abstract algebra. The concepts in question will be normality of a subgroup and construction of a quotient group. I will describe the APOS analysis and the pedagogy involved in helping students understand these concepts in terms of a specific subgroup of the group of all permutations of four objects. Students are asked to write computer programs for testing properties of a set with a binary operation that makes it a group and programs to determine if a subset of a group is a subgroup and if it is normal. They are also asked to write a general program that forms cosets and calculates the product of two cosets. The programs, written in the computer language ISETL, are surprisingly simple. I will show both the programs and describe how writing them relates to making the mental construction called for in the APOS analysis of these concepts. Finally, I will refer to some data that indicates the effectiveness of this approach for helping students learn these difficult mathematical concepts.

On the Role of Politics in the Development of Mathematics in Africa

M. E. A. El Tom

Columbia University, USA

A survey of the state of mathematics in Africa clearly shows that African governments have continued the colonial policy of investing very little in mathematics: 45 sub-Sahara African countries have entered the new millennium equipped with a total of less than 10 Ph.D.s in mathematics education and less than 100 Ph.D.s in mathematics. One purpose of the paper is to ask and suggest an answer to the question: Why invest in mathematics in Africa?

The proper context for addressing the legitimization question and the issues that arise naturally from it is the perennial 'crisis' of the continent. The view advanced by the World Bank and the IMF that Africa's predicament is essentially a problem of ' burgeoning balance of payments deficits, macroeconomic imbalances, and uncontrollable budget deficits' is found to be unproductive. The paper views the 'crisis' as 'a reflection of the failure of the state to create and nurture the conditions necessary for sustainable human development'.

It is suggested that Africa's ability to cope with its 'crisis' is critically dependent on the scope and quality of the continent's stock of human capital and on the state of its science and technology (S&T) base. Consideration of these two interrelated dimensions of development leads to the conclusion that the continent a) faces the dual challenge of considerably expanding opportunities for education as well as improving its quality under the constraint of limited resources; and b) needs to exert considerable efforts to strengthen a conspicuously weak S&T base. It is further suggested that Africa's need for mathematics arises essentially out of its fundamental need for 'development'.

It is to be expected that the challenges facing Africa in the areas of human capital and science and technology would have their counterparts in mathematics. Recent research and data obtained from responses to author's questionnaires make it possible to identify four major issues of mathematics education in Africa; a) the creation and strengthening leadership in mathematics education; b) upgrading the status of teachers of mathematics; c) implementation of effective programs for professional development; d) indigenisation of the language of instruction; and e) enhancing the relevance of school and university mathematics curricula.

Elsewhere (El Tom, 1995) I reported rather extensively on the state of mathematical research in Africa. The paper introduced the concept of 'publication matrix' and applied it to a limited set of data to gain insight into the level and structure of mathematical research in the continent. I observed that 'the level of mathematical research in Africa is, by any reasonable standards, low, and its structure is particularly weak.' The present paper updates this data and further extends it to cover all countries in the continent. The new data lend further support to my earlier observation, thus highlighting the urgency of adopting policies that promote mathematical research.

The argument is advanced that, in the final analysis, the establishment of a sufficiently diverse and vigorous mathematical community in Africa can only be achieved as part of a 'great inversion' of the patterns and priorities that have so far dominated the economic, social, cultural and political domains in Africa. The achievement of such a project hinges on the question of which social forces exercise effective political and economic power in the continent. In the meantime, African mathematicians and mathematics educators should work together to prepare the ground and sow the seeds for such an eventuality.

National Standards, Local Control of Curriculum: Setting the Course

of Mathematics Education in the United States

Joan Ferrini-Mundy
Michigan State University, USA

In the U.S., a country comprised of over 14,000 school districts, 2.7 million teachers, and 47 million public school children, public education remains the purview of local decision-makers and the constitutional responsibility of states. Interactions among local, state, and national mathematics education initiatives and policies have had an interesting historical path. We examine the impact of national mathematics standards (the four standards documents produced by the National Council of Teachers of Mathematics [NCTM]) over the past decade. In particular, we consider the complex interactions between national documents like NCTM has produced, and efforts to improve mathematics instruction at all levels.

In 1989, the National Council of Teachers of Mathematics (a 100,000-plus member professional organization concerned with mathematics education in grades kindergarten through twelve) issued the first national content standards for K-12 education in the United States - the Curriculum and Evaluation Standards for School Mathematics. This document, and its successors (the Professional Standards for Teaching Mathematics, 1991, and the Assessment Standards for School Mathematics, 1995) were highly publicized and widely disseminated throughout the membership of NCTM and to federal and state policy communities. Since curricular responsibility in the U.S. is not centralized, these documents offered goals, not mandates, for school mathematics education. In 2000, after a three-year development process, NCTM released Principles and Standards for School Mathematics, an update of the original standards.

In a country that does not have a national curriculum, the decision of a professional organization to produce "standards" and then to promulgate them widely invokes interesting questions about what implicit theory of action the organization might have had in mind for seeing its ideas enacted in practice. This talk will include:

· A brief description of the U.S. education system and its decentralized nature;

· A description of the roles of federal and state governments as they relate to mathematics education, including summary information about state standards and relevant policies, efforts to rate and evaluate standards, and the process of checking for alignment of assessments, curricula, and standards with documents such as the

NCTM Standards;

· A brief history of the national mathematics "standards" movement in the U.S., including discussion of the role of NCTM in initiating national standards and in revising them in the year 2000.

· Discussion of state standards, their role, their relationship to national standards, the ways in which they differ from national standards, and the complexities this creates for the coexistence of national and state standards.

· Some highlights of NCTM's recently released Principles and Standards for School Mathematics, which is available in both print and electronic forms, will be presented. We will discuss the document's intended audience, its structure, and its messages. And, the consultative process by which it was developed will be included, as well as some summary of various related plans and activities in the U.S. to use the document for the improvement of school mathematics education.

· Finally, we will comment on what has been learned in the 10 years since the 1989 Standards about how such professional documents seem to be interpreted, used, and critiqued in the U.S., with some analysis of the current situation and of the complex interactions among professional organizations, mathematicians, teachers in the field, the press, the public, and state and federal agencies in terms of setting the course of mathematics education in the United States.

Mathematics Instruction Unbound: The Contribution of Journal

L'enseignement mathématique

Fulvia Furinghetti
Universiti di Genova., Italy

The conference ICME 9 in Japan has been a good occasion to celebrate the first hundred years of the journal *L'enseignement mathématique*. To look at the past of this journal - in particular, the years from its birth (1899) until the First World War - allows to reconsider the ideas and the debates in which the modern mathematical instruction and mathematical education have their roots. Those years were rich of ferments and initiatives both in the world of mathematics and of mathematics instruction. Most of the main mathematical journals were already published and in 1897 the first International Congress of Mathematicians took place in Zurich. The nations were acquiring the modern organization and the problems of instruction were central in this organization. In many countries interesting journals devoted to mathematics teaching (at different school levels) were published. Moreover in the 1890s the first national associations of mathematics teachers were settled all around the world.

The founders of the journal *L'enseignement mathématique* are the Swiss Henri Fehr (1870-1954) and the French Charles-Ange Laisant (1841-1920). Some passages in their obituaries outline their interesting personalities. Laisant is described as "a man of science, educator, philosopher and politician", Fehr as "an exceptional educator", founder of the *Swiss mathematical library* and the *Swiss mathematical association*. Their biographies evidence a great social involvement in different directions.

In the "Committee of supporters" of *L'enseignement mathématique* we find important mathematicians, some of whom - Felix Klein for one - active in the study of problems of mathematical instruction as well as of teacher education.

The key ideas that made this journal notable in the international panorama were "internationalization" and "communication". In the presentation of the first number (1899, a.1, pp. 1-5) the founders pointed out that it was necessary "to join the great movement of scientific solidarity" alive in those days especially in the scientific community. Internationalism and communication were ideas spreading in society, as evidenced by the famous world exhibitions organized in those years. Also solidarity was an idea emerging in society. The founders pointed out the need of comparing the systems of instructions and of teacher education in the different countries. Moreover it was necessary that teachers communicate their ideas and know those of their colleagues.

The journal contained: general articles, news, bibliography and reviews. General articles were dealing with philosophical themes, themes of mathematics which may have impact in the teaching (at secondary and tertiary level), themes linked to psychology. Among the contributors there were important mathematicians. Due to the aims of the journal, among the general articles there were reports on the situation of the mathematical instruction in various countries. We see in this editorial policy the premises for the growing of the ideas inspiring ICMI (*International Commission on Mathematical Instruction*). These ideas were first proposed in the journal ('Réformes à accomplir...',, a.7, 1905, pp. 382-387 and pp. 462-472). ICMI was founded in 1908 and *L'enseignement mathématique* became its official organ.

The internationalization and communication were made explicit by the inquiries on mathematics teaching launched by ICMI through the journal. These inquiries originated reports discussed in international congresses, articles published in the journal, pamphlets and books. Among the themes concerning secondary school proposed in the journal there were the following:

* To which extent it is possible to take into account the *systematic exposition* of mathematics
* The question of the *fusion* of the different branches of mathematics
* The question of mathematical *rigor*
* To which extent the *first elements of differential and integral calculus* have been introduced in the various countries. At which level of rigor? With which methodology? Which applications of calculus are shown?

If we have in mind the trends of mathematical research - e.g. the development of analysis and foundational studies - we understand that mathematical research influenced the world of mathematical instruction at the beginning of the twentieth century.

It is notable another type of investigation carried out in the journal, which concerned the way of working of mathematicians. In the volumes of the years 1902 and 1904 thirty questions were proposed to the readers about their research methods, general "hygienic" rules useful to their intellectual work, etc. The answers were analyzed by Fehr himself and the Swiss psychologists *Édouard Claparède* and *Théodore Flournoy*. A part the anecdotal side, the interest of this inquiry is in having focused on the reflection about the nature of the mathematical activity and on issues related to psychological/affective factors. The idea underlying this inquiry links the journal to the developments of mathematics education which took place in the second half of twentieth century.

Reference
Furinghetti, F. (to appear). Mathematical instruction in an international perspective: the contribution of the journal *L'Enseignement mathématique*. *L'Enseignement mathématique.*.

Research on Student Teachers' Learning in Mathematics and Mathematics Education

Barbro Grevholm
Kristianstad University, Sweden

In a longitudinal study I follow the first group of students aiming to become teachers in mathematics and science for compulsory school, grades 4-9. The research focus is the students' development of concepts in mathematics and mathematics education.

Theories in mathematics education involve concepts as meaningful learning versus rote learning, conceptual knowledge or procedural knowledge, mathematical phenomenon seen as procedures or objects and conceptual change as important part of learning. In several theories mathematical concepts and the development of concepts are crucial. The method used is qualitative investigation of data from different types of documentation of students' cognitive development during the education program. Concept maps are used as tool for investigating students' answers in questionnaires and interviews and for the students to express their current concept structure.

Earlier research in Sweden on teacher education in mathematics

In Sweden few research studies have been undertaken concerning the learning of mathematics for student teachers and no earlier longitudinal study is known. Lindblad (1978) reports on students' mistakes during problem solving written in tests. The results caused debate on students teachers' background knowledge in mathematics, which later led to higher prerequisites (Ds U 1986:5). A similar study (Ljung 1987) conducted later was also showing unsatisfactory results. The conclusion was that subject matter studies must give a substantially deeper knowledge on the areas of mathematics that are taught in school (Ljung, 1987, pp. 36-37).

No other major studies on teacher education in mathematics in Sweden have been reported for a long period of time. A study on compulsory school student teachers, doing a course of modelling, shows that the students favoured the use of technology especially when solving complex mathematical modelling problems. When using software to select models the students became uncritical of the results they got from the computer and graphing calculator (Lingefjärd, 2000).

One of the research questions and some results from the study

How are the studies of mathematics and mathematics education influencing student teachers' development of concepts in these areas?

General tendencies in the observations are that students seem to slowly develop a professional language during the education, changes in concepts is a slow process and the pace of students' development is different. What the students have experienced and know when they enter the education is important for success during the education. One student can follow a course without changes in concepts while another seems to change substantially. A mathematical object is often seen in one way instead of many different complementing ways. Students can give easy examples of a specific concept and know the procedures and processes connected to the basic concepts but have difficulties in expressing themselves about the concepts. Students are vague and not enough specific when they try to explain how they understand a concept. Knowledge that students express through a concept map seems to be lasting. The figure shows a concept map of function (made by F14) in the beginning of the calculus course taken.

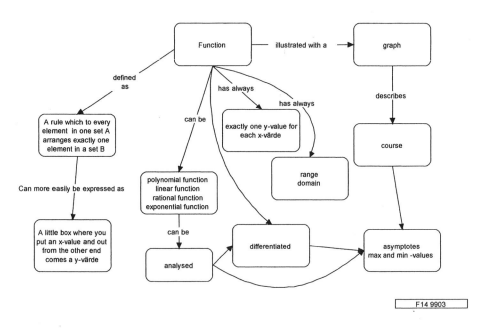

Can students experience more meaningful learning if we know more about their concept development? Can teacher educators design better learning situations for students when they know more about the cognitive development of students? Improvement of our knowledge on student teachers' development of concepts during the education might contribute in a constructive way to the redesign of teacher education.

Eliciting Mathematical Ideas from Students: Towards its Realization in Japanese Curricula

Yoshihiko Hashimoto
Yokohama National University, Japan

It is common for students in their mathematical studies to encounter problems that have unique answers that are uniquely determined. Due to these experiences, students often come to hold the belief that there is only one correct answer, and only one correct way to answer, to every problem. This can make it very difficult for classroom teachers to elicit certain mathematical ideas from students.

In this lecture, I would like to propose three 'open' methods for teaching mathematics and discuss how they are incorporated into the Japanese national mathematics curriculum.

THREE OPEN METHODS

The three open methods are open process, open-end product and open problem formulation.

Open Process

The open process is a teaching method that focuses on the different ways of solving a problem, the answer to which may be unique. Many actual examples from elementary, junior high, and senior high schools are described in Hashimoto and Becker (1999). Classroom teachers employing an open process organize lesson plans according to the following scheme:

a. introducing the problem or topic
b. understanding the problem
c. problem solving by the students
d. comparing and discussing
e. summary of the lesson

Making lesson plans is a very important aspect of the open process teaching method.

Open-End Product

Traditionally, problems are so well formulated that answers are either correct or incorrect. Such problems can be regarded as 'closed' or 'complete'. In contrast, problems that are formulated to have multiple correct answers are 'incomplete' or 'open-ended' (see Shimada, 1977, Becker and Shimada, 1997, where creating such problems is described in detail). Many books have been published, some even very recently, dealing with the issue Open-End Product.

Open Problem Formulation
In this method, students are encouraged to formulate or pose new mathematical problems from a given problem by using generalization, analogy, the notion of converse, or other ideas, and then to solve the newly formulated problems by themselves. This teaching method has also been referred to as "the developmental treatment of mathematical problems".

THE JAPANESE NATIONAL CURRICULUM
A new national mathematics curriculum will be put in force in Japanese elementary and junior high schools from 2002 and in senior high schools from 2003. Japanese textbooks must be made according to National Curriculum Standards. Mathematics problems utilizing the three open methods can be found in these textbooks. All elementary and secondary schools in Japan are required to use these textbooks in the classroom and generally speaking, classroom teaching depends on the content of the textbook. Hence classroom teachers using these textbooks will be naturally led to incorporate open teaching methods into their implemented curricula. I believe that this is a good result and important to the realization of new ideas. The fact that test problems are created by classroom teachers is a problem. But if mathematics teachers employ 'open method' problems, which can be easily picked up from textbooks, they are more likely to be able to change their student's views of mathematics.

In conclusion, students entering the 21st century will be able to look at things from different points of view if their ways of mathematical thinking are shaped by openness and open teaching methods.

References
Becker, Jerry P. and Shigeru Shimada, eds. *The Open- Ended Approach: A New Proposal for Teaching Mathematics.* Translated from the 1977 Japanese version by Shigeru Shimada, ed. Reston. Va: National Council of Teachers of Mathematics, 1997.
Hashimoto, Yoshihiko and Jerry Becker. " The Open approach to Teaching Mathematics - Creating a Culture of Mathematics in the Classroom: JAPAN" in Linda J. Sheffield edit, *Developing Mathematically Promising Students*, pp. 101-119, NCTM, 1999.

California's Back-to-Basics Policies and the 1999 Textbook Adoption

Bill Jacob
University of California, Santa Barbara, USA

In 1992, California adopted a new mathematics Framework. This Framework did not list content that students needed to study at each grade level. Instead it focused on classroom and program characteristics that would promote student learning of mathematics, emphasizing instructional approaches that would encourage students to take responsibility for their own learning, with teachers as facilitators rather than imparters of information. The Framework stated that, "Students construct their understanding of mathematics by learning to use mathematics to make sense of their own experience." (p. 33)

Following a number of years of controversy about the 1992 Framework and the NCTM Standards, California adopted a new Mathematics Framework in 1999. The messages of the 1999 Framework are quite different than those presented in 1992. The 1999 Framework promotes direct instruction leading to mastery of symbolic procedures. It proclaims the importance of balancing basic skills, problem solving, and conceptual understanding, but its views on problem solving and conceptual understanding differ greatly from those presented in 1992. The 1999 Framework also included the 1997 California Mathematics Standards which detail what topics should be studied at each grade level, and specifies the topics teachers should emphasize. Unlike previous documents, professors of mathematics played a dominant role in the development of the new Standards and Framework.

After a brief review of the history and discussions leading to the adoption of the 1999 Framework, this talk will focus on its impact during the following eighteen months. Of primary interest are the 1999 adoption of instructional materials and the recently launched professional development initiatives. Both are consuming unprecedented amounts of state money and will affect classrooms in California on a daily basis. The general picture that emerges is one of great variation, but at the same time it indicates that the 1999 Framework is leading to changes far more rapidly than did its predecessor. The primary impact has been to move the curriculum from one where students were "expected to think and reason in all mathematical work" to one where the majority of student effort in grades K-6 is devoted to rote learning of computational procedures required on state mandated tests.

Historical Sources in the Mathematics Classroom: Ideas and Experiences

Hans Niels Jahnke,
University of Essen, Germany

Reading historical sources in the mathematics classroom should lead to authentic mathematical experiences and introduce students to the cultural context of mathematics.

To attain this, a classroom climate is required where students are encouraged to generating their own hypotheses about a text and to thinking themselves into mathematical ideas of human beings who have lived in other times. This might cause students to reflect about their own views of the subject matter (for examples and reflections on reading sources cf. Arcavi & Bruckheimer, 1998; Fauvel, 1990; Furinghetti, 1997, IREM de Montpellier, 1995; Logarto et al., 1993).

The lecture will discuss two classroom experiences. In a selection of pages from John Bernoulli's Lectures on the Differential Calculus grade 12 students work on the notion of an infinitely small quantity and its application to determining tangents and extrema (Jahnke, 1995). Bernoulli wrote the Lectures in 1691/2 when he taught the new Leibnizian differential calculus to the Marquis de L'Hospital. In his view, calculus was based on two "axioms": 1. Any curved line can be considered as a straight polygon consisting of infinitely many segments of infinitely small length. 2. An infinitely small quantity like dx obeys the rule $x + dx = x$ where it is supposed that $dx \neq 0$ and x is a finite quantity.

In the experiment these axioms were considered as a way of building a model of curved lines designed by its inventors in order to solve a number of questions hitherto considered difficult or even unsolvable. Studying the source meant interpreting the assumptions and investigating how the model worked in the solution of problems. In the end, for many students this was the first time they really reflected on the conceptual foundations of calculus.

The second source to be discussed was read in grade 9 and started with the story of the famous tunnel of Samos (ca 530 B. C.) cutting through a mountain to supply the Samos fortress with water (Jahnke & Habdank-Eichelsbacher, 1999). The tunnel of about a km length was mined simultaneously from both ends, and the two teams met under the mountain. The underlying engineering feat must be highly evaluated, and since the discovery of the tunnel at the end of the 19th century, it was a much discussed question how Greek engineers did the surveying.

A possible answer is a source, about 600 years more recent. In a handbook describing the handling of a surveying instrument called dioptra, Heron of Alexandria (40 to 120 A.D.) treated the problem of "cutting through a mountain in a straight line if the entrances of the tunnel are given". The method used can be inferred form the figure below.

Both sources are of a different nature. Whereas the Bernoulli text is written by a great mathematician who has invented a new theory, the Heron text is sort of a textbook of engineering written for practitioners where it is not as important who the author was.

In the first source the main difficulty is to understand from the definitions, axioms and applications some theoretical concepts newly introduced by the author and his friends who themselves did not have full control of the theoretical consequences of their invention. Additionally, these concepts do not have a complete analogue in modern mathematics. The second source shows the way how a part of mathematics, well-known at its time, was explained to people working in practical conditions and with practical aims. Thus, the source does not intend to give exact explanations, but to be precise in regard to the sequence of steps which are to be followed. It was the task of the students to reconstruct from this recipe the underlying theoretical principles.

In both cases, the empirical analysis of the experience focussed on a number of questions: the students' specific knowledge and their general appreciation of history of mathematics; the strategies they applied in working with the source; especially, we were interested in their identification of key elements (drawings, formulae, important concepts); their ability to find examples and analogies for a concept, hitherto unknown to them, their ability to reproduce the content of a source in their own language.

All in all, the experiences showed that for a number of students, not all of them, reading a source was motivating in a measure that they were ready to invest considerably more time than usual. Mathematics will not become easier; on the contrary, this activity will demand and train a number of abilities frequently disregarded in mathematics teaching.

References
Arcavi, A. & M. Bruckheimer, 2000, Didactical uses of primary sources from the History of Mathematics, *Themes in Education*, 1, No. 1, pp.44-64
Fauvel, J.: 1990. *Mathematics through history,* Q.E.D. Books,York.
Furinghetti, F. 1997. History of mathematics, mathematics education, school

practice: case studies linking different domains. *For the learning of mathematics*, 17(1), pp.55-61

IREM de Montpellier (ed.) 1993. *Proceedings of the First European summer university on 'History and epistemology in mathematics education'.* Montpellier

Jahnke, H. N. 1995. Historische Reflexion im Unterricht. Das erste Lehrbuch der Differentialrechnung (Bernoulli 1692) in einer elften Klasse. *mathematica didactica* 18, 2, pp.30-58

Jahnke. H. N. & Habdank-Eichelsbacher, B. 1999. Authentische Erfahrungen mit Mathematik durch historische Quellen. in: C. Selter & G. Walther (Hrsg.) *Mathematik als design science. Festschrift fur E. Chr. Wittlnann,* Lelpzig: Klett-Verlag, pp.95-104

Logarto, M. J. jn M. J., Vieira, A. & Veloso E. (ed.) 1993. *Proceedings of the Second European summer university on 'History and epistemology in mathematics education '*(Braga, Portugal), two volumes.

Mathematical Artifact Production: Broadening the View of "Doing Mathematics"

Cyril Julie

University of the Western Cape, South Africa

In this paper we briefly consider the notion of doing mathematics. Based on some shortcomings of this movement, it is proposed that doing mathematics should be broadened to mathematical artifact production. This idea is explained and some insights are presented of the discoordinations South African teachers encounter when they engage in mathematics modeling as an exemplar of mathematical artifact production.

Doing Mathematics

Doing mathematics is one of the programs that emerged in reaction to the New Mathematics movement. According to Floyd (1981: 1) doing mathematics is akin to mathematical thinking and this she simply describes as "what mathematicians do."

Indicative in this statement is the observation that mathematicians do not proceed flawlessly from start to finish when they "investigate and solve mathematical problems." (Floyd, 1981: 1) although some processes and strategies they employ are identifiable. It is generally agreed that problem-solving and investigations are at the heart of doing mathematics. There is, however, not agreement that problem-solving and investigations are synonymous. Froebisher (1994: 155) attempts to clarify the differences between problem-solving and investigations by stating both approaches has at its centre a problem but problems can be differentiated between those "which have a set goal [and] are closed and convergent [and those] thought of as being open and divergent." The first type would fall under the notion of problem-solving and the second under investigations. Sierspinska (1996: 41), however, warns that ". . . 'openness' is not a property of a problem [but rather] the relation between the solver and the problem."

Notwithstanding this difference of import is that the goals to be pursued should be those determined by the learner and Lerman (1989) expresses the view that situations which enable students "to pose problems for themselves" (p.79) should be the desirable investigations that should be embarked upon. Although Lerman's proposal was made more than fifteen years ago it is still the case that concretely problem-solving and investigations, and hence doing mathematics, are manifested as puzzle solving; work with classical problems; calculational procedure finding where equivalent procedures are paraded as different procedures and the activities learners are confronted with are used as vehicles for concept formation. Thus the goals are implicitly determined by the context within which learners find themselves. In any case the matter of learners pursuing their own goals is much more complex than, say, simply confronting them with mathematical situations where they decide which problems to they would like attend to. I contend that with education and schooling structured the way it is, the possibility that learners pursue their own goals is scant. This touches the heart of what mass-based education is about. I would argue that mass-based education should be about the provision of epistemological access. By this is meant the way and how the existing store of human knowledge has been created in its historical context, how it has been and still are being used for a variety of purposes and how created knowledge can be used for purposes decided upon by its creators and collaborators.

Artifact production

In articulating the notion of epistemological access as the purpose of schooling and education it is clearly evident that knowledge is seen as a tool or product that is the outcome of the work of knowledge-makers. These tools or products are what I call artifacts and for mathematics they are referred as mathematical artifacts. As pointed out elsewhere (Julie,1998) the proposal that the production of mathematical artifacts should be accorded a more prominent role in school mathematics is not new. Essentially, mathematical artifact production entails that learners are afforded the opportunity to make those things that are found in the universe of mathematics. The goal is thus fairly clear to the learner: a thing which can qualify as an object of the practice must be made.

During the process of constructing the artifact issues such as understanding mathematical concepts and the stressing of the identified processes of doing mathematics are not of importance. Regarding the first-mentioned issue it is accepted that concepts can be used without fully understanding them (Papert, 1996). This occurs frequently mathematical practice as aptly demonstrated by Heaviside's (Griffiths, 1978: 16) reflection on his own work when he states that "I know of mathematical processes, that I have used for a very long time, of which neither I nor anyone else understands the scholastic logic. I have grown into them, and so understand them that way." It is also accepted that when one is constructing an artifact, the processes involved are in a sense naturally employed. Livingston (1986) in his discussion on mathematicians' work states this as follows: ". . .at the work-site, the mathematician is not interested in a theory of mathematical discovery; he (sic) is interested in making mathematical discoveries." These mathematical discoveries are the mathematical artifacts that are produced in mathematical practice.

The production of mathematical models by practising South African teachers

Elsewhere (Julie, 1998) it is argued that mathematical models of physical and social phenomena are artifacts produced in the mathematical sciences. In an ongoing project, the Applications of and Modeling in School Mathematics Project (AMSMAP), one of the aims is to describe practising teachers' behaviour as they engaged in the development of mathematical models. Preliminary analysis of data indicates that teachers experience a variety of discoordinations when producing mathematical models.

Inspired by Engestrom's (1987)(1993) notion of an activity system it is argued that the discoordinations have the origin in the historical development mathematics modeling teaching in schools.

Primary Arithmetic Based on Piaget's Constructivism

Constance Kamii
University of Alabama at Birmingham, USA

Piaget distinguished three kinds of knowledge (physical, logico-mathematical, and social-conventional knowledge) according to their ultimate sources. He showed scientifically that children acquire logico-mathematical knowledge, including number concepts, by construction from within rather than by internalization from the environment. Based on this theory, I hypothesized that children should be able to invent addition, subtraction, multiplication, and division without any textbook, workbook, drill, or conventional algorithms. This hypothesis has been amply verified in grades 1-3 (Kamii, 1985, 1989, 1994, 2000), and I am now working with fourth graders.

A new, scientific explanation of how children acquire logico-mathematical knowledge leads to (a) educational goals, (b) classroom practices, and (c) ways of evaluating results that are different from traditional ones.

Educational goals

My goal for children is to get them to think, in their own ways, to solve problems. This goal is different from the traditional aim of getting children to produce correct answers by internalizing "facts" and conventional algorithms.

Our sequence of objectives is also different from the traditional order of teaching computational techniques first and then giving word problems for children to apply these techniques. In a constructivist approach, we give word problems first and let computational techniques emerge out of solving word problems.

Method of "teaching"

I put quotation marks around "teaching" because we do not teach arithmetic in the traditional sense. We use three kinds of activities in the classroom instead of a textbook and workbook: discussions of everyday situations (such as taking attendance and voting to make decisions), solving word problems, and playing math games.

The two principles of teaching we follow are also different from traditional practices. First, we do not show children how to solve a problem because we want them to use what they know to invent new procedures. Children struggle to solve problems, but this struggle constitutes the constructive process. Second, when children give answers, we refrain from saying "That's right" or "That's wrong" and, instead, ask other children if they agree. The exchange of viewpoints is very important in Piaget's (1947/1950) theory, and children find truth not from the teacher but by debate among themselves.

I showed part of a videotape entitled First Graders Dividing 62 by 5 (Kamii & Clark, 2000) to illustrate what these principles look like in a classroom. In this tape, the children used repeated addition at various levels rather than division or multiplication. When one girl got an incorrect answer (of 13, with 2 cents left over), the teacher turned to the other children and encouraged the exchange of points of view. The other children had to think long and hard to figure out how the girl got 13, and the girl stood her ground until she was honestly convinced that 12 was a better answer.

Evaluation

Many data were presented to show the superiority of a constructivist approach in grades 1, 2, and 3. The data involved single-digit addition and double-digit addition, subtraction, and multiplication as well as a word problem. The first point made was that children who do their own thinking can logically explain how they got the correct answer. Traditionally instructed children do get correct answers, but not many of them can explain "carrying," "borrowing," cross-multiplication, and long division.

The second point made was that children who do their own thinking are far superior in their knowledge of place value. The reasons are: (a) Children who invent their own procedures use their knowledge of place value to figure out how to deal with multidigit problems, and (b) conventional algorithms "unteach" place value. When children invent their own ways of dealing with 16 + 17, for example, they usually do 10 + 10 = 20, 6 + 7 = 13, and 20 + 13 = 33, thus using their knowledge of place value. By contrast, the algorithm of "carrying" makes children deal with each column as if all the numbers were ones. After "carrying" the "1" of "13," most second graders think they are doing 1 + 1 + 1 (rather than 10 + 10 + 10)

References
Kamii, C. (1985(2000)). *Young children reinvent arithmetic(2nd edition)*. New York: Teachers College Press.
Kamii, C. (1989). *Young children continue to reinvent arithmetic, 2nd grade*. New York: Teachers College Press.
Kamii, C. (1994). *Young children continue to revinent arithmetic, 3rd grade*. New York: Teachers College Press.
Kamii, C., & Clark, F. B. (2000). *First graders dividing 62 by 5 (videotape)*. New York: Teachers College Press.
Piaget, J. (1950). *The psychology of intelligence*. London: Routledge and Kegan Paul. (Original work published 1947)

Exams in Mathematics (secondary school) - Russian Experience:

Traditions, Changes, Difficulties

Alexander Karp

University of Education, St. Petersburg, Russia

Written exams often seem to be outside the main stream of the international research. Although there are some papers devoted to the analysis of exams in different countries (e.g. Dossey, 1996), the examination tasks are usually considered (and rightly so!) to be ill-suited for the international comparison of results in the observed countries, for they are obviously too deeply rooted in the respective cultures. Moreover, written exams are often the subject of critique even within national borders, being viewed as the archaic tool for the measurement of abilities (Clarke, 1996). However the exams' connection with the national history of education and with the social history turns to be a positive rather than negative feature as soon as we change our focus and opt for the study of processes and experiences rather than the comparison of results.

This lecture is intended to focus on several aspects of studying exams. Exams are the practical and concrete manifestation of the syllabus, that's why they belong both with the administrative history of education (Schubring, 1988) and with its real history that is history of what is actually happening in the classroom. Exams form the bridge from secondary school to society and provide one of the best opportunities to investigate how the general demands put forward by society are being articulated in terms of specific requirements. How can we observe this phenomenon? What should be the subject of our study? Of course, themes of the tasks and the system of general organisation of exams (their duration, or level of centralisation, etc.) are of extreme importance. However, the investigation of the most meaningful issues (such as the level of difficulty or the ratio between the routine and creative procedures, or the restoration of beliefs of math educators -- the ideal student model) seems to be possible only when based on three interconnected principles. These are: historic systematicity (whereby for example, not separate questions but the history of use of such questions should be studied); synchronic systematicity (whereby the administrative and content aspects of exams at any given moment should be studied in interaction); and set of questions systematicity (whereby attention should be paid to the structure of the set of problems). This approach helps understand and formulate the social tendencies and expectations. The above mentioned principles can be applied internationally, notably, the study of exams as the reflection of social aspects of education has certain advantages in Russia, because of the acuteness of social problems in that country.

The analysis of changes in the system of exams shows how the Russian math education culture with its internationally renowned achievements (especially in teaching future mathematicians) and deficiencies (especially visible over last years) emerged. The main characteristics of this culture are: the belief that mathematics is important and relevant to everybody; high theoretical level and special attention to proving; high level of the requirements to the skills and mastery of algorithms; special attention to the knowledge of numerous concrete facts; as well as the lack of flexibility (both in revision of content and in taking in to account individual differences) and the near absence of teaching of applied mathematics.

Finally one of the attempts to meet the new challenges of math education will be discussed. It is based on the analysis of the morphology of the exam problems, their structural properties, and the ways of thinking fostered by these properties. The study of various forms of activity (generalisation, analogy, self-control, etc.) becomes more specific when based on sets of questions in their typical combinations. The emphasis on these aspects of exams is sure to influence the classroom teaching. This is of primary importance as the focus of math education should now shift from storing information to processing it.

References
Clarke, D. (1996). Assessment. in A.J.Bishop et al. (eds.) *International Handbook of Mathematics Education* .Kluwer Academic Publishers. Netherlands.
Dossey, J. (1996) Mathematics Examinations. in E.D.Briton, S.A.Raizen (eds). *Examining the examinations.* Kluwer Academic Publishers. Boston/ Dordrecht/ London.
Schubring, G. (1988). *Theoretical categories for investigations in the social history of mathematics education and some characteristic patterns.* Universitat Bielefeld, Institut fur Didactik der Mathematik, Ocasional paper # 109.

When Machines Do Mathematics, then What Do Mathematics Teachers Teach?

John Kenelly and Dan Warner
Clemson University, USA

Education is now charged with preparing students for careers dominated by powerful information technology. Routine and repetitive tasks no longer require human efforts and many mathematical procedures are done routinely on computer workstations. Evidence that mathematics instructions must change is overwhelming, but many are still searching for the answers to the fundamental question of how to teach mathematics in an age where many sophisticated mathematical operations can be done on machines. Watershed decisions at this level are best addressed with a historical perspective and the authors first looks at the "jump discontinuities" in mathematical that resulted from the contributions of Euclid and Newton.

With the recognition that mathematics instruction must move away from drill and practice, one refocuses on the other all parts of the mathematical triad - selecting, processing and interpretation. Much attention is and should be placed on the first of the triad, i.e., "planning the approach." Technology in the form of graphing calculators has opened the mathematics classroom to explorations. Students now routinely look for alternative approaches to problems and graphing calculators facilitate literally every member of the class taking their own cut at the problem. How many times have teachers said and students appreciate the statement that "there's more than one way to address the problem." The debate on how to best adapt instructional methods to new era is far from complete. In fact, it is safer to say that the arguments have hardly begun.

Along with the reduced emphasis on manipulations, there remains the question of how best to balance traditional means and modern approaches. Are teachers trying to hold on to old methods because of their needs or because of their teacher comforts?

Unfortunately, interpretation is still the orphan child. Everyone admits it need, but few suggest the means. The authors content that presentations through the vehicle of digital cameras should fill this critical gap. Building on the caption of "the first time I really understood it was when I taught it" the case is made for engaging students in frequent presentations. Using digital cameras to record investigations and attractive software for moving calculator screen directly from the calculator to the cameras without the need for a computer, we now have the tools. It is up to mathematics teachers to make presenting as much a part of mathematics instruction as it has made explorations on graphing calculators .

Narrative Elements in Mathematical Argumentations in Primary Education

Gotz Krummheuer,
Freie Universitat Berlin, Germany

In the discussion about conditions of learning it is more frequently stressed that the entire phenomenon of human learning is not spanned if one confines one's studies to the interior, mental processes of the learner. Learning is also a social process which takes place in the interaction between human beings (BRUNER, 1996, p. 22; see also BAUERSFELD, 1995, BRUNER, 1990, ERICKSON, 1982, and KRUMMHEUER, 1992). This insight led BRUNER 1986 to formulate the feature of a psychology which constitutionally considers social elements for psychic processes, as for example in the course of learning. He defines this as cultural psychology (p. 35) and explains that each individual development must be ex-pressible in the particular symbolic system of a given culture. For this, the members of a culture not only have the general means of their language but, additionally, they can also employ specific culturally accomplished ways to interpret the psychological disposition of individuals. BRUNER (1990) defines this as folk psychology (e.g. p. 33ff). Regarding the teaching- learning- process in a classroom situation he speaks of folk pedagogy (BRUNER, 1996, p.46). These two concepts include the mostly implicit basic assumptions of a culture about the psychological functioning of its members.

The narrativity of classroom culture

Especially with regard to primary education it is often stated that mainly basic cultural techniques such as reading, writing and arithmetic are taught and acquired. From the perspective of cultural psychology, this seems to be an insufficient point of view: Children do not only learn the contents of culture. Through their contributions in reading, writing, and calculating they also create "a" or "the" culture. Concatenating these two aspects one arrives at what could be described as classroom culture. Classroom culture is a culture of subject matter and a culture of learning. Participation in this double sense integrates the social constitution of learning.

According to our research the classroom culture of our primary schools is characterized by narrativity: frequently, the different contents are presented in a narrative style, and the social constitution of classroom-learning can be described in related models of participation in situations of story-telling. This is also relevant for mathematics classes, and the analysis of processes of interaction concerning this

148

subject matter can demonstrate the importance of this thesis in general. Especially, in mathematics classroom the social constitution of classroom-learning is the participation in the interactional accomplishment of argumentative, narratively structured sequences of actions. According to BRUNER (1990) one can identify four characteristics for such narrative accomplishments: its

1. "sequentiality"
2. "factual indifference between the real and the imaginary"
3. "unique way of managing departures from the canonical", and
4. "dramatic quality" (p.50).

Here, the first and third points are of special interest. The claimed narrativity of classroom-culture is seen in the patterned sequentiality of classroom-interaction. The specifity of an event, such as the elaborated solving process for a new mathematical task, is presented in relation to the canonical management of such events or problems.

The concept of "narration" is used here in order to describe a specific phenomenon of everyday classroom-conversation. It is not meant in the sense of literary science.

Social learning conditions in classroom

The basic insight of this research is that in a narratively accomplished classroom culture a proved folk psychology of learning becomes apparent which functions in these everyday classroom situations and which is based on narratively structured processes of collective argumentation.

This specific kind of "accounting practice" (GARFINKEL, 1967) emerges in the pursuing or novel creation of a sequence of working steps. With regard to ERICKSON (1986) it is called the "academic task structure" (ATS). This is a sequence of actions as it is accomplished by the participants in their process of in-teractional negotiation. In primary mathematics classes, this interactive realization occurs often in a narrative style: the conducted calculations are told according to the sequence of the ATS in as much as the necessary competencies can be integrated. Typically, the inner logic of the total approach within such narratively realized academic task sequences is not explicitly thematized, but it is expected as a specific achievement of the participants. They have to infer this inner logic from the specific presentation of the narrations (for more details see KRUMMHEUER, 1995, 1997). This does not usually happen successfully and often not in its entirety. Learning which is related to novel concepts and insights does not happen automatically. But, on the other hand, this kind of narrative classroom culture is characterized by a great stability in everyday primary school teaching and learning situations and there are many students who daily proceed successfully in their content-related learning development by participating in this kind of classroom culture.

References

Bauersfeld, H. (1995): "Language games" in the mathematics classroom: Their function and their effects. In: Cobb, P. & Bauersfeld, H. (Hrsg): *The emergence of mathematical meaning. Interaction in classroom cultures.* Hillsdale, NJ: Lawrence Erlbaum

Bruner, J. (1986): *Actual minds, possible worlds.* Cambridge, MA: Harvard University Press

Bruner, J. (1990): *Acts of Meaning.* Cambridge, MA; London: Harvard University Press

Bruner, J. (1996): *The Culture of Education.* Cambridge, MA: Harvard University Press

Erickson, F. (1982): Classroom discourse as improvisation. in: Wilkinson, L. C. (Hrsg): *Communicating in the classroom.* New York: Academic Press

Erickson, F. (1986): Qualitative methods in research on teaching. In: Wittroch, M. C (Hrsg): *Handbook of research on teaching.* New York: Macmillan, third edition

Garfinkel, H. (1967): *Studies in ethnomethodology.* Englewood Cliffs: Prentice-Hall.

Krummheuer, G.(1992): *Lernen mit "Format". Elemente einer interaktionistischen Lerntheorie. Diskutiert an Beispielen mathematischen Unterrichts.* Weinheim: Deutscher Studien Verlag

Krummheuer, G. (1995): The ethnography of argumentation. In: Cobb, P. & Bauersfeld, H (Hrsg): *The emergence of mathematical meaning: interaction in classroom cultures.* Hillsdale, NJ: Lawrence Erlbaum

Krummheuer,, G. (1997): *Narrativitat und Lernen. Mikrosoziologische Studien zur sozialen Konstitution schulischen Lernens.* Weinheim: Deutscher Studien Verlag

The Role of Personal Computing Technology in Mathematics Education: Today and Tomorrow

Oh-Nam Kwon

Ewha Woman 's University, Seoul, Korea

Why do we study mathematics? What is the purpose of learning mathematics? The purpose, of course, is educational. Education develops a student's potential. It helps the student to develop into a decent citizen, one who fulfills his or her given role in society. We study mathematics to gain a better understanding of and solve the mathematical problems that lie behind the incidents and phenomenon of everyday life. As with all other subjects taught in school, the purpose of teaching mathematics is to nurture citizens for productive life in the knowledge based society. Mathematics helps to foster problem-solving ability through the process of dealing with issues with various analytical methods. We also study mathematics to better grasp the structure of various phenomenon and to understand physical world.

Mathematics education is aimed at fostering a deeper understanding of things that we encounter in everyday life, such as shopping at the supermarket, the behavior of populations, the earnings rate on investments, the structure of building, the limits of computation, the performance of vehicles. The ultimate purpose of teaching mathematics, therefore, is to cultivate the ability to understand the mathematical order of life and nature. If this is the case, then the question is whether mathematics, in terms of content and method, is being taught in schools in such a way that gives students a real sense of the practicality and applicability of mathematics.

The attention of today's students, who are familiar with the mechanical world and encounter visual stimulation such as computers, TV, and three-dimensional graphics, cannot be held solely by using blackboards and textbooks. Indeed, there are many limits to paper and pencil-based education from the perspective of cultivating creativity and higher-order thinking in preparation for the 21st century: an age of pluralism as well as specialization and globalization. As is evident a study of mathematics education trends around the world, not only is the content of mathematics education being explored, but changes in teaching methods are being explored to determine the most effective way to teach mathematics.

The most versatile tool to realize these changes, the thing that can be most widely and most quickly introduced, is none other than digital technology. Technology has played a dominant role in the shift that has placed realistic problems at the center of the curriculum. The most economically viable approaches in recent times use graphic calculators with graphic, numeric and symbolic facilities. They have the great advantage of portability, allowing the student to use them anywhere and at any time. Personal computing technology, in the form of calculators, has already changed the curriculum in various ways and has the potential to change it much further, as does computer technology. By the introduction of real life situations into lessons, something that was not possible with paper and pencil environments, the importance and necessity of mathematics and its relation to the real world, can be highlighted. In the Standards 2000, National Council of Teachers of Mathematics emphasizes how much times have changed since the original Standards were published in 1989. One of the greatest changes has been the rapid development in hand-held technology over the past ten years.

In this lecture, the role of personal computing technology will be discussed in the context of mathematics education in the curriculum, with a focus on a rapidly changing society subject to globalization and digitalization. First, the concept of personal computing technology in mathematics education, including calculators, CBL and CBR, will be defined. The impact of hand-held technology on mathematics education is examined in relation to key variables: the nature and purpose of mathematics, as well as the current and potential roles of hand-held technology including resourcing, curricular influence, and teacher confidence. The results of research into the effects of hand-held technology use are also examined. Case studies of current practice in Korea are presented to exemplify several of the key issues in relation to course development and delivery. Moreover, the effects of spatial visualization using VRML will be discussed, and suggestions for the application of next-generation technology will be presented.

Computer technology and hand-held technology are converging and are designed to permeate the canonical curriculum. Finally, a framework for future developments is provided in connection with the emerging possibilities offered by mobile technology. Education must not only keep pace with the changes in society, and but go further: education must lead and promote change in society to ensure a better world for future generations

Reference
NCTM. (2000). *Principles and Standards for School Mathematics*. Reston. VA: National Council of Teachers of Mathematics.

New Technologies as a Bridge between Various Parts of Mathematics for Pre-service Students Teachers

Colette Laborde

University of Grenoble and University Institute for Teacher Education, France

Many university students encounter great difficulties in co-ordinating all mathematical resources they have and in moving from one setting to another one. One of their major difficulties certainly lies in the absence of flexibility between models as mentioned by several researchers. It is also very likely that they especially lack abilities to represent geometrically algebraic objects and operations.

As Robert (1998) thoroughly described, problems university students encounter in mathematics do not lie in a lack of knowledge but in the atomic nature of their knowledge. Students know a lot of isolated theorems and facts without being able to structure this myriad of elementary knowledge items. Several researchers stressed this absence of flexibility (Dreyfus & Eisenberg, 1996, Tall, 1996). Robert mentioned in particular that even graduate students in pre-service teacher education never question the coherence between calculus and geometry. She contrasts expert practice in mathematics and novice practice: experts are able to move in and around the problem to be solved, they vary parameters, change data, hypotheses, they move from one setting into another one, they consider the problem from several points of view, they establish relations between different ways of expressions. But only a small number of attempts is made at university level to foster the learning of such practice.

The availability of dynamic geometry software with direct manipulation deeply changes the situation in that they offer an environment in which it is possible to perform rapidly complex and precise constructions, to modify and change constructions very easily in case of error, to receive visual feedback especially when varying parameters of the situation. In a word, this kind of environment offers rich validation and exploration possibilities. By using them, students gain flexibility between geometry and algebra or calculus by enlarging their visual experience of algebraic and numerical properties.

Two examples of visual reasoning in advanced mathematics for preservice teacher students, made possible by the computer environment Cabri-geometry will be presented: the first one on solving discrete linear dynamic systems, the second one on qualitative analysis of behaviours of solution of differential equation. They illustrate this back and forth process between empirical observation in a computer environment and work at a theoretical level. They will also show how a geometrical model may give evidence of phenomena which would have remained invisible in the numerical model for a non expert.

The observation of preservice teachers gave evidence of difficulties of students in this back and forth moves between various models. But it shows also how visual phenomena observed on the geometrical model gave rise to questions and compelled the students to formulate theoretical questions. It turned out that students were not able to solve all these questions and the teacher played an important role in giving some hints. The paper will attempt to elicit

i) the contribution of technology in the solving processes of students,
ii) the conceptual difficulties of students revealed by technology,
iii) the critical role of the teacher in this kind of situation.

References

Dreyfus, T. & Eisenberg, T. (1996). On different factes of mathematical thinking. in R . Sternberg & Ben-Zeev (Eds) *The Nature of Mathematical Thinking.* Hillsdale, NY: Lawrence Erlbaum Associates.

Robert, A. (1998). Outils d'analyse des contenus mathématiques a enseigner au lycee et a l'universite. *Recherches en didactique des mathématiques,* **18/2,** pp.139-190.

Tall, D (1996). Funtion and Calculus. in A. Bishop et al. (Eds) *International Handbook of Mathematics Education.* Dordrecht: Kluwer.

History of Mathematics in Educational Research and Mathematics Teaching - the Case of Probability and Statistics

Ewa Lakoma
Military University of Technology, Poland

In recent years there has been continuing evolution in points of view on mathematics and its education. Our knowledge concerning the nature of the process of mathematics learning and mathematics understanding has been developing in a significant way (Freudenthal, 1983, Sierpinska, 1994). General aims of mathematics teaching have been undergoing essential changes. Mathematics - as a learning subject - has been acting as a tool for explanations of reality and for communication among people (Sierpinska 1998). In order to gain this aim, *a process of mathematics learning* must be organised respecting actual student's cognitive development. Thus, there is a need to explore and to understand natural processes of forming in student's mind such mental objects, which can be mathematised by adequate mathematical concepts.

History of mathematics helps to understand these processes (Freudenthal, 1983, Sierpinska, 1994). The case of probability and statistics teaching shows that reaching for history of mathematics turns out to be very fruitful (Lakoma, 1992, 1999). The *dual character of probability* concept - laws of chance versus degrees of belief - was perceived and described from historical point of view by Ian Hacking in his work "The Emergence of Probability" (1975). Analysis of this fundamental feature of this concept has become an inspiration for research in epistemology of probability in the process of learning in today's classroom (Lakoma, 1990). Giving historical perspective to the teaching of probability and statistics has become helpful, not only for exploring and for understanding the student's ways of probabilistic thinking, but also for inspiring the design of teaching approach, which takes into account the student's actual abilities.

An analysis of the historical phenomenology of probabilistic concepts (Lakoma, 1992, 1999) - in the sense of Freudenthal (1983) - led to the didactical hypotheses, which have been verifying on the basis of careful observations of classroom activities and deep analyses of students' dialogues and works (Sierpinska, Kilpatrick, 1998).

When studying students' activities and listening their dialogues, it is very useful, as well as in any live discussion in mathematics, to treat *mathematics as a language* (Bauersfeld, Zawadowski, 1981). It allows interpreting mathematics in statu nascendi in figurative way, not literally. Moreover, figurative interpretation of old historical ways of mathematical thinking is extremely helpful in searching for symptoms of understanding and creating mathematics in student's mind (Lakoma, 1990, 1998, 1999).

The main aim of this lecture is to present in a systematic way the methodology, sketched very briefly above, and the most important results of this educational research. The dual nature of the concept of probability serves not only as scaffolding to build a didactical proposal for a classroom practice but also as a tool for diagnosis and evaluation of a degree of maturity of student's probabilistic knowledge and understanding. The main results of this research allowed designing an approach to probability and statistics teaching from diachronic perspective - so called the Local Models' Approach. In this didactical conception taking into account the epistemological structure of mathematics lets students learn mathematics according to their individual potentialities (Lakoma, 1999, 1996-2000). Qualitative analysis of using history of mathematics in mathematics education, rather than quantitative one, seems to be useful to recognise an effectiveness of the process teaching.

References

Bauersfeld H., Zawadowski W., 1981, *Metaphors and Metonymies in Teaching of Mathematics*, Occasional Paper 11, Insitut fuer Didaktik der Mathematik, Bielefeld.

Freudenthal H., 1983, D*idactical Phenomenology of Mathematical Structures*, Reidel.

Hacking I., 1975, *The Emergence of Probability*, Cambridge University Press.

Lakoma E., 1990, *The Local Models in Probability Teaching (in Polish)*, doctoral thesis, Warsaw University, Department of Mathematics, Informatics and Mechanics, Warsaw.

Lakoma E., 1992, *Historical Development of Probability* (in Polish), CODN-SNM.

Lakoma E., 1999, The diachronic view in research on probability learning and its impact on the practice of stochastics teaching, in: Jaquet F. (ed.), *Proceedings of the CIEAEM-50*, University of Neuchatel, Switzerland, August 1998, pp.116-120.

Lakoma E., 1999a, On the historical phenomenology of probabilistic concepts - from the didactical point of view, in: Boye A., Lefort X. (ed), *Actes de la 7e Universite d'Ete interdisciplinaire sur l'histoire des mathématiques*, Nantes, France, 1997, pp.439-448.

Lakoma E., Zawadowski W. a.o., 1996-2000, *Mathematics 2001* (in Polish) - series of textbooks, teachers' guides, films, programs for students of age 10-16, WSiP, Warsaw.

Sierpinska A., 1994, *On Understanding in Mathematics*, Kluwer, Dordrecht.

Sierpinska Anna, Kilpatrick Jeremy (ed.), 1998, M*athematics Education as a Research Domain: A Search for Identity, An ICMI Study*, Kluwer, Dordrecht.

The Socio-cultural Turn in Studying the Teaching and Learning of Mathematics

Stephen Lerman
South Bank University, UK

It is taken for granted today that research on teaching and learning mathematics must take into account the social, historical, and cultural milieu of schooling and pupils and of mathematics. There are quite different interpretations, however, of how 'social' and 'individual' interact, what role the social environment plays in the development of the individual and in what sense the individual is unique, and therefore how that milieu should be taken into account in research. Research methods in education, as well as approaches to teaching, are built upon how one interprets knowledge, the process of learning and the role of teaching.

Until the last 15 years mathematics education tended to draw on mathematics itself or psychology, as disciplines that provide intellectual resources for the production of knowledge in the field. Studies in epistemology, ontology, knowledge, and knowledge acquisition focus on how the individual acquires knowledge and on the status of that knowledge in relation to reality. Theoretical frameworks for interpreting the social origins of knowledge and consciousness began to appear in the mathematics education literature towards the end of the 1980s. Shifts in perspectives or the development of new paradigms in academic communities are the result of a concatenation of factors within and around the community. In the title I have called these developments the social turn in mathematics education research. This is not to imply that other theories, mathematical, Piagetian, radical constructivist or philosophical have ignored social factors. We can recognise a philosophical orientation in the early 1980s, although preceded by Dawson (1969), which drew into mathematics education the quasi-empiricist theory of Lakatos, but was also coincident with a humanistic, democratic concern by many teachers and researchers at that time. Piaget's and von Glasersfeld's emphasis on social interactions as providing a major source of disequilibrium is also evidence of general recognition of the importance of a social perspective.

The term social turn in my title is intended to signal something different, however, namely the emergence into the mathematics education research community of theories that see meaning, thinking, and reasoning as products of social activity. This goes beyond the idea that social interactions provide a spark that generates or stimulates an individual's internal meaning-making activity. The social turn in mathematics education has developed from three main disciplines or resources:

157

anthropology (from e.g. Lave, Wenger); sociology (from e.g. Bernstein, Walkerdine); and cultural psychology (from e.g. Nunes, Crawford). In this talk I will indicate how these can be brought together into a fruitful and coherent research direction by a consideration of the unit of analysis for research in mathematics education. Fundamental to the social turn is the need to consider the person-acting-in-social-practice, not person or their knowing on their own. I will extend the unit of analysis to take account of the sense in which a social practice regulates the actions of the participants. I will frame this discussion by looking at aspects of situated theory, with critiques opening spaces for elaborations from sociology and from cultural or discursive psychology.

Perhaps the greatest challenge for research in mathematics education (and education/social sciences in general) from perspectives that can be described as being within the social turn is to develop accounts that bring together agency, individual trajectories, and the cultural, historical and social origins of the ways people think, behave, reason and understand the world. Any such analysis must not ignore either: it should not reduce individual functioning to social and cultural determinism nor place the source of meaning making in the individual. A further challenge specific to mathematics education is to account for individual cognition and difference and to incorporate the substantial body of research on mathematical cognition, as products of social activity. In the field of production of mathematics education there is a growing body of research using Activity Theory and other tools in this endeavour. In my talk I will give examples from my own research on learning and teaching in analysing classroom transcripts, looking at those interactions, not as windows onto the minds of the learners but as situated products of the discursive resources of the classroom, the previous networks of experiences of the participants, and the social relationships between them.

In Search of an East Asian Identity in Mathematics Education - the Legacy of an Old Culture and the Impact of Modern Technology

Frederick K S Leung,
University of Hong Kong, Hong Kong SAR

Introduction

In the majority of the past Century, East Asian countries, either through being colonized by or subject to heavy influence from Western countries, have basically adopted a Western model of mathematics education, both in terms of the mathematics curriculum and in teacher training. In the later part of the Century, with decolonization and a growing interest in Eastern cultures in the West, these countries have begun to re-discover their cultural roots.

The superior performance of East Asian students in recent international studies such as TIMSS, and the reported "failures" in mathematics education in many of the Western countries have further prompted East Asian scholars to re-evaluate their traditional cultural values in order to locate themselves in the international scene of mathematics education.

This paper attempts to analysis the various factors which are influencing the East Asian countries in their search for an identity in mathematics education. The discussion will help these and other countries as they contemplate the important questions of what sorts of teachers we should be producing, and what curriculum we should be designing for our students in order to prepare them to face the challenges of the IT era in the 21st Century.

Outline

The paper will examine the following characteristics and argue that they are distinctive features of mathematics education in East Asia. It is hope that a better understanding of these features will complement the strengths and weakness of other traditions of mathematics education.

1. Product (content) versus process

There has been a trend in recent decades to focus more on the process of doing mathematics (e.g. problem solving) rather than learning the mathematics content itself. The emphasis in East Asian countries however has been on both the content and the process (e.g. the emphasis on the two basics (basic knowledge and basic skills) in China). In fact, the underlying belief is that the content is fundamental. Without content, there is nothing for the process to be applied to.

2. Rote learning versus meaningful learning

East Asian students have been criticised as learning by rote. But recently educators have pointed out that the kind of repetitive learning in East Asian countries is actually "a route to understanding". Memorisation, even before thorough understanding, may have an important role to play in learning mathematics.

3. Studying hard versus enjoying the study

Pleasurable learning has been a slogan in some Western countries. Yet the traditional view in East Asian countries, especially in China, has been that studying is a serious endeavour, and one is expected to put in hard work, deriving content (or "happiness") only after the hard work. This is in sharp contrast to the attempts to simplify what is to be learn for students or introduce different sorts of activities in order to make the learning more pleasurable.

4. Extrinsic versus intrinsic motivation

Educators in the west have treasured intrinsic motivation, and considered the kind of extrinsic motivation derived from examination pressure as harmful to learning. Yet an optimal level of pressure is thought to be healthy in East Asian countries. We should utilise both intrinsic and extrinsic motivation in promoting students' learning of mathematics.

5 . Whole class teaching versus individualised learning

In the West, individual care is seen as the ideal, and it is only because of financial or other resource limitations that educators resort to large class, whole group teaching. Yet in the Eastern tradition, the role model of the teacher in a "direct teaching to the whole-class" setting is essential. Extreme modes of individual attention such as individualised learning programmes may prove to be harmful because most of the time the student is interacting with materials rather than interacting with or observing/listening to the teacher, thus losing the opportunity to model upon the teacher.

6. Competence of teachers: subject matter versus pedagogy

With the exponential growth of knowledge, it is believed that the teacher is no longer expected to be competent in the subject area. Her role should be that of a facilitator of learning rather than the source of knowledge. This implies that what the teacher needs is only competence in pedagogy, i.e., in helping students to acquire the knowledge that the teacher may not possess. In contrast, the image of the teacher in the East Asian tradition is still that she is an expert or a learned figure (a scholar) in mathematics. Recent studies have shown that actually without a thorough understanding of the knowledge, it is not possible to invoke the appropriate pedagogy. Student centre, teacher centre or knowledge centre? The above dichotomies point to the major dichotomy about who or what should be the centre in the teaching and learning process. Student-centredness is the basic tenor

160

in Western education theories, yet Chinese educators are reaffirming the importance of the teacher and the subject matter. This is perhaps the essence of an East Asian identity in mathematics education.

Automated Reasoning and Educational Intelligent Platform

Li Chuan Zhong, Zhang Jing Zhong
Guangzhou University, China

(1) Newly advances in research for the automatic inference and education technology

There are two ways in research of automatic inference. First one, it is in research for the general rules and methods; the another is oriented to some certain specific problems. Experienced for years, the latter is more effective than the former. There are two events known all over the world to be illustrated this fact. First, symbol calculation software are prevailing, and second, Deep Blue computer system beat the world champion of chest. The latter caused a sensation, while the former made practical effects significantly. From 1980's, a great deal of advanced intelligent works and mental labors are decreased instead of increased the applications of symbol calculation software in computer. Consequently, this fact eases up the crisis of shortage of scientists and mathematicians who are in consequence of quality drop in mathematic education, and it raise the efficiency in the scientific and technological working.

The elementary geometry is nearly one of the most ancient disciplines. Though it is oldest one, mechanically problem solving has been progressed slowly until the passed few years. Triumphantly, not only can we judge the truth or false of proposition in elementary geometry by computer, but also can generate some proofs that easier understood and tested. The triumph of automatic inference in the branch of geometry has opened much wider fields for some scientific disciplines. A series of results in automatic inference may spread to following areas:

a. Such basic scientific researches as physics, chemistry, biology, and so on;
b. Some complicated calculations in the High-tech;
c. To strengthen and reinforce CAD with intelligence by geometrical inference and plot automation;
d. To develop education technology.

Among them, the last project is new direction worth serious considerations. Literally, education technology is interdisciplinary field across education and technology. Technologically, it integrated and incorporated with multimedia, network, and artificial intelligence. The earliest rush was for multimedia. Much educational software was named "multimedia education software" that betrayed the view people held that impossible for education technology without multimedia.

162

Then the network was the favorite for everyone. Leaders and workers emphasized Tele-education, thus many schools and colleges were busied over the Internet in campus. In contrast to that, the artificial intelligence is still necessary to be developed.

Why is the software not able to satisfy the need for teaching? The key problem is most of the education software without intelligence. That kind of software, practically, is only an electronic pager, a set of exercises, or curriculum video broadcasting. Most students preferred to use reference books for review rather than operating education software, because reading books comes cheaper and more comfortable for eyes than staring at the screen of computer. Most teachers think that it is no suitable software for teaching in class, because commercial software is not friendly, could not be modified to fit varied situations, not able to add the experience accumulated by themselves.

What kind of good education software they want? What kind of capability the software should be possessed of?
The middling students hope that the software is able to answer their questions encountered in the study, not merely a set of fixed exercises. The leading students expect that the software provide an environment for them to gain the abilities of innovation, do not want that it is only a knowledge injector. The teachers desiderate that the software play a role of capable assistant, not a video tape or VCD, so it can answer questions asked by students, can free them from most of routines to let them manage the more innovative work by themselves. The software must be equipped with multimedia editor supported by a knowledge database to facilitate preparing lectures and making classware.

Unfortunately, it is long way to go to match the requirement right now. The approach to change the situation is to employ the artificial intelligence, especially the automatic inference, to research and develop the intelligent platform for education software.

(2) The basic structure of Educational Intelligent Platform
The intelligence platform for education software we conceived is oriented to discipline, such as platform for plane geometry, platform for physics studied in junior high school, and so on. It consists of nine subsystems, as follows:

1 . Discipline knowledge database: it stores the knowledge required by syllabus in its memory.
2. Expression system for knowledge element: Some intuitive figures, images, and symbols in this system, such as circle, line segment for geometry; pulley, ammeter for physics are called as knowledge elements.
3.The question generator system that connected with knowledge elements.

4. The automatic inference system based on discipline knowledge logical rules.

5. The automatic inference system based on the knowledge base of discipline.

6. The temporary information base based on the knowledge of discipline and automatic inference system.

7. Based on multimedia the preparing lecture and making classware system used for teacher.

8.The classware broadcasting system supports classware demonstration independently.

9. The system that supports self-taught, preview, review, and self-test for students.

Does Practice Make Perfect?

Shiqi Li

East China Normal University, China

熟能生巧, corresponding to an English proverb Practice Makes Perfect, is an ancient Chinese idiom. Many teachers in China as well as in East Asia believe it and consider it a principle for mathematics teaching and learning. However most mathematics educators in the West think understanding is the most important goal. They adopt an attitude of negating drill and practice and regard it as a purely behavioral manipulation. The issue of practice first versus understanding first is nearly the same dilemma as the question of which came first, the chicken or the egg. It is meaningful to reflect on the traditional way of teaching and learning and show what possibilities it possesses for developing understanding.

Action and Reflection - The Form of Learning

Now it is widely accepted that teaching mathematics means teaching mathematical activities. Why is activity necessary? First of all, mathematics learning is empirical or quasi-empirical action (Lakatos, 1976). The behavior of manipulative practice is a fundamental behavior for mathematics. Students will do mathematics themselves and acquire knowledge through their practical activities. Most of activities are manipulations of mathematics objects. It implies that mathematics concept would be a tree without roots or a river without source if there were no real or mental manipulation.

But a mathematical object is actually a mental object. They are built through man's activities. To construct it, more important thing is a leap in thinking, i.e., reflective abstraction (Piaget, 1971). The basis of reflection is manipulative activities. Without manipulation the following reflection cannot be put into effect. So students' manipulative practice will lay a foundation for their reflective abstraction. In short, practice makes perfect, perfect will be formed on solid basis of practice.

Concept Process and Object - The Content of Learning

As Sfard et al. (1991,1994) pointed out, in mathematics especially in algebra, a lot of concepts are both operational process and structural object. So a concept is of dual nature. According to the further investigation, the cognition of concept usually begins with process, then shifts to object. They co-exist as a whole in mind and play different roles in appropriate contexts. Only at this moment has understanding been accomplished entirely. The duality of mathematics concept brings the duality of mathematical thinking and comprehension. Metaphorically, a mathematical concept is like a large, smooth ball which is difficult to manage. The process of concept is a possible gap to touch. Routine practice gives a starting point for concept cognition. Students could know the inherent relation through manipulation and open the door to their successive learning.

Broadly speaking, a concept is one of the links of a chain of concepts. Concept as an object will play a pivotal role. It manipulates some objects at certain level and is manipulated by the processes of other concepts at higher level. There is a cognitive crux between these levels. In fact it is a strange loop in the reification of concept. If a concept is not operated by processes at higher level, it will seem no necessary to be reified and it will not become an object. On the other hand, if what to be operated is not an object, these operations will be operations without objects. If student is forced to do these operations, s/he can follow the rules but does not make sense of it. However some chances for comprehension are provided by these operations. Students could attempt to explore underlying meanings through their imitative practice and find opportunities to insight into the process, and make object explicit from mechanical manipulation. Mathematical algorithm or process is indeed a really driving force. It encourages students thinking and prevent learning from stopping. If we insist that students should not have routine practice and solve problems until they have understood related concepts, they may lose any opportunities to be engaged in learning. In short, the operations at higher level bring a bird's eye view to look at a concept from higher standpoint so as to promote the reification of object. The operations beyond one's understanding may be what we usually mean -- Whenever you do not understand a concept immediately, please follow the process and practice it, familiarize yourself with it. Then you could achieve better understanding gradually.

Concluding Remarks
Briefly, the discussion above reveals that the mechanism of routine practice is not simply interpreted as mechanically imitating and memorizing rules and skills. Manipulative practice is the genetic place of mathematical thinking and the foundational step of concept formation. The reasonableness and effectiveness of practice lies in its necessity. The mechanism and positive role of Practice makes perfect are confirmed in this meaning. However it implies at the same time that it is insufficient for concept formation to have proficient practice only. On the other hand if there is no balance between the stage of process manipulation and the stage of object formation, immoderate practice may delay students' development of comprehensive. Practice will make stupid. Improper routine practice also can course students' negative believes, attitudes and emotions. As a result, practice makes them boring.

References
Lakatos,J.(1976) *Proofs and Refutations --The Logic of Mathematical Discovery.*

Cambridge University Press, London.

Piaget,J.(1971) *Genetic Epistemology*, W. W. Norton, New York.

Sfard,A.(1991) On the dual nature of mathematical conceptions: Reflections on processes and objects as different sides of the same coin. *Educational Studies in Mathematics*, **22**, pp.1-36.

Sfard,A. and Linchevski,L.(1994) The gains and pitfalls of reification -- The case of algebra. *Educational Studies in Mathematics*, **26**, pp.191-228.1

Enhancing the Mathematical Knowledge of Primary Teachers

Lim-Teo Suat Khoh

National Institute of Education, Nanyang Technological University, China

Introduction

The National Institute of Education is the sole teacher education institute in Singapore and it provides pre-service pedagogical training for all teachers in Singapore. Annually, the Institute graduates nearly 1000 teachers for the primary schools and about 700 pre-service teachers for secondary schools. There are 3 pre-service training programmes for Primary school teachers in Singapore but in this lecture, I shall be discussing only one of these namely, the BA/BSc with Dip Ed, a four-year undergraduate programme with pedagogical training as well as in-depth content knowledge in two academic subjects.

As in many countries, most teachers in primary schools are normally responsible for teaching nearly all subjects of the school curriculum, namely, English, Mathematics, Science, Social Studies, Art, Health Education, etc. As such, unlike those trained for teaching Mathematics at secondary schools, primary school teachers have very diverse mathematics backgrounds and some can be relatively poor in their mathematical understanding of the concepts they are expected to teach. School leaders and curriculum specialists in the Singapore school system have expressed such concerns in this area. Local research in the area of teacher knowledge has also indicated concerns about content knowledge of teachers, especially in the disciplines of science and mathematics.

In response to these concerns, the Curriculum Content (CC) courses were introduced to the BA/BSc with Dip Ed programme from the 1998-99 academic year to provide the knowledge base for the curriculum subjects which the trainees will be trained to teach. The CC course is aimed at building up the trainees' own knowledge and understanding of the subject and is not to be confused with the Curriculum Studies (CS) courses which deal with methodology and pedagogical issues of teaching/learning the subject. The trainees are required to do 3 CS courses in English, Mathematics and a third subject area. Linked to each of the CS areas which are 8 unit (96 hour) courses, a CC course of 3 units (36 hours) is included as from 1998.

The CC Mathematics Course

The CC Mathematics course was thus intended to supplement the mathematics methodology course by providing foundation conceptual understanding which is closely related to the primary Mathematics syllabus. It was modelled on an in-service module taught in the July 1998 semester and was taught for the first time in the January 1999 semester and for the second time in the January 2000 semester. The course ran over 12 weeks with contact time of 3 hours per week. The trainees were not taught in the traditional mode of lectures and tutorials but in classes of about 20 per class.

Based on the content of the primary mathematics curriculum, the following topics were included in the course:

· Historical numeration systems
· Place-value systems using different bases
· Operations and number systems
· Divisibility
· Basic concepts in Statistics
· Historical results in geometry
· Mathematical discussion and establishment of geometrical results taught at primary levels
· Modeling of word problems using equations and links to the "model method" used in Singapore schools.

Problems Encountered

One of the most difficult problems was the mixed backgrounds of the students. As an undergraduate course, we had to maintain rigour and standard. However, about half of the students did not have a strong mathematical background and were used to doing mathematics in a very procedural manner. Overall, they were not used to discussing mathematics concepts or understanding abstract structures. Although the approach taken was based on exploration and discussion, some of the students had great difficulties in coming to grips with the concepts.

In the 1999 cohort, 18% of the students did not pass the course while in the 2000 cohort, the failure rate was 10%. Student feedback from the 1999 cohort was very mixed. Those who liked mathematics felt that the course was enlightening and helpful but those who found the course difficult found it unlike their previous encounters with mathematics and could not see the relevance of the topics in spite of the lecturer's having explained the rationale of each topic to them. Some of the students explained that they had mathematics phobia from the past and did not realise they would still have to do mathematics at university level. Comparatively, more than one group of in-service teachers who had taken a similar course gave feedback that such a course was very useful in providing them with a stronger foundation for teaching mathematics in the primary schools.

Conclusion

The staff who conceptualised and taught the CC Mathematics course still feel that it is an important and crucial component in the training of primary teachers. In fact, the National Institute of Education is now reviewing the other pre-service programmes for primary teachers and such CC courses will very likely be incorporated in these programmes as well in the near future.

Modeling the Teacher's Situation in the Classroom

Claire Margolinas

Institut Universitaire de Formation des Maitres d'Auvergne, France

My intent is to demonstrate how the teacher is caught in a network of different constraints. Some of these constraints derive from the problem offered to the pupils, the manner in which they react and the answers they give. Others derive from the teacher's representation of the act of teaching in general, but also from mathematics and the mathematical theme to be dealt with (and more precisely the plan assigned to an individual lesson). The teacher's actions correspond to maintaining a balance, something which can be difficult among the differing constraints. The teacher's difficulties can correspond to a lack of knowledge on a specific level, and it is therefore important for teacher training to be able to identify this competence.

1. Two Complementary process: devolution and institutionalisation

The theoretical framework of French mathematical education is built around the concept of didactical system. A didactical system is set up when the intentions of teaching and learning exist (Brousseau, 1998). It includes the object of the study, the person who wants to study it and, if necessary, the person who will help to study it (Chevallard, 1997). Some of these didactical systems exist inside an educational system, which organises the encounter among knowledge, pupil and teacher. In this description, the teacher is not the central actor in the system; that is based on the interaction between student and knowledge.

Inside the theory of didactical situations (due to Brousseau), we were initially concerned by the definition, the study and the empirical observation of situations in which the pupil was supposed to learn almost without the help of the teacher. The concept of adidactical situations is the most important theoretical issue in this theory.

The fact that the teacher was not established a priori as an essential part of the research was, paradoxically, a great help in determining the necessary roles for the teacher. The importance of the teacher was stressed in two complementary processes: devolution and institutionalisation.

The term devolution is imported from the vocabulary of justice, where it defines the act of a king who delegates part of his regal power to the chamber. In the context of the classroom, devolution is the process in which the teacher delegates the power to solve a problem to the pupils. During the initial part of the process (the devolution phase), the teacher explains the task to the pupil, without providing any indication about possible ways of solving it; the teacher encourages the children to enter into the solving process. In fact, devolution of the situation is not reduced to this particular phase, but exists during the entire solution process, because the pupils can, for instance, realise that they do not really understand the task, or they maybe discouraged, etc. That is why I speak about the devolution process and not only about the devolution phase.

The term institutionalisation refers to the didactical system as an institution, and in general to the different institutions that are related to mathematical knowledge: professional mathematicians, instructional programs, etc. The more typical moment of the institutionalisation process is the institutionalisation phase, the final part of the process, during which the teacher helps to decontextualise and formalise the knowledge learned in the previous didactical situations. But this particular phase cannot take place if nothing is set up beforehand, to reveal for instance the necessity of formulating actions and a common vocabulary.

2. A more detailed model
When a teacher gives a problem to be solved to the pupils, he or she sets up a particular situation for the pupils. More precisely, the interpretation of the problem, which can differ from pupil to pupil, places the pupils in different situations. Without adding any details, we can say that the pupil is interacting with the problem at different levels, from the more simple (interaction with the material) to the more complex (dealing with proof, for instance). Most of the results of these interactions are not visible to the teacher, and even if some element existed which could be observed (an observable), it would require some knowledge from the teacher to interpret what he or she sees. Thus, even when teachers are only observing pupils, their intellectual activity can be very important and their observations often modify the course of the actual lesson or the future lessons.

The observations of the teacher are part of his or her situation, for they can modify decisions. We can say that during the devolution process the task of teacher is not only to give or to delegate the problem to the pupils, but also to receive information from them.

In the didactical situation, when for instance institutionalising certain knowledge, the teacher will be constrained by her or his knowledge gained from observing the interaction between pupils and problem.

But teachers are also constrained by their representation of the act of teaching, of mathematics in general, and by the general ideology of the educational institution in which they are teaching. These general beliefs about teaching can determine some of their actions in situations (for instance, a decision to leave the students

172

more or less to work on a problem by themselves). A little less generally, the teacher also has some general beliefs about the mathematical knowledge that he or she has to teach, and finally, has a definite plan for the lessons to be taught.

In the didactical situation, the teacher will make some decisions that can be explained only by the necessity of the general plan, and not by the possible and actual situation.

What I will exemplify in this lecture is that:

(1) there are some tensions between the different levels of constraints;
(2) what is commonly referred as the 'experience' of the teacher can be described as knowledge of different levels.

3. Consequences for the transmission of situations and the training of teachers
It is well known that it is difficult for a researcher to transmit a situation to teachers. This difficulty is often explained by the different representations of teaching between the researcher and the teacher (for example, a constructivist versus an empirical representation). In the model described above, this level is only one of the determinants of the teacher's situation. Therefore, it is not sufficient to explain the difficulties of transmission of situations.

In the observations that I have made, the teacher is normally oriented in his or her decisions by the lesson plan; this level of specification is more important than the others. But if the reactions of the pupils reveal an unpredicted interpretation of the problem, the possibility for the teacher to react accordingly and to adjust the plan depends on knowledge of the specific problem that has been proposed to the pupils. Observation of some teachers that have chosen to work together show that this level of knowledge (observation knowledge) is not spontaneously shared, and that it handicaps the 'inexperienced' teacher, that is one who is teaching with this particular problem for the first time. The problem for the training of teachers is therefore how to develop competence of the teachers in the various levels.

References
Brousseau, Guy., 1998, *Theorie des situations didactiques,* ed. La Pensee Sauvage, Grenoble.
Chevallard, Yves., 1997, Familiere et problematique, la figure du professeur, *Recherches en Didactique des Mathématiques*, vol 17 n°1 pp. 17-54, ed. La Pensee Sauvage, Grenoble.
Margolinas, Claire., 1998, etude de la transmission des situations didactiques, *Actes du colloque "Recherche(s) et Formation"*, Grenoble fevrier 1998, ed. IUFM, Grenoble.

Crucial Issues in Teaching of Symbolic Expressions

Tatsuro Miwa

Japan

Symbolic expression is a most important and indispensable means of communication and thinking in mathematics and regarded as mathematical language.

Nature of Symbolic Expression and Its Use

From the viewpoint of language, relation between "signified" and "signifier, symbolic expression" is considered. A transition process from signified to signifier is a process "to express" and its inverse process is "to read". A transition process between two symbolic expressions is "to transform" and this is done formally. Roles of these processes in the use of symbol expressions are sketched in a triangular diagram which I call Scheme of Use of Symbolic Expressions.

As to language user, pointed out is that illiteracy comes out when education of language is not done adequately and this is serious for symbolic expression as it leads to non-use of mathematics and shutting off the gate to academic and professional career in future. In addition, noted is that language is rooted deeply in culture and user is influenced largely by their cultural background.

Symbolic expression is used in almost all strands of mathematics in secondary level and above. Speaking more correctly, without symbolic expression it is impossible to develop quantitative reasoning in the areas. In sciences which use quantitative methods, symbolic expression is essential as seen typically in physical sciences.

Symbolic expression is particularly effective in pattern-finding and generalization as well as problem solving in a broader sense. Pattern-finding is done by seeing a situation not as unique but as an element of a certain set. This assumes generation of variables and to express with use of symbolic expressions is most appropriate for number patterns. Generalization means "construction of variables" and it presupposes existence of certain invariant. Generalization of propositions concerning numbers requires use of symbolic expressions.

In problem solving symbolic expression is used effectively not only in mathematically formulated problems but also ill-formulated ones. The typical in the former are applications of equation and inequality. For the latter, symbolic expression is used in problem formulation and its solution. Mathematical modeling is a typical example. Then specifying and using of vital relationship among various quantitative relations in the problem is crucial and symbolic expression is suitable for the work.

Teaching of Symbolic Expressions at Introductory Stage

According to the principle that symbolic expression is foundation of mathematics for all, teaching of it at introductory stage, in particular, is desirable to be organized so that language aspect and its use are combined systematically. The principle denotes that it is crucial to ensure foundation for all to use symbolic expression as means of communication and thinking in mathematics. This may be interpreted immediately that students become competent to generate symbolic expressions and manipulate them. It is true only partially. I find an evidence that not a few students are reluctant to use symbolic expressions. To be competent does not necessarily lead to the will to use and to become skillful at expressing and manipulating alone does not form foundation of mathematics for all. To use metaphor, becoming skillful is compared to training of grammar and spelling in writing. What to communicate and think and for what purpose are important as well. A desirable approach demands to unify generation and manipulation of symbolic expressions and use of them systematically. Pattern-finding and generalizations as well as problem solving are good examples of use of symbolic expressions.

Three processes in language aspect of symbolic expressions are core part of teaching of it at introductory stage. In a process "to express" both sides of signified quantities and signifying expressions must be taken into consideration. Here focused on are difficulties in generation of symbolic expressions of quantities which students can calculate numerically and understanding of meaning of letters in expressions. In process "to read", symbolic expressions are referred to everyday language, numerical values and figures according to situations. Further, it is assumed that the process includes arrival at deeper understanding and new vision out of which we can make discoveries and gain insight in the situation. In process "to transform", we must obey transformation rules, which imply existence of invariant. As long as we obey the rules any form is allowable, and transformation is guided by user's goal.

The three processes are considered not to be isolated but connected and making good use of their connection is effective in teaching and learning.

Obviously teaching of symbolic expressions is based on that of arithmetic in elementary school. Many students' misconception and misunderstanding in symbolic expressions originate in their arithmetic learning. Among what students are expected to master in arithmetic the followings are very important:

· rational number concept and its relation to division;
· quantitative relations and their relationship to arithmetic operations;
· ratio and proportionality.

175

Among various factors in teaching of symbolic expressions, certainly most influential is technology, let alone teacher. It promotes students' mathematical activities and helps them develop mathematical thinking. However, technology itself does neither take the place of symbolic expressions nor help generate symbolic expressions directly. Today collaboration of symbolic expressions and technology facility is most desirable.

Mentoring in Mathematics Teaching and Teacher Preparation in Zimbabwe

David Kufakwami Jani Mtetwa
University of Zimbabwe, Zinbabwe

The main aim of this paper is to stimulate discussion on mentoring that might lead to generation of fresh research questions. A more specific aim is to examine more closely the challenge of mentoring within the mathematics subject area and consider its implications for the training and education of mentors within the currently evolving schemes of preparing mathematics teachers in Zimbabwe.

The discussion begins with a brief consideration of the role of mentoring in teacher professional development in general, then moves on to consider mentoring within mathematics teaching. The main issues raised here are captured in the questions, "What is mathematics?" or "What does it mean to do mathematics?" become central. Here, we see that there is a wide variety of conceptions or beliefs about the nature of mathematics as a subject. Different conceptions of mathematics may in turn lead to different conceptions and practices of mentoring, an observation that takes us to a consideration of characteristics of mathematics teacher mentors.

It is proposed here that a mathematics teacher mentor needs to possess, among other things, a good command of content knowledge, pedagogic content knowledge, and curricular knowledge. Content knowledge refers to the depth of understanding of the concepts, skills, and processes that constitute the subject content of mathematics. But what does deep understanding of mathematics mean? This question compels us to examine and draw from the profiles and lived experiences of productive mathematicians. We pose the related questions, "What is the nature of expert mathematical knowledge and how do mathematicians do mathematics?" A discussion of these and similar issues leads us to the conclusion that mathematics teacher mentors may need to be able to "behave like mathematicians" in so far as their mathematical knowledge structures and processing are concerned. It is also these abilities that the mentors need to inculcate in their mentees.

Pedagogic content knowledge refers to the knowledge of translating mathematical content knowledge into forms that make them accessible to learners in a variety of contexts. In this regard examining profiles of expert mathematics teachers could offer useful insights for the process of developing mathematics teacher mentors. The difficulty one encounters here is that many aspects of pedagogic content knowledge are tacit and not available in explicit forms for interrogation. Thus the problem of

177

how mathematics teacher mentors could be assisted to develop pedagogic content knowledge and in turn pass on that knowledge to their mentees remains open for more exploration.

Curricular knowledge is essentially knowledge about the other two, i.e., content and pedagogic content knowledge. Curricular knowledge is easier to develop in mentors as it is largely informational in character.

The paper ends by looking at the implications of the issues raised and discussed here for mentor-mediated mathematics teacher preparation in Zimbabwe. The main observations to highlight are that:

(1) A large number of Zimbabwean mathematics teachers show indications of possessing a kind of mathematics content knowledge that can best be described as textbook content knowledge. This kind of knowledge is often re-productive and procedural (a-la-Skemp) in nature, as opposed to the deeper knowledge that is often characteristic of productive mathematicians.

(2) Zimbabwean mathematics teachers are drawn from a wide range of training backgrounds and wield different paper qualifications that attract different perceptions of status. This raises a real and practical issue of whom can be mentored (or is willing to be mentored) by who with regard to differences in, for example, paper qualifications, age, length of teaching experience, and gender.

(3) Teacher preparation in Zimbabwe has been and is still driven by a supervision/evaluative model rather than a developmental/supportive model that is more consistent with the concept of mentoring.

(4) Mathematics learning and instruction in Zimbabwe is driven by an examination orientation rather than by a learning orientation. This gives the whole enterprise an instrumental character that engenders beliefs and conceptions of learning mathematics that may be peculiar to such an orientation.

These observations clearly make the process of developing mathematics teacher mentors problematic and therefore a formidable challenge for mathematics teacher educators in Zimbabwe.

Computer Science and Toward an Approach in Research on Mathematical Education

Huynh Mui
Thang Long University, Vietnam

1. Computers are increasingly being used as instruments in mathematical education. Many programming languages and packages of computer-aided instruction are available, which leads to new easy and exiting ways of learning mathematics. However, these efforts are only aiming at how to use computer science, e.g. for searching appropriate tools to apply mathematics or to develop the teaching techniques. As it is generally known, computer science had essential departure in mathematics, and some mathematical basic concepts are being introduced in many programming languages. The two disciplines are both rapidly developed, but in parallel and almost separately.

2. During the last decades, digital signal processing and digital logic are becoming more and more flexible in logic capability of digital computer systems. The hardware circles repeated revolutions to bring an explosion in hardware capabilities. In this situation, toward a vital approach in mathematical education, the main point is to bring mathematics back again to computer science: how to establish the mathematics of digital objects, the objects constructed by digital signals, and how to teach mathematics under such computer languages.

3. There are two critical concepts in computer science: data type and objects. A type is a collection of values. For example, the integer type inclusively consists of all integers between -32768 and 32767. An operation is a process that accomplishes some task on a given type. For example, addition is an operation, which produces the sum of two integers. A data type consists of a type and a set of operations that can access on the data of that type. In the integer data type, the type is integer, and some of its operators are +, *, div, :=, =, <, and some others like Reading, Copying, Searching from a certain file in some variables, etc. An Object is a collection of fields of various data type together with a collection of operations that operate on those fields.

By this way, one can formulate some mathematical concepts. For example, rational number is an Object with Data declarations: nominator, denominator (of integer type) and Operation definitions: IsDenominatorZero, Addition, Multiplication, etc.

4. The concept of objects is quite similar to the concept of algebraic systems in

mathematics, i.e. the sets equipped with operations. The essential difference is that operations in programming languages also include the process to manipulate the data, to reach the results by data processing. In mathematics, operations generally required certain properties, which is taken as axioms to proceed the logical reasoning process.

The significance of the concept of Objects has led to the development of powerful approach to problem solving in computer science in the last decade. Object is of great generality: objects run over all entities, from low-level ones as integers. Note that, in mathematics, one can originally start from very undefined terms, especially from the notion of empty set.

5. Obviously, many basic mathematical concepts, like the real numbers, the infinity, the continuity, the curves, etc cannot be inserted to the computer science. But, a lot of efforts have been done to simulate these objects, e.g. the advent of graphic high standards, the calculation of π of far more than one hundred millions digits. It is necessary now to study digital objects as Abstract Data Type of digital signals in computer science, and to establish mathematics of digital objects. To this end, one needs to realize the 'digitalisation' of analytical and geometrical concepts: the real number by approachable rational numbers, the point by pixel, the continuity by digital continuity, etc.

6.Many among us learned to program and spent many years doing the same thing in assembly language, Fortran, Pascal, C, etc. As always, we build program, choosing instruction statements one by one, putting them together to make a program. In a certain sense, this does not mean mathematically anything. In fact, a most common viewpoint in our mathematical circles view results obtained by computers are not allowable as mathematical results, although the computer science circles consider software as an abstract and mental activity akin to mathematics. We need to develop an programming languages environment in which one can introduce mathematical concepts by precise definitions (including operational procedures) as objects, formulate lemmas or theorems as procedures, particularly establish abundant database of objects related to mathematical basic data, in such a way that they can verify by themselves such procedures and database. It is important to make the mathematicians accept these materials as believable references, and let them think of the objects defined by programming languages as objects in their minds.

Can College Mathematics in Japan Survive?- A Project of Reform -

Yukihiko Namikawa
Nagoya University, Japan

1. Mathematics education at Japanese universities is in crisis

Now in Japan the total education system is in a severe crisis, and so is the case of mathematics education at universities. We consider this crisis by restricting to the education of college level (or general education), by which we mean math education for the 1st and 2nd year students, not only for students of math major but those who need mathematics in their majors such as physics or engineering.There are three aspects of the crisis. First we are facing a remarkable decline of mathematical knowledge and ability of fresh students. Secondly we had a big change of systems in universities including the system of general education. The last one is the mismatch or insufficiency of math education for further study of major.

2. Project of reform of math education of college level

In April 1994, we established a working group in the Mathematical Society of Japan to overcome this crisis. From 1995 we began a systematic study on it with the support of the Grant-in-Aid of the ministry of education in Japan. So far we made several investigations to clarify the situations. The results were much more disastrous than imagined before start and still conditions are going worse. We could, however, make clear where problems come from and what should be done to solve them. According to three aspects we organized three groups of study: to investigate the system of college level education in each university with the involvement of mathematics in it; to investigate the mathematical ability of students; to study what kind of mathematics is needed in majors, e.g. in physics, in engineering, in economics, in teacher education and in computer sciences. Here we shall report on the first and second subjects.In order to carry out the investigations we have organized a network connecting our study group and universities (mainly department of mathematics and those who are involved in math educations of college level). The electric mailing system of this network is also used to distribute important informations concerning education (in general).

3. Vanishing of colleges of general education

One of the biggest changes occurred in the university reform (mainly in national universities) was the vanishing of colleges of general education with full-time staff for it. Instead the whole university is supposed to be responsible for the general education. But the investigation shows that there is a decline of the level of education in fact.Moreover there will be a new big change caused by the decrease of rate of birth. In private universities they have begun to cut the positions of

181

mathematicians who are in charge of general education by replacing them with temporary ones.

4. Remarkable decline of mathematical ability of fresh students

The most surprising result was the one of the questionnaire to universities on the math ability of fresh students.Among (just) 100 answers given by the organizations which have teaching staff in charge of college math education (e.g. department of mathematics), 78 answered that the ability is declining (unchanged - 9, improved - none!).Moreover as declining abilities and knowledge they mention those of mathematical description, abstract and logical thinking, poor intuition, lack of understandings (proof and meaning) of concepts, formulae and theorems. They are almost all fundamental abilities of mathematics to be acquired at school. As attitudes of students many answers mention the passivity (lack of motive, lack of initiative) and not a few answers point out a decline of literacy of Japanese.A careful analysis of answers shows that the decline began around the latter half of 1980's. The cause would be twofold. The first is the change of the style of math education at schools, namely drill training to solve test problems without understanding and with lack of training to write logical answers. The second is a non-systematic cut of contents of math education at the change of the national standard in Japan.

5. Problems in elementary and secondary educations of mathematics

Such a decline is also a reflection of problems of education in general. Here is the reason why we should be involved in the whole education at schools, though universities are even responsible for some of the problems (e.g. entrance examination). Here we can only give a list of main problems related to ours.

1) weakness of literacy (both usual language and mathematics);
2) reduction of contents in the national standard and decrease of percentages of the number of pupils at high schools who take mathematical courses but obligatory ones;
3) lost of the sense of reality of what they have learned (relation with usual life);
4) decline of the level of understandings of mathematics in teachers.
These problems are related to other subjects. The first is to Japanese and English, the next two are to natural sciences and the last is in general.

6. How to overcome the problems

Here again we can only give the list of indications:

1) improvements of the education in universities appropriate for the situations including that of entrance examinations;
2) cooperation with other majors, natural science in particular, and that of educators and researchers together with proposals to national policy of education.

In 1998 we established a liaison committee of academic societies of mathematics, physics, chemistry and biology including both educational and research (pure and applied) and we are cooperating in the exchange of informations and in common activities such as a public appeal or an open symposium.

Student's Levels of Understanding Word Problems

Jarmila Novotna
Charles University, Czech Republic

In the paper I focus on the following aspects: grasping word problem assignments levels of understanding and students' solution strategies and their relation to their understanding of the solved word problems. This is a part of broader research project aimed at the following questions: What is going on between the posing of a word problem and the students' answer? What kinds of experience will help students to perform well on word problems? What sort of practice may help?

In the presented research the following methodology was used: Comparative analyses of textbooks and other materials for teachers, qualitative analyses of written student's solutions, and analyses of audio-recordings and protocols of individual interviews.

In the process of grasping a word problem, the solver absorbs, sifts and uses a sequence of information. The grasping process has five basic components: a) *identifying separate pieces of information* during the first reading of the problem; b) *determining what the question was asking*; c) *searching for a unifying view*; d) *looking for and hopefully finding all relationships* relevant to the solving process; e) *getting an overall insight* (finding how all the pieces of information are mutually connected). The grasping process is serial. A student usually reads the assignment (once or more times) and tries to record information (components a) to d)). Component e) runs in parallel to the first four. Less successful solvers may be unable to grasp a word problem as a whole and only cope with parts of it. Thus, they may confuse the relationships among different pieces of assigned information.

In this research, I look at the levels of a student's understanding of word problem assignments through three variables: 1. *attaining the grasping process components and its quality* (levels of understanding of the assignment are related to the successfully finished components of the grasping process; the components are not necessarily expressed in a student's solution in an explicit way, they may be hidden in implicit steps); 2. *how many times the solver refers back to the assignment* (a scalar variable); 3. *quality of the grasping process* (grasping with understanding, incomplete understanding if the solver only grasps a part of the assigned information, prothetic grasping if no understanding occurs in a particular stage of the grasping process). Using the three variables, the grasping process is described by the following table:

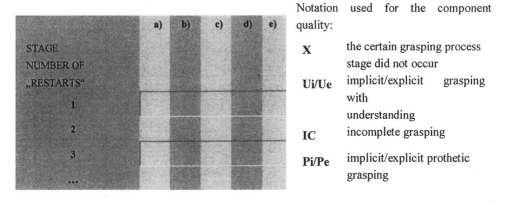

	a)	b)	c)	d)	e)	Notation used for the component quality:
STAGE NUMBER OF „RESTARTS"						**X** — the certain grasping process stage did not occur
1						**Ui/Ue** — implicit/explicit grasping with understanding
2						**IC** — incomplete grasping
3						**Pi/Pe** — implicit/explicit prothetic grasping
...						

The table gives two types of information - what happened during one reading of the assignment and how the individual components developed during the whole grasping.

The level of the solver's understanding of the word problem structure strongly influences his/her solving strategy. In this analysis, I consider the following three items for the characterisation of the chosen solving strategy: (i) if the solution was found accidentally or after gaining an insight into the problem structure; (ii) if the solution was based on the identification of key words/word groups in the text or on the insight into the problem structure; (iii) how the use of symbolic algebraic description in the word problem assignment influences the grasping processes and/or the solving strategy.

The use of symbolic algebraic description in the word problem assignment influences the grasping processes and/or the solving strategy. Four stages of dealing with the assignment containing one element of the language of algebra, are presented: (1) The solver ignores data which are not assigned as concrete numbers. (2) The solver is aware of the fact that he/she is asked to work with letters but he/she is not able to understand the meaning of the symbols in the given context. (3) The solver is aware of the nature of data assigned as letters but the symbolic algebraic description of the situation is not yet fixed in his/her knowledge structure and he/she substitutes concrete numbers and thus changes the problem into a pure arithmetical one. (4) The solver is able to work successfully with data assigned in both arithmetical and algebraic languages.

Teaching Geometry in a Changing World

Iman Osta
Lebanese American University, Israel

The teaching of mathematics is witnessing substantial changes, with the widespread use of computer technology. The new tools are reshaping the kind of mathematical knowledge needed by prospective citizens, laypersons, workers, specialists or researchers. They are also affecting the methods and approaches to math teaching.

Geometry might be one of the most affected disciplines by this drastic change, for many reasons related to its very nature, among which: the dual aspects of geometry (deductive and intuitive), its heavy perceptive components, the need in its teaching for sophisticated types of representations (not only coded or symbolic, but also and mainly figurative or semi-figurative), etc. The used technology has special impacts on every one of these aspects.

A thorough look through the history of geometry education would show big shifts between two extremes, as to the use of graphics, drawings, sketches or other types of representations. Geometry teaching has oscillated between two perceptions of geometry as a school discipline: The first perception sees it as a context for developing a pure deductive, logical and axiomatic construct, and the other one looks at it as the study of space through the study of figures, shapes, configurations, etc.. The second view relies heavily on graphic representations, on intuition and perceptive abilities as ways to reach the deductive formal level of dealing with geometry. In-between these two extremes, many approaches to geometry occurred, such as: analytical, differential, utilitarian, and other approaches.

The paper aims at developing a prospective view on how the new technological tools would affect the teaching of geometry in the near future: the type of expected school geometry, the possible goals of a geometry curriculum, the content, and the teaching approaches of school geometry curriculum.

The hypothesis of this paper is that the kind of tools available to geometers and geometry teachers affects to a large extent the prevailing nature of geometry in school math curricula, as well as the methods of its teaching. The very nature of geometric concepts to be developed depends on the tools that are available and used in their representation.

The example of the circle represented in different contexts can show us how the conceptualization of the same geometric object varies when we use different tools. While school curricula stress the definition of the circle as being the "set of points that are equidistant from a fixed point", they favor the use of compasses in representing it. However, the circle drawn using compasses suits better a conception of the circle as being the section of a cone by a plane. The plane is the plane of the paper on which we draw, and the cone is the virtual cone generated by the rotation of the pencil-arm of the compasses around the pin-arm, this latter representing the axis of the cone.

Drawing the circle using a string and a pin would suit much better the common definition above: "set of points of the plane that are equidistant (length of the string) from a fixed point (the tip of the pin).

Other conceptions of the circle may be privileged in other environments: under Logo, the representation of the circle corresponds to the definition: "A circle is the limit of a regular polygon as its number of sides tends to infinity and the length of its side tends to zero". Under such environments, we may even have circles that are more "circular" than others. Various dynamic geometry tools adopt various types of representations, embedding cognitive systems with which students interact. They create mid-way representations between concrete objects and abstract geometrical constructs, by their powers of animation, visualization, transformations, etc.

The key questions are do the different ways of representing a certain geometrical concept affect the way students learn it? How wold the embedded representations in interactive dynamic geometry software affect the students' learning of geometry? Should new geometry curricula integrate (implicitly or explicitly) the availability and accessibility of these tools? Would the goals in a curriculum be set as to build an "intelligent partnership" between students solving geometry problems and cognitive systems embedded in the Dynamic Geometry software?

Mathematics for Mathematics Teachers -On Statistics-

Han Shick Park
National University of Education, Korea

I highly recommend that materials directly related to school mathematics should be included in the pre-service and in- service curriculum for secondary school teachers.

In this paper, I would like to explain the statistics unit structure in the secondary school mathematics curriculum in Korea. I would like to propose the statistics materials that need to be taught pre-service and in-service teachers. In the secondary school curriculum, statistics and probability are combined as one unit, but in this paper I would like to limit the discussions to statistics only.

Statistics for mathematics teachers consist of descriptive statistics and inductive statistics. Descriptive statistics is for junior high school teachers, and inductive statistics is for senior high school teachers. In Korea, the same certificates of mathematics teachers are given to both junior and senior high school. There is no separate certificate for senior high school teachers. The following topics are suggested for descriptive statistics and for inductive statistics.

(A) Descriptive Statistics
1. Statistics for one variable
(1) Frequency distribution
To construct tables of frequency distribution with unequal width of class and find out the shape of frequency distribution curves.
(2) Representative
To define the arithmetic mean, median mode, geometric mean, harmonic mean, and m-trimmed, m-Winsorized mean.
(3) Degree of scattering
To define standard deviation and variance, mean deviation, quartile deviation and range to study their characteristics.
(4) Skewness and kurtosis
To define skewness, kurtosis and to study their characteristics.
2. Statistics in two dimensions
(1) Correlation table
To construct a correlation table for a set of data and to study scatter diagrams and correlation diagrams.
(2) Correlation
To study the definition of coefficient correlation and to calculate it. Then, to study its characteristics.

(3) Regression line

To study the definition of regression line and to calculate it. Then, to study its characteristics.

(4) Spearman's coefficient of rank correlation

To study the definition of Spearman's coefficient of rank correlation and to calculate it. Then, to study its characteristics.

(B) Inductive Statistics

1. Probability distribution

(1) Discrete probability distribution

① Probability table and graph

② Mean, variance and standard deviation

③ Binomial distribution

④ Poisson distribution

⑤ Moment generating functions(m.g.f.)

(2) Continuous probability distribution

① Probability density functions

② Mean and variance

③ Normal distribution

④ Moment generating functions

2. Sampling

(1) Population and sample

(2) Random digit

(3) The central-limit theorem

(4) The normal approximation to the binomial distribution

3. Statistical inference

(1) Confidence intervals for the mean of normal distribution

(2) Confidence intervals for p in a binomial distribution

(3) Confidence intervals for the population means

4. Test of significance

(1) Significance tests

(2) Two types of errors

(3) Maximum likelihood method

(4) Others

 In conclusion, I would like to emphasize again that materials directly related to school mathematics should be included in the pre- and in-service curriculum for secondary school teachers. Although it is often assumed that if one understands advanced mathematics, one will automatically know junior or senior high school mathematics, I would like to stress that this is not always the case.

Mathematics Education for and in the Dominant and Other Cultures:

A Multicultural Inquiry

H. Sakonidis
Democritus University of Thrace, Greece

The technological advancements of our time and the economic and political dominance of Western societies suggest that success and survival in the world of the future will depend to a large extent on one's ability to be "literate" in mathematics. Thus, it is possible that mathematical ability will become a criterion for discrimination against a person or a group, being used as a filter into employment and professional development. In this context, taking into account relevant research findings, the socially or culturally "different" persons or groups, particularly in Western societies, will be the most vulnerable.

For many years, mathematics was considered universal, objective and unrelated to the social and cultural conditions within which it is developed and practiced. The formal presentation of school mathematics backed this view and did not address the culture with which pupils identify and through which they learn. However, recent developments in the field have come to suggest that mathematical learning and teaching constitute a particular social and cultural process (Bishop, 1988). This view imposes a new framework of thinking about mathematics education, which draws on the mathematical practices in which pupils are engaged in everyday life, both in and outside of school. Such a perspective addresses the needs of minority children and the demands made on them, as well as the pupils of the dominant group in   society.

The education of the minority groups have captured the interest of researchers and educators alike in the last thirty years or so. However, it is only recently, under pressure emerging from population movements in certain parts of Europe, that some governments, becoming more conscious of the presence of "other" groups in society, have been forced to recognize the urgent need to adopt a multicultural agenda in their educational system. Unfortunately, so far, most efforts towards this have been predominately concerned with language teaching and learning. Subjects such as mathematics, being considered more or less independent of social and cultural issues, have been left out of this agenda, thus torpedoing the multicultural approach altogether.

In the Greek educational system, the largest minority group consists of about 120,000 Muslims living in the northeastern part of the country. The Laussane

Treaty, signed between Greece and Turkey 77 years ago, governs the operation of minority primary schools, where about 53% of the weekly timetable is taught in Turkish (e.g., Mathematics and Science) and the rest in Greek. The textbooks for the subjects taught in Turkish are produced and approved by the Turkish government, whereas the ones used for the instruction in Greek by the Greek government. The teaching personnel of the minority primary schools consists of 373 Christian and 419 Muslim teachers, almost 40% of the latter being only graduates of the secondary minority schools.

Thus, Muslim children, living in a conservative, mainly agricultural Muslim community, surrounded by an Orthodox Christian population, attend classes in a rather complicated educational environment compared to that of the rest of the population. A recent study (Vakalios, 1997) has shown that the dropout rate of minority children is much higher than that of the general population and that their limited knowledge of the Greek language seems to constitute a barrier for them in accessing higher education. Furthermore, it has been found that the achievements of the minority secondary pupils are lower than those of the Christian pupils, especially in mathematics, science and Greek Language. These findings suggest that minority children are likely to encounter difficulties later on in their professional and social incorporation into the wider society.

The results of some preliminary studies on the characteristics of the mathematics education provided for these minority children are reported here. These studies were designed and carried out as a part of a large, ongoing study on the way in which Greek Muslim children make mathematical meaning in an educational environment, where two rather distinct cultures meet, the one holding a dominant role in the wider society and the other dominating at a local level. The results show that the educational environment of these children is rather downgraded and definitely not related to their everyday lives. This situation presents problems and difficulties for the Muslim pupils in general and in mathematics in particular, as they struggle to come to terms with the cultural values associated with mathematical activities in three different cultures (Turkish, Greek and their own). Furthermore, they enter school with a culturally distinct view of reality, which causes further frustration and confusion about what exactly is relevant when mathematical contexts are discussed or modeled.

References

Bishop, A.J. (1988) *Mathematics Enculturation*, Dordrecht: Kluwer.
Vakalios, A. (1997) *The problem of intercultural education in western Thrace* (in Greek), Gutenberg: Athens.Greece

Mathematics Education for Gifted Students in Korea

Hyunyong Shin, Inki Han
Korea National University of Education
Gyeongsang National University, Korea

The needs for the special math program for the gifted children can be considered from two sides of perspective; personal and national. On the personal side, it would be the satisfaction derived from developing individual's potentials and interest to the fullest; whereas, developing the children with exceptional aptitude in math by means of compatible curriculum would have a significant impact in the fields of math and science and decisively contribute to the nation's competitive edge.

Recently, the issue relating to the special learning program for the gifted children has been gaining momentum in Korea. Consequently, interest and support by the government have been initiated. Numerous researches on the theory and practice of the special education have been implemented at the elementary and middle school levels[13, 14].

In this talk, we discuss what is going on in Korea for mathematics education for gifted students. We introduce some national institutes for gifted education[9]. The National Academy for Gifted Students that will be established soon is also mentioned briefly[8].

The curriculums for the aforementioned institutes are discussed.

The main focus of this talk is on the report of a project for expanding creative mind in gifted education. In fact, under the auspices of the Ministry of Education, this author participated, from December of 1997 to November of 1999, as the researcher-in-charge, and as a hands-on field experiment personnel, in developing a tangible study program that is pioneering and suitable to the special math education program for the gifted children in Korea. One unique characteristic in developing the teaching materials was actively utilizing many basic concepts of cryptology[3] and superstring theory[4], along with careful use of calculators and computers. Researching through various bibliographic materials on the initiative factors has been productive in extracting many factors attributable to the formation of initiatives. Consequently, such findings have contributed positively in developing about 100 hours of study materials for the grade, middle, and high school levels that are vital to instill the sense of initiative among the students. The study materials, in turn, have been validated through the teaching and learning processes. In this research, the following supportive issues were taken into consideration in developing the study materials:

1 . The Study Topics That Would Inspire the Motivation to Solve the Problem.
Example: Fix the entangled exercise equipment.
2. The Study Topics That Is Conducive to Developing the Factors of Initiative.
(1) Sensitivity toward the Task
Example: Explain, in mathematical expression, the principle of ladder climbing.
(2) Fluency in Thinking
Example: The 1998 Game
(3) Flexibility in Thinking
Examples: From Pascal's Triangle, find number patterns as many as possible.
(4) Originality of Thinking
Example: A basic concept of cryptology - A probabilistic proof
(5) Perseverance
Example: (To be presented in the full paper)
3. Exercises for Self-motivated Study
Example: Find the counterfeit coin using the balance scale.
4. Diversification of Study Tools
Example: Adventure for Mersenne primes utilizing computer and internet
5. Study Tools to Stimulate Cooperation and Competition

Example: (To be presented in the full paper)

In conclusion, we report our experience on the use of technology, philosophy, and the role of teachers in gifted education. The advent of computer and other technology could be of great advantages not only in enhancing the study effects and creativity, but in the constructive point of view as well. However, as Dong-A Daily News (a Korean daily newspaper)[2] and Jane Healy[1,5,6] and Tien[15] have pointed out careless utilization of technology may result in a severe adverse impact. Naturally, utmost study and care are mandatory in utilizing technology. We think about Paul Erdös[7, 12] and John Nash[10] as good examples of the gifted. We may propose a philosophical problem on the gifted education. As everybody agrees, it is the teachers that play the most important role in education. It is also oviously true in the gifted education. Before we start to run a special program, the teachers who will be involved in the program should be ready.

References
[1] J. Becker, [ME] *Computers rot our children's brains,* private communication by email, May 2, 2000.
[2] DONG-A DAILY NEWS, *Too Much Computer Spoils Kid's Math Grades,* November 6, 1998.
[3] M. R. Fellows, N. Koblitz, *Combinatorially based cryptography for children* (and

adults), pre-print through internet, 1998.

[4] B. Greene, *the elegant universe,* W. W. Norton & Company, New York, London, 1999.

[5] S. B. Harvin, *Outsmarting Ourselves: How computers can fail children,* NEW YORK TIMES, December 11, 1998.

[6] J. M. Healy, *Failure to connect: How computers affect our children's mind - For better and worse,* Simon & Schuster, New York, 1998.

[7] P. Hoffman, *The Man Who Loved Only Numbers,* Hyperion, New York, 1998.

[8] KEDI, *Proposed Math Curriculum for Gifted Children,* Commissioned Research(CR), KEDI. Seoul, Mar. 20, 1999.

[9] KEDI, *Development Research on Science Education for Gifted Children,* CR 99-15. Seoul: Bong-Mun Publishing Co., 1999.

[10] S. Nasar, *A Beautiful Mind,* Simon & Schuster, New York, 1998.

[11] J. S. Renzulli, *The enrichment triad model: A guide for developing defensible programs for the gifted and talented,* Mansfield Center, CN: Creative Learning Center, 1997.

[12] B. Schechter, *My brain is open,* Simon & Schuster, New York, 1998.

[13] Shin Hyunyong, Han Inki, Kim Won-Kyung, Shin In-Sun, Research on Revised Plan for Teaching Math to the Gifted Children, *Journal of Korean Society of Mathematical Education, Series E: Communications on Mathematical Education,* Vol. 10, 2000.

[14] Shin Hyunyong, Han Inki, Lee Chong-Wouk, Program for Developing Creativity among Gifted Math Students in Grade School, *Journal of Korean Society of Mathematical Education, Series E: Communications on Mathematical Education,* Vol. 10, 2000.

[15] D. Tien, *Using MATLAB in teaching advanced engineering mathematics,* Submitted to but not presented at ICMI-EARCOME 1 , 1998.

Designing Instruction of Values in School Mathematics

R. Soedjadi
Surabaya State University, Indonesia

Nowdays, mathematics has been rapidly growing. Many new mathematical topics developed and new results found. The major reason for this rapid growth is its wealth of applications. This rapid growth will certainly effects the contents of school mathematics for the students. If some new topics should be included in the school mathematics, in the same time, some "old" topics should be excluded from it. Beside, mathematics educators must be aware that a lot of students after graduation may not directly use mathematics in their real life, but most of them may use mathematical way of thinking in facing their real life, and furthermore, this can effect their life attitudes. Mathematics teaching is not only based on the cognective achievement, but it is also based on the increasing of affective and psychomotor achievements.

Mathematics educators should reconsider that the main purpose of teaching mathematics is not simply for transforming mathematics as much as possible to the students. Mathematics is taught to the students for helping them putting their logical reasoning in order, performing their personalities, and being able to use mathematics and their mathematical reasoning in facing real life situation. This implies that the mathematics teaching process should be designed so that it covers the cognitive, affective and psychomotor fieds. This means teaching of values in mathematics teaching process must be developed by mathematics educator.

By selecting the topics that will be included in the school mathematics curriculum it is hoped that content of the curriculum will not be too loaded. And so, there will be enough time for the teachers to design mathematics instructions that contains values education. Even though the affective and psychomotor purposes can be achieved by chance in any mathematics instruction, but is necessary designing mathematics instruction that leads to the achievement of affective and psychomotor pruposes.

It is believed that not every teaching method is suitable for teaching all mathematics topics in any circumferences and situations. The quadrilateral topics for junior high school students include Parallelogram, Rhombus, Rectangle, Square, and Trapezoid.

In this paper we focus our attention on Parallelogram, only. The strategy is "activating students" through Bruner's learning phases. Bruner's learning phases, inactive-iconic-symbolic, can be well designed and applied in teaching mathematics.

One possible such design is described in the next sections for teaching
QUADRILATERALS (especially, parallelogram).

Inactive
Triangle ABC is rotated by student around O (AO = OB). 180°.

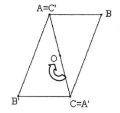

Figure-1   Figure-2

Found the parallelogram ABCB'

Iconic
Just by observation the parallelogram ABCB' - analyze the same object of ABCB'

Symbolic
Write the same symbol for the same object of ABCB'

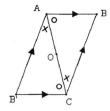
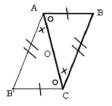

Figure-3   Figure-4

To construct some definitions of parallelogram ABCB' by students. (by the same
angles or same sides or parallel sides) **Take one of the definitions as the convension
and use this for the next activities.**

VALUES : 4
1. Free opinion to the object
2. Free to construct the definition, - but all true.
3. Make the convension, -democracy for starting the deductive reasoning

Some Characteristic Features of Wasan: The Japanese Traditional Mathematics

Osamu Takenouchi
Osaka International University, Japan

Wasan is the mathematics specially developed in Japan in the Edo period (1603 to 1867). Though we see many splendid monuments from long ago such as shrines and temples, and we think that to build them there must have been good mathematics already in those days, we are not able to find any literature which communicates to us the existence of the study of mathematics before the Edo period. In the Edo period, we find many remarkable works of mathematics. But, we no longer make studies of mathematics in the style of Wasan because when the Edo period terminated, the government made a decision to pursue the teaching of mathematics in the European style, and researches began to be made in the new style.

Wasan inherits from the Chinese mathematics. In general, culture was first imported from China into Japan, and our ancestors developed proper Japanese culture after that. There was well developed mathematics in old China, and several books are known to have been imported and they became the basis of Wasan. For example, I will mention Sangaku Keimo (算学啓蒙, Suanxue quimeng, 1299) and Sanpo Toso (算法統宗, Suanfua tongzong, 1592) which had the most important influence.

Japan was isolated from other countries in the Edo period except for China and Holland because of the policy of the Tokugawa shogunate which ruled Japan. So Wasan was forced to make special development of its own separated from the mathematics from abroad.

Very peculiar in Wasan is the use of the Soroban, or Japanese abacus. The Soroban was put into practical use in China in the 13th and 14th centuries. And after it was brought from China in the 16th century, its way of use was well studied, and it spread all over Japan, everywhere in the government, in the commercial activities, in the study of mathematics, and in the family. It now spreads all over the world. In many countries there are people who learn the use of the Soroban, though its usefulness is replaced by electronic calculators and computers. We find the development of Wasan in three directions.

(1) Mathematics for citizens

First attempts were made to educate citizens in the calculations for their daily needs and for their commercial activities. About 1625, several books were published for this purpose. Among others, the most important one is Jinkoki, which was used throughout the Edo period. There were other books similar to it, and the number of them comes to about 400.

(2) Academic studies

In the domain of pure mathematics, the first person who should be named is Seki Takakazu (1640?-1708). He made many remarkable works. His main works are considered to have been done in 1670 to 1690. To mention some of his works:

a. The summation formula of powers of natural numbers. He established a formula which is now known as Bernoulli polynomial.

b. Determination of the lengths of arcs of a circle. He used for that the acceleration method which is now common in numerical analysis.

c. Establishment of determinants. He mentioned determinants of order 3, 4, and 5. The theory of determinant was also studied by Tanaka Yoshizane (1651-1719) who made up a theory which is similar to that which is now commonly used.

Takebe Katahiro (1664-1739) was also eminent. He collaborated with Seki. As his remarkable achievement, I will here mention the establishment of a power series expansion to calculate the length of an arc of a circle. Seki made an asymptotic formula for that, but did not arrive at the notion of an infinitely continued power series. Likewise research, that is to find the power series expansions of various quantities, became a main flow of Wasan.

Takebe also worked to establish a good calendar. The calendar was imported from China long ago, and it was still being used. As it became unrealistic, to better the calendar was an urgent problem. Though several attempts were made, they could not obtain a satisfactory result.

The successors of Seki and Takebe made a big school. Other than those who belonged to this school, there were good mathematicians. But, since in Europe many geniuses worked out highly advanced mathematics, their works cannot be compared with those.

(3) Sangaku

Something very peculiar in Wasan is a custom to present wooden tablets to shrines and temples. These are called "Sangaku". This custom seems to have begun at about 1690, and it continued up to quite recently. On these tablets, one or several problems are proposed, and the answers and the processes to get them are given. It is said that about 1,400 Sangaku were presented to shrines and temples in various districts, but, among them, only 900 are left.

Sangaku may have been presented with various aims. Some of them were to offer the joy or thanks to God or Buddha for his achievement. Others were to show off his presence to the public.

It is often said that in mathematics in Japan or China, there are no proofs. Really, there are neither axioms, nor postulates. Only the way to lead to the answer is shown. Of course, to establish a good theory of mathematics, it is indispensable to make rigorous reasoning. Compared to European mathematics, the reasoning was not explicitly given in the books of Wasan. So, from another point of view, we can say that the study of mathematics in Japan and in China must have been very severe. If the way of reasoning is explicitly given, then one has only to follow that way. If such a way is not explicit, one has to find the way by himself. Only those gifted persons who were able to find the way could advance into the research of mathematics. The lack of proofs is by no means the lack of rigor.

Reinventing the Teacher- the Teacher as Student; the Teacher as Scholar: the Teacher as Teacher

Peter Taylor, Nathalie Sinclair
Queen's University, Canada

We will talk here about teaching, but at the centre of our discussion must be mathematics, because without the subject, there is nothing to teach. We must go beyond mathematics, of course, because the task of the teacher is not so much to work with the subject as to bring it into the classroom, and this requires a particular kind of intimacy with and understanding of the discipline. Our thesis is that what is central to this understanding is what we call "method", more precisely, mathematical method, the way in which mathematicians do mathematics.

Method refers to the manner in which scientists or artists take apart the universe, the way in which they seek to understand their world; it governs their choices--what to think about and how to think about it; what to do and how to do it. It is more concerned with general strategies than with particular results.

A method-based curriculum selects its examples with an eye to these general strategies rather than the need to cover a particular body of results. Such a curriculum has an openness which invites the teacher and the student to be active participants in shaping their own learning. Make no mistake that this shift in structure has enormous implications for the way in which the curriculum unfolds in the classroom and for the shape of the resource materials. This is not surprising when one realizes, for example, that that the skeleton has an enormous influence on the behaviour of the organism. The archeologists can tell us unbelievable things about the daily routine of an individual whose million-year old skeleton they have found intact.

In a curriculum structured on method, the examples are chosen with regard to the methods or ways of thought that they illuminate and the ordering of examples follows this lead, rather than being based on the development of the knowledge base. Of course method and knowledge are closely related and evolve in parallel, and it will be quite natural (and necessary!) to provide a coherent development of knowledge at the same time. However, in a method-based curriculum, what we pay attention to is the quality, coherence, transparency and completeness of the examples not of the knowledge base that they might draw upon. As a consequence there will be components of knowledge which are omitted or which appear in only a restricted version. In our debates with colleagues they are quite worried about what they call "gaps" and when these arise they insist on filling them in. This is insulting to a method-based curriculum which requires an artistic restraint at just this point. We are reminded of the old adage that the mark of a good teacher is not what she says but what she is prepared to leave out.

There is a good analogy here with the use of a parable to convey a general truth. The teacher does not choose to give a parable because she thinks that the student is not clever enough to understand the abstract principle or that the parable is the more important; it is rather because the parable in its everyday immediacy has a flexibility and an openness that the general principle lacks.

It would be wrong to jump to the conclusion that for us knowledge is somehow tainted and a curriculum based on knowledge is bound to cause the entire subject to spoil. In fact the mathematical knowledge we now possess is nothing short of awesome and there's no reason it could not be the basis of a wonderful curriculum. The problem is that in mathematics, at least at the high school level and perhaps the first year or so of university, a knowledge-based curriculum seems almost inevitably to degenerate into a list of propositions and technical skills and without an inventive teacher with superior resource materials, this squeezes the life out of the subject. We identify three phases of a teacher's life and our thesis has important implications for each of these.

The Teacher as Student

Our focus here is on the undergraduate preparation of the intending mathematics teacher. The centrality of method represents nothing less than a paradigm shift in curriculum structure. To meet this, we believe that new programs (not just new courses) are needed--programs that emphasize method rather than content, exploration and discovery, true ownership of the ideas, and a solid confident mastery of a fundamental set of results and techniques. The design and execution of such programs represents a formidable creative challenge. For example, how should the curriculum be parceled? The traditional answer is to construct courses which follow standard fields: calculus, linear algebra, differential equations. But too often in this approach the big unifying ideas are lost in the press to cover the standard results of the field. We advocate a structure based on method rather than on content. The development of such a curriculum will require considerable imagination.

Are we advocating programs for secondary teachers which would separate them off from other mathematics majors? In fact, we hold this to be undesirable and we believe that our approach would work well for all or most such majors. The measure of freedom (and responsibility) it would give to all students would allow them to construct the learning profile that they are willing and able to engage.

The Teacher as Scholar

To what does the teacher owe her fundamental allegiance? To her students--we car all agree on that. What else? To the curriculum? In fact, no, not to the curriculum--to the subject, to the discipline. The curriculum is an importan instrument but it is always provisional, always subverted by technical demands always subject to the periodic buffetings of academic and political forces. It is the discipline itself, ripened in the sweet soil of art, culture and human wisdom tha must ultimately be served, a discipline that still grows, that still excites, tha generates an energy and a passion that no student can be indifferent to. Now t serve the discipline, and at the same time to balance the needs of the curriculum and the "rubrics" of assessment, she needs a deep understanding of the subject and a sense of herself as its keeper and bearer. In short, she must be a scholar. It takes scholar to resolve discrepancies and contradictions between the curriculum and the subject, to stand firm before those in authority over her, authority that comes from the culture as well as from the organizational hierarchy. It takes a scholar to be certain that her joy and love of the subject are what her students deserve.

A scholar is really a special kind of artist, and therefore the way of the schola requires care, dedication, imagination, and of course time, time to read, time to write, time to exchange ideas with colleagues, to play with concepts, to reinvent the universe. To find time and space enough for this, we might have to change much o the culture, at least in North America.

The Teacher as Teacher

We have already pointed out that the school culture, certainly in North America typically fails to support the image of the teacher that we are building, rather i pours into the system a heavy mixture of content and assessment expectations, and public accountability. If we hope to attract more bright energetic and imaginative students into the teaching of math and science, we need to project an image of the profession as one with a promise of challenge and innovation.

202

The Intuitive Rules Theory: Comparison Situations and Infinite Processes

Dina Tirosh, Ruth Stavy and Pessia Tsamir
Tel-Aviv University, Isreal

Many teaching and learning theories assume that knowledge about children's mathematical and scientific thinking could significantly improve mathematics and science education. This assumption has driven intensive research on students' conceptions and reasoning in mathematics and science education. Most of this research has been content-specific, and aimed at detailed description of alternative concepts and reasoning.

In the course of our work, we have observed that students react in similar ways to a wide variety of tasks that share some common, external features. We have so far identified four types of responses, two related to comparison tasks (More A-more B and Same A-same B), and two to subdivision tasks (Everything comes to an end and Everything can be divided endlessly). Responses of the type More A-more B are observed in students' responses to many comparison tasks, including classic Piagetian conservation tasks (conservation of number, area, weight, volume, matter, etc.), tasks related to intensive quantities (density, temperature, concentration, etc.) and other tasks (e.g., free fall, infinite sets, size of cells). In all these tasks, two objects (or two systems) that differ in a salient quantity A are described (A1>A2). The student is then asked to compare the two objects (or systems) with respect to another quantity B (B1=B2 or B1<B2). In these cases, a substantial number of students responded inadequately according to the rule More A (the salient quantity)- more B (the quantity in question), claiming that B1>B2. We suggest that students' responses are determined in great part by the specific, external characteristics of the task, which activate the intuitive rule More A - More B, and not necessarily by their ideas about the task-specific content or concepts.

Responses of the type Same A-same B are observed in many comparison tasks. In all of them the two objects or systems to be compared are equal in respect to one quantity A (A1=A2) but differ in respect to another quantity B (B1≠B2). A common incorrect response to all these tasks, regardless of the content domain, was B1=B2 because A1=A2. We regard all these responses as specific instances of the use of the intuitive rule Same (amount of) A- same (amount of) B. Responses of the types Everything comes to an end and Everything can be divided endlessly are often given to successive division tasks. In a series of studies, we presented students of different ages with various tasks related to the successive division of mathematical and

203

material objects. Students were asked whether the described successive division of a specific object would ever come to a halt. The majority of the younger students provided 'finite " responses to all tasks. Many of them explained their judgment by claiming, in line with one intuitive rule, that Everything comes to an end. The older students, who were already aware that theoretically, subdivision processes may continue endlessly, tended to provide "infinite " responses to both the mathematical and material object tasks claiming, in line with the other intuitive rule, that Everything can be divided endlessly.

In our lecture, we introduce the Intuitive Rules Theory, which accounts for many incorrect responses to mathematics and science tasks. This unique theory has strong predictive power, that is, when a certain task is described, it is possible to predict how students will respond on the basis of the external, specific features of the task and a small number of intuitive rules. We will describe the four intuitive rules and discuss the following issues:

- What are the origins of the intuitive rules?
- Do these rules apply only to mathematics and science tasks?
- Can we explain all incorrect responses as resulting from the intuitive rules?
- What factors affect the application of the intuitive rules?
- What are the educational implications of this theory?
- How can teachers use their knowledge about intuitive rules to improve mathematics education?
- How can this theory be used to improve mathematics and science teacher education?

Real-World Knowledge and the Modeling of School Word Problems

Lieven Verschaffel
University of Leuven, Belgium

For several years it has been argued by many mathematics educators that the current practice of word problems in school mathematics does not at all foster in students a genuine disposition towards mathematical modeling. A major criticism in this respect, which is the focus of this lecture, is the following. Rather than functioning as realistic and authentic contexts inviting or even forcing pupils to use their common-sense knowledge and experience about the real world in the different stages of the process of solving mathematical application problems, school arithmetic word problems are perceived as artificial, puzzle-like tasks that are unrelated to the real world.

In this lecture, which relies heavily on the book Making sense of word problems that I just finished together with B. Greer and E. De Corte (Verschaffel, Greer, & De Corte, 2000), I report and reflect upon a series of studies that have been done to investigate this phenomenon of "suspension of sense-making" when doing word problems within the culture of mainstream mathematics education.

The lecture is divided into three parts. Part 1 reviews the basic observations and research findings with respect to the phenomenon of "suspension of sense-making" After having described some earlier examples of striking evidence of students' lack of sense-making in school mathematics, I review the studies by Greer (1993) and by Verschaffel, De Corte, and Lasure (1994) with students in Northern Ireland and Belgium, respectively, as well as some replications by others with students in other countries, which all provided additional and more systematic evidence that after several years of traditional mathematics instruction students have developed a tendency to reduce word-problem solvlng to selecting what they take to be the correct arithmetic operation with the numbers given in the problem, without seriously taking into account their common-sense knowledge and realistic considerations about the problem context. Afterwards I present two related but distinguishable lines taking this research further. While the first line of research investigated the effects of several forms of "scaffolding" aimed at enhancing students' alertness to the problematic nature of the problems used in these two original studies and their replications, the second looks at the effectiveness of attempts to increase the authenticity of task presentation or test setting.

Having presented and discussed in Part 1 the available studies documenting and probing the phenomenon of students' tendency to tackle arithmetic word problems with apparent "suspension of sense-making", Part 2 provides a critical analysis of the way in which word problems are currently taught in typical mathematical classrooms, -- including a study of (pre-service) teachers' performance on the same word problems given to students in the studies of Greer (1993) and Verschaffel et al. (1994) discussed earlier, and of these (future) teachers' views about these problems. Afterwards I review a number of recent studies that have gone beyond ascertaining the state-of-affairs. These design experiments illustrate how by immersing students in a fundamentally changed learning environment they can acquire what can be considered to be more appropriate conceptions about, and strategies for doing, word problems. A common feature of the approach followed in these design experiments is that word problems are not conceived as artificial, puzzle-like tasks that can always be unambigously solved by performing one (or a combination) of the four basic arithmetic operations with the given numbers, but as genuine exercises in realistic mathematical modeling.

Having discussed the empirical evidence in the first two parts of the lecture, the third and last part turns to a wider discussion of some theoretical issues related to the process of mathematical modeling, a further analysis of the features of the (mathematics) educational system that lie at the roots of what we consider to be the outcomes seriously detrimental to many students' understanding and conception of mathematics, and suggestions for reconceptualising the role that word problems might play in mathematics education and how the approach to teaching them might be changed accordingly.

Reference
Verschaffel, L., Greer, B., & De Corte, E. (2000). *Making sense of word problems.* Lisse, The Netherlands: Swets & Zeitlinger.

Mathematics Education -Procedures, Rituals and Man's Search for Meaning

Shlomo Vinner

Ben Gurion University of the Negev, Isreal

The community of mathematics education is making intensive efforts to understand the mathematical behavior of students and teachers and to use the insights it gains in order to suggest curricular, instructional and technological improvement. The focus of the intensive efforts to understand the mathematical behavior is mainly cognitive. Even if there is an attempt to consider motivational aspects it is usually related to cognitive domain, for instance, how to create an environment which will pose intellectual challenge to the students, how to make mathematics relevant to their life or how to arouse their curiosity. My claim is that human behavior has so many aspects which are not cognitive that focusing mainly on the cognitive aspect can be misleading. It is true that some attention is also drawn to emotional aspects of learning mathematics, like negative feelings, mathematical anxiety or lack of confidence but the picture is still far from being complete. My attempt in this talk is to discuss some essential aspects of human behavior which usually are not considered as relevant to mathematical behavior. Yet, I believe, they may explain many typical phenomena in mathematical behavior which keep the mathematical education community quite busy. When trying to explain human behavior various explanatory principles can be used. The two explanatory principles that I have chosen to use in this lecture are the following:

1. The principle of human needs.

2. The principle of psychological schemas (cognitive or emotional)

I am going to elaborate on them shortly and to suggest that they can be used in order to explain some phenomena in the domain of mathematical education.

1. The principle of human needs
The idea here is that the human behavior, as well as human thought, is determined by the human needs. The needs, are determined by some physiological mechanisms in our body which have developed there through the course of biological evolution. These mechanisms gave evolutionary advantage to the individual who had them and thus these individuals and their offspring's survived. Some of these mechanisms have been identified by molecular biology or biochemistry while others are yet unknown. For instance, biologists know a lot about the mechanisms of some

physiological needs (like sexual desire, hunger and thirst). On the other hand, they know nothing or almost nothing about needs considered to be purely psychological such as the need for emotional stability, the need for positive feedback, curiosity (the need to know), the need for certitude and many other needs that we can identify in human beings. In the beginning of psychoanalysis (Freud) the tendency was to establish the explanation of human behavior on minimal number of needs (Freud spoke about sex and aggression and used the term Tribe the translation of which into English is drive). Another characteristics of this tendency was the assumption that the needs are universal, namely, they exist in every human being. Today, there are also other tendencies which do not restrict the number of needs. They also allow the assumption that some needs are not necessarily universal, namely, some people have them and other people do not. The principle of human needs as an explanatory principle is quite simple. At a given situation, if a need is identified then the actions of the individual are considered as a means to satisfy this need. It is not so clear what makes a psychological request to be considered as a psychological need but it seems to me that the request for meaning can be considered as a human need. The reason for that can be the fact that meaning is so often associated with various human domains where people look for meaning. They speak about the meaning of life, about meaningful relationships, about meaningful professions and so on. In the cognitive domain they speak about meaningful learning, about meaningful problem solving and about conceptual understanding and so on. The lecture will point at some contexts outside and inside the mathematical education domain where the need for meaning finds various ways of expressions. Inside the community of mathematical education, the tendency of emphasizing concepts, argumentation and meaningful problem solving as the essentials of mathematics education can be considered as one of the expressions of the need for meaning.

2. The principle of psychological schemas (cognitive or emotional)
The assumption here is that our mind contains many different schemas which are formed there during our life. Some of them are innate and others are acquired. (The underlying assumption is that they all have neurological basis but biologists know almost nothing about it.) By means of these schemas we learn, we process information and we react to different kinds of stimuli. One of the most dominant schemas in our mind is the ritual schema. We can even regard it as a super schema which contains many subschemas for many particular rituals, such as various religious rituals, military rituals, school rituals and other social rituals. A ritual is a sequence of words or acts we have to carry out in a certain context. The meaning of the words or the acts is very often not clear to the people who take part in the ritual. Very often, accomplishing a ritual is supposed to give the individual a certain social recognition. Thus, a ritual can be considered as a procedure, the accomplishment of which grants the individual with a certain social credit. It is claimed very often that

208

Mathematics is considered by the majority of people as a collection of unrelated meaningless procedures. One of the main claims of the lecture is that for many people doing mathematics is activated by the ritual schema. In other words, consciously or unconsciously, many people behave in mathematical contexts (mathematics classes, homework assignments and examinations) as if they take part in a ritual the elements of which they do not understand. This will be illustrated by examples from the context of mathematical proof, algebraic procedures, solving equations and other common mathematical activities. Thus, there are two essential conflicting elements in the human psychology which are active in the domain of teaching and learning mathematics: the need for meaning and the ritual schema. Therefore, this will be the claim of the lecture, as it happens with many other conflicting tendencies in human beings, there is no chance that one tendency will take over the other one. The educators will continue with their call for meaningful learning, where as the masses of students will prefer the ritual (procedural) approach. This is exactly like the case of religion, where some leaders emphasize moral behavior as the essence of religion but the masses and other leaders consider rituals as its essence.

Children's Understanding of Basic Measurement Concept: A Cultural Perspective

Catherine P. Vistro-Yu

Ateneo de Manila University, Phillippines

The purpose of this lecture is to discuss children's understanding of basic measurement concepts from a cultural point of view. In particular, I wish to discuss children's understanding of unit, length, area, and perimeter vis-a-vis how parents' knowledge of the said concepts influence the manner in which children learn those concepts themselves and also in conjunction with the school environment and culture. The basis of this discussion is a study that was conducted on ten 3rd and 4th grade students and their parents who were given measurement tasks, outside of the regular class setting. Four of these students study at a private, Catholic grade school, three study at a private, Montessori grade school, and the rest study at a public central elementary school. All ten students were given measurement tasks and interviewed individually following the measurement activities, except for two students who were interviewed together after working independently on the tasks. The students were also asked to fill out a simple information sheet.

There were ten measurement tasks given to the students. Four of these can be classified as standard problems. Of the six non-standard problems, three were construction exercises, one required an extension and reorientation of a measurement procedure, and another involved the ambiguous word "big", while the last is a simple application of the concept of perimeter.

Results of the experiment show some interesting similarities and differences among students from the different school systems. Students from the public central elementary school displayed a correct conceptual understanding of all four concepts. On the other hand, some students from the two private schools could not explain the concept of perimeter either because they could not remember (Catholic students) or they have not studied it (Montessori students). The students' performance of the tasks indicates that most of them rely on formulas, in spite of the availability of non-standard measurement tools during the activity. This was also especially evident during the interview sessions as they often mentioned the formulas that apply to the problems. Individually, the students differed in their performance on the non-standard problems and their reasoning. It was at this point that some began relating personal experiences either at home or in school to explain their actions. Furthermore, in explaining their answers and procedures, some used the local translation of the concepts except for unit, whose direct translation in the

210

Filipino language is the same as that for measurement.

The motivation for analyzing children's cognition of a basic mathematical concept such as measurement sprang from the call by Filipino educators and psychologists for the development of a culture of science and mathematics in the Philippines. Naturally, this must first involve knowing how interactions between parents and their children influence the manner in which the children appropriate school knowledge. Certainly, there are other factors that operate around the Filipino learner. While a primary concern is for us to understand how Filipino children actually learn it is still helpful to look at research and theoretical constructs generated in other countries that would help us in our endeavor. The Vygotskian framework of studying children's cognition by looking at the sociocultural context that they come from is particularly useful here. Special emphasis is placed on children's learning of measurement concepts and procedures as taught informally in the home, by the parents or an older sibling whether consciously or unconsciously, and how this informal instruction interact with the formal learning of the same concepts in school. The nature of interaction between parents and their children, i.e. the level of involvement in their children's learning of concepts can shed light to the problem and must therefore be described. The qualitative methodology ,specifically, the clinical interviews approach, was used in analyzing the data gathered form the children, their parents, and teachers.

It was, therefore, necessary that in the present study, parents of the ten children were involved in the investigation. Some of these parents were asked to answer or discuss their possible answers to the same set of measurement tasks given to the children. They were consequently interviewed to discuss further their understanding of the concepts. Initial analysis of the parents' performance on the measurement tasks indicates a direct relationship between a child's success in the tasks and that of a parent or sibling. Furthermore, there appears to be a congruence or similarity between a child's conceptual understanding of the concepts and that of a parent or sibling. Parents believed that informal procedures learned at home helped children understand some of these concepts.

Although the study is not conclusive, the results can benefit both teachers and parents. There are implications for both curricular and instructional changes that could recognize the importance of children's informal learning of concepts at their homes, which may prove to be useful in their understanding of the concepts. The study also has implications for parents. At 3rd and 4th grade, children still seek the guidance of a parent or an older sibling in their schoolwork and lessons. An awareness of how their own understanding of concepts interact with what children formally learn in school can help them guide the children much more effectively.

Mathematical Modelling In Middle School Education of China

Shangzhi Wang, Qixiao Ye

The Capital Normal University, Beijing Science Technology University, China

In the first part of this paper we will introduce the activity of " Chinese Middle School Mathematical Modelling Competition" from 1997-2000. The activity consists of three parts:

1) We offer some open mathematics application problems and let some students bring them to go home and use three days to solve them by using any tools and references. We translate some problems from Chinese into English. Many problems are very open, that means that according to analysis of real situation students can give some models to solve them. We'd like to say that students enjoy this kind of problems very much.

2) To ask some students to complete a little papers in which the students need to find some problem in their real life and to use their mathematics and subject knowledge and methods to solve them. It is very surprises to us that we receive more than 4000 papers of students some of that are very excellent. We are very glad to introduce some papers of students in our talk.

3) To ask some students to complete an examination of mathematics application problems. We will give some examples. There are more than 70000 students which attend the activity and they are very glad to enjoy it.

In second part we will talk about the problem of creativity and practical ability of students. This is a very important problem in the mathematical education, in particular in Chinese mathematical education.

Recently The Education Ministry of China build a very big engineer to push forward the education reformation of China. One task of them is to make the new standard of curriculum including the new standard of mathematics curriculum. In the third part of the paper we'd like to introduce some idea and thinking in the task., especially about the creativity and practical ability.

In the last part we talk about teacher's problem in the activity of " Chinese Middle School Mathematical Modelling Competition" and introduce a new course "Middle School Mathematical Modelling" in The Continue Education Engineer of mathematical teachers of middle schools.

Visual Forms in Mathematics: Thinking, Communicating, Learning

Walter Whiteley
York University, Canada

While this topic begs for visuals and the presentation will include a lot of visuals, both static and dynamic, this abstract is not visual, due to the problems of technology and the restrictions of space (issues for the presentation itself).

Why use visuals in mathematics?
Mathematicians make rich and varied use of visuals in our private work. However, we often hide much of this visual reality when we present in public. Reasons for this current style include: a bias that abstraction and clear thinking is lost with diagrams; diagrams are unreliable; and the past technology which made text and formulae easier to produce and transmit. However, our visual intelligence is too richly connected, physically and intellectually, not to be used widely in mathematics and mathematics teaching. Our awareness of this gap is the first step in change.

The use of visuals outside and inside of mathematics is increasing, with new technologies for easier creation, for richer expression, and with dynamic tools such Geometer's Sketchpad. Increasingly, 'scientific visualization' is used to display of large data structures for communication and analysis of the patterns. What had been private and vague, is coming out in a wide range of clear shared visual communication in mathematics.

In the cognitive theories of 'multiple intelligences', such as those of Howard Gardner, mathematics is primarily linked with number and logic. People whose strength lies in visual areas are streamed away from mathematics. Those remaining in mathematics after secondary school may be weak in visual reasoning and the associated skills which are key elements of the practice of mathematics. Incorporating the visual components and the visually oriented people is essential to inclusion of the needed diversity within the mathematical community.

Together these factors remind us that strong visual literacy is a core ability our students need to do mathematics.

How can we teach the use of visuals?
The studies of visual intelligence tell us that: we create what we see. We grow up with a rich and flexible capacity to interpret visual input. We will illustrate a few of these processes to emphasize that: we can change what we see.

Central in all perception is the capacity to ignore most input. Conversely, among the input available, we actually 'see' what we are 'paying attention to'. A novice and an expert do not 'see' the same things, pay attention to the same features, or follow the same searches, when faced with information in visual form. We need to learn, in detail, how an expert moves their attention over a visual form - and how someone can learn to follow similar sequences of attention, perception, and meaning.

A visual is no more transparent than the controls of a multi-function telephone. Many visuals are filled with learned conventions and specific associations which make them effective tools for experts. Learning to use visuals takes the same thought, practice and evolution as learning algebra, or other mathematical skills. The challenge is to generate learning activities and conventions that will bring the students to see what mathematicians see - that will change what students see.

Two aspects of learning of geometry are relevant to learning to use visuals. The first is the developmental van Hiele model, which reminds us of the necessity, in each new area, of working from the bottom up with concrete examples and vocabulary, before assuming students can work at more abstract levels of material. I find a similar evolution in the learning visuals, particularly the use of complex conventions. The second aspect is that we all learn to see and interpret in 3-D first, and 2-D is a very artificial experience, particularly when used to give conventional representations of either 3-D or of concepts that are not themselves primarily visual.

Some examples of visuals in mathematics
I present a selection of visuals and the use of visual reasoning in mathematics drawn from my own practice and teaching. Not surprisingly, given its visual content and my own background as a researcher in applied geometry, I begin with some examples from geometry. What do I 'see' in geometry? Transformations!

In spite of the practice encoded in many North American high school geometry materials, congruence is a transformation, in reasoning and practice. We consider some congruences of parallelograms and butterflies (isosceles trapezoids) as illustrations of the role of transformations in appropriate definitions, constructions, and proofs for such objects. This illustrates a visual hierarchy of symmetries of quadrilaterals based on subgroups of the transformations of the square - a hierarchy which extends to spherical and hyperbolic geometry. We offer some sample problems where transformations are the obvious visual approach, although common materials use a disjointed approach which I describe as 'trolling for triangles'.

Central to the role of transformations in visual geometry is the 'modern' definition of a geometry captured in Felix Klein's Erlanger Program: geometry is the study of the properties invariant under a group of transformations . We review a core of

Klein's hierarchy of geometries - from topology to Euclidean geometry. This is actually connected, as Piaget noted, to the sequence of learning of children (from topology to Euclidean geometry). It should direct the sequence of topics in geometry as well.

We consider a basic form for visuals for algebra: the connection between area and sum . This connection appears in manipulative like algetiles, in the visual proofs of algebraic identities ("Proofs without Words"), in the calculus of areas, and in advanced mathematics. Yet it is something which needs to be 'learned' in concrete situations even by Canadian university students.

I briefly survey some visuals of what I 'see' when I: do proofs; do simple differentiation,; and other problem solving. I will also offer a basic counterexample in which vision deceives many observers - a cautionary tale about what to use diagrams for, and what practitioners have learned not to use diagrams for.

Throughout the presentation, we illustrate with dynamic geometry materials. These new programs permit experienced mathematicians to make visible to students the kinds of visual play which were formerly hidden in our minds and in crude sequences of diagrams. They have also become part of own practice of geometry.

Conclusions for mathematics Teaching
What we see is learned and visual mathematics must be as carefully taught as any other part of mathematics. There is a need for consistent visual conventions and practices, from a young age, including learning of plane representations of 3-D and a wide range of transformations. What we see changes: (i) the questions we ask; (ii) the processes we use to study them; (ii) the answers we give; and (iv) the ways we communicate.

It is worth the effort to thoughtfully include visual literacy and expertise in our teaching of mathematics. It is honest to the real form of mathematics and it is inclusive in its impact on learners.

Mathematics Instruction through the Production of Manipulative Materails

Kiyoshi Yokochi
Guest Prof. at Beijing Normal University, Japan

1. Summary

I will explain the following through the several experiments of mathematics instruction through the production of manipulative materials, with many Photos.

(1) The pupils and the students create compact mathematics through producing manipulative materials.
(2) The pupils and the students learn several new mathematics necessary for this international age, through producing manipulative materials.
(3) The pupils and the students learn the mathematical culture through producing manipulative materials.
(4) In these days, it is very desirable to learn mathematics in the reality. The learning through producing manipulative materials falls under the condition.

2. Creating Compact Mathematics

Since 1986, I have made the sophomores create a compact mathematics on constructing miniature cars or cottages with paper. Some results are as follows.

(1) In Japanese schools at any level, the teaching of solid geometry is poor. However the above students were convinced of the importance of solid geometry.
(2) They were convinced that mathematics relating to trihedarl angle is not only abstract, but also has the reality of constructing interesting objects.
(3) They came to want to learn the other compact meaningful mathematics.

3. The Development of Drawing Methods in Ancient Pictures and Drawing the Beautiful Pictures with Them

Since 1989, I have proposed the introduction of "Cultural History of Mathematics" in the schools. As a theme of the field, I have studied the development of the drawing method of solids in ancient pictures in China and the West since 1991 and taught some results of my study to the students in several universities. At the same time, I have asked them to draw the beautiful pictures with the drawing methods.

On the other hand, last year, Mr. Munenori Shimono, a mathematics teacher at

Shirakawa Senior High School in Gifu Prefecture, taught the above content in brief to his third grade students under my instruction. In this case. he taught mathematical structure of the drawing methods with the computer. Therefore, the students drew the beautiful pictures of the real buildings with the computer.

4. Mathematics of the Globe with an Apple and Making the Sundial with Paper
The development of the learning on this theme has three steps since 1997. The learning content at each step was as follows.

4.1. The Stay in a Summer Camp
The stay in a summer camp for " Making Mathematics With Prof. Yokochi" has been held at Naoba in Niigata Prefecture each year sponsored by Asahi Press since 1995. The attendants are primary school pupils. In 1997 and 1999, the learning content for the 5th and the 6th grade pupils was mathematics of the globe.

4.1.1. The Latitude and the Longitude
First, the pupils regard an apple as the globe. Then, they think of the meaning of the latitude and the longitude with an apple.

4.1.2. Time Difference and Distance between two Cities
Next, they make a little globe with styrofoam and learn time difference produced by rotation of the globe. Then they measure the length of the equator with a kite string. And with the length, they decide the distance between several two cities. At last, they solve several problems like the following.

The plane left Paris at 22:00 on Monday. At what time will the plane arrive in Beijing?

4.2. The Ninth Grade Students at Junior High School attached to Yamagata University
On Nov. 24, 1999, the realtime collaborative distance learning (abbreviation: DL) for about 60 minutes between the ninth grade students at Junior High School attached to Yamagata University and the tenth grade students at Hildegard Wegscheider Oberschule in Berlin. The teachers are Mr. Masaru Tanaka in Japan and Mr. Peter-Maria Lischka in Germany, respectively. The learning content was an equator-type sundial and the learning method was so called "students teaching students". Therefore at the DL Yamagata's students addressed to Berlin's students with their sundials.

4.2.1. The Teachers' Preparation
4.2.2. The Students' Preparation
First the students learned mathematics on the movement of the sun and the earth theoretically. Then they made the sundial.

4.2.3. DL

5. Conclusion

(1) The learning with manipulative materials makes the learning of the following fields possible: the new mathematics necessary for the future; several mathematics at higher level.

(2) Through the production of manipulative materials, the pupils and the students can learn mathematics meaningfully and vividly.

(3) Through the production of manipulative materials, they can learn mathematical structure of several problems accurately.

Working Groups for Action

WGA 1: Mathematics Education in Pre- and Primary School

Chief Organizers: Linda Sheffield(USA),
Ann Anderson(Canada),
Associate Organizers: Christoph Selter(Germany),
Shizumi Shimizu(Japan),
Wan Kang(Korea),
Local Assistant Organizer: Keiko Hino(Japan),
Liaison IPC Member: Jerry Becker

To capture the dynamic discussion of about 250 participants in Working Group for Action 1: Mathematics Education in Pre-and Primary Schools (WGA1) is a formidable challenge in a brief report such as this. Our hope, however, is that through a summary of topics and highlights of our speakers' positions and our members' discussions, we might what the readers' appetites and they may follow up for more detail on our web site http://www.nku.edu/~sheffield/wga1.html. Because of the brevity of the report, we caution readers not to oversimplify or overgeneralize the points made but to remember that a sentence in this report will inevitably fail to reflect the depth and breadth of the thoughts and dialogues it seeks to summarize.

Day One
The topic for the first day was Understanding and Assesing Children's Mathematical Thinking. We explored issues involved with coming to know and understand children's mathematical thinking and doing, as well as determining standards for assessmentand accountability. To do so, we posed two focus questions: "How might we best understand or asses children's mathematical reasoning: through formal ,standardized means or through more informal methods? And "What should be the main purpose this: understanding children's thinking or assessing ,standardizing and reporting results?"

The two major presenters for this topic were Ian Thompson of Great Britain and Hanlie Murray of South Africa. Discussion leaders were Graham Jones of Great Britain and alluded to the National Numeracy Strategy. The focus of his talk, however, was on levels of sophistication of children's strategies used for mental calculation of two digit numbers gathered through in-depth assessment carried out by teachers trained in the use of a Learning Framework in Number. Dr. Murray also indicated that their research in South Africa is providing evidence of children's thinking in whole numbers and decimal fractions and they too have developed a model for the development of number concepts. To complement Dr. Thompson's talk, however, she focused her presentation on ways of capturing children's thinking, with examples ranging from altering written tests slightly to ask children to explain their reasoning to one-to-one interviews with children. In addition she spoke of children's use of "theorems in action" to make a calculation easier and the use of children's drawings as a source of insight into their thinking as well as their beliefs.

Discussion and Reactions: Following these presentations, participants shared their opinions and experience in small group discussions, from which the following points were gleaned. It became apparent that standardized testing varies internationally. Some countries(e.g., Great Britain, United States)have increased external assessment leading to school ranking, and so on. Other countries(e.g., Hong Kong)are trying to move away from them; still others(e.g., Norway, Japan)currently have no standardized testing per se.

There seems to be strong support for Informal/Formative assessment and some groups. Delineated approaches such as oral interviews, portfolios, projects, observations(games), self-evaluations, and questioning during classroom discussion as ways and means to carry out such assessment in our mathematics classrooms.

Concerns about standardized testing revolved around the pressures it places on children and teachers, its potential to mislead and the influence on curriculum- i.e., the "teaching to the test" phenomena. Concerns around more in-depth assessment revolved around the logistics of listening to individual children when dealing with large class size and overcrowded curriculums.

Day Two

The topic for second day was *Developing Children's Mathematical Power.* Here, we examined building on children's mathematical understanding, encouraging the development of their mathematical thinking, and using appropriate tools to develop mathematical reasoning. Our focus turned to three questions: "How might we best develop children's mathematical power: via establishing a good classroom culture or by using good tasks?"; "What are some examples or prototypes of these ?"; "Should technology take a major role?"

The two major presenters were Nobuhiko Nohda of Japan and Erna Yackel of the United States. Discussion leaders were John Edgell from the United States, Munirah Ghazali of Malaysia and Yoshinori Hayakawa of Japan, and Agnes Macmillan of Australia. Dr. Nohda described the "Open Approach" used by some teachers in Japan. The Open Approach is defined as a method of teaching in which activities of interaction between mathematics and students are open to varied problem solving approaches. He clarified characteristics and provided examples of three types of Open Approach problems(i.e., Process is open, End products are open, Ways to develop are open), used by teachers to support children's mathematical thinking. Dr. Yackel shared the underpinnings of their research with Inquiry mathematics classrooms, namely the symbolic interactionist perspective that meaning is constituted as individuals interact with one another. She then focused on the explication of social and socio-mathematical norms developed in such classrooms. An important thesis in her talk is that as children learn to explain and justify their thinking to others they develop intellectual autonomy.

Discussion and Reactions: From discussions following these two presentations, the following points regarding the focus questions serve as highlights. Many participants supported a strong connection between classroom culture and task activities and asserted that both a supportive environment as well as good tasks are needed. Others felt that clarifying what is meant by culture is important and that in some ways the classroom culture-the valuing and responding to children's thinking-is more important than the task posed.

Some groups discussed examples of "good" task and shared personal successes. In attempts to think of criteria for identifying such task (i.e., clear, non-ambiguous, challenging, open-ended), others tried to define mathematical power. (i.e., critical thinking, Questioning, logical reasoning, solving non-routine problems and so on), pointing toward issues of resources and teacher's ability or power to support children's power. Technology was discussed by some and although all agree it has a place, words of caution regarding its importance lines in "how mathematics learning is best supported" rather than "technology for technology sake". Reference to the power of "low tech tools" (i.e., manipulatives) was also made less we forget that hands-on experiences possess value as well as computer/calculator experiences.

Day Three
The topic for the third day was *Supporting Teachers in Understanding, Assessing, and Developing Children's Mathematical Abilities.* We looked at developing support systems for both new and experienced teachers, with a focus on the question, "How might we best support teachers: via solid mathematical content or by helping teachers to learn how children think?"

The two major presenters for this topic were Hsin-Mei E.Huang of Taiwan and Barbara Clarke of Australia Discussion Leaders were Nobuki Watanabe of Japan, Alena Hospesova of Czech Republic and Joan Cotter and Tad Watanabe from the United States. Dr. Huang discussed some of the difficulties involved in professional development aimed at getting teachers to change from a direct-teaching mode to a more cognitively-based approach to teaching. She stressed the importance of teachers listening to students' approaches to solving problems and using appropriate task-based assessment. This was echoed by Dr. Clarke who presented a framework that focused on a clear understanding of Key mathematical "growth points" in children's learning using examples from the Early Numeracy Research Project in Australia. She emphasized teachers developing knowledge of students through one-to-one mathematical interviews. This emphasis on knowledge of student's thinking and reasoning was a common theme throughout the work of this group.

Discussion and Reactions: Discussion following these two presentations was lively and varied, but the following points were expressed by several of the participants. There seemed to be a consensus that teachers' mathematical power is important (and perhaps a prerequisite) but that pedagogical power is critical. Teachers themselves must be comfortable with the mathematics they teach before they allow children the freedom to construct mathematical knowledge.

Several statements were made that teachers needed to see cognitively-bases teaching and learning in all university classes including those from the Mathematics Department as well as those from Education. Teachers frequently teach the way they are accustomed to learning and lecturing about change is not the way to make it occur. Pre-service teachers also need several experiences with children, and need time and support in reflecting on those experiences.

Participants also noted the need to provide time for in-service for teachers for such things as visits to other classrooms, forming learning communities and lesson study groups, viewing and discussing videos of model classrooms, and involving parents, administrators, policy-makers, and other community leaders. Several also noted that some state-mandated assessment worked against teachers' efforts to develop powerful mathematics students.

Next Steps

WGA 1 participants expressed a desire to continue the work of the group between ICME meetings. Some of the suggestions included developing aproposal for a special issue of *Educational Studies in Mathematics* to disseminate the main papers presented. There was also interest in continuing and expanding the web page for the group. Currently the WGA 1 web page at http:// www. nku. Edu/ Sheffield / wga1.html has links to all the major papers as well as most of the Papers by Distribution. Since ICME 9, names, countries, research interests, and email addresses of WGA 1 members who are interested in international discussions and collaboration have been added to the site. Plans include adding links on the site to national curricula, exemplary mathematics projects, and to primary mathematics education discussion groups.

Suggestions for Further Research in Pre and Primary School Mathematics Education

The following are a few of suggestions from the participants for needed research in this area.

- The impact of technology specific to primary mathematics education
- The connection of primary mathematics education to administration and government policy issues such as those related to funding and assessment
- The connection of research to classroom practices and vice versa
- Critical mathematics and pedagogical core content (big ideas) for both students and teachers.

Overall, as our discussions evolved, it became clear that our focus in mathematics education in Pre and Primary schools seems to have switched to children's thinking and doing mathematics-and away from content analysis per se-thus giving rise to such issues of how (or whether we need) to determine or describe 'core curriculum', scope and sequences, and so on. Also, we feel our discussions around surrounding technology went beyond the discussions around calculators which arose at ICME8.

Major Presentations:
Murray, Hanilie., *In-depth Assessment of Children's Mathematical Reasoning.*
Thompson, Ian., *Mental Calculation and Mathematical Thinking.*
Yackel, Erna., *Creating a Mathematics Classroom Environment that Fosters the Development of Mathematical Argumentation.*
Nohda, Nobohiko., *A Study of "Open -Approach "Method in school Mathematics Teaching.*
Clarke, Barbara., *Supporting Teachers in Understanding, Assessing and Developing Children's Mathematics through Sharing Children's Thinking.*
Huang, Hsin-Mei Edith., *Supporting Elementary School Teachers In Understanding, Assessing and Developing Children's Mathematical Abilities In Taiwan.*
Papers by Distribution*
Day One
Jones, Graham., *Assessing and Understanding Children's Statistical Thinking.* Australia
Ghazali,Munirah&Zanzali, Noor Azlan Ahmad., *Assessment of School Children's Number Sense.* Malaysia
Partove, Edita., *Assessment :An Important Part of Mathematics Teaching.* Slovakia
Huang, Hsin-Mei E., *Investigating Children's Analogical Reasoning in Solving Mathematics And Science Problems.* Taiwan
Doing, Brian & de Lemos, Molly., *Hops, Steps and Jumps: Looking at Numeracy Progress in The Early Years.* Australia
Walls, Fiona., *The Effect of Time-constrained Testing Activities on Children's Developing Beliefs and Attitudes in Learning Mathematics.* New zealand
Cotter, Joan A., *Visualization and Explicit Number Naming as a Foundation for Children's Early Work in Mathematics.* USA

Day Two

Hayakawa, Yoshinori., *Abacus Numerals for Effective Leaning.* Japan.

Edgell, John., *An Example of a Child Becoming Mathematically Empowered and An Example of a Group of Children Not Becoming Mathematically Empowered.* USA

Bonotto, Cinzia., *Mathematics in and out of Schools: Is it Possible to Connect These Contexts?* Italy

Macmilla, Agnes., *Numeracy Play: How Mathematical Is it?* Australia.

Anderson, Jim. Anderson, Ann. & Shapiro, Jon., *Parents Using Picture Books to Support Mathematical Thinking.* Canada

Holden, Ingvill Merete., *Playful Mathematics in Primary School.* Norway .

Motoya, Yoshiko., *Drawing of Two Crossed Bands.* Japan.

Day Three

Watanabe, Nobuki., *Developing Children's Space Cognition-Leaning of the Geometry of the Globe.* Japan

Huang, Hsin-Mei E., *Investigating of Teachers' Mathematical Conceptions andPedagogical Content Knowledge in Mathematics.* Taiwan.

Hospesova, Alena., *Spporting Teachers in Understanding, Assessing, Developing Children's Mathematical Abilities.* Czech Republic.

WGA 2: Mathematics Education in Junior Secondary School.

Chief Organizers: Ferdinando Arzarello(Italy),
Alwyn Olivier(South Africa),
Associate Organizers: Rick Billstein(USA),
Keiichi Shigematsu(Japan),
Suwattana Utairat(Thailand),
Local Assistant Organizer: Nanae Matsuo(Japan),
Liaison IPC Member: Julianna Szendrey.

1. A brief statistics

The group has had more than 100 participants and the program has been organised as follows in 3 two-hours sessions:

3 half-an-hour lectures:
- F.Arzarello, *Critical issues for Mathematics Education in the Junior Secondary School*;
- P.Boero, *Approaching Mathematical Theories in Junior Secondary School*;
- R.Billstein, *On United States Curriculum's Answer to The Transition from Junior Secondary School to Senior Secondary School*;

5 twenty-minutes presentations:
- Maurice Starck, *First Reduce A Triangle...(An Exploration around The Thales Property)*;
- Koji Nakagomi, *Gathering Circles, It Is The Teaching Material Which Keeps Creativity and Variety*;
- Veronica Diaz & Alvaro Poblete, *Solving Types of Problems: Its Evaluation in Geometry in Chile*;
- Hironori Osawa, *Exploration of The Best Baton-Passing in The Relay Race. An Example of The Development of Integrated Learning Focused on Mathematics*;
- Harry Silferberg, *The Conceptual Geometric Knowledge of Pupils in The Upper Level of Comprehensive School in Finland*;

2 fifty-minutes workshops:
- Gill Beeney, Roger Beeney, Pamela Leon, Jane Smith & Carolyne Starkey, *Supporting Interactive Teaching in Junior Secondary School*;

3 parallel eighty-five minutes subgroup discussions:
- Unifying concepts
- Curriculum
- Goals and Methods

1 plenary final seventy minutes discussion.

2. Critical issues for mathematical education in the junior secondary school

In most countries of the world, school education from grade 6 to grade 10 is featured by transitions: from compulsory education to jobs and/or vocational school education; from school-for-all to different schools (or curricula). Furthermore, there is the transition from child to adult behaviours of learners within the 11-16 age range. Mathematics education plays a special function in these transitions: it must ensure the acquisition of crucial tools for life and many professions; it must prepare students for further studies in scientific and technological areas; it is supposed to pass over relevant components of modern scientific culture.

The problem of transition must be investigated and discussed from different points of view, e.g.: *mathematical, cognitive, cultural, political.*

- From a ***mathematical*** point of view, the main problem of transition is featured by the necessity of introducing important and challenging issues, which appear as unifying and crucial in the present historical moment (which is itself also featured by deep transition aspects, social and political). A crucial question concerns the status of mathematical knowledge in Jun. Sec. Schools (JSS in short). On the one hand, it has not any longer the empirical and episodic features of the elementary school. On the other hand it cannot yet have the character of a structured theory, like possibly at the senior level. But what must it be in the positive? For example, the transition to the new status of mathematical statements compels teachers both to introduce new topics (e.g., algebra, functions, etc.) and to approach old ones in new ways (e.g., geometry, number systems). This transition involves the way all mathematical topics (from numbers to geometry, through algebra, statistics, probability, etc.) can be approached. Typical items to contrast are: *Simple-Complex; Arithmetic-Algebra; Induction-Deduction; Intuitive-Proof; Processes-Products.* They often underline the two faces of the same coin, a coin which must be tossed in JSS.
- From a cognitive point of view, the transition deals with the change from the child to the adults behaviours within the perspectives of continuing school at a higher level or of entering the working world. Some consequent problems to investigate are the following:

a) How to balance the learning of mathematics with the developing knowledge and interests of students, particularly when their attitude towards mathematics has been negative because of different complex reasons (previous school experiences, mass media images, etc.)? b) How to develop a situated teaching of mathematics within suitable fields of experience that connect a deep real level of mathematical knowledge with that of students and teachers in a positive interaction framework? c) In many countries there is a big jump between the way maths are framed from elementary to secondary school: how can the different types of interactions in the class [student(s)-student(s), teacher-student(s)] be organised within different pedagogical frameworks?

227

- From a *cultural* point of view, the learning of mathematics evolves differently in the different countries, because of cultural reasons. One must distinguish between general and specific issues. Typical general issues are: a) how the technological evolution changes the ways mathematics can be taught; for example, is it worthwhile to investigate how the new technologies allow concepts and images to interact at a new level? b) the stereotyped ways of looking at maths inside and outside school influence the ways. It is taught: how do these change in the passage from elementary to secondary teaching? Examples of specific issues are: a) how is the teaching of maths influenced by the organisation of the school, particularly by the changes which learners encounter in their own country passing from the elementary to the secondary level? b) how is the teaching of maths determined by that of other disciplines as natural sciences, first language, etc.?

- From a *political* point of view, the transition concerns the school organization and its evolution. Within this framework, crucial questions are: a) which the specific tendencies and the general features of the teaching of JSS maths in different countries? b) which suggestions mathematical education research can give to politicians in order to improve mathematics teaching in the school; c) what suggestions can be made to help those responsible for school organization in the various countries?

In general, we can remark that mathematical theories and theoretical and cultural aspects of mathematics (like the systemic character of mathematical knowledge and the role of mathematical models in shaping scientific knowledge of the physical world) represent a challenge for mathematics educators all over the world. Neither *abandoning* them in curricula designed for most students, nor insisting in *traditional teaching* of them seem to be good solutions. The former means dismissing the school in its task of passing over scientific culture and models of rationality to new generations. The latter is scarcely productive and impossible to keep in today's school systems.

An interesting and important area of investigation is opened to mathematics education research: on what theoretical and cultural aspects of mathematics should the efforts be concentrated? how must they be implemented in curricula? how to ensure a reasonable success in classroom activities about them? In relationship with these "transitional" characters of mathematics education in JSS, we need to consider epistemological questions (what does it mean "theoretical status of mathematical knowledge"? How can we distinguish mathematical theories from other scientific theories?) and related cognitive and didactical questions (how can students approach theoretical knowledge? How can they arrive to distinguish some features of mathematical theories and other scientific theories?).

228

3. Research issues and recommendations

Within the above frameworks, some main research issues can be put forward, some as recommendations and some as a starting point for future ICME 10 studies, namely:

a) The so called *mathematical war* between those who support programs to make children think critically and solve problems and those who support programs that stress basic skills. An example is given by the revision of 1989 Standards by the NCTM in USA (Principles and Standards for School Mathematics, 2000). Here the old emphasis on the mechanics of mathematics-i.e. memorizing tables, rules and equations- has gradually been replaced in many schools by a curriculum that encourages kids to explore math through estimation and real-life experience, such as the stock market. Scores in some states are falling: students who never memorized rules are finding it can cripple them later. This poses the problem of making students comfortable with numbers. JSS is crucial with this respect: a main issue seems to be how to nurture creativity in students, giving them also the tools to get it. Here is an example from the new NCTM Standards (grades 6-8) towards such a direction:

Suppose you have a box containing 100 slips of paper numbered from 1 through 100. If you select one slip of paper at random, what is the probability that the number is a multiple of 5? Of 8? Is not a multiple of 5? Is both a multiple of both 5 and 8?

b) Which competencies for the 21st century? "An educational system for the 21st century must produce learners who read and think critically, express themselves clearly and persuasively, are able to solve complex problems, and become self-sustaining, lifelong learners" (from: *How People Learn: Brain, Mind, Experience and School*, Wash. D.C., Nat.Sci. Acad. Press, 1999). Some of the conclusions drawn in the book seem important for JSS, namely: focusing on 'conditioned' knowledge (not just content but also contexts); looking at competencies that build foundations for later learning; stressing learner environments which are learner-, knowledge-, community- centred. Another issue for future research is how focusing the possible different approaches to transition: it seems that there are two main ways, namely contents-oriented and systemic-oriented. Moreover aims and goals for teaching are culturally dependent; it should be useful a comparison between different states and within a state (between different subjects), to investigate which are the most critical, which the most robust.

c) New standards and testing. An article on the New York Times (11.07.00) says that success in the new jobs doesn't depend on mastery of one uniform body of knowledge as measured by standardized tests. Instead, many of them require an ability to learn on the job....Yes, people need to be able to read, write and speak clearly. And they have to know how to add, subtract, multiply and divide....Our challenge is to find different measures of the various skills relevant to the jobs of the new economy. It's our job not to discourage our children but to help them to find their way." In any case, formative assessment should be an important aspect of teaching and learning.

d) What about the standards in the transitional period that features JSS? Testing in transitional ages is very delicate. Typically when one tries monitoring the acquiring of such new delicate mathematical objects, where symbols, concepts, everyday language interact in a complex and often contradictory way. In such cases, quite often results got by pupils in some specific objective tests seem to contradict their general performances: namely, clever pupils get less marks than good ones. An explanation of this seems to be the more complex level at which clever pupils look at some problems, which in fact become more difficult for them than for lower pupils, who do not even perceive such deeper aspects. This is not an exceptional in developing age.

e) Methodologies: the new, the old and other. The debate of the new math war reduces everything to a contrast between the old methods and the new constructivist ones. But there are elements which are difficult to get in a constructivist approach to theoretical knowledge and difficult to mediate through a traditional approach. They concern concepts and contents which are typical of JSS. Examples: (i) contents (especially, counter-intuitive conceptions) which are difficult to construct individually or socially; (ii) methods (for instance, mental experiments) far beyond the students' cultural horizon; (iii) kinds of organisation of scientific discourse (for instance, scientific dialogue; argumentation structured into a deductive chain) which are not a natural part of students' speech. Moreover classes should be structured heterogeneously (de-tracking) and girls should get extra attention.

f) Unifying concepts and ideas. They are those that give depth (contrasted with breadth) to the curriculum. For example, they concern:

- The transition from arithmetic to algebra: why and how? Variables and functions, as concepts and as symbols do have a deep novelty with respect to the epistemological status of arithmetical knowledge and language, to which students have been acquainted during the elementary school; all this puts on the table the problem of the transition from arithmetic to early algebra. In particular the concept of linear ($y = kx$) and anti-linear ($y = k/x$) functions seem crucial as new organising concepts.

- The transition to the theoretical thought from empirical knowledge: an important issue is the transition from argumentation to proofs and from empirical statements to theorems within a mathematical theory as contrasted with respect to other scientific theories such as physics or biology. Another issue is that of systematicity, contrasted to the episodicity of usual elementary teaching. Both issues can be nurtured and developed in the long term in the school, provided the teacher gives attention to students' verbalisation activities, namely to their communication skills, both oral and written.

- New technologies: which support to Visualisation (e.g., Dynamic Geometries) and to Symbolic languages (e.g., Spreadsheet)? More generally: which experimental evidence that computers, web,...do increase math learning ? What and how to assess ? In any case, technology should be carefully incorporated in the school, provided teachers receive a training in its use, above all from a cultural point of view.

- Which activities and methodologies nurture students' creativity? For example, a crucial issue seems that teachers give open problems to students, to develop their conjecturing abilities and their skills of flexible patterns of thinking.

WGA 3: Mathematics Education in Senior Secondary Schools

Chief Organizers: Abraham Arcavi(Isreal),
Michele Artigue(France),
Associate Orgaznizers: Christine Knipping(Germany),
Wong Khoon Yoong(Brunei),
Maria Trigueros(Mexico),
Wataru Uegaki(Japan),
Local Assistant Organizer: Masami Isoda(Japan),
Liaison IPC Member:Setphen Lerman.

In most countries, now, senior high school mathematics teaching has to face many difficulties and challenges. The aim of WGA 3 was to exchange ideas and discuss about these, and also to actively contribute to the development of future collaborations.

The work was organised in the following way:

1. A first collective session where, in order to introduce the theme, three plenary speakers, from three different regions of the world: Brunei Darussalam, France, USA, were asked to summarise the main characteristics of present high school mathematics education in their respective countries, the ongoing debates and problems to face.

2. Two subgroup sessions, in order to favour interactive work. On the basis of the proposals we had received, three subgroups were organised, respectively devoted to curricula (coordinated by Martin Kindt from Netherlands), technology (coordinated by Kaye Stacey from Australia), and rich content teaching experiences (RCTE in the following), coordinated by Maria Trigueros from Mexico.

3. A final collective session including subgroup reports of the WGA activity, identification of guide lines for future research and development work, organisgation of further collaborations and exchanges WGA participants.

The first session

The three plenaries reflected three very different perspectives: a centralised curriculum in a country with a long tradition in mathematics education (France), a decentralised approach in a large country coming to grips with disagreements about different views of mathematics education (USA), and the case of a small country trying to blend the adoption of external influences with local perspectives (Brunei Darussalam).

In his plenary, Dr.Wong Khoon Yoong described mathematics education in Brunei and evidenced the difficulties generated by the adoption of an external curriculum.

232

Brunei Darussalam is a small Islamic country in the Borneo Island. It gained full independence from Britain in 1984. The national ideology is called the Malay Islamic Monarchy (MIB) concept, which emphasises the teaching of Islam, the priority of the Malay language, and loyalty to Monarch and State. The national education policy provides 12 years of free education in the 1-6-3-2-2 pattern, inherited from Britain, but with recent modifications. Mathematics, taught in Malay in grades 1to 3 and in English from grade 4 onwards, is a compulsory subject in primary and secondary schools. The language switch is one reason why there is a sharp drop in mathematics performance from grade 4 onwards.

At the upper secondary level, a differentiated curriculum is offered, although a common core covers some standard topics in numbers, measurements, algebra, geometry, trigonometry, statistics, and probability.

Teachers, until recently mostly expatriates, have to abide by the mathematics content as defined externally, but they have freedom to establish the teaching sequence. Exposition and drill and practice are the main modes of instruction.

Efforts are being made to incorporate the local culture and values into the mathematics curriculum. Dr.Wong Khoon Yoong described an example in which the central mathematical topics (percentages and proportions) were described in a problem in which some desirable cultural values were stressed (e.d. adherence to Islamic laws, savings for emergencies, and helping the unfortunate). He ended his presentation by introducing some questions for discussion among which the following: what can be learnt from this very particular situation, and conversely, what can be offered to Brunei high school mathematics education by the reflection developed in other contexts?

In her plenary, Professor Joan Ferrini-Mundy presented the USA context and challenges in the light of the newly revised National Council of Teachers of Mathematics (NCTM) Principles and Standards for School Mathematics. She identified the following seven challenges for improving high school mathematics education.

Deciding what to include in the secondary mathematics curriculum: in the absence of nationally mandated curricular goals, as is the case in the US, initiating substantial curricular changes is complex and controversial.

Meeting the needs of all students: keeping post-secondary options open for students often results in a blurring of the traditionally separate tracks as they face the difficult task of coordinating recommendations from national and state organisations with arrangements that will serve both the college and vocationally inclined students.

Increased availability of technology: how can curriculum and instruction make best use of the widespread availability of graphing calculators and computers, as well as access to the World Wide Web? How to cope with the speed of technological evolution?

Interest in curricular integration: despite the history of offering separate courses in algebra, geometry, and precalculus, there is some interest in "integrated" curricula. Such instructional materials pose interesting challenges of change for the schools.

Choosing a curricular "target": traditionally, the college preparatory track has been geared as preparation for calculus. Yet, "aiming for calculus" maybe changing in favour of other "targets" (discrete mathematics, probability, statistics) and lead to reconsider the precursor curricula.

Shortages of qualified teachers: a serious and worsening problem in the US is the ongoing shortage of secondary teachers adequately prepared to teach mathematics.

Articulation with post-secondary education: difficulties at this level are especially reflected in the increased enrolhment in university remedial mathematics courses.

As stressed by Joan Ferrini Mundi, these challenges are exciting opportunities for research and development, making the US context for work in secondary mathematics education a stimulating and diverse enterprise.

Professor Luc Trouche, chose an historical perspective, by contrasting the contexts and values of the main reforms undertaken in France, during the 20th century. Through an analysis of similarities and differences, this historical perspective helped him to point out the specific difficulties high school has to face now, and better understand the resulting general feeling of crisis. The main points he stressed were the followings: a less investment of the mathematical community into educational issues; a greater complexity of the mathematical field itself; a different vision of the role played by mathematics and more generally scientific knowledge in society; a different school population, now very diverse both from a social and a cultural points of view and with a different relationship to school; a technological evolution whose speed makes integration by the educational system very problematic.

He presented then some main features of the reform which is now taking place in France (it begins in 2000-2001):

- *looking for a better adaptation to societal needs*, and especially what is needed for behaving as an educated citizen living in a democratic country (emphasising statistics and probability),
- *looking for a better adaptation of high school to the evolution of school population*, by diversifying teaching strategies, institutionalising group work and individual help,
- *looking for a better adaptation to the complexity of mathematical knowledge and learning processes*, by presenting the curriculum as a web, by introducing TPE (cross-curricular personal work on a given subject related to physics or biology and maths),
- *looking for a better integration of technology*, from calculators to internet.

But, as stressed by L.Trouche, these curricular changes can be more counterproductive than productive, if some minimal conditions are not fulfilled, in terms of material means of course, but also in terms of pre-service and in service teacher training.

The subgroup's work
The curriculum subgroup
There was a strong interest in sharing, comparing and contrasting how the curriculum is structured and actually works in different countries. Several participants overview or comment from their home countries experiences. For example, France where high school mathematics tries to adapt to a wide range of students, in the framework of a national integrated curriculum driven by content; Colombia where there are national guidelines which emphasise working from "rich problem situations" to promote exploration, modeling, practicing and inventing around five content oriented areas: numeric, spatial, measurements, variational and stochastic thought, but where there is no official syllabus and little is known about what actually goes on in the classrooms; the Netherlands with the application-oriented curriculum developed by the Freudenthal Institute; Latvia where the syllabus is the same for all, and streaming is associated with different levels of rigor.

These national presentations served as the background against which several topics were debated, for example:
- What content should be taught? (What specific areas of contents should be preferred? What role for processes, strategies, modeling and applications?)
- How to arrange the structure of the curriculum? (Emphasis on mathematical contents or on more general processes? How to get an adequate balance?)
- How can the need of all students be met? (How to organise streaming?)

The technology subgroup
The subgroup tried to foster the reflection initiated by the plenarists, by analysing and discussing some interesting experiences reported by the participants. These reflected the present diversity of technological uses: project where students are engaged in the production of videos connected to math history or real-world applications of mathematics, project where new mathematical contents such as fuzzy set theory are introduced in relationship with the realisation of technological products, tele-tutoring projects addressing specific high-school situations such as in-hospital temporary assistance, project whose aim is to explore the feasibility of offering new mathematics subjects that incorporate the extensive use of Computer Algebta Systems (CAS), project linking Japanese and Australian high schools through internet and opening students to other mathematics cultures. Small groups discussions led to stress the following points:

- the potential offered by technology, both for copying with the individual and social dimensions of learning, and the new opportunities provided now by internet,
- the evolution of mathematical needs induced by technological evolution,
- the necessity of overcoming the na?ve vision that technology automatically fosters conceptual thinking,
- benefiting from technology requires the design of specific situations and specific expertise from teachers. This fact makes teacher training a key issue for the integration of technology.

The teaching practices subgroup

In this subgroup, there was a general agreement about the necessity of introducing more RTCE into high school teaching. Several interesting examples were provided by the participants and used to foster the reflection. Discussions focused on the characteristics that a teaching experience must have to be considered as a RTCE and to the way RTCE can be managed in classroom situations. These discussions were followed by considerations about the role of problem solving and the use of models in RTCE and the relationship between mathematics and other disciplines and culture.

Several points arose, among which the followings:

- RTCE can be developed on pure mathematical situations or on real situations that involve modeling, and both are useful and important. In the case of real problem situations, it is important that students have to built models by themselves.
- Wider spread of technology is an opportunity for developing RTCE because students can explore with a wider variety of problems and problems conditions.
- Cultural diversity can be seen as a mean for finding interesting situations where mathematical problems arise from different cultural perspectives and allow students to get a better understanding of each other.
- The use of RTCE provides an opportunity to explore students conceptions and needs. But it was also stressed that integration of RTCE into teaching practices cannot only be achieved through curricular changes. Teachers, who already suffer from a curriculum overload and pressures from the school systems and pre-university examination, have to be helped by adequate teacher training and resources. Research has here an crucial role to play, especially because it is an important source of knowledge about students' conceptions and strategies.

The use of reading materials for promoting RTCE, and the conditions to be fulfilled in order to make this use efficient and of a reasonable cost were also widely discussed.

Some concluding remarks

Presentations and discussions in the WGA 3 showed that, in spite of an evident cultural diversity, mathematics high school teaching met similar difficulties all around the world. Teaching has to adapt to the massification of high school teaching and to find the ways of addressing new and very diverse categories of students. It had also to adapt to the increasing speed of technological evolution. But these sessions also evidenced the richness and diversity of resources offered by research and innovation and the necessity to better benefit from these, to better exchange and communicate. For that reason, we decided to maintain the site open for the WGA3 on the web site of the IREM Paris 7 (www.irem-paris7.fr.st). The reader will find there more information about the WGA 3 activities.

WGA 4: Mathematics Education in Two-Year Colleges and Other Tertiary Institutions

Chief Organizer: Marilyn Mays(USA),
Associate Organizers: George Ekol(Uganda),
Auxencia Limjap(Philippines),
Yoshitaka Sato(Japan),
Local Assistant Organizer: Sayuri Takahira(Japan),
Liaison IPC Member: Lee Peng Yee.

Introduction

For the first time in the history of the International Congress on Mathematical Education mathematics educators from two-year college and tertiary institutions other than universities came together to discuss common interests. Over 70 individuals participated from at least 10 countries. The educational institutions represented included Colleges of Technology, Junior Colleges, Community Colleges, Universities of Technology, Polytechnics, and Colleges of Engineering. Each of these institutions has functions unique to that type of institution and that country, but all serve the needs of students beyond secondary school in an environment unlike the university.

This working group met in three two-hour sessions during the Congress using a meeting format that provided participants and other interested parties as much information as possible about the institutions that are the focus of the WGA. They invited the presentation in shortened versions of all papers proposed that were appropriate for the group. Approximately thirty papers were proposed and twenty-three were selected for ten- or twenty-minute presentations. Other papers were selected for PbyD. The papers fell into three groups: (1) special programs, pedagogy, and other general issues; (2) introductory courses including but not limited to developmental (remedial) mathematics; and (3) advanced and engineering related courses. (See "Papers and Authors.")

The participants found many similarities in their institutions and many commonalities in their concerns. Regardless of the missions of these institutions, students are focused on immediate goals of an education relevant to the world of work and are often underprepared for their course of study. These and other topics are discussed in more detail below in "Issues and Concerns." The participants for WGA 4 were overwhelmingly in favor of the continuation of the working group. The feeling of community was strong among the participants as was the appreciation of the visitors for the hospitality of our Japanese hosts.

A special issue of the Community College Journal of Research and Practice will be published early in 2001 and will contain many of the papers presented at ICME 9. A listserv is being established for all participants and others interested. (See journal publication and listserv information at the end of this report.)

Meeting Format

The format of the meetings was as follows:

Day 1: All participants met as one group.
· Welcome and introductions;
· Brief overviews of the role of two-year or non-university tertiary institutions in the participating countries by representatives from each of those countries;
· Distribution of papers chosen for Presentation by Distribution (PbyD);
· Presentation of papers on special programs, pedagogy, and other general issues.

Day 2: Participants divided into two groups to gear presentations.
Group 1: Introductory courses, including, but not limited to developmental or remedial.
Group 2: Advanced and engineering related courses.

Day 3: The participants met together.
· Opportunity for questions and comments on PbyD papers;
· Discussions of the issues and problems of common concern to WGA 4 participants;
· Development of report to be presented to the International Program Committee (IPO);
· Discussion of continuation of WGA 4 and changes that might be made in content and format.

Papers and Authors

The following papers are listed in groups, alphabetically by the family name of the first auther.

Special Programs, Pedagogy, and Other General Issues:

The Syllabus and Adult Learner: Integrating Technique with Content; BAKER, Robert; University of Alaska, SE-Ketchikan Campus, USA

A Learning System of Mathematics on a Computer Network; KATSUTANI Hiroaki; Toyota National College of Technology, Japan

Mathematics Education in Singapore Polytechnic; LOW-EE Huei Wuan; Singapore Polytechnology, Republic of Singapore

The Games on Eduler Graphs and Mathematical Education; NAKASHIMA Izumi, Gifu National College of Technology; YASUTOMI Shin-ichi, Suzuka National College of Technology, Japan

The Critical Role Of Two-Year Colleges In The Preparation Of Teachers Of Mathematics: Some Strategies That Work; WOOD, Susan; Reynolds Community College, USA

Attempts of the Mathematical Education Corresponding to Various Academic

Abilities, YASUTOMI Shin-ichi, KAWAMOTO, Masaharu, Suzuka National College of Technology, Japan

Method and Effectiveness of An Individual Exercise of Fundamental Mathematics; YOSHIOKA Takayoshi, NISHIZAWA Hitoshi, TSUKAMOTO Takehiko; Toyota National College of Technology, Japan

Introductory Courses, Including, but Not Limited to Developmental/Remedial:

Using Self-Paced Learning in the Mathematics Classroom for Adults Returning to Education in the Introduction to Higher Learning Programme at Whitireia Community Polytechnic in New Zealand; ABBOTT, Anne; Whitireia Community Polytechnic, NZ

The Ostentatious World of Algebra; CHANG Ping-Tung; University of Alaska, Anchorage, Matanuska-Susitna College, USA

Learning for the Future: Increasing Success Rates in Basic Skills Mathematics Courses at the Community College Level; FORD, Jan, LEU, Inwon; Cuyamaca Community College, USA

Level of Precision in Pre-University Mathematics Courses: A Case Study; KLYMCHUK, Sergiy; Auckland University of Technology, NZ

Teaching in Context; LAUGHBAUM, Ed; The Ohio State University, USA

The Diagnostic of Collegiate Students' Knowledge of Fractions; LEE, Brenda; Wu Feng Institute of Technology and Commerce, Taiwan

Interinstitutional Collaboration to Maximize the Effectiveness in Teaching Developmental Mathematics Classes; WAYCASTER, Pansy; Southwest Virginia Community College, USA

Advanced and Engineering Related Courses:

Visual Images as Educational Materials; ASO Kazutoshi; Ishikawa National College of Technology, Japan

Developing and Implementing an Integrated, Problem-Based Engineering Technology Curriculum in the South Carolina Technical College System; CRAFT, Elaine L., South Carolina Technical College System; MACK, Lynn G., Piedmont Technical College, USA

A Study on a Coordinate of a Point of Tangency, the Generalization of a Multiple Root and the Richness of the Mathematical Teaching Materials; KOSHIBA Toshihiko; The Anan College of Technology, Minobayashi-tyo, Japan

An Experience of Cross-curricular Integrated Learning in Mathematics and Physics; SAEKI Akihiko, UJIIE Akiko; Kanazawa Technical College, Japan

What is Computer Mathematics? What Should Be Taught and Who Should Teach?; SHIBATA Masanori K.; Tokai University, College Circle, Takanawa Campus, Japan

A New Style of Mathematical Education in Colleges of Technology for Networked Society; TAKAGI Kazuhisa, ITOH Kiyoshi, NAGAOKA Kouichi, KATSUTANI Hiroaki, KAWAKAMI Hajime; Kochi National College of Technology, Toyota National College of Technology, Akita University, Japan

Some New Ideas on the Mathematics Education in Colleges of Technology in Japan;
UMENO Yoshio; Ichinoseki National College of Technology, Japan
<u>Presentation by Distribution Papers</u>:
Preparing Students Mathematically for the Twenty First Century; GORDON,
Sheldon P., State University of New York at Farmingdale; GORDON Florence S.,
New York Institute of Technology, Farmingdale, USA
Ten Year After: Anatomy of a Math Contest; KREVISKY, Steve; Middlesex
Community College, USA

Issues and Concerns

Various issues and concerns were raised during the presentations and the
discussions that followed. Authors had been asked to submit the three issues most
important to them and their colleagues. The organizers collected these and compiled
a list that was distributed at the meeting in Japan. The working group agreed to
focus their discussions on three of these issues as follows:

· Faculty Development. The group recognized the need to guarantee the professional
growth of faculty at their institutions. Since most faculty in these institutions are
not required to have a background in education subjects, mathematics pedagogy
becomes a real concern. In addition, they must keep pace with current trends in
mathematics education like learner-centered instruction, technology-based
curriculum, teaching in context, and distance education. They should also have the
capability to address the needs of their clientele and be aware of research and
effective practices in teaching adult learners and offering relevant course work. The
working group seeks the support of administrators in drawing a clear faculty
development program for their teacher. This program may include subsidy to the
workshops and conferences organized by professional groups on mathematics
education. Institutions might work with area business and industry to provide
internships for faculty members in the workplace so they get first-hand experience
that can be shared with their students.

· Mathematics Curriculum. The group realized the need to design curricular
programs that cater to the needs of the students and the community. These
programs should motivate students to engage in meaningful learning and should
prepare them for the workplace. The mathematics they learn should have strong
content base and enhance their numerical literacy, critical thinking, and logical
reasoning. They should become proficient at applying problem solving skills in real
life situations. Since information technology requires proficiency in discrete
mathematics, faculty should consider including more discrete mathematics in the
programs.

· Need for Research-Based Information. Improvement in the educational system of
two year colleges and other non-university institutions is possible if relevant
research is conducted. This includes research of curricular programs responsive to

the needs of the community, effective teaching strategies, student profile and demography, and teacher preparedness to address specific student needs. Research results should be disseminated at the national and international levels to ensure effective exchange of information.

Summary

The number of papers proposed and number of participants were significant evidence of the need for this working group. Participants will continue to communicate and interact by means of the journal and listserv. While the group acknowledged the diversity of their interests as well as the commonalities, they felt that it was important to continue to meet together. The venue employed for this Congress allowed opportunity for those sub-groups with divergent interests to meet separately for a portion of the time. Participants are already looking forward to a continuing dialog and to meeting again in 2004.

Community College Journal of Research and Practice; Editor D., Barry Lumsden, University of North Texas; P.O. Box 311337; Denton, TX76203, U.S.A.; lumsden@coefs.coe.unt.edu.

WGA 5: Mathematics Education in Universities

Chief Organizers: Lynn Steen(USA),
Qixiao Ye(China),
Associate Organizers: Derek Holton(New Zealand),
Urs Krichgraber(Switzerland),
Tatyana Oleinik(Ukraine),
Neela Sukthankar(Papua New Genea),
Local Assistant Organizer: Tetsuro Kawasaki(Japan),
Liaison IPC Member: Gila Hanna.

In recent years, as college and university mathematics have become increasingly engaged in issues of education, ICME has recognized this emerging interest by offering several forums for analysis of university issues. A 1998 ICME-sponsored Study Workshop on mathematics education in universities formed the foundation for the working group WGA 5 at ICME 9. Discussions in WGA 5 revealed a variety of serious issues facing university mathematics education, including widely reported declines in the number of students choosing to specialize in mathematics; demands for strengthening the preparation of K-12 teachers of mathematics; and challenges posed by new clienteles of non? specialist students.

The working group heard seven papers in plenary session (including a report on the 1998 ICME Study Workshop) and sixteen short presentations in three subgroups arranged on the themes of Applied and Advanced Mathematics; Preparing Teachers of Mathematics; and Teaching and Learning Mathematics.(These papers, and names of the organizing committee, are listen at the end of this report; abstracts of the papers can be found on the Internet at www.stolaf.edu/people/steen/wga5.html.) Three major themes emerged from these papers and the ensuing discussion:

Repositioning
Participants in WGA 5 reported increasing strains on university mathematics education from many different sources. Governments have become increasingly assertive in setting priorities for universities, priorities that often favor basic and practical courses over the traditional core mathematics curriculum. Students too are different? fewer mathematics specialists, more non-specialists seeking mathematics as a service (rather than a major) course. Individuals from different countries reported that students now arrive at university with weaker skills, or at least with different skills: less fluency with algebra but more experience with technology, less maturity in traditional mathematics, but mare familiarity with group projects.

Changing patterns of employment mean that many older students are returning to study college-level mathematics, either to complete an unfinished degree or to develop proficiency needed for career advancement. They, as well as traditional students, are increasingly interested the world. Thus mathematics for modeling and joint programs such as computational science, financial mathematics, and bioinformatics are becoming increasingly popular, thereby adding to the pressures bearing down on traditional mathematics programs. Some participants reported that client disciplines are reducing their requirements for mathematics coursework in favor of teaching mathematics as embedded aspects of their own disciplines.

One participant summarized these changes as a "collapse of privilege" for traditional university mathematics. Increasingly, departments find that they now must defend their position and resources in an increasingly competitive marketplace of ideas.

Teaching
The engine driving response to there pressures in college and university mathematics departments is a new (in some institutions, unprecedented) thoughtfulness about teaching. This focus is motivated in part by the loss of unquestioned status, but even more by the pedagogical challenges posed by students with non-traditional preparation and goals who are now studying mathematics. University faculty everywhere are exploring new approaches to pedagogy and debating the relative merits of different strategies. Many have become engaged in the "scholarship of teaching," a systematic reflection on their own pedagogy in the context of broader studies in educational research.

This concern for teaching reaches broadly into all aspects of mathematicians' professional lives. Increasingly, mathematicians are becoming engaged in the preparation of K-12 teachers of mathematics, especially in finding innovative means of linking students' mathematical studies with their pre-service teaching experiences in order to develop profound understanding of elementary mathematics. Mathematicians are introducing programs to help graduate students become effective teaching assistants and to help them balance their responsibilities as students, researchers, and teachers. These efforts have led one major university to make teaching a part of the research thesis by requiring that the results of the thesis be taught to others.

In many departments of mathematics the responsibilities of a professor now include, in addition to mathematical competence, an addition area of expertise? perhaps technology, perhaps pedagogy, perhaps an important contemporary field of application. These complementary skills also help mathematicians become teachers in a broader area, as they now, more urgently than even before, need to teach not only their students, but also the broader public? including university administrators and government officials? about the prevasive nature of mathematics in today's society.

Transitions
Many participants raised issue related to transitions that were disturbing the traditional order of university education. One is the increasingly challenging transition students undergo in shifting gears from a secondary school perspective to the independence and rigor of a university context. The difficulty and importance of this transition suggests to some that a genetic, developmental approach to pedagogy in early years of university may be essential to smooth the transition to formal, deductive mathematics. Another is the transition that faculty need to make as mathematics shifts from its historic manual and mental methods to those that are increasingly technological. A third is the transition that departments need to make as their students shifts from being primarily specialists to predominantly generalists. Departments everywhere struggle with the challenge of maintaining integrity of mathematical programs and at the same time meeting the needs of diverse client departments.

Another transition that departments are now beginning of focus on is that which students face as they shift from learning-oriented undergraduate programs to graduate training which encompass balanced responsibilities in learning, teaching, and research. Since most graduate students will become teachers of mathematics, either in secondary or tertiary systems, it is especially important for the future of mathematics that this transition go well.

Future Themes
It is clear from the vigor of discussion that mathematics education in universities a theme of sustaining importance for ICME. But it is also clear that particular issues may benefit from special attention in the future, separate from general discussion. These include:

· *Graduate Education in Mathematics.* The increasingly pervasive nature of mathematics challenges graduate program to expand in diverse arenas, thus risking loss of focus. The nature and quality of both secondary and tertiary mathematics depends on the ability of graduate programs to meet multiple responsibilities, a task of increasing difficulty in a world filled with attractive alternatives.

· *Policy.* As governments become more active in setting goals for higher education, traditional disciplines frequently lose status in comparison with programs designed to meet the needs of the new economy. Faced with increasing demands for public accountability, mathematics departments must find new and effective ways to demonstrate their value in the Internet age.

· *Technology in Higher Education.* In recent years technology has become both sufficiently powerful and sufficiently common that it now is an integral(rather than merely optional) component of undergraduate mathematics. Learning to rightly use these powerful mathematical tools poses many issues fore university mathematics that deserve thoughtful consideration.

· *Fragmentation*. As mathematics become more pervasive in its applications, it also is increasingly dispersed to other departments, programs, faculties, institutions, and now to the Internet. No longer are mathematics departments the primary locus of mathematics education is now under other auspices. This change creates an immense new challenge for university mathematics education.

Plenary Presentations

Holton, Derek (New Zealand): *Challenges for University Mathematics Education: Reflections on the 1998 ICMI Study Workshop.*

Burton, Leone (England): *Forging Links Between Researching and Teaching Practices.*

Gardiner, Anthony (England): *Mathematics Graduates' Perceptions of Proof, and their Abilities to Recognize and Construct Simple Proofs.*

Goroff, Daniel (United States): T*he Impact of Graduate School Policies and Practices on Mathematics Teaching.*

Kyle, Joseph (England): *Supporting Academic Practice for Mathematics, Statistics and Operational Research (MSOR) in the UK.*

Anthony, Glenda (New Zealand): *Undergraduate Mathematics Teaching and Learnig: Research Review for Australia.*

Pagon, Dushan (Slovenia): *New approaches to Teaching Mathematics at the Universities: Experiences from Slovenia and Czech Republic.*

Working Group A: Applied and Advanced Mathematics

Hazanov, Sergei(Switzerland): *Mathematics for Engineers: Indispensable and Superfluous.*

Klymchuk, Sergiy(New Zealand): *Role of Mathematical Modeling and Applications in University Mathematics Service Courses: An Across-Countries Study.*

Nishimoto, Toshihiko(Japan): *Reform of the Mathematics Education for the Faculty of Engineering.*

Tazawa, Yoshihiko(Japan): *Some Numerical Approach in Teaching Differential Geometry.*

Brandell, Gerd(Sweden): *Smoother Transition from Secondary to Tertiary Level: Demand for Adaptation and Renovation of School and University Mathematics Education in Sweden.*

Ye, Oi-Xiao(China): *China Mathematical Contest in Modeling(CMCM)and the Reform of Math Education in China Universities.*

Working Group B: Preparing Teachers of Mathematics

Brown, Suzanne(United States): *Supervising Mathematics Students Teachers.*

Langbort, Carol(United States): *Developing Leadership in Mathematics Education through a Masters Degree Program.*

Lovric, Miroslav(Canada): *"Teaching Mathematics" Course at McMaster University: An Innovative attempt at Improving Quality of Teaching.*

Novotna, Jarmila and Marie Kubiniova (Czech Republic): *Didactics of Mathematics: The Influencing Factor in Mathematics Teacher Training in Universities.*

Oleinik, Tatyana (Ukaraine): *The Development of Mathematics Education of Teachers in Ukarine.*

Working Group C: Teaching and Learning University Mathematics

De Carrera, Elema F.(Argentina): *Mathematics Education at the University: An Item Difficult, to Enter On.*[Presented in Writing]

Murphy, Teri Jo (United States): *The Preparation Needs of New Graduate Teaching Assistants.*

Nakata, Mie (Japan): *Four Clues to Teaching Mathematics: Good or Right and Complexity or Abstraction.*

Safuanov, Ildar (Russia): *The Genetic Principle in Teaching University Mathematics.*

Shield, Milo(United States): *Satistical Literacy: A Pre-Stats Bridging Course.*

WGA 6: Adult and Life-long Education in Mathematics

Chief Organiser: Gail FitzSimons(Australia),
Associate Organisers: Diana Coben(UK),
John O'Donoghue(Ireland),
Lynda Ginsburg(USA),
Local Assistant Organiser: Akihiko Takahashi(Japan),
Liaison IPC Member: Heiz Steinbring.

This working group for action replaced the successful1996 ICME-8 WG 18, *Adults Returning to Mathematics Education*, inaugurated in recognition of the growing importance of this complex field which spans all educational levels.(See FitzSimons(ED.),1997,for papers.) The 1996 UNESCO report *Learning: The Treasure Within* made the following observations.

"···educational is at the heart of both personal and community development; its mission is to enable each of us, without exception, to develop all our talents to the full and to realize our creative potential, including responsibility for our own lives and achievement of our personal aims"(p.19)

"···it seems to us that the concept of an education pursued throughout life, with all its advantages in terms of flexibility, diversity and availability at different times and in different places, should command wide support. There is need to rethink and broaden the notion of lifelong education. Not only must it adapt to changes in the nature of work, but it must also constitute a continuous process of forming whole human beings—their knowledge and aptitudes, as well as the critical faculty and the ability to act. It should enable people to develop awareness of themselves and their environment and encourage them to play their social role in work and in the community"(p.21)

"The concept of learning throughout life thus emerges as one of the keys to the twenty-first century. It goes beyond the traditional distinction between initial and continuing education. It meets the challenges posed by a rapidly changing world. ...The need [for people to return to education in order to deal with new situation in their personal and working lives] is even becoming stronger. The only way of satisfying it is for each individual to learn how to learn" (p.22)

A forum such as ICME provides an excellent opportunity for international exchange of ideas as well as the solidarity and co-operation sought by bodies such as UNESCO. The concept of equity is crucial and respect must be accorded adult and other learners in terms of their cultural, linguistic, social, and other backgrounds; their voices must be heard. Life-long Education is being increasingly linked by governments to the concept of work. However, it should be recognised that the

248

concept of work encompasses no only paid work in the official labour market (full-time, part-time, or casual)but also, for example, that which takes place in the home and the community (paid and unpaid). As well as formal institutions each of these are potential sites for life-long education. It also follows from the quotations above that social needs are no less important than economic.

Over 60 people participated in this WGA during the three days of meeting in Tokyo.

The stated goal of the was to propose a set of recommendations related to mathematics education in relation to lifelong education. This orientation offered a very broad scope for presentations. Work is being undertaken in many countries to develop systematic and critical foundations for this research which needs to be grounded in the work those practicing in the field. The group welcomed the contributions of educators with experience of teaching mathematics to adults, whether on a formal or an informal basis, as well as those with observations and recommendations on the amelioration of compulsory schooling towards an ethos of life-long education, taken in the broadest sense in being of benefit of both the individual and the community at large.

At the programme evolved it become apparent that there were several distinctive themes, pertinent to countries at varying levels of industrial development. These included adult teaching and learning, family education, education for the workplace, distance education, professional development, and research and policy. The programme was structured to accommodate plenary session as well as parallel sessions.

Presentations

The following presentations were made:

Mexican Adults' Knowledge about Basic School Mathematics: Silvia Alatorre, Natalia de Bengoechea, Ignacio Mendez,&Elsa Mendiola, National Pedagogical University, Mexico City/ National Autonomous University of Mexico

Adult Learners of Mathematics: Working with Parents: Rosi Andrade &Marta Civil, The University of Arizona, USA

What Might Good Practice Look Like in On-Line Teaching for Numeracy and/or Mathematics?: Jennie Bickmore-Brand, Murdoch University, Australia

Without a Bridging Mathematics Course, Can Distance Education Students Survive?: Sakorn Boondao, Thailand

Life-Long Learnig and Values: An Undervalued Legacy of Mathematics Education?: Philip C Clarkson (Australian Catholic University), Alan J Bishop, Gail E FitzSimons and WeeTiong Seah (Monash University)

Forging Links for Community Development : The Roles of Schools and Universities M.A.: (Ken) Clements, Universiti Brunei Darussalam

The Changing Adult Numeracy Curriculum in England: Diana Coben, School of

Continuing Education, University of Nottingham, UK

An Educational Programme for Enhancing Adults' Quantitative Problem Solving and Decision Making: Noel Colleran(City of Limerick Vocational education Committee),John O'Donoghu e& Eamonn Murphy(University of Limerick),Ireland

Mathematics and Lifelong Learning :In Whose Interests?: Gail E. FitzSimons, Monash University, Australia

Developing a Video Case Study to Engage Numeracy Teachers in Reflection on Their Practices: Lynda Ginsburg, University of Pennsylvania, USA

An Analysis of "Mathematical Museums" from Viewpoints of Life-long Education : Yoichi Hirano & Katsuhisa Kawamura, Tokai University, Japan

Mathematics and Key Skills for the Working Place: Henk van der Kooij, Freudenthal Institute, The Netherlands]

The Need for Innovative Math Curriculum in Japanese Primary and Secondary Schools: Introducing Polythetic Learning as an Approach Compatible with Lifelong Education: Tadato Kotagiri, University of the Ryukyus, Japan

Numeracy in the International Life Skills Survey: Myrna Manly and Dave Tout

The Context of Nursing Mathematics: D.F.(Mac)McKenzie, Unitec, New Zealand

A Summary of Research on Adult Mathematics Education in North America during the Past Twenty Years: Katherine Safford-Ramus, Saint Peter's College, Jersey City, USA

Language in Mathematics for Adult Second Language Learners: Beth Southwell, University of Western Sydney, Nepean, Australia

Fosterning a National Desire of Learn Mathematics and the Establishment of a Mathematics Aptitude Certification System: Tashiyoshi Takada, The Mathematics Certification Association of Japan(SUKEN)]

What is Numeracy? What is Mathematics?: Dave Tout, Language Australia, the National languages and Literacy Institute of Australia

'Competence' as a Construction in Adult and Mathematics Education: Time Wedege, Roskilde University, Denmark

The abstracts are currently available on the Adults Learning Mathematics website: www.alm-online.org. It is intended that the full papers be published by the end of 2000.

For further details contact the CO:Gail.Fitzsimons@Education.Monash.edu.au or the ALM web address.

Recommendation

The final, extra session allowed time specifically for participants to make recommendations about life-long education in mathematics, as well as about the organisation of ICME and this working group in particular. The following is a synthesis of recommendations taken from the this session, recognising that this working group represents an emerging field concerned with extremely diverse populations of learning in terms of variables such as age, and educational, social, cultural, and political backgrounds.

The following recommendations were made concernig the **functioning of ICME meetings:**

1. Participants supported the continuation of this WGA in 2004, but with title amended to: *Adults in Life-long Education for Mathematics.*

2. We commend the Report-Back sessions, but would like the ICME Organising Committee to please attenpt a further strengthenig of the links between WGAs and TSGs.One mechanism for this may be brif updates on the progress of each group to be published in the daily newsletter.

Political aspects of Life-long Education to be considered:

1. We need to aware that the discourse of lifelong/education have been appropriated by economically-oriented goverments.

2. We need to be aware of the risks associated with following government agendas in order to gain funding for research and/or programme delivery. Such agendas may, for example, be framed in the rhetoric of recognising urgent unmet community need while simultaneously demanding mathematics (or numeracy) curricula and pedagogies that are inappropriate-that is, not grounded in adult or lifelong education research (see, e.g.,Coben O'Donoghhue & FitzSimons (Eds), 2000).These risks are well illustrated in the metaphor of Diana Coben: "It is like stepping on a rake-head!"

3. We need to be aware of the relationships between the sectors of education, especially as education becomes commodified. For example, adults do not need simply 'school mathematics' (again) , even if dressed in 'adult' contexts.

Conversely, as highlighted by several presenters, school mathematics itself may be broadened in scope, in cognitive and affective domains, to encourage the formation of positive attitudes spanning a lifetime towards the study of mathematics.

Research aspects of Life-long Education to be considered:

1. Whose interests are we, as adult and lifelong mathematics educators, serving? Is it government(s)? Industry? Individuals?

2. Where does mathematics actually occur in industry?

3. How does mathematics education fit in with government and industry priorities? For example, it may be perceived that adults sre being enabled to critique government policy. Or, that adults are being empowered to make their own career decisions rather than complying with decisions with decisions made elsewhere.

4. Ethics is a critical issue in Adult and Life-long Education. There is always an opportunity cost to adults in terms of time and/or money invested in undertaking study, and researchers need to be cognisant of this fact. Some adults, especially inhabitants of social institutions, have few if any rights over videotapes, audiotapes, or transcripts of dialogue.

Possible research questions:

1. Is a broad mathematics education better than narrow training in improving

economic and social productivity/output?

2. Are we, as adult educators, being caught up in a mathematics-technology juggernaut? What might constitute a circumspect approach to the uses of technology as a tool and endpoint of teaching?

3. Is there a function for adult mathematics education to involve the general public, not least decision-makers, in education processes concerning the realities of mathematics — as disinct from the 'school mathematics' remenbered by most?

4. To what extent can learners in a system determine their own goals?

Other observations:

1. Education for lifelong learning goes beyond a narrow context (e.g., 'semi-skilled' jobs).

2. The conceptual shift from 'mathematics' to 'numeracy' nay afford the opportunity for a broader curriculum.

3. Parents, together with friends and other relations, who have experienced an enjoyable, successful, interesting, and engaging mathematics education are likely to support and encourage children's learning through socialisation and enculturation.

4. The timescale for adult education may be too restrictive under managerialist philosophies of education, as is the focus on small packages of atomised curricula. Adult education requires a long-term commitment to achieve its goals. However, longer time spans for formal education do not imply more time in the formal classroom. Education may take place formally, informally, or non-formally.

Conclusion

This WGA, Adult and Life-long Education in Mathematics, was broadly situated to encompass political, cultural, social, epistemological, pedagogical/andragogical discourses. Our thanks goes to all who participated in this group, particularly to those who made presentations, and especially to Akihiko Takahashi and the ever-helpful technical assistants in Tokyo who ensured its smooth functioning.

References

Coben, D., O'Donoghue, J.,&FitzSimons, G.E.(Eds).(2000).*Perespectives on Adults Learnig Mathematics:Research and Practice*.Dordecht: Kluwer Academic Pulishers.

Delors,J.(Ghair).(1996).*Learning: The Treasure Within*. Paris :United national Scientific, Cultural and Scientific Organization (UNESCO)

FitzSimons, G.E.(ED.)(1997).*Adults Returning to Study Mathematics:* Papers from Working Group 18,8th International Congress to study mathematical education, ICEM-8.Adelide: Australian Association of Mathematics Teachers

WGA 7: The Professional Pre-and In-service Education of Mathematics Teachers

Chief Organizers: Peter Sullivan(Australia),
Ruifen Tang(China),
Associate Organizers: Toshiakira Fujii(Japan),
Konrad Krainer(Austria),
Joao Pedro da Ponte(Portugal),
Local Assistant Organizer: Koichi Kumagai(Japan),
Liaison IPC Member: Tania Campos.

One of the pressing challenges for mathematics teacher educators is to identify the language, concepts, principles, and practices that can be the shared basis of professional dialog. Of course, in seeking commonalties in professional knowledge, educators of mathematics teachers have a substantial challenge .this challenge is compounded in that virtually all of the issues of interest to teacher of educators. ICME 9 saw active discussions on curriculum processes, mathematical topics, mathematical thinking and creativity, perspectives, on what constitutes knowledge, the role of technology in learning and doing mathematics, social and political factors, equity, and assessment of learning .These topics are all of interest to teacher educators and teachers alike. There are, nevertheless, topics of particular interest to teacher educators. WGA 7 sought to provide a forum for discussion and elaboration of these.

The basic question of WGA 7 were:
What are the key influences on processes and practices of mathematics teacher education?
What are the possible future directions for teacher education?
What are the directions in research in mathematics teacher education and in what way can that research contribute to improvements in teacher education?

The working group sought papers that reported on projects or developments in contributing countries that addressed these questions, as well as commenting on influences on teacher education, including constraints, the methods used, content of courses, including mathematics, pedagogy, and curriculum, methods for evaluating both students and programs, and program structure.

In the first session, there were three plenary presentations that established the context of the working group. The papers were:
Konrad Krainer, Institute for Interdisciplinary Studies of Austrian

Universities(IFF): *Teacher education as research? A trend in European Mathematics Teacher Education.*

Kathleen Hart, University of Nottingham: *Using Research to Inform Teacher Education.*

Tang Ruifen, Zhao Xiaoping, Wang Jiyan, & Chai Jun, East China Normal University: *Recent Developments in Mathematics Teacher Education in China.*

Krainer compared six European initiatives in teacher education, Hart described a research based curriculum and teacher development project in Sri Lanka, and Tang summarized general directions on teacher development in China.

In the second session, there were six parallel streams to allow for prepared presentations reporting on initiatives in teacher education. The first stream addressed issues in pre-service teacher education. The presentations were:

Patricia Baggett & Andrzej Ehrenfeucht, New Mexico State University: *Partnership Mathematics Content Courses for Prospective and Practicing Elementary and Middle School Teachers.*

Susie Groves, Deakin University, Australia: *Numeracy across the Curriculum: Recognising and Responding to the Demands and Numeracy Opportunities inherent in Secondary Teaching.*

Denise Mewborn, University of Georgia: *The Role of Mathematics Content Knowledge in the Preparation of Elementary Teachers in the US.*

H.J.Morris, University of Wales Swansea, United Kingdom: *Questions Braised by Testing Trainee Primary Teachers' Mathematical Knowledge.*

Andrea Peter-Koop, Brend Wollring, University of Munster and University of Kassel Germany: *Integrating Student Teachers in Interpretative Classroom Research Projects.*

These discussions on pre-service education highlighted differences in approaches. For example, there are countries where there is active political interference the evaluation of the quality of programs and of individual graduates, others where there is active community interest in the content, countries where pre-service education is well funded, and still others where the community has considerable trust that educators can prepare teachers appropriately. In all cases, though, there was a sense of the multidimensionality and complexity of pre-service teacher education, and the need for ongoing renewal of the content and processes of teacher education and of the educators themselves.

The second stream addressed the professional education of teachers. The presentations were:

Alan Bishop, Barbara Clarke & Sue Bennett, Monash University, Australia: *A Research and Development Project on National Professional Standards for Excellence in Teaching Mathematics .*

Patricia Campbell, University of Maryland: *Teacher Enhancement and Education*

Reform: High Stakes in the United States.
Rosalyn Hyde, The Mathematical Association: *Training Teachers: Whose Job is It? An Overview of In-service Training for Mathematics Teachers in the UK.*
Tapio Keranto & Keijo Vaananen, University of Oulu: *Making Master's Theses Serve the Professional Growth of Prospective Mathematics Teacher and School Mathematics Better.*
David Miller & Derek Glover, Keele University, United Kingdom: *The Completion, Content and Continuing Use of the Career Entry Profile in Mathematics Teacher Education.*
Sue E. Sanders, University of Wales Swansea: *What Do UK Schools Think Makes a Good Mathematics Teachers?*
The focus of these discussion were beyond process of in-service teacher education and addressed issues of incentives, certification, and structural renewal and recognition of teachers. This is clearly an emerging issue of importance for teacher educators.

The third stream focused on in-service teacher education. The presentations were:
Ping-Tung Chang & John Downes, University of Alaska Anchorage and Georgia State University: *In-service Training for the Math Teacher of the 21st Century.*
Naomi Chissick, Ort Schools, Israel: *In-service Teacher-training: Implementation of New Teaching Practices in High Schools.*
Fan Lianghuo, Nanyang Technological University: *The Development of Mathematics Teacher's Pedagogical Instructional Knowledge.*
Auu Pietela, University of Helsinki, Finland: *On a New Approach to Implement Primary Teachers' In-service Training in Mathematics.*
Ron Smith, Deakin University. Australia: *Connecting Teacher Beliefs and Features of Effective Professional Development.*
Patricia Wilson, University of Georgia: *Approaches to Mentoring Student Teachers in the United States.*
Even though practices in in-service teacher education are diverse, there seemed to be common assumptions across various countries. There was agreement that in-service professional development should focus on education rather than on training, and extend over multiple sessions rather than be limited to a single session. Further, the focus and emphasis should be negotiated rather than imposed, with opportunities for participants to contribute actively rather than passively receive. One key difference among countries seemed to be the extent to which there is a systematic requirement for teachers to participate in formal professional development. Such requirements seem to stimulate more innovation in the approaches to professional development programs.

The fourth stream addressed innovative methods in in-service teacher education. The presentations were:

Eliane Cousquer, Universite des Sciences et Technologies de Lille: *A Multimedia Laboratory in a Training College in France.*

Maarten Dolk, Fredenthal Institute, The Netherlands: *Between Theory and Practice: Students in the Netherlands Developing Practical Knowledge by Investigating Primary School Mathematics .*

Cristina Gomez, University of Wisconsin-Madison: *The Struggles of a Community of Mathematics Teachers: Developing a Community of Practice in an Urban Bilingual High School.*

Pi-Jen Lin, National Hsin-Chu Teachers College, Taiwan: *An Approach to Enhancing Teachers' Professional Development: An Experience of Taiwan.*

Pessia Tsamir & Dina Tirosh, Tel Aviv University and the Kibbutzim Teacher College: *A Mathematics Teacher-training Program: Teaching Pedagogical Content Knowledge.*

Tang De Xiang, Ningbo Education College, Zhejiang, China: T*he Experiment of High Level Training Mode of Mathematics Teachers.*

The projects reported on were diverse ranging from two very exciting uses of multimedia in teacher education, to descriptions of collaborative partnerships between researchers, teacher educators, and practitioners.

The fifth stream addressed the context of teacher education. The presentations were:

Barbro Grevholm, Kristianstad University: *Teacher Education in Transition? The Case of Sweden.*

Valery Guusev & Iidar safuanov, Moscow State Pedagogical University: *Modern State and Changes in Mathematics Teacher Training in Russian Federation.*

Yuh-Chyn Leu & Fou-Lai Lin, National Taipei Teachers College and National Taiwan Notional University: A *Review on Teacher Education Research Projects brought about by the Elementary Mathematics Curriculum Reform in Taiwan.*

Tibor Marcinek, Comenius University, the Slovak Republic: *On Initiatives with Impact on Education of Mathematics Teachers in the Slovak Republic.*

Derek Woodrow, Manchester Metropolitan University, UK: *Redefining the Teacher's Role: Developments in Teacher Education and Training in England.*

Education is socially and culturally determined, and so is teacher education. This stream explored some of the factors influencing directions and initiatives in teacher education.

The sixth stream addressed the mathematics education of teachers. The presentations were:

Toshihiro Homma, Kobe Shinwa Women's University: *Education of Mathematical Thoughts(Ideas).*

Yasuo Iijima, Mutsumi Ojima, Ibaraki University: *On the Improvement of Training of Mathematics Teachers-Especially in the Area of Teaching Geometry.*

Oleg Ivanov, St Petersburg State University, Russia: *Special Mathematical and Methodical Training in Mathematics Teacher Education.*

Roza Leikin, Greisy Winicki, The University of Haifa, Israel: *Defining as a Vehicle for Professional Development of Mathematics Teachers.*

Gina Mantero, Altair School, Peru: *Methodological Case Study in the Formation of Mathematical Concepts.*

Wei Sun, towson University: *Mathematics Curriculum in the Teacher Education Program in the People's Republic of China.*

These discussions highlighted one difference between those interested in elementary education (ages 4-11) and those interested in secondary education (age 11-18) with a strong focus by the letter group on the content and processes of mathematics. Issues considered within this stream included the study of old topics in new ways, the consideration of new topics, the role of technology, the nature of mathematical creativity and problem solving, and appropriate assessment mechanisms.

The final plenary presentation by:

Joao Pedro da Ponte, Brunheira Lina, University of Lisbon, Portugal: *Analysing Practice in Preservice Mathematics Teacher Education.*

Synthesised the work of the group, as well as describing the goals, methods and processes of a pre-service secondary teacher education program in Portugal.

In the final session there was discussion of the implication of the work of the group, and especially of methods for further dissemination of the written contributions.

In summary, there were 41papers presented at the working group, many of which were outstanding in both originality and insight. The presenters were from 21 countries. There were 4 plenary addresses, 36 co-ordinated presentations, and two papers presented by distribution only. All papers were distributed in paper form and twenty disk copies were made available for those who could not access the electric versions. An editorial team was established to explore avenues for publication of the contributions to the group.

WGA 8: Research, Practice and Theory of Mathematics Education

Chief Organizers: Deborah Loewenberg Ball(USA),
Ruhama Even(Isreal),
Associate Organizers: Chris Breen(South Africa),
Lyn English(Australia),
Luciano Meira(Brazil),
Local Assistant Organizer: Toshikazu Ikeda(Japan),
Liaison IPC Member: Nobuhiko Nohda.

General Description

This working group focused on connection between and among mathematics education research and mathematics, the foundation disciplines, and practice, The practice. The premise was that insularity from any or all of these critical domains is a threat to the quality and progress of the field. We organized our work to examine how productive fostered, we explored actual and possible connections between mathematics education and other disciplines. We investigated how mathematics education research interacts with mathematics as a disciplines, as well as with theory and practice of scholarship in other fields, with an eye on practice, we also explored new approaches to research that seek to bridge traditional divides among theory, basic research, and problems of teaching and learning. We set out to learn about productive interactions among disciplinary communities in the context of research in mathematics education. We asked: What are some of the barriers to such interactions? What special roles do mathematics and mathematicians and mathematics as a discipline have? and what roles might they have? in mathematics education research? We asked similar questions about the roles of other disciplines. We examined what is entailed in deriving questions about the roles of other disciplines. We examined what is entailed in deriving questions directly from issues of practice and in working closely with practitioners. We considered what is afforded and what pitfalls exist in designing theoretically-focused experiments in practice. We discussed: How do these sorts of efforts affect the definition of research problems in mathematics education and the development of methods? How do they affect the claims of research and what counts as "evidence" for those claims? Approximately 130 participated in this working group, from over 25 different countries.

Session 1

Deborah Ball introduced the two focus problems, the key questions, and the program for the four sessions of the working group as summarized above. Next Ruhama Even described a case where the same mathematics lesson was analyzed in two different ways, using two different theoretical framework. The two analyses led ifferent conclusions and explanations about what was going on in the class. The arge group was then split up into small groups of 3-5pople for short discussion of he case. This introductory activity helped to orient the participants into the themes f this working group and encouraged them to get acquainted with one another. The hird part of this session was devoted to a keynote presentation by Willibald Dörfler Austria).For the last part of the session the large group was split up into three maller groups chaired by Jo Boaler (USA), Lyn English(Australia)and Gerald joldin (USA).The groups discussed issues raised in the session in light of the key uestions presented at the beginning of the session.

Keynote presentation 1: "Mathematics, mathematics education and mathematicians -an unbalanced triangle" by Willibald Dörfler (Austria)

Willibald Dörfler argued that the scientific discipline of mathematics education is evoted to studying the relationships between mathematics and human beings, oth taken in their entire variety. He explained that researchers in mathematics ducation study and investigate mathematics as it is learned, practiced, produced, nd used by people. He identified this as a meta-study of mathematics, and he roposed to term this "mathematicology"(much as musicology is the study of music s a human activity). Mathematicology, Dörfler claimed, seeks to develop theoretical escriptions and models of mathematical activities and processes as human activity. After illustrating potential uses of this kind of research about mathematicians and f mathematics educators. He claimed that this separation is sharper and more brupt in mathematics than in other disciplines, resulting in few functioning and nutually enriching relationships between mathematicians and mathematics ducators. Dörfler concluded his presentation by proposing that mathematics ducators work to create increased collaboration between mathematicians and ducators by looking for issues in mathematics that have features analogous to spects of mathematics education, the role of the human agents is increasing ommunication and connections between mathematicians and mathematics ducators.

Session 2

The second session began with a keynote presentation by Luciana Bazzini (Italy)on vork conducted by Maria G. Bartolini Bussi and herself. Then the large group was plit up into three smaller groups chaired by Jo Boaler (USA), Lyn Inglish(Australia) and Gerald Goldin (USA). The smaller group work began with hort presentations by participants whose proposals have been accepted for resentation at the meeting. The groups continued to discuss issues raised in the irst and second sessions in light of the key questions presented at the beginning of he work.

List of Accepted Short Presentations

259

What Most Needs to be Researched in Mathematics Education? by Christopher Ormell(UK).

The Importance of Connecting Mathematics Education Research and Practice or Scholarship: Experiences of a Teacher Working in both Fields by Karl Josef Fuchs (Austria).

Proof in Geometry: Researching and Teaching by Ornella Robutti, Federica Olivero and Domingo Paola(Italy).

A Method of Research on Mathematics Education-For a Theory based on Practice by Hirokazu Okamori, Keiichi Onishi and Yuichi Mori(Japan).

"Achieving coherence in mathematics instruction: Theoretical and practical considerations" by Jinfa Cai(USA).

The Relationship between the Culture of Small-scale Peasant Economy and School Mathematical Education in China by Zheng Lian(China).

"Dialectical" Synthesis in Qualitative and Quantitative Research by Chris Day (England).

The Challenges Doing Mathematics Education Research in Developing Countries : A Malawian Experience by Catherine Panji Chamdimba(New Zealand).

Culture and Cooperation: A Three-year Program for Teacher Enhancement in Mathematics Education in the Bedouin Schools by Ruth Shane(Israel).

Pre-service Teachers' Conceptual Understanding of Transformations of Functions During Student Teaching after a Technology-rich Mathematics Education Program by William Leonard Jr. and Beverly Rich(USA).

Pre-service Teaching after a Technology-rich Mathematics Education Program by William Leonard Jr. and Beverly Rich(USA).

Keynote presentation 2: "Research, practice and theory in didactics of mathematics" by Luciana Bazzini.

At the beginning of her presentation, Luciana Bazzini highlighted the complex and often asymmetric relationships between the field of mathematical didactics and other research fields, such as the history of mathematics, psychology, mathematics and educational studies. She described two sets of problems. One set of problems is related to the difficulties of dialogue between the scientific communities of professional mathematics and professional didacticians of mathematics. The second set is rooted in the dialectic nature of the Theory-Practice relationship within the field of didactics of mathematics. Brazzini then described two research projects developed in Italy that address these problems: one focused on theoretical thinking in geometry and the other on algebraic problem solving. The starting point of inquiry in both projects is deep analysis of the nature of mathematics. The researchers themselves have been educated as mathematics. Also, there is a strong involvement of teachers working in their own classrooms in both projects cooperating with the university researchers in all phases of the research studies.

The findings of the research are then applied university courses for prospective teachers. Luciana Bazzini concluded her presentation by suggesting to address a symmetrical question to thee one presented by the organizers of the working group: "What special roles do didacticians of mathematics and didactics of mathematics as a discipline have, and what roles might they have, in research in mathematics?"

Session 3 & 4

The last session comprised the third and fourth sessions. The session began with a plenary panel, organized by David Clarke (Australia), presenting international perspectives on relating research and practice in mathematics education. For the second part of the session, the large group was split up into several smaller groups to discuss several key questions and issues that emerged in previous sessions. Representatives then reported back to the whole group about their discussions. Two commentaries concluded the sessions. Hyman Bass(USA) and Barbara Jaworski (UK) were invited before the conference to serve in the role of commentators, and each of them provided about the course of the few days' work.

Panel Presentation and Discussion: International Perspectives on Relating Research and Practice in Mathematics Education

Participants: David Clarke(Australia), Beatriz D'Ambrosio(USA), Koeno Gravemeijer (The Netherlands), and Frederich Leung/Patrich Wong(Hong Kong).

The panel presentation and discussion addressed the question: "How mathematics education research and theory is and could be connected to practice? "This question was addressed from the perspectives of research and practice in Europe, Australia, Asia, and the US. Each presenter raised specific issue related to connecting research, theory and practice in their country and illustrated theses issues with examples from a project (or projects) with which they were familiar.

Panel Presentation 1: Adressing the Situated Nature of Practice in Classroom Research

Clarke focused on the issue of how research can adequately address the situated nature of "practices", the questionable legitimacy (and value) of dichotomizing teacher and learner practice, and how "practice-oriented" research might optimally inform the profession. In particular, it was argued that research into teaching and learning as separate bodies of practice misrepresents both and is unlikely to provide insight into mathematics classrooms or, ultimately, to inform the actions of practitioners in a constructive or effective fashion. The topic was then situated with respect to Australian research.

Panel Presentation 2: Diadactical Phenomenology Applied to Early Statistics

Gravemeijer described a research method called developmental research that has been the main mode of research for several decades within the Freudenthal

261

Institute in the Netherlands, and with it the domain-specific instruction theory for realistic mathematics education (REM) is being developed. Within this type of research, Theory development is grounded in very practical down-earth teaching experiments. This offers opportunity for a natural connection between practical wisdom and scientific knowledge. The focus of the presentation was on the elaboration of "didactical phenomenology" in relation with the design of an instructional sequence on an introduction in statistics in grade 7 and, as carried out in a teaching experiment at Vanderbilt University (Nashville, USA).

Panel Presentation 3: The Teacher-Researcher: Bridging the Gap between Research and Practice.

In this presentation D'Ambrosio proposed that the "teacher-researcher" is as means of bridging the gap between research and practice. The notion of helping teachers acquires a disposition towards research as an integral part of their practice seems to be an important component in bridging the gap. The focus of the presentation was on the work that currently being carried out in teacher education to bring beginning teachers to an understanding of how inquiry into student learning contributes to the quality of their work with children.

Panel Presentation 4: The Relationship between Educational Research and Curriculum Development in Mathematics-the Case of Hong Kong.

Wong, presenting for Leung and himself, explained that mathematics curriculum in Hong Kong is centrally developed. It was developed in the late 70s with no base in rigorous educational research. Recently, the Government acceded to concerted requests from researchers and enthusiastic practitioners, and formed committee to conduct a "holistic review" of the mathematics curriculum. Academics and teachers were recruited to serve on the committee. Based on their recommendations, the Government commissioned two research projects to inform the curriculum review. One is a comparison of curricula in major countries; the other is to solicit the views of various stakeholders on the mathematics curriculum.

Conclusions

Our discussions of the plenary lectures, and of the short presentations, as well as our continued probing of the group's core questions led to a greater appreciation of the following:

1. Some contemporary researchers are designing projects that aim to develop both knowledge and practice. This is different from developing theory and then "putting it into practice."

2. Many of these projects involve researchers, mathematicians, and teachers working together. These can serve to provide resources for others to learn to build such bridges among key communities, as a means for improving the work.

3. Multiple perspectives on practice can help to illuminate aspects of teaching and

learning that are often invisible to researchers and practitioners working alone. One approach is to use multiple perspectives in complement with one another.

4.Disciplines that can contribute to mathematics education research include psychology, sociology, history, political science, economics.

5.Mathematics has a special role to play in developing ideas, tools, and, lenses for mathematics education research. (e.g., Dörfler's mathematicology)

6.Working to develop relations among theory, research, and practice will require ongoing concerted effort and learning. We can use ICMI, PME, and other professional organizations to create opportunities and support for such development.

WGA 9: Communication and Language in Mathematics Education

Chief Organizer: Barton, Bill(New Zealand),
Associate Organizers: Maria Luisa Oliveras(Spain),
Armin Hollenstein(Switzerland),
Local Assistant Organizer: Hideyo Emori(Japan),
Liaison IPC Member: Tadao Nakahara.

Prior to the conference, the papers being presented in this Working Group were published, and this book was made available free of charge to Working Group participants on arrival in Japan. This book *Communication and Language in Mathematics Education* is available from the Chief Organizer at b.barton@auckland.ac.nz. The pre-publication of papers allowed the Working Group to spend a shortened time listening to presentations, and a longer time discussing the issues. This Working Group met three times, the first and last sessions as a full group, and the middle session as two groups.

The First Session

The initial session began with the Organizers presenting a plan for the conference. It was noted that this Working Group title encompassed a wide range of topics. It was therefore proposed that the group develop a unifying framework for these various contributions. It was further suggested that the Framework consist of key research questions. It was assumed that our various perspectives would us to ask these questions in various ways, thus generating our specific research questions.

The overview presentation was give by a former Chief Organizer of this group, Heinz Steinbring. He first noted the two aspects of this Working Group: Mathematics IN different languages, and Mathematics AS language. Previous Working Groups had concentrated mainly on the latter of these two aspects. He then focused on the special role of symbols in the epistemology of mathematics, where a symbol may be algebraic or geometric. A triad of symbol, concept and object was presented in which mathematical knowledge is to be seen in the relationships between the three elements.

Drawing on the work of Luhmann and de Saussure, Steinbring drew out two assumptions commonly made during communication in the mathematics classroom: that mathematical signifiers refer to only one thing; and that there is a direct bridge between mathematical communication and an individual's cognitive learning. He concluded "When mathematics is seen as a rather rigid, logically correct and unified body of knowledge identified with its symbol system then mathematical communication in the classroom breaks down to a mere transport of symbols

264

carrying definite, unequivocal meaning. Only when mathematical symbols and signs are interpreted as intentionally expressing relationships and structural connections, mathematical communication could become a vivid social process in which all partners have to construct their mathematical understanding by actively interpreting the signifiers conveyed by other communication partners."

Finally Steinbring interpreted the theoretical approaches of constructivism, objectivism and interactionism in terms of this understanding of mathematical communication, demonstrating the complexity of research questions in the area of Mathematics AS Language.

The discussions following this presentation, chaired by Norme Presmeg, made clear the variety of interests within the group, so the latter half of the session was taken up with six small-group discussions focusing on the meaning each group wanted to give to the words 'language' and 'communication', and on how they phrased their research questions. The results were summarized and made available to participants in the following session. Regarding 'language' and 'communication' the variety of responses led to agreement to maintain a broad perspective on both these ideas. The major research questions generated were discussed again in the second session? See below.

The Second Session
The second session of the Working Group has held in two parts, one group focusing on Mathematics AS Language, and the other on Mathematics IN Different Language. Each group heard four presentations, each followed by considerable discussion.

Group A heard papers from Ann Assad, Liz Bills, Fritz Schweiger and Carl Winslow. Assad reported on a study of two elementary school teachers as they implemented increased communication within their mathematics classes through promoting talking and writing about mathematically rich investigations. The results were that, in both classes, the students became better problem solvers, acquired a variety of ways to express themselves mathematically, and began to enjoy doing mathematics.

Bill's contribution examined the role of teacher's language in the enculturation of students into mathematics as a practice, i.e. into a set of values, processes and ways of thinking. An analysis of transcripts of two teacher's lessons with pre-University students revealed a number of aspects of their language use. The teachers maintained a careful balance between two apparently opposing needs: to represent the world of mathematics so that the students are enculturated into it; and to recognize that this world may appear alien to the students and that the teachers need to position themselves with the students in this alienation. Enculturation firstly takes place through emphasis on new concepts and their associated vocabulary. One teacher did this by stressing definition and the other by emphasizing use. Secondly enculturation takes place through particular expressions of agency: use of passive and impersonal forms, vague referents, and the interchangeable use of personal pronouns. Several questions needing further investigation were elaborated.

Schweiger's contribution concerned the grammar of mathematical symbolism. He noted that the correct use of mathematical signs are often learned without being taught in an explicit way, but that the use of calculators, computer algebra, and word processors increases the awareness of such rules. He was concerned with the general semiotic principles of this grammar, and discussed the principles of serialisation, similarity of configuration and alphabetic correspondence, disjointness, symmetry and duality, wellformedness, and iconicity and semantics of symbols.

Winslow's paper discussed some technical aspects of mathematical discourse which are related to the role of transformation in the sense of structural linguistics. Using an analysis of a theorem statement and proof, he demonstrated an analysis which exposed the deep semantic structure of mathematical writing.

Group B heard papers from Nuria Gorgorio, Hajime Hayakawa, Hideo Emori and Norma Presmeg. Gorgorio reported on a project working with new immigrant and minority children in Barcelona, examining the nature of the multilingual situation, and the cultural conflicts that arise is such situations. Some of the questions which arose were: Is mathematical achievement confused with linguistic ability? What benefits for mathematics learning are observable in bilingualism? What beliefs about mathematics are associated with cultural groups?

Hayakawa reported on a project to create a bilingual web-based environment where Japanese students could learn mathematics and English simultaneously. The results indicated that the mathematics learning was the same for Japanese students using bilingual or Japanese-only programmes, but the English learning was enhanced. English-only programmes were not as effective. The study further indicated that more time was needed in bilingual programmes, and that the technical difficulties needed further work.

Emori focuses on the mental spaces that are constructed while solving mathematical problems collaboratively. By analyzing each communication in a participant's mental space, he demonstrated the mechanism of how each message combines together and how people make sense of a chained communication as one story. He proposed an "Emergent Chain model" consisting of four levels of communication to help make sense of mathematical classroom communication.

Presmeg presented an overview of theoretical perspective which can be used in research on language and communication in the mathematics classroom, with a commentary on the opportunities they present and the dangers they bring. This led into an extended discussion of the research questions generated the previous day. The discussions of both groups concerning a research framework were summarized as follows:

What is mathematical communication?
 · What makes mathematical communication mathematical?
 · In what ways is it a transformation of representations amongst symbolic language, natural language, geometric figures, concrete object, graphs, etc?
 · How does language link to mathematical concept? (e.g. What is the role of symbols for students learning mathematics in a language which is not their native language have to link their existing concepts with concepts formulated in a foreign language?)
 · How does language link to mathematical symbols?
 · What are the common aspects of mathematical communication in a multilingual situation?

Are there kinds of communication that hinder or stimulate mathematical learning?
Communication between peers:
 · What communication takes place when students solve problems together?
 · How do we get students to communicate about mathematics?
 · How can teachers facilitate communication between students?
Communication between teachers and students:
 · How can teachers facilitate conceptualization with his/ her use of language?
 · How can teachers communicate without giving the answers?
 · How do we get authentic discourse?
 · Who has the power of communication and language in the classroom?
 · How can the different meanings of student and teacher be resolved?
What are the special aspects of symbolic communication?
 · Do conventional symbols reflect a particular (Western) syntax (cf Wasan)?
 · What can we learn about symbolic aspects of language from a study of language?
 · Is a complete description of mathematical symbolic language possible given cultural considerations?

What can teachers do about communication?
 · What changes does the teachers need to implement in the didactic contact in order to facilitate horizontal communication that simulates critical mathematical learning?
 · How can teachers and educators make students aware of language issues in order to promote appropriate responses?

Does the mode of communication change: mathematical questions; mathematical methods; mathematical answers?

· What metaphors are students using and how do they relate to teachers' metaphors?

· In what ways are students' or teachers' metaphors potential obstacles or scaffolds to the development of mathematical thinking?

· How does the structure and syntax of language(s) interfere with, or help, the learning of mathematics?

· Do some languages reveal mathematical relationships/ structures/ concept to different degrees than others (and does this impede or promote understanding)?

How is mathematical knowledge/ understanding revealed through language?

· In what way is mathematical language a cultural tool?

· How are changes in students' conceptual thinking over time evidenced in their language and body language?

· How effectively can communication and learning take place in spite of language deficiencies or differences?

What are the effects of bi/ multilingualism on mathematics learning?

· How are mathematical ideas expressed in different languages?

· What different mathematical expressions are privileged by different languages?

· How do these different mathematical expressions relate to formal mathematics?

How can mathematics be used to communicate?

· Can mathematics be used as a bridge between different languages?

How should we go about researching these questions?

Which of these questions are significant or worthy of our effort in the sense that having answers to them would help mathematics teachers and learners?

The Third Session

The final session began with two unscheduled short presentations: Iben Christiansen spoke briefly about the book that she and Anna Chronaki are editing with the same title as this Working Group. Ken Clements also spoke about the recent Australasian review of research in this area written in conjunction with Nerida Ellecton as a chapter in the mathematics Education Research Group *Australasia Research in Mathematics Education* in Australasia 1966-1999. This was followed by the two final paper presentations, the first by Helle Alrø and Mikael Skanstrøm, the second by Chris Bills.

Alrø and Skanstrøm reported on a case study which followed up their Inquiry Co-operation Model developed in earlier work to help analyse the role of dialogue in the learning of mathematics. They followed two students as they worked on a problem, and look specially at their patterns pf communication when they made progress in their work and when they got stuck in their problems. They observed the important role of teacher interference in this process.

Bills' reported on a pilot for a longitudinal study to investigate the development of young children's mental representations which are formed as a result of their interaction with their teacher's external representations. The results suggested that children's mental representations are influenced by the external representations, and, furthermore, that children express their methods of calculation in metaphoric language which indicates the re-presented experience.

This last paper generated considerable discussion about the role of metaphor in mathematical communication, a issue which seemed to be central to many of the perspectives represented in the group. Final discussion turned to the research framework proposed initially. It culminated in the development of one key research question which generated all the questions posed above. That is:

How are epistemological constructs in mathematics formed in various social situations through language and communication?

It was agreed that this question, and the derivative framework could be used between now and the next ICME as a focus for joint work.

In summary, the major topics discussed were: the dynamics of classroom communication; the place of metaphor in mathematics; the potentials and problems of multilingual communication; theoretical descriptions of dialogue; and the special nature of symbolic and visual communications.

WGA 10: Assessment in Mathematics Education

Chief Organizer: Ole Bjorkqvis(Finland),
Associate Organizers: Marja van den Heuvel-Panhuizen(Netherland),
Max Stephens(Australia),
Local Assistant Organizer: Miho Ueno(Japan),
Liaison IPC Member:Gilah Leder.

The agenda of WGA 10 was the study of a broad spectrum of purposes and modes of assessment in mathematics education. This included new developments in large-scale assessment programs, assessments for certification, and assessment by teachers as part of day-to-day classroom instruction. Emphasis was also placed on the balance and mutual influence between different types of assessments and effective ways of promoting change in educational and social reality by means of assessments in mathematics education. There were to be reports of studies analyzing difficulties and promising practices in the alignment of assessments and goals of mathematics education as well as studies describing the technical aspects of producing valid and easily applicable types of assessment.

The interest for this particular WGA was large enough to warrant a division into subgroups. The themes of the subgroups were chosen to accommodate the variety of topics as well as possible. The first session and the last (extra) session, however, were common to all participants.

During the introductory session the working procedures of the group were decided upon, and there were two survey lectures that came to serve as references in much of the work that followed. Dylan Wiliam (United Kingdom) gave a lecture on "The Relationship between Formative Assessment and Summative Assessment", and Norman Webb (USA) another one on "Alignment of Assessment and Content Standards". The final session included, in a similar manner, a lecture by David Clarke (Australia), "Is Assessment Capable of Being an Engine for Systemic reform?", in which many of the common threads were tied together.

A particular feature of WGA 10 was an "Interactive Symposium on Multi-Focus Assessment", which was arranged in parallel with the subgroups during the third session.

Assessment and Educational Policy
The subgroup on Assessment and Educational Policy engaged in discussions that were flavored by accounts of national experiences. It was apparent that there are considerable differences between countries with regard to assessment as part of educational policy. There were, however, trends that could be identified at an

international level, too, and the report of the subgroup included some conclusions and findings that describe the situation as of 2000.

- There is insufficient clarity regarding how to measure the cost of assessment. It was argued that the cost of assessment should be measured not only in money, but also in time and student lack of other learning.
- The concept of alignment between expectations and assessment has come into frequent use and become an important tool in the way educational policy is being studied. Methods of measuring alignment are being developed.
- Where expectations and assessment are well aligned there is a strong causative influence on classroom practice, and where this alignment is lacking or weak, assessment practices, particularly mandated or high-stakes assessment, appear to exert a far more coercive influence on classrooms.
- At a surface level, the influence can be rather quick. Specific terminology and practices associated with mandated or high-stakes assessment is soon found in mathematics instruction in schools.
- Assessment is a powerful mechanism for the social construction of competence. New assessment schemes in mathematics contribute to this development.
- Educational policies that neglect professional development of teachers (e.g., with respect to new assessment schemes) seem bound for failure. The teacher is the key agent for successful implementation of policy, and identification of the kind of teacher support needed should be a key element of any educational policy.

Methods and Outcomes of Assessment
The WGA 10 contributions that related to Methods and Outcomes of Assessment described experiences and results with new and traditional types of assessment schemes in several different countries. The conditions for obtaining valid and reliable information that serves specific purposes were analyzed in reports of theoretical studies.

- The importance of careful work with individual items was emphasized. Attempts are being made to minimize misinterpretations of the outcomes of assessments due to technical imperfection.
- There is, however, still a problem with mathematical content categories being poorly defined. Individual items of very similar kind may, e.g., in one connection be classified as "algebra", in another as "problem solving".
- There is a need for development of the assessment of mathematics in integrated school contexts.
- There is a high current interest in assessment methods investigating the strategies of students.
- A central role of formative assessment is to show the learner what to do to improve. The formative function of assessment, rather than the summative, must be

paramount in the day-to-day work of the classroom. Record-keeping should be integrated into classroom activity, so that evidence of achievement can be re-interpreted for summative functions.

- The tensions between formative and summative functions of assessment might be mitigated by, e.g., broadening the basis for assessment, lessening the predictability of the items, placing the focus on quality assurance rather than control, and basing formative assessment on a developmental theory of learning.

Assessment and Professional Development
Work within the subgroup of Assessment and Professional Development had, at its disposal, reports of experiences of professional development of teachers. Notably there were examples of ambitious international cooperation in this field. Some of the results identified or supported recently established practical knowledge:

- The power of rich assessment tasks, which engage teachers in personally meaningful professional development, provide them with efficient professional tools and open up new views of school mathematics.
- The value of involving teachers in posing or creating assessment tasks and in developing rubrics for scoring items.
- The efficiency of using student work samples to elaborate student misconceptions and solution strategies, and to further the teacher's understanding of children's needs.
- How to use "the other" in assessment tasks (e.g., another person to whom you wish to explain a solution strategy). It provides a sense of purpose and more altruistic goals. There are indications of increased perfomance where this is used.

General Results and Future Work
During the final session it was concluded that many of the assessment issues from ICME-8 in 1996 still exist, but in a new environment being shaped by information and communication technology. It is not easy to predict how ICT will affect assessment in the future. TIMSS has had a clear impact across nations, in most cases serving as a catalyst for thinking about assessment and educational policy. The importance of international cooperation was emphasized by many of the participants in WGA 10. The similarity of the problems across nations and the need felt for more efficient dissemination of new ideas seemed to indicate that WGA 10 really should be functional for a longer time than the congress itself. This would be a natural conclusion to draw from the word "action" included in the title, but it was also articulated with reference to the importance of assessment to the whole field of mathematics education.

The first steps towards such a continuation of work were thus taken. A publication of contributions to WGA 10 will be available, and an electronic network of participants will make it possible to keep up contact until ICME-10 in Copenhagen.

WGA 11: The Use of Technology in Mathematics Education (Computers, Calculators, IT Media)

Chief Organisers: Rolf Biehler(Germany),
Barry Kissane(Australia),
Associate Organizers: Sergei Abramovich(USA),
Rosihan Ali(Malaysia),
Shoichiro Machida(Japan),
Local Associate Organiser: Tomoko Yanagimoto(Japan),
Liaison IPC Member:Claudi Alsina.

The past several ICMEs have found it appropriate to devote part of the formal structure of the congress to technology, so that the inclusion of WGA 11 at ICME 9 was a continuation of a strong recent trend, evident in many countries. In the past decade, computers have become increasingly accessible to schools and pupils at home, sophisticated calculators have assumed very great importance in many countries and the Internet has changed from being an academic activity linking a few universities to having key significance in an increasingly wired world. In such circumstances, the subtitles of this working group are especially relevant, highlighting these three key aspects of work in mathematics education. This working group attracted close to 300 participants, from more than 30 countries, suggesting that the questions and issues associated with technology in mathematics education continue to be prominent ones internationally.

Internet supported preparation for the congress: WGA 11 was organized to accommodate a wide range of educational and research activities associated with technology in mathematics education. An open Call for Contributions was made around a year before the congress. This Call was widely publicised electronically and a web site was established so that intending participants could obtain detailed information on the structure and likely range of activities planned. A number of submissions was received, reflecting a wide range of activity. The submissions themselves were used to structure the work of the WGA 11 into four distinct subgroups, described in some detail below.

Because of unavoidable time and space limitations at ICME, an organisational structure different from those of previous congresses was chosen. Participants whose contributions were regarded as relevant to the WGA 11 aims and sufficiently interesting for presentation to an informed international audience were invited to prepare a paper for electronic distribution prior to the congress. Abstracts of these presentations were placed on the WGA 11 web site several months prior to the

273

congress, with full papers available on the web about 2 months prior to the congress.

The full versions of papers were password-protected prior to the meeting, to preserve the integrity and viability of ICME 9, on the advice of the ICME 9 Secretariat. Registered delegates to WGA 11 were informed and thus were able to engage in depth with the professional work of the contributors well in advance of attendance, permitting short presentations at the congress itself to be given on the assumption that a significant proportion of the audience had already had access to the paper. While there was, unfortunately, a small number of delegates without (known) email and a small group whose web access was not adequate to take advantage of this method of academic communication, this innovation appeared to be successful for the great bulk of participants, and is recommended for future meetings. Password-protection of papers was lifted immediately after the congress, so that delegates who had chosen to attend other working groups could read them. A month following the congress, papers were removed from the web site, to allow revisions and for publication purposes.

Paul Goldenberg (USA) was invited to give a plenary presentation to WGA 11, concerning the quest for "common notions" about technology in mathematics learning. The idea of common notions has roots with Euclid's 'self-evident' truths, and offered some starting points for delegates to consider the debates about technology in many countries. He proposed for discussion some examples of what all might accept as important for students to be able to do without access to technology. If such starting points can be agreed upon, he argued, we may be able to make progress with the many educational issues associated with technology. By its nature, such a conversation did not conclude at the congress, but it is hoped that it will continue on a wider platform after the congress.

Working sessions of the 4 subgroups: Following the plenary, delegates joined one of the four subgroups for approximately three more sessions, before coming together again for a final, short, plenary session. Most delegates chose to remain in a particular subgroup, which captured their interests most strongly, although there was also some movement between subgroups. Presenters in subgroups generally made generous allowances for discussion, on the assumption that delegates were already somewhat familiar with their work. Altogether, 48 presentations were made in subgroups, involving presenters from 21 countries in six continents.

Subgroup 1: Internet, multimedia, hypertext as a support for mathematics learning and teaching was presided over by Shoichiro Machida (Japan) & Hans-Georg Weigand (Germany). Invited papers were contributed by: Nina Boswinkel & Frans Moerlands (The Netherlands), Bryan Dye (UK), George L.Ekol (Uganda), Shoichiro Machida (Japan), Tohsuke Urabe (Japan), Jenni Way (UK), Hans-Georg Weigand

(Germany), Mary Jean Winter (USA) and Wei-Chi Yang (USA).

Presentations focussed on the development and use of web sites for teachers and for students, on the use of the Internet for teacher education purposes and on the role of hypertext in mathematical communication. The development of significant web-based resources for large audiences of pupils and their teachers was described. A variety of educational purposes are involved, including the provision of enrichment material for pupils, learning outside regular classroom environments, lesson preparation and professional communications. It is clear from the work of this subgroup that the Internet is of increasing interest to teachers, pupils and even the general public as an educational resource for mathematics education.

Work involving use of the Internet within teacher education, activity that might be expected to increase in prevalence over the next few years, was reported. Aspects of the changes to mathematical representations for electronic communications across a range of cultural settings were discussed, reaching a conclusion that considerable work remains to be done on the optimal design of electronic communications in mathematics. It was also noted that there has been relatively little empirical work reported so far on the impact of the Internet on student learning in mathematics. This is clearly a matter of some significance in a climate in which a great deal of public attention has been aroused and considerable public and private resources have been expended on developing the necessary hardware and software. We hope that the next ICME will see more substantial evidence of the impacts of this work on various settings for mathematics education reported and discussed.

Subgroup 2: Integration of (algebraic and graphics) calculators into the mathematics curriculum and assessment was presided over by Barry Kissane (Australia). Invited papers were contributed by R.M. Ali, Z. Zainuddin & A.I. Md. Ismail (Malaysia), Roger Brown & Einir Wyn Davies (Wales, UK), Michael Cavanagh & Mike Mitchelmore (Australia), Penelope H. Dunham (USA), David H. Haimes (Australia), Toshikazu Ikeda (Japan), Tom G. Macintyre (Scotland, UK), Regina Moeller (Germany), Nuriye Sirinoglu & Yasar Ersoy (Turkey), Sang Sook Choi-Koh (Korea), Vlasta Kokol-Voljc (Slovenia), Len Sparrow & Paul Swan (Australia), Henk van der Kooij (The Netherlands) and Bert K. Waits & Franklin Demana (USA).

Papers addressed the significance of hand-held technologies in school mathematics, reported on empirical work associated with them and also focused on their implications for assessment, particularly formal assessment practices. The subgroup agreed that calculators derive their significance for mathematics education from their potential accessibility to a wide range of students. Thus, for example, a very significant impact on curriculum thinking and school practices associated with the development of graphics calculators for mathematics in the past decade in the USA was noted. Several presenters discussed and described recent curriculum developments associated with graphics calculators. The significance of calculators for identifying and provoking pupil misconceptions was discussed, together with the need to accommodate such possibilities in teaching. Presenters were keen that their work not be seen as a criticism of the technology, but rather as providing insight for teachers and researchers into student thinking, possibly not previously revealed. With one exception, presenters focused attention on the use of calculators for older students, those of secondary school age or beyond.

There is a need for technology use in teaching and learning to be coherent with technology use in assessment, including high-stakes assessment. Participants agreed that the challenges for curriculum and assessment are considerable for hand-held CAS devices such as algebraic calculators, and we look forward to more work in this area being reported at the next ICME.

Subgroup 3: Software tools as cognitive technologies for mathematical learning and thinking, perspectives for computer rich curricula was presided over by Rolf Biehler (Germany). Invited papers were contributed by: Charlotte Krog Andersen (Denmark), Raouf N. Boules(USA), Tilak de Alwis (USA), William Finzer (USA), Nicholas Jackiw (USA), Bernhard Kutzler (Austria), Jean-Baptiste Lagrange (France), James E. Schultz (USA), Pumadevi Sivasubramaniam (UK), Eno Tonisson (Estonia), Yoshiaki Ueno (Japan), Tomoko Yanagimoto (Japan) and Rose Mary Zbiek & M. Kathleen Heid (USA).

A range of different software types were explored from a pedagogical point of view. Computer Algebra Systems (CAS) are rapidly increasing in importance, as they become more widely available, and a number of contributors described the significance of this sort of software in tertiary mathematics and secondary school mathematics curriculum development. The need to adapt CAS for educational purposes, the relative advantages of innovative pedagogically designed software with dynamically manipulating opportunities such as Fathom and Geometer's Sketchpad for geometry and statistics, and a vision for an overall Mathematics Office, which would contain all the different tools without conflicting interfaces, syntax and semantics was put forward as important points against a more pragmatic predominance of existing CAS and algebraic calculators. Discussions were concerned with how to use software tools to support learners with relatively simple tasks versus giving access to more advanced mathematical topics for bright students.

It was felt that more work was needed on the development and subsequent evaluation of 'Substantial Learning Environments' to make the many creative ideas still more adapted to practical conditions and to know more how pupils and teachers make use of the ideas. in the future. It was clear from the meeting that access to suitable software for education is uneven, across countries and across the range of pupil interests and abilities.

Subgroup 4: Conceptual and professional development of learners and teachers in technologically enriched classrooms was presided over by Sergei Abramovich (USA). Invited papers were contributed by Sergei Abramovich (USA), Christian Greiffenhagen (UK), Michael de Villiers (South AfricaJudy O'Neal (USA), Merrilyn Goos, Peter Galbraith, Peter Renshaw & Vince Geiger (Australia), Lulu Healy, Sandra Magina & Nielce M. Lobo da Costa (Brazil), Yasuyuki Iijima (Japan), Masami Isoda & Akio Matuzaki (Japan), Inchul Jung (USA), Hari P. Koirala, Jacqueline K. Bowman, Marsha Davis & Linda) Espinoza Edmonds (USA), Heinz Schumann (Germany) and Behiye Ubuz (Turkey).

Three themes were evident in presentations. In the first place, classroom practice needs to be studied and also to be re-designed to understand and account for the influence of technology. Several informative empirical studies were presented that were routed in theoretical work in the socio-cultural perspective. Secondly, the professional development of teachers continues to be a concern, especially as technologies are rapidly evolving. Innovative projects and research studies addressing this concern were presented. Finally, new kinds of interactivity have been spawned by recent software developed for educational purposes. The best examples of the latter continue to be concerned with geometric activity, although others (for data analysis and calculus, for example) were discussed as well; some of these were also the subject of presentations in Subgroup 3. A concern was how to relate the visual and the experiential potential of computers to developing mathematical thinking, proof and reasoning in the more usual sense.

Follow up activities A publication, drawing on the original papers presented at the conference, following a refereeing process, is planned to reflect the variety of significant work taking place in this crucial area. We confidently predict that the significance of technology for mathematics education will continue over the next several years and expect it to be again prominent in ICME10. We hope that a greater range of work will be reported at that time, especially involving the further development of software environments for mathematics learning and their empirical evaluation.

http://wwwstaff.murdoch.edu.au/~kissane/ICME-9.htm

WGA 12: The Social and Political Dimensions of Mathematics Education.

Chief Organiser: Chistine Keitel(Germany),
Gelsa Kninjik(Brazil),
Associate Organisers: Marilyn Frankenstein(USA),
Hanako Senuma(Japan),
Renuka Vithal(South Africa),
Local Assistant Organizer: Minoru Ohtani(Japan),
Liaison IPC Member: Cyril Julie.

Prior to the congress, the COs and AOs of WGA 12 prepared a discussion paper with possible question to be dealt with in presentations and discussions, and a proposal for the structure and format of WGA 12. Since early in the preparation of the sessions, it was possible to keep contact with presenters and registered participants via email and to distribute abstracts of presentations and the time schedule of the programme. 20 papers from 14 different countries have been accepted for presentation at WG A 12, but many more had been submitted by colleagues who could not afford to attend ICME 9. During the congress WGA 12 had 45 permanent participants. The presentations and the group of participants have been divided into two subgroups: Subgroup 1: "Social and political views about mathematics and mathematics education and Mathematics for All ", and Subgroup 2: "Mathematics education in the global village and politics for social justice and equity"

Prior to the congress, a WGA-12-booklet containing the discussion paper, the programme of WGA 12 , the timetable and the abstracts of all presentations in English and Japanese, prepared by the LO, has been distributed. At the beginning of the presentations, the participants discussed two major goals for the working in WGA 12 which have been used as frame for all discussions and have been taken up once more in the final discussion in the last session of WGA 12:
- Developing social and political dimensions of mathematics education academically and as a serious field of study
- Analysing and questioning associations, organizations, and conferences of mathematics education socially and politically

Participants of WGA 12 decided that the final report of WGA 12 should address our concern about how we could ensure the autonomy and professionalisation of mathematics educators and their active role in their associations or organizations. The question has been put forward provocatively: "Do we speak for ourselves and are we really autonomous in our professional and organizational decisions?" In the following list, issues, concerns and themes are summarized that have been continuously addressed in the presentations and discussions with respect to the two major goals of WGA 12:

Issues, concern and themes addressed in presentations and discussions:
- mathematics education and democracy
- challenges and perils of globalisation
- promises and pitfalls of IT :socio-political realities and fictions
- social and political views about mathematics and mathematics education
- Mathematics for All
- contradictory demands and measures for new qualities of mathematics and mathematics education research
- social and political conflicts. Poverty, violence and instability? consequences for mathematics education and research
Questions concerning formats, structures and management of the growth and developments of mathematics education as a discipline discussed in the final discussion:
- How could equity and social justice concerns become more prominent and visible at ICME and in ICMI? (participation by whom, choice of plenaries, decisions about organizers of WGA or TSG etc. by whom etc.)
- How to increase a broader participation of different countries?
- How to improve transparency of criteria and decision processes and to make it a more democratic participatory program? (site of congresses, selection of themes of WGA or TSG, selection of speakers...)

Summary of the presentations of WGA 12
Alatorre, Silvia, National Pedagogical University, Mexico City: *Mexican Adults' Knowledge about Basic School Mathematics.*
The findings of a survey were reported that was conducted among Mexican adults and in which twenty problems of Basic School Mathematics were posed , covering mainly Arithmetic. Two samples were taken in Mexico City each of 792 subjects aged 25-60 (which covers three national primary school curricula) and representative of the city's population in that age group. Each subject received one of two versions (A or B) of the questionnaire and also gave general data. The issue of adults' numeracy has been discussed.

Bishop, Alan, Monash University, Australia: *Democratising Mathematics Education: Supporting Promising Eevelopments*
The presentation stated that the current mathematics education situation in most countries is non-democratic. The curriculum is a mechanism of governmental control, rather than educational enlightenment. The commercial textbook 'business' community controls the materials available to teachers. Assessment is primarily a

mechanism for selecting the mathematical elite. But the presenter also showed that there are promising developments however: the increasing availability of personal technology, the growth of the vocational education sector, the informal sector growth through the Internet, the increasing professionalisation of mathematics teacher associations, the growth of collaborative research. He emphasized that the challenge for all of us is how to support developments like these from within our own often highly politicised educational contexts, and with our own limited resources.

Burton, Lerne, University of Birmingham, United Kingdom: *Mathematicians on Mathematics*
Mathematics is seen, and understood, as a defined body of knowledge with associated skills, objective and independent of human action. In a study undertaken with 70 practising research mathematicians, Leone Burton has found out that the working practices and consequent epistemologies is seen and understood more generally. In this presentation she gave an overview of her study and its educational implications. Christiansen, Iben maj, Aalborg University, Denmark: Reasons to teach mathematics: which hold, which do not?
The presenter underlined that there could be many reasons to teach science and mathematics. It is often stated that investment in mathematics, science and technology will increase the global competitiveness and economic productivity of nation. However, this is but one possible incentive to develop these fields in production and learning. Sjoberg suggests four types of possible arguments for science education: The economical argument: Science education as a presentation for working and further education in highly technological and science-based society. the use argument: science education to improve practical mastering of daily life in a modern society. The democracy argument: Scientific knowledge is important for making informed opinions and for responsible participation in democracy. The cultural argument: Science is an important part of human culture, similar arguments are used for mathematical education. She discussed the extent to which mathematics education can actually serve to further these purposes, in order to challenge some of the myths regarding this issue. This raised a discussion about which types of mathematics education could meet which objectives.

Civil, Martha, University of Arizona, USA; Planas, Nuria, Universitat Autonoma de Barcelona, Spain: *Towards the Participation of ALL Students in the Mathematics Classroom*
This paper is concerned with politics for social justice in relation to gender, class, race, and ethnicity. The presenters approached this sub-theme from two different contexts-Spain and USA. Though the contexts and educational policies are different, they found themselves confronting similar questions and issues when it comes to the mathematics education of minority, economically disadvantaged students. In

particular, both are concerned by how to develop classroom-teaching environments that promote the mathematical participation of ALL students. The theoretical approach is grounded on a socio-cultural view of education.

In their presentation, they provided some background for their common research interests in the chosen sub-theme. Then they presented brief illustrations from each country (Spain and USA) to raise some common questions that did bring up a provocative discussion in the working group.

Frankenstein, Marilyn, University of Massachusetts, USA: *Developing a Critical-Mathematical Literacy though Using Real-Life Applications*
This talk did not focus on how outside political forces impose on and shape mathematics education, but rather on how a critical mathematical literacy can reveal the nature of those outside political forces. The presenter argued that in order to 'read the world' using mathematics, it is necessary to use real real-life applications. Even when teachers use real data in their mathematics curricula, the math problems created can be contrived, and/or context-narrow, and/or can ignore the politics involved in the choice of which real-data, of importance to whom. This can result in obscuring and/or distorting various aspects of the world that the data are describing. In her talk, she illustrated these criticisms of real-life math word problems and presented examples of real real-life applications, problems that are studied in a broad enough context so learners can see how understanding basic math literacy can illuminate the meaning of real-life. The problems involved using numbers to describe the world; understanding the meaning of numbers that describe aspects of the real-world; verifying/following the logic of an argument that uses numbers to support its point; using calculations to restate numerical descriptions of the world; and, understanding how numerical descriptions of the world originate and are summarized in various forms. Finally, she commented on the non-neutrality of knowledge and on the question of teaching difficult, pessimistic information.

Gorgorio, Nuria; Planas Nuria ,Universitat Autonoma de Barcelona, Spain; Bishop, Alan J., Monash University, Australia: *Constraints in the Mathematics Classroom Coming from the Socio-political Level*
In this paper, the authors presented some constraints arising at the pedagogical level derived from decisions and actions (or sometimes lack of decisions and actions) taken at the social and political levels. They showed how some restricted views of the educational community about minority students have important influences on their mathematical achievement. In particular, they presented data from their project that show that, too often, teachers associate the idea of 'immigrant student' with the idea of 'disruptive student'. From their perspective, they tried to understand the 'disruptions' taking place in the mathematics classroom in the light of the idea of 'cultural conflict'. The construct 'cultural conflict' appeared to be useful

not only when analyzing the social dynamics of the mathematics classroom with minority students, but also when trying to understand the educational bureaucrats' and politicians' attitude towards cultural diversity. During their presentation they showed some episodes taken from the data that stimulated and promoted a general discussion in the working group.

Judak, Murad, American University of Beirut, Libanon: *The Internet and Standards as Cultural Carriers and Barriers in Mathematics Education*
Referring to his talk at ICME-6, entitled "Religion and Language as Cultural Carriers and Barriers in Mathematics Education"(Jurdak, 1989), the presenter reminded us that religion and language are two factors whose effect on mathematics education was discussed mostly in the context of developing, that is, the receiving end of technological cultural production. In his presentation, he focused on standards and Internet in the industrial countries, that is, the main source of cultural technological production. Somehow, standards and internet are counterparts of religion and language in the sense that the first sets benchmarks of what is acceptable and the second, being a delivery system of information, is a meta-language. The definition of culture as defined by White(1959) was used as White identified four component of culture: technological(manufacture and use of tools), ideological(beliefs and values), sentimental(attitudes and feelings), and sociological(customs and institutions) to substantiate his thesis.

Keitel, Christine, Freie University Berlin, Germany: *Social and Political Dimensions of Mathematics Education-An Introduction*
In her introduction to the Working Group in Action 12 "Social and political aspects of mathematics education" the chief organizer underlined that WGA 12 wants to explicitly address and analyse new (and old) policies concerning mathematics education in various parts of our world: policies that care for providing the essential and appropriate teaching and learning opportunities and that ensure access to all levels of institutionalized schooling in the elementary, secondary and tertiary sector of education as well as non-academic adult education; that search for appropriate social measures and conditions for creating and carefully establishing practices guided by principles of social justice and equity. She expressed her hope that WGA 12 could come out with an interesting discussion which stimulate the participants not only individually, but also might create some teams who decide to work together and plan to present some joint projects that they would do in the future!

Knijnik, Gelsa, Universidade do Vale do Rio dos Sinos-UNISINOS, Brazil: *Reseaching on Mathematics Education in a Political Perspective*
The paper discusses political and social implications of mathematics education research, analyzing methodological and theoretical aspect of what the presenter has been calling an Ethnomathematics approach. This consists of: the investigation of

the traditions, practices and mathematical concepts of a social group and the pedagogical work which is developed in order for the group to be able to interpret and decode its knowledge, to acquire the knowledge produced by academic Mathematics; and to establish comparisons between its knowledge and academic, thus being able to analyse the power relations involved in the use of both these kinds of knowledge. Based on the work she had developed the Brazilian Landless Movement, and could exemplify in concrete arguments about those implications.

Matos, jose Manuel, Universidate Nova de Lisboa, Portugal: *Variations in Children's Mathematical Knowledge*
The purpose of this presentation was to -as a brainstorming experiment- the consequences for mathematics education of a strong research programme on the sociology of mathematical knowledge especially by discussing the effect of the concept of variation of mathematical knowledge on research in mathematics education.

Meaney, Taisin, University of Auckland, New Zealand: *Understanding and Achievement: Ways of Discussing Technology and Social Justice in Mathematics Education*
This paper compared the frames used to discuss technology innovations and those used to discuss social justice within mathematics education. These two areas are of interest because technology has had significant influence on what and how mathematics has been taught in the last twenty years and new developments in this area are likely to continue this influence. Mathematics educators involved in social justice on the other hand are interested in why some group of students succeed and others do not. Although both groups have advocated changes to the mathematics curriculum, there appears to have been little discussion between the two groups.

Meyinsse, Joseph, Southern University, Baton Rouge, Louisiana, USA: *Predictors of Mathematics Achievement among African-American Eighth Graders'*
This study examined the factors that influence African-American eighth graders' performance on standardized mathematics tests. Specifically, the difference between high and low achievers' beliefs and attitudes towards mathematics, academic self-perceptions as well as perceptions regarding teacher, school, and parents on their performance levels were examined. Mukherjee, Arundhati, India: Towards a Flexible Mathematics Curriculum-a Userfriendly Approach.
The knowledge of mathematics, its technique and supporting roles in other fields were broadly discussed in this paper. Formulation of a mathematics curriculum providing equal opportunities, satisfying expectation of all type of users irrespective of their social, economic and cultural background was suggested for both primary and secondary level. Need for providing a built-in flexibility was stressed. For

example a mathematics course at the same level has been presented as serving equally a 'future farmer' as well as a 'would be' research scholar in agronomy by choice of the respective module. The author confronted the participants with the question how can this local context be viewed through the global window? He asked countries facing similar situation to work together through exchange of ideas, mutual experimentation, use the same model with a variation in approach suiting local need and condition. Other countries already working in the line should also contribute their own bit so that congress like ICME are more meaningful and significant in the sphere of mathematics education.

Resek, Diane, San Francisco State University, USA: *Designing a Secondary Mathematics Curriculum for All Students*
For the last ten years the author has been working with a group of mathematicians and teachers to develop a secondary mathematics curriculum for all secondary school students which focuses on problem solving, as well as conventional skills. By "all secondary school students", I mean the middle 95% are meant as there are probably a very few students at both ends of the spectrum that need a specialized curriculum. The Curriculum is designed to be taught in heterogeneous classrooms. This new curriculum, the Interactive Mathematics Program, has already been extensively field-tested with diverse populations and has been rewritten three times on the basis of feedback from classroom teachers. Students in the program have been evaluated using a variety of measures. The project collaborators have discovered characteristics that must go into such a curriculum and crucial elements that are needed for its successful implementation in order for it to be successful with all students and that will be reported.

Sethati, Mamokethi, University of Wits-Johannesburg, South Africa: *From Searching on or with to Searching on and with Teachers: Problems of Ethics in Mathematics Education*
This very stimulating and provocative presentation addressed special issues of ethics of research in mathematics education, and in particular the different methodologies in empirical research that do not respect ethical criteria when collaborating with students and teachers as objects, not as subjects in research.

Trap, Allan, DLH, Denmark: *Postmodern Enlightenment, Schools and Learning. Is It Meeting the Concrete or Meeting the Abstract that Educate?*
The presenter claimed that a crisis in educational institutions makes the enlightenment discussion reappear: What is the purpose of an educational institution? What is educating, building and forming humans? In short what is enlightenment or "bildung"? Wishing not to convince but to inspire by pointing at contingency and other wiseness this paper discussed late feudal, postfeudal, late modern and postmodern enlightenment. What has changed, and what has not? And

what is the basis of enlightenment today?

Valero, Paola, Royal Danish School of Educational Studies Copenhagen, Denmark: *Between the Sword and the Wall: The Issues of Democracy in Secondary School Mathematics Education*
The presentation started in stating that many of the current reform trends in mathematics education in different countries in the world include a "politically correct" discourse about the contribution that the mathematical formation of students in school should have in the construction and consolidation of democratic societies. But she also showed that the distance between these intangible formulations and mathematics education practices in the everyday functioning of the school as a whole generates questions about the real possibilities for actually bridging that gap. The intention of the presentation was to illustrate these general formulations with observations from three schools and to discuss some key points in the complexity of contradictory forces in the organization of school mathematics.

Vithal, Renuka, University Durban-Westiville, Southafrica: *A Pedagogy Conflict and Dialogue in Mathematics Education*
This paper reported on research in which the attempt to realize what may be called a social, cultural, political approach to a mathematics curriculum through the practice of project work in a mathematics classroom gave rise to a theorising of a pedagogy of conflict and dialogue. Drawing from a theoretical landscape which pulls together notions from ethnomathematics, critical mathematics education aspects of gender, race and class, and South Africa's own historical educational legacy of people's mathematics from the Apartheid era, the contradictory and co-operative nature of both conflict and dialogue were explored, and placed in a special relationship described through the concept of complementarity. A pedagogy of conflict and dialogue recognises the structures, authority, differentiation and mathematics disciplinary concerns of teachers and schools as it opens and strives toward giving meaning to issues of democracy, freedom, and equity in the diverse contexts of teaching and learning mathematics.

Timetable and structure of the organization of presentations and discussions:
DAY 1: Tuesday, August 1, 14:00-16:00:
14:00-14:20:Introductory presentations to WGA 12
14:20-14:45: Introductory discussion of WGA 12, deciding about subgroup-division
14:45-15-15: Presentations in subgroups
15:15-16:00: Discussion in subgroups
DAY 2: Wednesday, August 2, 14:00-16:00:
14:00-15:00: Presentations in subgroups
15:00-16:00: Discussion in subgroups
DAY 3: Saturday,August 5, 14:00-17:30:

14:00-15:30:Presentations in subgroups
15:30-16:30: Discussion in subgroups
16:30-17:00:WGA 12-Summary and final discussion of perspectives and actions

WGA 13: History and Culture in mathematics Education

Chief Organizers: Jan van Maanen(Netherland),
Wann Sheng Horng(China-Taiwan),
Associate Oragnizers: Ryosuke Nagaoka(Japan),
John Fauvel(UK),
LAO: Shinya Yamamoto(Japan),
Liaison IPC Member: Mogen Niss.

Structure and themes

The Working Group concentrated on the following five major themes, which were identified in the call for papers. For each theme a keynote speaker was invited. The keynote lectures were discussed in subgroups, in which further short presentations were given as well.

• Aspects of multidisciplinary work

Central question: How may mathematics education be improved by attending to the possibility of cross-disciplinary work with other subjects and teachers? Both positive and negative aspects should be considered.

In the keynote lecture Mangho Ahuja (Southeast Missouri State University, Cape Girardeau, MO 63701, USA) spoke about *Traditional versus multidisciplinary teaching*. He compared two teachers in their approach of the Pythagorean theorem, one taking the traditional path and the other who introduced the topic through activity groups in a broad range of fields. Teachers of other disciplines got involved via the questions that they received from the students, although they had been much reluctant to cooperate when they were asked beforehand. The outcome of the multidisciplinary project was positive. Costs are high, certainly when the curriculum does not provide incentives for this type of approach.

• Effectiveness of history in teaching mathematics

Central question: What evidence have we that using history or broader cultural dimensions in mathematics education improves the quality of that education?

Karen Michalowicz (The Langley School, McLean VA, USA) spoke in the keynote lecture about *Developing historical modules for use in the high school classroom*, a project funded by the National Science Foundation, which she is carrying out together with Victor Katz (University of DC, Washington DC, USA). Six teams, each of three teachers and a university professor, have worked together during the last two years in order to produce resources for classroom lessons, in a variety of fields. The modules are now distributed and are being field tested by an independent agency. The first impression, from telephonic interviews with students, is that 'history works', especially with respect to the students attitudes, since students think that mathematics taught in this manner is considerably more interesting.

· Probability theory and statistics

Problem definition: An important subject whose historical dimension has been too little attended to (except at a rather simple anecdotal level) is that of probability and statistics. A fuller consideration of the contribution that its history could make to statistics education is overdue.

The keynote speaker was Arthur Bakker (Freudenthal Institute, Utrecht, NL). He discussed *the history of early statistics and its didactical implications*, concentrating on a historical and then a didactical phenomenology of average values. These constitute a large family of notions that in early times were not yet strictly separated. There are many parallels between history and the development of students' conceptions. Classroom observations indicate the importance that students discover many qualitative aspects of average values before they learn how to calculate the arithmetic mean and the median. From history, it is concluded that estimation, fair distribution and simple decision theory can be fruitful starting points for a statistical instruction sequence.

· The dance and poetry of mathematics

Problem definition: An aspect of mathematics education which historical-cultural studies are well able to support is its creativity, fun and beauty. Spelling out in, one detail how this may be achieved will be a useful service to teachers.

Hisako Kikuchi (Higashiyamagata Junior Highschool, Yamagata, JP) reported in his keynote lecture *Sangaku as a teaching material* about joint work with Ikutaro Morikawa (Yamagata University, Yamagata, JP). Sangaku is one of Japan's indigenous mathematical customs from the Edo period. Many mathematicians of this period would try to set original problems for themselves and solve them. Doing so, they produced plates with colorful figures and dedicated them to a shrine or a temple. This custom showed not only appreciation for God, but also pride in one's mathematical ability. Sangaku appeared to be a fruitful medium for working with students, who studied constructing and solving problems through the making of sangaku. Students' appreciation of mathematics increased, as well as their confidence in problem solving.

· Culture

Problem definition: It is important to discuss the breadth of the idea of culture and to discuss how gar it needs to be narrowed, and in what directions, in order to make progress with bringing proposals for how mathematics teachers may be supported and encouraged.

The keynote lecture Mathematics education: *Cultural perspective and underpinnings in the Indian context* was given by Dilip K. Sinha (Visva-Bharati, India). He reviewed a series of aspects of Indian mathematical culture, which ranged from early work discussed by Colebrook to the fairly contemporary notes by Ramanujan. Although current mathematics education in India is predominantly shaped by western perspective, one can also recognize in it the essence of Indian culture, in that recent perspectives on mathematics education keep on developing with these three categories: grassroot, esoteric and applicable.

Further presentations and discussion
After the keynote lectures further work was done in three subgroups:

The first group was chaired by Costas Tzanakis (University of Crete, Greece) and went on with the theme of *multidisciplinary work*. The discussion explored what multidisciplinary work might be in the context of mathematics education. The conclusion was that there should be an emphasis on mathematics, and that the teacher should adjust the work to the social context of the students. Important parameters are the educational level of the students, the subject, the time available, and the teacher's own experience. Multidisciplinary work is possible in practically any subject. Examples signaled were: calculus, differential equations, probability theory and statistics, combinatorics, vector analysis and functional analysis, but also subjects like number theory, group theory and topology. The subjects may relate to non-mathematical topics as: physics and natural sciences, philosophy, music and arts, logic and linguistics, drama, literature and history.
Specific examples of actual implementations were presented by Oscar Joao Abdounur (Brazil), about *Historical aspects of ratio and proportion in music and mathematics education*; Costas Tzanakis, about *Elaborating on abstract algebraic concepts on the basis of physical ideas and concepts*: special relatively on the basis of elementary matrix algebra and group theory and Paul Manning (USA) on *Intersections of mathematics and the humanities discovered by accident: language, literature, philosophy*.

A second group, chaired by Karen Michalowicz, went on with the themes *Effectiveness of history in teaching mathematics and Probability theory and statistics*. Short presentations were given by Catherin Murphy (USA), about *A historical course for teachers*; Rebecca Kessler (USA), about A *module about Archimedes for the mathematics classroom*; Osamu Takenouchi (Japan), about *History and mathematics teaching in Japan*; Phyllis Caruth (USA), about A *module about the history of combinatorics and statistics for the mathematics classroom*, and Bernd Zimmermann (Germany) about *Appealing geometrical problems from Al-Sizji*. The subsequent discussion was mainly about effectiveness. The conclusion was that there are many ways to implement history, some of them needing special attention and care. For example, one should be critical when students use information that comes from the internet. History can have a function, it was agreed, either to enrich mathematics (e.g., if you know a subject already, to do it once more but in a different manner), or to introduce a subject to students. It can be applied in order to develop a new learning trajectory, it can produce heuristics for problem solving, and many more useful things. Historical games ware also discussed as a positive contribution in mathematics lessons.

The third group, chaired by Florence Fasanelli (Washington DC, USA) and Jan van Maanen, Worked on the broader cultural perspective, as reflected by the final two keynote lectures. Short presentations ware by Lawrence Shirley (USA) about *Using costumes and connecting to local peculiarities* and Man-Keung Siu (Hong Kong) about his course *Mathematics: a cultural heritage*. A variety of aspects of culture came up for discussion:
· the clash between western and eastern mathematical traditions,
· the influence that the prevailing culture may have on individual students, or on groups of students (e.g. the gender problem is closely linked to the mathematical culture),
· paying attention to the specific culture of the region, or the culture of an ethnic subgroup of a mathematics class, can have a positive influence, for example in increasing the self-confidence of the group,
· cultural happenings (visits to a museum, dream, etc.) often attract criticism from colleague-teachers and parents, so one should be prepared for that. On the other hand enthusiasm of students is one of the best and most convincing arguments for doing these types of activities, certainly with the parents,
· The relation between culture, history and mathematics education is under-researched, and is worth further research.

Looking back
On this Working Group some general conclusions may be drawn. The first is that the relation between history and mathematics education is still an area in which many developments take place. The systematic production and testing of historical modules, as described by Michalowicz and Katz, is on example of a type of research with a practical outcome that is very important. The value of making a connection with local culture was brought forward more than once, and with reports of positive results. Increasing confidence with students is one of the key-words connected with the positive evaluation.

As always positive results require input. The balance between cost and result was discussed, and although it was agreed that the costs are still high, many participants appeared willing to invest in this manner. One of the reasons was their own pleasure in preparing historical material for students, but the main reason was that they noticed many positive effects with students. In some countries the curriculum is not supportive of this work. Further work has to be done on national levels.

More history at ICME 9

As an appendix I shall list here the other historical activities at ICME 9.

There were regular lectures by Niels Jahnke (Germany) about *Historical sources in the mathematics classroom: ideas and experiences*, by Osamu Takenouchi (Japan) about *Some characteristic features of Wasan, the Japanese traditional mathematics* and by Ewa Lakome (Poland) about H*istory of mathematics in educational research and mathematics teaching?: a case of probability and statistics.*

Then there were two sessions of the International Study Group on the relations between History and Pedagogy of Mathematics (HPM), with the following speakers: Bjørn Smestad (Norway) on *History of mathematics in Norwegian textbooks*, Peter Ransom (UK) on *Teaching geometry through the use of old instruments*, Osamu Kota (Japan) on *John Perry and mathematics education in Japan*, Yoichi Hirano, Kathihusa Kawamura and Shin Watanabe (Japan) on *Mathematical exhibits at museums from viewpoints of mathematics education*, Nobuyuki Watanabe (Japan) on *A practice of the cultural history of mathematics in elementary school*. The second HPM-session was concluded by the installation of HPM's new chair for the period 2000-2004, Fulvia Furinghetti (University of Genova, Italy).

And finally, the book History in mathematics education: The ICMI study, edited by John Fauvel and Jan Maanen, and published by Kluwer Academic Publishes (Dordrecht 2000), was launched with presentations by several chapter-coordinators (Fasanelli, Jannke, Michalowicz, Nagoya, Siu and Tzanakis).

Topic Study Groups

TSG 1: The Teaching and Learning of Algebra

Chief Organizer: Zalman Usiskin(USA),
Associate Organizers: Romulo Lins(Brazil),
Teresa Romano(Mexico),
Anna Sfard(Israel),
Local Assistant Organizer: Hiroshi Hosokawa(Japan),
Liaison IPC Member: Stephen Lerman.

Summary report

This report is divided into two parts, the mechanics of the organization and presentation of the study group, and the content of the presented papers.

Mechanics: Two weeks before the conference, 109 ICME attendees had registered for TSG 1. About 100 people attended the first of the two sessions of TSG 1; about 60 attended the second session. Each of the two sessions was organized in the same way. A few minutes were devoted to introductory remarks from the chief organizer. Then five papers were presented for 10 minutes each followed by questions of clarification. The last of these papers was by an associate organizer to allow also for comments on the preceding papers. Then, in the remaining time (20 minutes the first day; 15 minutes the second), there was discussion. The order of presentation of the papers was roughly in order of the grade levels; this proved to be effective.

This TSG could easily have used a third time slot for discussion. Furthermore, it is likely that many presentations in the WGAs would have been appropriate for this TSG.

On the other hand, it was quite useful not to have been split by grade or age level. It was felt to be quite informative for participants (and presenters) to see the broad range of algebra in mathematics schooling, from primary to college. We are pleased to thank the local arrangements committee for supplying helpers who were extraordinary with their prompt attention to the equipment in the room and other needs of the presenters.

Content: One strong theme was the teaching of algebra to primary-school-aged children(ages 6-9). Four papers dealt with student work and two additional papers dealt with training teachers to teach algebra(or algebraic thinking, depending on one's view) at this level.

Carraher presented video segments showing third students reasoning about additive relations. The findings that students of this age may be capable of dealing with algebraic reasoning, but instruction must address the tension between fixing values and treating them as variable quantities. Schliemann explored the notations developed by a third-grade student participating in an algebra study at a public school in Boston(USA). This student's written production, actions, and words suggest that young children's notations can constitute precursors of conventional algebra representation and can become tools to further understanding and thought processes. Falcao presented the results of a study of 8- and 9-year-old children in a public school in Recife(Brazil). The results suggest that algebraic activity does not need to wait until arithmetic development to be implemented; in fact, arithmetic immersion may present some obstacles to algebra. Lins argued that these results imply an early start to the study of algebra, as opposed to what Piagetian constructivism would suggest. He felt that we should grant algebra learning the same understanding we grant to first-language acquisition: flexibility with mistakes and errors; assessment of progress based on social functionality rather than skill; and opportunity to engage in "algebraic cultures" with various aspects and modes of creating meaning.

Thompson addressed the training of primary school teachers to incorporate algebra in their teaching. She felt that rather than making algebra or algebraic thinking a chunk of the curriculum, it may be more effective to help elementary teachers consider ways to extend topics and activities outside of mathematics to include algebraic ideas. She gave a number of examples of the use of children's literature in helping teachers engage in algebraic thinking. Malara reported a multi-year study of teachers and students in middle school in which algebra is approached as a language both in its syntactical aspects and in translation and production/communication of thought. Very positive results were found with both teachers and students in the use of algebra in proof and argumentation in arithmetic. Strong results were found also for the solution of algebraic problems without student knowledge of the laws of algebra; this provides reason for both teachers and students to face syntactical questions in themselves and independently from the context.

Within the same domain of innovative ways of teaching algebra and analyzing students' algebra practices, Ikkyu Yanagimoto proposed the use of a "Framework of representing thinking activities" to help students to construct and express their thinking. Narratives play an important role in this teaching model and the idea is that both students and teacher take advantage of this way of working in the classroom. An example involving the solving a simple equation using this framework was provided by the author.

A second strong theme was the use of technology in the teaching of algebra at the secondary school and college levels. Thompson reported results from two studies conducted by the University of Chicago School Mathematics Project with students in a second-year of algebra study. These results suggest that an intensive use of graphing calculators with corresponding textbook support influences students' practices to prefer graphic representations when solving algebra problems and stimulates students to use a wider variety of strategies to solve problems than used by students who study similar material from a traditional textbook. Pagon, based on his experience in the Tempus Joint European Project and in the T3 project, expressed a number of reasons to promote the use of Computer Algebra Systems(CAS) such as Derive, Maple, and Mathematica for the teaching of algebra: as a way to motivate students to learn mathematics (and sciences); as tools to help students to better understand mathematical objects and their properties; and as self-learning and self-evaluating tools.

Rojano reported on partial and preliminary results from a study carried out in Mexico on the incorporation of new technologies to the school culture (the case of spreadsheets and graphing calculators in the secondary school algebra). Results from a pre-questionnaire, administered before the experimental work with new technologies took place, revealed student preference to use arithmetic and natural language to express a problem situation or a generalization task (such as a pattern in number sequences). After two years of use of spreadsheets and the TI-92 calculator in their algebra courses, students participating in this study preferred to use algebraic spreadsheets and numeric codes, rather than the natural language. This tendency to choose other "symbolic" languages instead of the mother tongue can be attributed to pupils' use of an intermediate code (between natural language and algebra) with a clear numeric basis (that of the spreadsheets or the calculator) to cope with word problem solving and generalization tasks.

As a whole, the set of contributions in the technology block informs us that the use of CAS, graphic environments and spread sheets are proving to have a significant impact on the variety of strategies used by students when they solve problems, the sort of representations they choose, the sort of language they prefer to use to cope with word problem solving and generalization activities, their motivation to learn mathematics, and the content of the algebra curriculum.

Papers presented
Carraher, David, Ana Schliemann,and Barbara Brizuela(USA), *Bringing Out the Algebraic Character of Addition and Subtraction: Some Issues in Generalizing from Instances and in Instantiating Variables.*
F Falcão, Jorge Tarcísio da Rocha, Anna Paula Brito Lima, Cláudia Roberta de Araújo, Mônica Maria Lins Lessa, and Monica Oliveira Osório(Brazil), *Introducing Algebraic Activity in Elementary Level.*
Lins, Romulo(Brazil), *Some Key Issues in Early Algebra Education.*

Malara, Nicolina(Italy), *The Approach to Algebraic Thought in Compulsory School: Teachers Training and Classroom Processes.*

Pagon, Dushan(Slovenia), *New Approaches to Teaching Algebra, Based on the Use of CAS.*

Rojano, Teresa(Mexico), *A Study of the Use of Multiple Information Technologies in the Learning of Algebra.*

Schliemann, Ana, Barbara Brizuela, and David Carraher(USA), *Notations as Representations of Algebraic Thinking and as a Tool for Algebraic Learning.*

Thompson, Denisse, and Sharon Senk(USA), T*he Use of Problem-Solving Strategies by Second-Year Algebra Students: The Case of the University of Chicago School Mathematics Project Advanced Algebra.*

Thompson, Denisse(USA), *Helping Elementary Teachers Develop Children's Algebraic Thinking.*

Yanagimoto, Ikkyu(Japan), *The Structure of Learning Process Focused on "The Framework for Representing Thinking Activities".*

TSG 2: The Teaching and Learning of Geometry

Chief Organizer: M.Alessandra Mariotti(Italy),
Associate Organizers: James Wilson(USA),
Oleg Mushkarov(Bulgaria),
Local Assistant Organizer: Takahiro Kunioka(Japan),
Liaison IPC Member: Jerry Becker.

The discussion was organized around few short presentations which aimed to introduce different aspects related to the theme of the Topic Study Group.

The first session was opened by Peter Bryant reporting on a collaborative (British and Brazilian) geometry project aimed to look at the basis for young children's understanding of geometrical relations. Two hypotheses were confronted: the first related to Piaget's theory stresses the importance of external relations, the relations between the figure and surrounding space, while the second, related to van Hiele's theory, stresses the internal structure of geometrical figures. The results showed that children either do not bother about position at all or, when they do, they concentrate on internal relations, like length and angle.

Difficulties related to recognition of internal relationships in a geometrical figure were also considered in the following intervention of MORIKAWA Ikutaro; in particular a proposal was presented aiming to introduce pupils (8th grade) to the link between properties recognition and deductive reasoning.

The issue of the role of new technologies and their potentialities arose in the following presentation by Walter Whiteley; the author's examples highlighted different components of geometrical thinking, deductive reasoning and problem solving. The theme of problem solving was resumed by HAN Inki who presented a theoretical framework for studying geometrical problem solving.

The first session was closed by the intervention of John J. Edgell, who presented some activities from one of the formative, field research programs that he is carrying out with students at grades K-S at the public school levels. As the author said such research projects have impacted the preparation of pre-service teachers of mathematics and in-service teachers training programs.

Thus the focus moved from the learners to the teacher, and the second session opened on a new issue, concerning primary and high school teachers and their awareness of the importance of geometrical resources when dealing with the teaching of other branches of Mathematics. A research project was presented by

Regina Maria Pavanello, it concerned Brazilian teachers, both with and without a degree in Mathematics. Data analysis showed that the teachers, including those with a degree in Mathematics, had difficulties in distinguishing the geometrical aspects involved as, for instance, in the equal partition of continuous integers.

Students' cognitive models and instructional materials were compared in the following presentation by José Manuel Matos. The relationship between students conceptions and school geometry was also considered in the next presentation. Different paradigms, coming form an epistemological analysis, were described by Alain Kuzniak, and used to describe different approach to geometry for prospective teachers.

Experience with geometry for prospective elementary school teachers was then approached by Barbara Pence, who raised the issue on whether a dynamic geometry environment can help these students build their own interrelated system of geometric objects. Different proof schemes were described as they could be observed in students responses to a final examination test

The relationship between empirical and deductive approaches was directly approached in the following presentation by Fujita Taro, who examined the role of experimental tasks in the textbook *Elementary Geometry* (1903) by Godfrey and Siddons. Although the final objective of such tasks was preparation for deductive geometry, Godfrey recognized general educational value of experimental verification in geometry teaching.

The analysis of such particular case introduced the issue of the complex choice required in setting up school curriculum. An interesting contribution on this same issue came from the last presentation, by Keith Jones. The complexity of the question of how to construct an appropriate geometry curriculum is a long-standing one is based on the fact that there are just too many interesting things to include so some decision has to be made as to what to include and what to exclude. Jones presented three perspectives on the issue of the design of the school geometry curriculum and the following final comment inspired by an essay on geometry written by Sawyer, that I like to take as a final conclusion of this report too.

《In an elegant essay on geometry, Sawyer(1977, In Praise of Geometry. In W.W Wilson, *The Mathematics Curriculum: Geometry*. Glasgow: Blackie) concludes that "In the subject matter of geometry we suffer from an embarrassment of riches. We have so many tools for the discussion of geometric problems? Euclid transformations, coordinates, matrices, calculus. However, it is noticeable that no one of these is the magic key that unlocks all doors. An eclectic approach seems in order; pupils should learn the power and limitations of each". Such an "eclectic" approach does not necessarily have to result in pupils experiencing geometry as a

298

kind of "inconsistent bazaar".》

Further investigation are needed in order to set up general criteria for building up curricula, which can take into account the complex of different perspectives involved.

Schedule of the presentations at the TSG2 "Teaching and Learning Geometry"
First session
Copying Geometric Figures: How Children Make Sense of It? Peter Bryant, Tereziha Nunes, Sandra Magina, Tania Campos, Brazil
As Introduction to the Deductive Geometry, Morikawa Ikutaro, Yamagata University, Japan
Dynamic Geometry Programs and the Practice of Geometry, Walter Whiteley, York University, Toronto, Ontaro, Canada
Realization of Search of Solving Geometrical Problems, Han Inki, Gyeongsang National University, Korea
A *Formative Field Research Study with Second, Third, Fourth Grade Chinese-American Students on Accessing Geometry from a Measurement:Tessellation, Cube, Simplex, Construct Perspective*, John J. Edgell, Jr, Southwest Texas State University, USA
Second session
Geometry and the Construction of Mathematical Concepts, Regina Maria Pavanello, State University of Maringá, Brazil
Cognitive Models for the Concept of Angle, José Manuel Matos, Faculdade de Ciencias e Tecnologia, Lisbon, Portugal
On an Intrinsic Approach of Geometry Taught at School, Alain Kuzniak, IUFM d'Alsace, DIDIREM Paris VII, France
Proof Schemes Developed by Perspective Teachers Enrolled in Intuitive Geometry, Barbara J. Pence, San Jose State University, USA
Roles of Experimental Tasks in the Teaching of Geometry. An Examination of Elementary Geometry(1903) by Godfrey and Siddons, Fujita Taro, University of Southampton, UK
Perspectives on the Design of the School Geometry Curriculum, Keith Jones, University of Southampton, UK

TSG 3: The Teaching and Learning of Calculus

Chief Organizer: Paul Zorn(USA),

Associate Organizers: Thomas Judson(USA),

Osamu Kota(Japan),

Tsuneharu Okabe(Japan),

Local assistant Organizer: Tamotsu Kiuchi(Japan),

Liaison IPC Member: Jerry Becker.

Summary and overview. Calculus has remained for a long time an essential foundation for further work in mathematics, the sciences, engineering, business and economics, and many other areas. New technologies, new teaching methods, and new educational research have led in recent years to new approaches to content and pedagogy of calculus courses, and sometimes to controversy. Participants were invited to share ideas, experiences, and opinions, from a rich variety of mathematical, educational, national, and cultural perspectives. Sessions included brief talks and presentations, a panel discussion, and some free and active discussion of key ideas and issues raised by speakers and presenters. (These elements are summarized below.) Ms. Mikiko SASAGO provided useful translations between Japanese and English.

More than 70 people, representing about 20 countries, participated in all or part of TSG 3 activities. Meetings were held in two 90-minute sessions, on 1 and 2 August 2000, at the Chiba Institute of Technology.

Panel discussion. The first day's session began with an informal panel discussion on aspects of calculus teaching and learning around the world. The panelists, all professors of mathematics, were Y.K. Kim(Korea), U. Kirchgraber(Switzerland), H. Mui(Vietnam), and K. Ueno(Japan). Panlists were invited to describe various aspects of calculus teaching and learning in their own countries, and to identify any question of special current interest in their countries.

An interesting exchange and discussion ensued. Following are some samples of what we learned.
1. The fraction of all students who take some course with "calculus" in its title varies significantly from county to country, with very high figures in Japan and Korea and a smaller fraction in the United States.
2. Students in Europe and Asia are likely to meet calculus ideas first in secondary school. In the U.S., by contrast, many students first see calculus in colleges and universities.
3. The type and amount of technology in use in calculus courses varies widely, from

little or no use in some countries to widespread use in Switzerland and the U.S.

4. University entrance examinations and centralized national curricula are important in many countries in determining what calculus is taught and when students encounter it. In particular, several participants described Japan's system of rigorous university entrance exams as a force working against the possibility change in mathematical teaching and learning. Some other countries, such as the U.S., have much less centralized systems? But perhaps at some cost in confusion and lack of uniformity.

5. Many countries are in the process of changing mathematics curricula or introducing technology use at the secondary level. In some cases these changes will reduce the amount of time students spend on calculus, so that time can be made for other topics, such as the mathematics of information technology.

Two special presentations. The second day's session began with two special presentations. First was a report by T. Judson(USA) and T. Nishimori(Japan) on their qualitative study, conducted partly in the U.S. and partly in Japan, comparing the procedural and conceptual knowledge of calculus students in Japanese and American high schools. They demonstrated the written exam they've administered to students in both countries, and gave instances of students' answers both to the exam and to general interview questions. The work remains in progress, so conclusions are not available, but it will be interesting to discover whether students in the two countries perform similarly or differently on various calculus-related tasks.

The second special presentation was by T. Okabe(Japan), who described an approach to teaching calculus based on graphical and computer-graphical images. A visual approach, using images familiar to students from everyday life, can both motivate students to learn and help them gain deeper insights into the essence of important calculus ideas, which are often slighted in traditional approaches to the subject. The concepts of gradient and differential, for example, are better understood through carefully chosen images and exercises than through formal symbolic manipulation alone.

Brief papers. There were 5 brief paper presentations over the two days:

1. C. Dolores Flores(Mexico) described a planned research project with Mexican undergraduate students. Many students have difficulty with the basic variational ideas at the heart of calculus. The project aims, therefore, to design and implement strategies for improving students' success with variational thinking and effective use of variational language.

2. C. Rondero Guerrero(Mexico) described his research in epistemology and didactics of calculus, which focuses on inter-relations between discrete and continuous variationl processes. This important connection deserves more explicit

attention in calculus teaching; an integration method called the "potential mean" was described as an illustration.

3. K. Kataoka(Japan) described a carefully designed assignment for high school calculus students, who combined paper-and pencil and technology tools to deeply investigate properties of one function - chosen by each student. The experience helped students master the important connections between derivatives, concavity, and the increasing/decreasing behavior of functions.

4. J. Stupp(Israel) discussed the ability of 11th and 12th grade students to cope independently with an open-ended problem - to characterize all possible third-degree polynomial graphs. Students found the task valuable but surprisingly difficult.

5. D. Wu(USA) described various strategies for using the software Mathcad to improve learning in beginning calculus. Examples included curve sketching and finding extrema of a function on an interval; with graphical and symbolic tools at hand, students can investigate such problems more quickly and deeply than they could do otherwise.

Three key questions. In discussion, the group paid special attention to three questions:

1. *When should calculus students first meet the epsilon-delta formalism?* The topic is difficult, many people felt, especially as regards the use of quantifiers. So the topic should be delayed until at least a second encounter with calculus.

2. *How should technology be used in calculus courses?* Technology is an unavoidable fact, said many, and so will inevitably make its way into courses. But technology often makes teachers' work harder, not easier. National curricula often slow the process of integrating technology, especially in secondary schools.

3. *When is calculus best studied: in secondary school or later?* Most participants preferred to delay calculus until better basic skills have been acquired and the function concept is well understood.

Discussion of these topics among TSG 3 participants continues by e-mail. An informal TSG3 proceedings is also planned, to be distributed among participants.

TSG 4: The Teaching and Learning of Statistics

Chief Organizer: Susan Starkings(UK),
Associate Organizers: Theodore Chadjipadelis(Greece),
Michimasa Kobayashi(Japan),
Tae Rim Lee(Korea),
Local Assistant Organizer: Toshiyuki Nakano(Japan),
Liaison IPC Member: Peng Yee Lee.

The aim of this topic group was to elucidate problems, with potential solutions, involved in the teaching and learning of statistics at all levels of education. Further details of this organization can be obtained from their web site www.cbs.nl/isi/iase.htm

The format of the sessions allowed speakers to put forward their own countries, and in some cases joint countries, research findings. Many issues were brought to light with possible methods of teaching proposed. At the end of each talk delegates had the opportunity to ask the speakers questions on their presentations. These questions were not only interesting and the replies informative, but showed that the delegates at ICME have a real concerned over the way students learn statistics. Two sessions were scheduled by the ICME organizing committee. Two sessions did not appear to be enough time for all the issues raised to be fully explored, however, many delegates carried on discussions well after the sessions had ended. The speakers presented issues on a variety of topics and presented views from many different cultures. The findings from the research carried out was diverse, from many levels of education and in total added to the flavour of the sessions content and debate.

Listed here is a brief outline of the talks with the author's e-mail addresses to enable contact with the authors for further information. It is hoped that the full text will be edited and published by the International Statistics Institute on behalf of the IASE.

Session 1
Paper Title: Structural Equation Models Relating to Attitudes about Achievement in Introductory Statistics Courses: A Comparison of Results from the USA and Israel
Joe Wisenbaker, Janice Scott University of Georgia, USA & Fadia Nasser, Tel Aviv University, Israel.
Joe started off the session by giving an overview of the difficulties that many students, particularly those in the social and behavioural sciences, encounter while

taking introductory statistics courses. Those identified were classified as cognitive factors such as mathematical ability and background, and non-cognitive aspects of statistics education. Comparative results of students from Israel and the USA were then presented. It was clear that further research in this area would be desirable.

Paper Title: The Teaching and Learning of International Statistics in Transitional Country: Case of Ukraine
Ruslan Motoryn, Kiev National University of Economics, Ukraine
Ruslan presented the Ukraine's prospective in statistical education. He described the syllabus content of his country's courses. The transition from planned to market economy in areas of productive forces was described. Ruslan wanted to convey that help from developed countries was required for transitional countries to appreciate and use the techniques available. Resources in these types of countries was still very sparse and that statistical education was still of a formal nature and very mathematical in content. He was sure this was going to change in the near future. Advice form other countries would be much appreciated.

Paper Title: Conceptual Challenges Facing A-Level Statistics Students: Teacher and Examiner Perspectives
James Nicolson & Gerry Mulhern, Queen's University Belfast, UK
This study investigated students' conceptual challenges among A-Level statistics teachers and examiners. This was carried out by using a questionnaire which was either written or via semi-structured interviews. The questionnaire comprised of two sections: (1) free-response questions and (2) an attitude scale which was designed to assess agreement with specific statements regarding possible conceptual challenges. 49 participants completed the questionnaire and these results and findings were presented to the delegates.

Paper Title: How Do We Arouse Students' Interest in Statistics?
Hiroaki Hirabayashi, Osaka Women's Junior College, Japan
Hiroaki's stated that many students in his college disliked statistics and that in order to arouse students' interest appropriate teaching material needed to be developed. He outlined why it was thought that these students lost interest in statistics. This presentation centered on using computerized statistical models used for estimation purposes which proved to be entertaining. These models were very complex in their mathematical structure and that by using computers the students fear of statistics was reduced and interest in the subject was revived.

Session 2
Paper Title: The Use of a Multimedia Tool in Teaching Factor Analysis to Business School Students. Is there a Statistical Significant Improvement?
Corinne Hahn & Patrick Dassonville, Chambre de Commerce et d'Industrie de Paris, France

Corinne's presentation was about the teaching of factor analysis to students from non scientific backgrounds. This was not considered an easy task to do and that new ways of teaching this topic should be considered. The first stage in this project was to create a multimedia tool and the second was to evaluate the efficiency of this tool. Corinne gave a brief introduction on the teaching of statistics in French Business Schools and then went on to describe the pedagogical program integrating the multimedia tools developed. Two groups of students were followed one using the tool the other group using traditional teaching methods. The findings of this piece of research was describe in full outlining the advantages and disadvantages. The project overall was seen as a success and advocated the use of the multimedia tool.

Paper Title: Assessing and Fostering Children's Statistical Thinking
Graham Jones, Illinois State University, USA, Bob Perry, University of West Sydney, Australia, Ian Putt, James Cook University, Australia & Steven Nisbet, Griffith University, Australia
In this presentation Graham Jones discussed how the teams research had built and used a cognitive model to support instruction in data exploration. The talk examined the formulation and validation of a framework that described students' statistical thinking on four processes. He also described and analysed various teaching experiments with young children that used the framework to inform instruction. The teams conclusion is that more research to build learning trajectories that link different levels of children's statistical thinking identified in the framework.

Paper Title: Multimedia and Multimedia Databases for Teaching Statistics
Hans-Joachim Mittag, University of Hagen, Germany
Nowadays the use of multimedia resources and WWW supported learning environments is a crucial issue in education that was presented by Joachim. His talk was supported by his own techniques that are used in Germany. He advocates that statistics seems particularly suitable for illustrating the benefits of a multimedia based teaching. In particular the modularization of many courses bodes well in this environment. This use of animated text books with on line help is useful for students to learn at a distance. For the full potential of this technique to be usefully employed a systematic co-operation between different educational institutions, co-ordinating their development and exchanging ideas will be necessary for (a) its future development and (b) the implementation of such techniques.

Paper Title: Co-constructing Statistical Knowledge
Carolina Carvalho and Margarida Carvalho, University of Lisbon, Portugal
Carolina and Margarida's research was carried out in Portugal but the findings that were presented were certainly understood and emphasized with by delegates at the

session. The main focus of this research was to analyze peer interactions in order to understand their role in students' performances when they were solving statistical tasks. A deep analysis of their discourse was presented. The way in which students solved tasks proved to be interesting and illuminated many aspects of learning statistics. It was found that above all peer interactions was the most powerful way of implementing new strategies for solving problems. This study was supported by Portuguese educational authorities and further work into this is ongoing at the present moment in time. The authors would be more than happy to receive enquiries or other research into this area.

Summary

Common questions at the sessions focused on the following areas.

1. How much mathematics is needed to be able to do statistics?
2. Developing and transitional countries need help to move into the new realm of statistical education being advocated by developed countries.
3. That appropriate use of technology could enhance the students understanding of statistics.
4. Co-operation between educational institutions, the development and exchange of ideas is paramount to the successful implementation of multimedia resources.
5. Research, from various countries, should be presented and that knowledge gained form these studies can be used to enable educators to improve their own teaching material and methods of delivery. It was agreed by all that further research into how students learn statistics would be advantageous and that new innovative ways of teaching statistics is desirable.

A well attended topic group with much food for thought being presented and a lively discussion took place with the delegates. Unfortunately due to the political upheaval in Fiji our speaker from this country Parul Deoki could not be with us on this occasion. Similarly speakers from Argentina and Pakistan due to economic problems were unable to attend. Due to the keen interest in statistics and statistical education future ICME topic group sessions in the area of statistics is certainly advisable.

TSG 5: Teaching and Learning Aids and Materials(Hands-on) in Mathematics Education

Chief Organizers: Jin Akiyama(Japan),
Salvador Guerrero(Spain),
Associate Organizers: Mari-jo Ruiz(Philippines),
Soledad A.Ulep(Philippines),
Local Assistant Organizer: Toshinori Sakai(Japan),
Liaison IPC Member: Julianna Szendrei.

The TSG5 workshop was held on August 1 and 2, 2000 at the Chiba Institute of Technology. There were more than two hundred participants in each of the two sessions.

In keeping with the goal of TSG5, each paper discussed models that provide opportunities for experimentation and discovery in the classroom. The papers covered all levels, from basic to tertiary education. The following is a list of the speakers and a short description of the papers they presented. A brochure, containing the papers presented, was distributed to all the participants and is still available on request.

August 1, 2000

1. Title: Nonstandard Ways of Teaching Standard Mathematics II- Miscellaneous Properties of Circles -
Authors: Jin Akiyama[1], Toshinori Sakai[1], Norio Torigoe[2], and Yasuo Watanabe[1]
Affiliation: 1. Research Institute of Educational Development, Tokai University, Tokyo, Japan.
2. School of Science, Tokai University, Kanagawa, Japan
Description: The paper discusses models that can be used to teach properties of circles: the relationship between central and peripheral angles, the existence of inscribed and circumscribed circles, the Sine Theorem, the Alternate Segment Theorem, Ptolemy's Theorem, and the Addition Theorem for the Sine Function. A number of the models were actually presented during the talk.

2. Title: Practical Activities for Post-16 Mathematics
Author: Ruth Forrester
Affiliation: Edinburgh Centre for Mathematical Education,University of Edinburgh, Scotland
Description: The paper discusses a number of practical activities on a theme of parabolas for use with 16 and 17-year old pupils, covering the full range of different attainment levels. Pupil and teacher attitudes are compared: male/female,

urban/rural and Scottish/English. The ethnographic/illuminative evaluation methodology is used.

3. Title: Open-ended Problem Solving and Computer Instantiated Manipulatives (CIM)

Author: Akihiko Takahashi

Affiliation: University of Illinois at Urbana-Champaign, USA.

Description: The paper discusses research designed to explore whether Computer Instantiated Manipulatives(CIM), provided by the Internet can replace hands-on activities in order to enrich open-ended problem solving. The study focuses on a comparison between physical-manipulative based and computer-based activities.

August 2, 2000

1. Title: Lego Project --- Mediational Means for Mathematics by Mechanics

Authors: Masami Isoda[1], Akira Suzuki, Yutaka Ohneda, Masahiko Sakamoto, Naoto Mizutani[2], Nobuaki Kawasaki[3], Tatsuo Morozumi[4], Shigeki Kitajima, Norifumi Hiroi[5], Kazuhiro Aoyama[6]

Affiliations: 1. Institute of Education, University of Tsukuba, Japan.

2. The Junior High School Attached to the University of Tsukuba, Japan.

3. The Senior High School Attached to the University of Tsukuba, Japan.

4. Faculty of Education, Shizuoka University, Japan.

5. Master Program of Education, University of Tsukuba, Japan.

6. Doctor Program of Education, University of Tsukuba, Japan.

Description: This paper describes the significance of the LEGO Project, in which mechanical structures made with LEGO, represent mediational means of higher order mathematical concepts. LEGO mechanics used in this project were exhibited during the workshop period.

2. Title: Color as a Tool in Teaching Mathematics

Authors: Rene P. Felix, Reamar Eileen R. sales-Cacdac, Philippines

Affiliation: University of the Philippines

Description: The paper presents two situations where colors can be used as aids in the teaching and learning processes. First, the use of colors to clarify and illuminate concepts in the study of symmetry groups is discussed. Then, the construction of infinitely many origami tessellations from a single crease pattern, rephrased as the problem of construction in terms of colorings, is shown.

3. Title: Paper Folding for Polygons and Polyhedra

Author: Derek Holton

Affiliation: University of Otago, New Zealand

Description: This was an interactive session where participants were provided with strips of paper and taught how to make polygons and polyhedra without the use of glue.

TSG 6: Distance Learning in Mathematics Education

Chief Organizers: David Crowe(UK),
Klaus-Dieter Graf(Germany),
Associate Organizers: Seiji Moriya(Japan),
Jerry Uhl(USA),
Local Assistant Organizer: Ikuko Osawa(Japan),
Liaison IPC Member: Claudi Alsina.

TSG had two meetings, both of which were well attended. What follows is a necessarily brief summary of the talks: further details and pointers may be obtained from the TSG 6 website at http://mcs.open.ac.uk/icme.

On Tuesday (chaired by Dr.Crowe) we began with a talk by **Prof. Bernard Hodgson** of Laval university, Quebec, who described an experiment in teaching remote students(mainly prospective primary or secondary school teachers). The university and other remote centers were equipped with videoconferencing facilities(the costs being met by Laval, another university and some local sponsors). Bernard taught two full semester courses to students located 100 km from Quebec City: one was on geometry, the other on history of mathematics. At the same time the courses were taught to students on the campus at Laval. On some occasions he traveled to the remote site, so that the Laval-based students used the teleconference. In this way he was able to overcome some of the frustrations associated with lack of direct contact: but it is not clear that such a method could scale easily to larger numbers of students(his class sizes varied between 10 and 38). Despite the constraints he reported that the experiment was judged a success, and this approach is considered viable.

A joint presentation by **Prof. Masami Isoda** (Tsukuba University) and **Brian Woolacott** (Scotch College, Victoria) described collaborative problem solving tasks between 8 groups of high school students in Japan and Australia. A typical problem for 15-16 year old students involved predicting the motion of a point governed by mechanical linkages, and they were permitted to use Geometers SketchPad or Logo to assist their discussions. The project was undertaken in October-November 1999 with the participation of 66 students, between 14-16 years of age. All students enjoyed the project and wanted to continue their communication after the project had finished. Several important cultural factors were exposed. For example, before the project the Japanese students had the belief that mathematics is a common language shared throughout the world. After the project, the students had changed their minds and now believed that mathematics in Australia is different to mathematics in Japan. The results also explain how students' mathematical beliefs changed according to the quality of communication.

Dr. Tony Gardiner (Birmingham) gave a stimulating presentation in which he described experiments with the use of text for good mathematics students. He argued that text remains the most common and most portable medium for teaching and learning mathematics, and that its 'linear' structure mirrors the sequential/deductive structure of mathematical calculations and arguments. However, print struggles to incorporate "non-linear" ingredients ? such as how one begins to tackle a problem one cannot solve. Thus printed text makes it easy to present a mathematical method or solution; but has difficulty when it comes to explaining how that solution might be obtained by someone who had never met a similar problem before. In a number of books Tony has tried to overcome this traditional limitation of printed texts by choosing material in such a way that the commentary offered, or the sequence of problems presented, is compatible with the thinking processes of almost all readers, and is sufficiently convincing to carry them along. The most convincing examples to the observer are likely to be at upper secondary or undergraduate levels, where the reader may be assumed to be willing to read text. Examples were given to illustrate the above general points.

Prof. Kiyoshi Yokochi (Beijing Normal University) gave the first of a sequence of three talks that described an ongoing collaboration between schools and universities in Japan and Germany. In fact the first steps in distance learning were taken between schools in Japan, and involved students at third grade. Typical exchanges involved the construction of paper models, and the measurement of wind speed. These were later extended to solid modeling (in clay) with associated discussion of the mathematical idea of curvature. Folk culture was used as a vehicle for discussion of curvature, with students measuring curved lines on photographs of local scenes. Following the success of these experiments within Japan, the idea was extended to a collaboration between schools in Japan and Germany. The theme was 'students teach students', and one topic was Pythagoras' theorem, including several different proofs. Yet another topic was sundials, and the mathematics underlying their usefulness. As a result of these projects we know that distance learning can encourage creativity, improve the learning of mathematical ideas and moreover extend the appreciation of students for different cultures. Prof. Yokochi's talk was illustrated with some beautiful photographs and images of the students' work which, together with full details of his paper, may be seen at the TSG6 website.

Prof. Seiji Moriya (Yamagata University, Japan) continued with this theme, describing applications of the Computer, Communication and Visual(CCV) educational system in distance learning between schools in Japan, and also between Japan and Germany. A problem for investigation is identified in a collaborative context, and then work continues by iteration of (non-interactive) local lessons interspersed with communal interactive lessons. Despite some of the technical limitations of using ISDN lines, the response of students was extremely positive. Prof. Moriya advocates adapting the curriculum to promote cultural interchanges between students from different nations. He also noted that for educational research to move forwards it is necessary for teachers from universities and schools to meet 'at the same table'.

The first day was brought to a close by **Prof. Klaus-Dieter Graf** (Freie Universitat, Berlin), who added his experiences of the German-Japanese collaboration. He then gave a thoughtful summing up of the afternoon's activities which included a philosophical view of the importance in modern society of trans-national interaction and collaboration at the school level.

The Wednesday session (chaired by Prof. Graf.) was also well attended, and commenced with at talk by **Prof. Masahiro Nagai** (Japan) on the design of an environment supporting collaborative learning on school mathematics using the "distribution network". He claimed that much useful mathematical knowledge is created by collaborative learning, and that the Internet offers a way of facilitating this process. The distribution network is an environment designed to foster such active learning. Since 1998 he has installed a web-based database using the idea of Computer Supported Intentional Learning Environments(CSILE) which was developed at the Ontario Institute for Studies. Using CSILE, students choose a subject and pose questions, entering them into the database and are able to build knowledge and understanding by accessing input and participating in discussions concerning the subject. Significantly, the role of the teacher in such a process changes from provider of knowledge to guide and facilitator. This form of asynchronous collaboration was found to be cheaper and more effective than video-conferencing. The program was extended to include schools in other parts of Japan, and a fascinating variety of mathematical questions ensued. Full details may be found via the link on the TSG 6 website.

Next **Dr. Charita Luna** (Mindanao Polytechnic state College, Philippines) described her use of distance education for upgrading mathematics educators. In this study the effectiveness of videotaped lectures was compared favorably with face-to-face delivery. Despite students' views that the video technology was less satisfactory, they were able to re-view the tapes to clarify doubts. Moreover in pre- and post-tests on Logic and Set Theory the students using the videotapes were found to perform as well as those who had face-to-face lectures.

Dr. Thomas Lingefjard (University of Gothenburg, Sweden) gave an account of the SEMI project(Strategies for Examination when teaching Mathematics over the Internet). At present about 10% of in-service education at university level in Sweden is conducted by distance learning. Given the wide variety of mathematical topics that need to be covered this presents a challenge on how to conduct assessment. In particular the availability of technology (as calculator or computer) challenges the necessity (and feasibility) to examine some traditional topics. An account of the use of FirstClass as a medium for collaborative investigation was accompanied by a description of some open-ended but practical problems that may serve as a true test of attainment in the new era. A complete account of the findings of the project may be downloaded by following the link on the TSG 6 website.

Dr. David Crowe then presented an account of his work (conducted jointly with Liz Murphy) in supporting distance education students at the Open University. The OU has many students on the mainland of Europe, and distance prevents these from having access to face-to-face tuition. Electronic conferencing is seen as one way to ameliorate this, and the University uses the FirstClass system (with over 100,000 students currently online). However it is difficult to conduct a mathematical dialogue when confined to pure text, and a proposed solution is to use computer algebra documents (in this case Mathcad) as a way of enriching the exchange of messages. Preliminary data indicates that this is beneficial to both retention and success rates.

The final presentation came from **Prof. Jerry Uhl** and **Debra Woods** (University of Illinois, Urbana-Champaign) who described the distance learning aspects of the Calculus and Mathematica Program. Jerry showed some interesting examples of one of their modules on linear algebra, and mentioned some of the thinking that had gone into the pedagogic design of these modules. Debra then told us about her experience with students taking the courses, and described how the program is administered. A notable feature is that 'mentors' are drawn from those who have successfully taken modules in the past. It is also interesting to note that the program runs on a cost recovery basis, receiving no subsidy.

It is impossible to do justice to all the interesting and varied talks in such a confined space and I trust that the presenters will forgive me for having summarized their contributions in such a drastic way. However much more detail can be obtained from the TSG6 website quoted above, which will be available for the foreseeable future.

TSG 7: The Use of Multimedia in Mathematics Education

Chief Organizers: Katsuhiko Shimizu(Japan),
Gunter Krauthausen(Germany),
Associate Organizer: Xu-Hui Li(China),
Joost Klep(Nethrland),
Local Assistant Organizer: Yoshinobu Soeda(Japan),
Liaison IPC Member: Claudi Alsina.

Purposes and Scope of TSG 7:

With a rapid dissemination of digital technology in education, schools and classrooms are equipped with computers, a various kind of media. Multimedia, especially ICT, is expected to bring innovative practices, new styles and accesses in/to mathematics education. The purposes of TSG 7: The Use of Multimedia in Mathematics Education are to overview the current researches and developments on the use of multimedia in teaching and learning mathematics, and also to provide an opportunity to exchange opinions and ideas in this field. TSG 7 has dealt with following questions about sensible use of technology and multimedia in mathematics education from primary to university, pre- and in-service mathematics teacher education:

- experiences of software development,
- concrete experiences or evaluations of its use,
- merits and limits of technology and multimedia,
- theories of learning mathematics with technology.

The concept of "Multimedia" refers a broad scope of use of technology: computer with a various features, Internet, audio-visual and video technologies, broadcasting etc. TSG 7 planned to accept almost all types of above technologies, single or mixed use, real or virtual classrooms in mathematics education.

Program: TSG 7 is conducted under following program.

Plenary Lecture:

Eric Hart: *K to 12 The NCTM Standards 2000 Illuminations Website Project.*

Short Presentations:

Alena Hospesova: *Spreadsheets in Education of 10 Year Olds and Their Teachers.*

Sinikka Lindgren: *Pre-service Education for Elementary School Teachers: Mathematics and Multimedia.*

Jiye Deng: *The Networks Use of Innovative Researches and Practice in the School Mathematics Education.*

Xuhui Li: *The Use of Technology in Chinese Mathematics Education.*

Azita Manouchehri: *Technology in Secondary Mathematics Teacher Preparation: Challenges and an Alternative.*

Eliane Cousquer: *On Line University UEL http://www.univ-enligne.prd.fr in Mathematics Education.*

Tapani Jussila: *Using Mathematical CAL Software with African Students.*

Nancy Priselac and Mary Downtown: *Multimedia Enhanced College Instruction: Using Tower Activity, Graphic Calculators and Technology to Support Students Learning.*

Kwok Percy Lai Yin: *Socio-cultural Perspectives on the Integration of Information and Communication Technology (ICT) in Mathematics Education in East Asian Classrooms and Schools.*

General Discussion:

Presentation by Distribution:

Wim Matthijsse: *FlexWis, Multimedia in Mathematics Education.*

What We Learned from TSG 7:

Theme that are dealt in this TSG 7 can be categorized in followings:

1) Classroom uses in elementary and secondary mathematics education.
2) University courses in classrooms and on Web.
3) Teacher education in pre-service and in-service levels.
4) Distribution and exchange of information on mathematics education.

Also a various styles of use of multimedia are reported. These styles are followings:

1) Visual and dynamic presentation in teaching and learning, and representation of mathematical concepts.
2) Effective individualized instructions (CAI courses and Web).
3) New cognitive tools for mathematics learners.
4) Powerful dissemination tool for mathematics teachers, learners (Internet, CD etc.).

Participants in TSG 7 become to recognize the following state of use of multimedia in mathematics education based on a panel, short presentations and discussion.

1) It is observed that multimedia has become a powerful and indispensable tool in mathematics education.
2) Several innovative approaches have emerged by the use of multimedia, especially by ICT technology. The styles and approaches in teaching and learning mathematics have been changing.
3) Mathematics classes, students and teachers have started to go beyond regular classrooms and schools.

On the other hand, participants in TSG 7 also realized several problems with the uses and researches in multimedia. Many presenters have reported merits of multimedia use, but these are mainly personal impressions or expectations. Scientifically speaking, an assessment will be needed on "How better are these uses of multimedia in mathematics education, compared with traditional styles, in what points?" The researchers in this field expect and believe that Multimedia, ICT could improve mathematics education. But, even in participants, it is not easy to understand, at a glance, that "Exactly on what aspect of mathematics teaching and learning a use of multimedia does contributes". Researchers in this field should be aware of sharing and communicating an advantage and a good effect of use with others, especially with the users. In other words, a use of technology does not have demonstrated its advantage enough.

To Where We Go From ICME 9 TSG 7:
An understanding in the use of multimedia in mathematics education is deepened through this TSG 7. From children's use of spreadsheet to mathematics education on the web, from elementary level to university level, and in pre-service and in-service mathematics teacher education, multimedia has become powerful and indispensable tool in mathematics education. It is observed that innovative pedagogical approaches, new styles and accesses are made possible by the multimedia computers and Internet. The presentations of TSG 7 also revealed its advantages and limitations. Multimedia started to change the nature and the way what and how student learn and teacher teach mathematics. Researchers and developers in this field should continue to present theories and good models of multimedia use in mathematics education. Without good models and theories that explain and predict advantages and effect of using multimedia, users, that are mathematics teachers and students do not start and continue to use it in their classroom.

However, multimedia is only a tool for use to learn and teach mathematics. Therefore, a good use and a bad use depend on how and for what we use it in mathematics classes. This is the reason why this topic study group is established and maintained in ICMI activities. This endeavor should be continued in future ICMI to provide its good use to mathematics education community.

TSG 8: Vocational Mathematics Education

Chief Organizer: Clive Kanes(Australia),
Associate Organizer: Rudolf Strässer(Germany),
Local Assistant Organizer: Kosaku Sato(Japan),
Liaison IPC Member: Cyril Julie.

Discussions in this topic study group proceeded widely across matters relating to theoretical and practical interests involving vocational mathematics. However, two focal areas for study emerged strongly: curriculum development projects in the area of vocational mathematics and studies; and investigations into relationships among vocational mathematical knowledge, the curriculum and workplace. Within these areas key themes for investigation, analysis and debate in reports and discussions included:

●new curriculum programs for teaching topics in vocational mathematics
●the use of new technologies in teaching vocational mathematics (graphical calculators, multimedia tools)
●investigations concerning the institutions of vocational education and the status of vocational mathematics within these; and
●analyses of the relationship between workplace knowledge and the vocational mathematics curriculum

Papers presented engaged a variety of theoretical and analytical paradigms and techniques; some relied heavily on quantitative techniques of applied education research, others made use of ethnographic and other qualitative data. Theoretical paradigms also ranged widely.

Authors included contributions from Australia, Denmark, France, Great Britain, Sweden, and The Netherlands.

Titles of papers and authors are listed at the conclusion of this report. A brief outline of the content of presentations, organized by focal area for study (see above) follows.

Curriculum development projects in the area of vocational mathematics
Patrick Dassonville and Corinne Hahn explored the use of a multimedia tool in teaching Principal Components Analysis at the *Ecole Supérieure de Commerce de Paris*. The teaching method described provides an approach to the question to what extent we should teach the theoretical bases of the methods used in the workplace and illustrates a successful new curriculum tool in vocational mathematics.

316

Lisbeth Lindberg and Leif Maerker Bräcke reported on a curriculum development project whose aim is to improve the articulation between vocational goals and further education in mathematics in the upper secondary school within the Swedish system. This study was funded by the *Swedish National Agency for Education*.

Henk van der Kooij reported on curriculum project for vocational sector engineering students (age group 16-20) in The Netherlands. Addressing the issue that many mathematical issues taken for granted in general education are of no use in vocational settings, while other aspects of mathematics turn out to be very important, the project explored ways of addressing the particular learning needs of students. A was the integration of the graphing calculator in the learning processes of students who had a poor understanding of algebraic concepts.

Pieter van der Zwaart and Monica Wijers reported on progress of their WINST project which is currently being conducted jointly by the *Freudenthal Institute* and the *National Institute for Curriculum Development in The Netherlands*. The aim of the project is to investigate the possibilities for integration of mathematics, science and vocational subjects in pre-vocational secondary education.

Relationships among vocational mathematics knowledge, the curriculum and workplace

Cynthia Nicol reported on a Canadian case study into the integration of vocational and academic mathematics curricula at provincial and district levels. With calls for reform in mathematics programs to connect mathematics, school, and work this study examined the nature of the school-to-work connection drawing upon Dewey's idea of education through occupations. Through interviews conducted with parents, teachers, government and university representatives, multiple meanings and purposes of applied mathematics courses were found. An analysis emerged of the social processes which account for the developments and changes in the applied mathematics curriculum and point to the complexities and challenges of connecting mathematics, school, and work.

In her paper Gail FitzSimons critically analyzed a selection of curriculum documents used in Australian vocational education during recent years. Her paper argues that these documents do not adequately recognize the current realities of the workplaces for which they are intended in terms of changing technologies of production, both managerial and physical.

In their study, Geoff Wake & Julian Williams raised questions which should considered when developing mathematics curricula for both pre-vocational and vocational students. Conclusions are based on findings of how college students can (ore cannot) use mathematics to make sense of workplace practice in a range of different vocational areas. Information is obtained about mathematical thinking

317

students could find useful in the workplace. Their paper also offers insight into how mathematical content might be more effectively organized in a vocational curriculum.

In Tine Wedege's paper, the concept of qualification provided a framework for didactic reflection on the relation between adult education and work. Her study of semi-skilled workers' mathematics activities illustrated that there are systematic differences between numeracy at work and mathematics in school. Solving tasks and problems was given as an example.

In his paper Clive Kanes focused on how numerical workplace tasks are actually performed in a particular workplace context. Its main conclusions were that numerical workplace task performance is very much a local-cultural practice; and that numerical knowledge as a form of knowledge abstracted from a context of application has limited general significance for issues in vocational mathematics.

Papers presented/distributed were as follows:
Dassonville, Patrick (ESCP-EAP, France) & Hahn, Corinne (NEGOCIA, France), *Teaching Mathematics in Vocational Education at the University Level: The Case of Business School Students in France.*
FitzSimons, Gail E.(Monash University, Australia), *Text and Pretext in Vocational Mathematics Education.*
Kanes, Clive (Griffith University, Australia), *Towards the Ethics of Numerical Workplace Task Performance.*
Lindberg, Lisbeth (Göteborg University, Sweden) & Maerker, Leif (Bräcke Upper Secondary School, Sweden), *The KAM-Project.*
Nicol, Cynthia (University of British Columbia, Canada), *Mathematics Education through Occupations: Challenges of Implementing Applied Mathematics in Schools.*
van der Kooij, Henk (Freudenthal Institute, The Netherlands), *Mathematics in an Engineering's Setting: A Real Challenge.*
van der Zwaart, Pieter (National Institute for Curriculum Development (slo) Enschede, The Netherlands) and Monica Wijer, (Freudenthal Institute, The Netherlands), *The WINST-Project: Integrating Math, Science, Vocational Subjects and the Occupational Practice.*
Wake, Geoff & Williams, Julian (Centre for Mathematics Education, University of Manchester, United Kingdom), *Can Workplace Practice Inform Curriculum Design?*
Wedege, Tine (Roskilde University, Denmark), *Numeracy in Semi-skilled Jobs.*

Full papers can be obtained from the individual authors. A joint publication of the papers is under preparation. Further details are available from the CO via email from C.Kanes@mailbox.gu.edu.au

TSG 9: Mathematical Modeling and Links between Mathematics and Other Subjects

Chief Organizers: Werner Blum(Germany),
Peter Galbraith(Australia),
Associate Organizer: Iben Christiansen(Denmark/South Africa),
Local Assistant Organizer: Koji Yamazaki(Japan),
Liaison IPC Member: Mogen Niss.

Introduction

The content theme of TSG9 has played a prominent role at all ICMEs? However in reviewing developments in the field we can note shifts in emphasis within the educational debate about this topic. Some of the main trends in the eighties were summarized and discussed in Blum and Niss(1991).

Some of the main trends in the nineties have been, in our view:

(a) continued extension of the use of electronic technology (including pocket computers and graphical calculators as well as formal computing); (b) a renewed interest in philosophical and epistemological questions; (c) a focus on assessment of various kinds; (d) an increased focus on students' learning; (e) facilitating links between mathematics and other subjects.

The invited speakers addressed topics that linked with one or more of the above themes. Each session contained a period of plenary discussion, there was an initial introduction to the Topic Group in session 1, and a summing up at the end of session 2.

First session:

1. *Examples of Modeling in the School Curriculum*: Tomoko Yanagimoto (Japan)
TIMSS data indicate that high performance by Japanese students on tests is accompanied by expressed antipathy, and depressed opinions about the usefulness of mathematics. Challenges to cultivate the ability to solve realistic problems, has implications for the way in which teaching and learning is conducted. Some preliminary teaching experiments involving modeling have produced positive impacts on student perceptions regarding the usefulness of mathematics, and an increased sense of student ownership of problems.

2. *Research Studies into Students' Learning*: Jo Boaler(USA & UK) and Rudolf vom Hofe(Germany)

Boaler discussed curriculum outcomes from two schools: one of which used a traditional textbook approach, and the other open-ended projects at all times. The "project" students outperformed the "textbook" students in both examination and practical real world applications of mathematics, employing a deep conceptual understanding, in contrast to the shallower and procedural approach of the "textbook" students. It was affirmed that views and approaches adopted by students are strongly determined by the experiences and practices of learning setting.

Vom Hofe described how a computer algebra system MathView provided support for modeling real world situations-specifically involving function representation in introductory calculus. A goal of identifying characteristics of successful modellers was pursued by comparing individual learning strategies, received descriptively by students, with prescriptive conceptual models and concept images activated by the students, in the interplay between mathematics and real situations. The propensity for IT to elevate manipulation at the expense of reflection was flagged as a warning.

3. *Problems in Linking Mathematics to Other Subjects*: Henk van der Kooij (Netherlands)

In addressing philosophical and practical challenges van der Kooij drew attention to alternative ways in which variables are viewed: as pure numbers without meaning (in mathematics), as physical entities with dimensions and units on applications. Pure approaches that ignore dimensions and real entities are confusing for many students when working with applications in other subjects. A contradiction therefore exists between these two appearances of algebra, with consequences for the application of mathematics outside itself.

Second session:

1. *Assessment Developments and Issues in Mathematical Modeling Contexts*: Gloria Stillman(Australia-secondary level) and Chris Haines(UK-tertiary level).

Stillman identified two types of task that commonly appear in school-based assessment: (a) unsupervised tasks, completed over a period of time, and involving work both in school and at home, (b) supervised tasks that are conducted in class time under formal test conditions. Unsupervised tasks offer opportunities to develop full modeling ability but this is curtailed by the tendency to use high scaffolding, in which the solution pathway is structured. Such an emphasis, understandable at the outset, is disappointing when opportunities are not taken to move progressively towards greater use of more open modeling tasks. Concerns about the ownership and trustworthiness of assessment of unsupervised modeling, mean that the development of alternative assessment methods, with complementary checks on authenticity, remain a priority.

Hanes drew attention to a gap that has emerged in the scope of assessment-based studies, in that while substantial research has addressed the matter of student achievement in modeling, little attention has been paid to recognizing and assessing attainment levels of students at identifiable intermediate stages of a modeling process. With an aim of testing such skills in 20-30 minutes items were introduced and analyzed using a set of responses from groups of tertiary students to a 12-item questionnaire designed for this purpose. Analysis indicated that the items were generally robust, provided consistent results, and could contribute to an appropriate rating scale. Results are encouraging, in establishing items effective for examining the interface between the real world and a mathematical model, and between the mathematical model and its formulation, solution, and interpretation phases. Work is continuing.

2. *Theoretical and Epistemological Questions Related to Teaching Mathematical Modeling and Applications*: Stavros Papastavridis(Greece) and Morten Blomhoj & Tomas Hojgaard Jensen(Denmark).

Papastavridis shared an innovative teaching model (Context Orientated Teaching). This approach contains two components: viz Theory comprised respectively of action types (Questions, Heuristics, Concepts, Conjectures, Proofs), and Praxis. A problem is posed (taken from a practical context) and questions influenced by the context are used to direct the process. Heuristics involving a variety of approaches are applied, and concepts specific to the context may emerge. Conjectures are stimulated and their evaluation calls for the exercise of proof. The process was illustrated by an example in which exploratory work gave way to conjecture, and proof of the result for a particular case was followed by generalization. Broader issues continue to be considered, such as changing the order in which context oriented actions are invoked, and conscious variation of contexts.

Blomhoj and Jensen focused on different roles of modeling and problem solving in which each needs the other for maximum effectiveness. The two competences are mutually supportive, and it remains to achieve a balance under conditions in which time is a scarce resource. A university course based on the above theoretical complementarity was described. Students have found that modeling contexts change the nature of the mathematics and express frustration when "they don't know where they are going", but also comment that for the first time mathematics achieves meaning for them. At the same time mathematizing within models at times reveals new insights into mathematical concepts. Research invoking both sociological and cognitive perspectives is required.

Summary

Looking across the presentations we can identify several themes that have been addressed by the speakers. These include:

Goal setting: (to develop insights into experiential reality; to develop modeling competences; to learn 'pure mathematics'; to learn science; to give students focus and good experiences)

Issues of Learning: (identifying successful learning contexts; significance of situated cognition; identification of competences; meaning and beliefs)

Issues of Teaching: (supporting the development of modeling competences; using connections to other disciplines, the contribution of technology; the role of teacher beliefs)

Issues of Curriculum: (the place of modeling; role of project work)

Information and Communications Technology (ICT): (advantages and disadvantages; finding means to further enhance modeling capacities)

Issues of Evaluation: (forms of assessment; evaluation procedures; contextual factors)

Future Research

The presentations together with more than a dozen 'Papers by Distribution' imply a future research agenda that includes the following needs. Further analysis of learning and teaching to increase our understanding of how skills of modeling and applications are learned; research that connects and integrates across the different perspectives represented in the presentations; development of reliable evaluation techniques; creation and refinement of research methods to address problems in the field.

Reference:
Blum, W. & Niss, M. (1991). Applied Mathematical Problem Solving, Modeling, applications, and Links to Other Subjects-state, Trends and Issues in Mathematics Instruction. *Educational Studies in Mathematics* **22**: pp.37-68.

TSG 10: Trends in Mathematics and Mathematical Sciences: Their Reflections on Mathematics Education

Chief Organizer: Néstor Aguilera(Argentina),
Associate Organizer: Hajime Yamashita(Japan),
Local Assistant Organizer: Mariko Giga(Japan),
Liaison IPC Member: Mogen Niss.

The activities of the group centered around short presentations and discussions on them. Even with some last minute cancellations of contributions, the time resulted-as always-too short to get a better grasp of some of the ideas presented.

Serguey Pozdnyakov (Russia) gave the initial talk. Under the general title *Influence of Computer Science on Teaching Mathematics*, he presented a synthesis of very interesting papers by leading Russian researchers, among them those of M. Bashmakov on *Mathematical Education Needs Deep Mathematical Ideas*, N. Kossovski on *The language of Continuous Mathematics should be Transformed at the. Present Stage of Computer Generation*, S. Lavrov on *Applied Sciences Research Influences the Mathematics Courses more than Pure Mathematics Studies*, G. Litnitov on *Computational Mathematics should be Taught Differently*, Y. Matiyasevich on *The Appearance of Experimental Mathematics*, J. Romanovsky on *Secondary School Mathematics should be Shaped by the New Developments in Computer Science and Applications*, V. Ryzhik on *The Development of Applied Mathematics Is a General Trend which Influences Secondary School Geometry Teaching* and A. Slissenko on *Computer Science and Mathematical Education*. These and other papers were interviews done by the journal *Computer Tools in Mathematics*, as part of a special issue on occasion of the ICME 9 and the Mathematical Year. It was very interesting to notice that, unlike other countries, in Russia many computer science courses at the university level are taught within mathematics departments, thus the papers don't make a strict distinction between mathematics and computer science.

The next two talks, by Hajime Yamashita (Japan) on *Fuzzy Theory and Mathematics Education* and by Hiroshi Kanaya and Mikiharu Terada (Japan) on *Introductory Fuzzy Modeling and Secondary Education*, presented very different views on how fuzzy set theory could be used. Prof. Yamashita presented a method for instruction/cognition analysis applying fuzzy graph theory and its practical effectiveness on a case study. On the other hand, Profs. Kanaya and Terada presented concrete fuzzy electrical appliances which the secondary students build in order to introduce to them the ideas of fuzzy set theory.

On the second meeting, Mariko Giga (Japan) presented in her talk *Fractal, the Variety*, how she introduces students in medical school to fractals. According to her report, these students are excellent, like biology and are interested in mathematics, and thus it seemed appropriate to introduce them to fractals, based on the idea that these are a model of growth.

Christopher Ormell (England) gave a talk on *Some Reflections on Platonism - Titanic*, presenting some of the ideas which are more fully described in his work A new spirit in mathematics, trying to convey in the title and talk that most people don't realize that a change is needed.

The third talk, Mathematics Education in the New Curriculum in Japan (at high school), from Viewpoints of the Application of Mathematical Sciences, was elaborated by Yoichi Hirano, Akira Yamagami, Susumu Tani and Katsuhisa Kawamura (Japan). The authors reported on the aim of the reform planned by the Japanese Ministry of Education for 2002. According to the records, more than half of the children don't like mathematics, and the aim of the reform is to ameliorate this educational crisis. With the new curriculum, teachers will be asked to introduce heuristic subjects with which students can feel wonder and understand the mathematical principles experimentally.

On the other hand, the use of computer systems has been asked in almost all kinds of education and "information science" will be a subject required in high school. The authors then gave two examples in nature rich in mathematics: the Nautilus Shell (involving the logarithmic spiral) and the sunflower (involving Fibonacci numbers), proposing to study these with the help of the computer (e.g., using spreadsheets to find regression curves), and even presenting computer programs for better understanding the mathematics involved.

In conclusion, the subjects touched by the talks pointed more to the influence computers and applications of mathematics might have on the education of mathematics, rather than the influence that developments in abstract mathematics might have. Of course, this might be a biased sample, but for instance challenges as the "Millennium Prizes" of the Clay Institute were mentioned only because of the "P = NP" problem (related to computer science), and there was little mentioning of the importance of proofs on education. Instead, in the presentations there was a clear tendency on the use of computers to introduce and develop mathematical knowledge.

The chief organizer wishes to specially thank the local organizer, Prof. Yamashita, whose efforts decisively contributed to make the meetings of this group a success.

TSG 11:Problem Solving in Mathematics Education

Chief Organizers: Erkki Pehkonen(Finland),
Young Han Choe(Korea),
Associate Organiers: Jinfa Cai(USA),
Junichi Ishida(Japan),
Kaye Stacey(Australia),
Local Assistant Organizer: Toshiaki Yabe(Japan),
Liaison IPCMember: Nobuhiko Nohda.

Article

We decided on the one hand to have a panel discussion where some specialists from different parts of the world discussion on problem solving and where the audience has an opportunity to be active in the discussion. On the other hand, we wanted to offer a forum for all interested in problem solving to share their experiences. Therefore, the second session was split into parallel subsessions, in order to give enough time for everybody who wants to share their ideas orally. We though that paper sessions and oral sessions are not excluding each other, but they are complementary ways of sharing ideas. Additionally, we wanted to emphasize discussion. Such meetings are learning environments for us teacher educators, and learning takes place best when learners are actively working on the topics to be learned. In the case of adults, it mean that the sessions cannot a compound of only lectures, but there should also be possibilities for discussions.

When the conference chair asked from us a ten-line summary of the implementation of TSG-11, we concluded the following lines:

"Problem solving in teaching of school mathematics is being stressed getting more and more all over the world. The rise of the constructivist view point in learning has further increased its importance. One of the points in learning has further increased its importance. One of the points of emphasize in the TSG will be empirical research and development work done on teaching problem solving all over the world. The group will give its participants an opportunity to hear specialists' ideas on the state-of-art in problem solving and will offer them a forum to present their own ideas. Furthermore, there will be enough time for discussions, since according to the constructivist view of learning, communication forms an essential part of the learning process".

Practice of TSG 11

The two time slots (each 90 min) of TSG 11 were used, as follows: The first session which was named Problem Solving in Action was panel discussion with four specialists from different continents (Asia, Australia, Europe, North America). In the beginning, each panelist gave a short introduction (5-10min). After these introductory words, the audience had an opportunity for the rest of the time to participate with short questions and the panel with short answers.

The panelists were, as follows: Prof Jinfa Cai (USA) "Problem-Based Mathematics Instruction: Promises and Challenges in North America", Prof. Susan Leung (Taiwan) "Problem Solving in Asia", Prof. Kaye Stacey (Australia) "Trends in Researching and Teaching Problem Solving in School Mathematics in Australia", Prof. Bernd Zimmermann (Germany) "Problem solving in Mathematics Education in Europe". The chair of the panel was Prof. Erkki Pehkonen (Finland).

The second session which was named Teaching Problem Solving Around the World was planned to be an overview of problem solving implementations in different parts of the world. At the end, there were 20 participants who wanted to have an oral presentation on their experiences of problem solving teaching. Since we wanted to give everybody at least 10 min time for their presentation and 10 min for a follow-up discussion, only four presentations were able to be in one 90 min time slot. Therefore, we needed five parallel groups to meet in separate rooms.

Group 1 Group 2 Group 3 Group 4 Group 5   CHAIR: Jerry Becker(USA) CHAIR: Kaye Stacey (Australien) CHAIR: Lieven Verschaffel (Belgium) CHAIR: Barbro Grevholm (Sweden) CHAIR: Peter Sullivan (Australia) MAIN TALK: Tony Gardiner (UK) MAIN TALK: Junishi lshida (Japan) MAIN TALK: Oleg lvanov (Russia) MAIN TALK:Qiping Kong (China) MAIN TALK: Ngaiiing Wong (China) George Ekol(Uganda) Markku Hannula (Finland) Hsin-Mei Huang (Taiwan) Murad Jurdak (Lebanon) Monica Laporta (Brazil) Siew-Eng Lee (Malaya) Talma Levitan (Israel) Ikutaro Morikawa (Japan) Ban-Har Yeap (Singapore) SergeyRakov (Ukraine) Ildar Safuanov (Russia) Hah Ping Tan (Taiwan) Cholis Sa'dijah (Indonesia) Cristina Maranh A (Brazil) Juana Wilson (USA)

In a retrospective consideration, we might state that we succeeded in our plans. There was a rich variety of presentations around the world which can be seen in the table above. And it seems that the participants were satisfied. Many persons shared us already at ICME 9 their satisfaction on the implementation of TSG 11. The proceedings of the presentations in TSG 11 will be published next year (2001) in the Publication Series of Department of Teacher Education at the University of Turku (Finland). The title of the publication will be Problem Solving Around The World, and each presenter has space up to five pages and the panel members up to ten pages.

TSG 12: Proof and Proving in Mathematics Education

Chief Organizer: Paolo Boero(Italy),
Associate Organizers: Guershon Harel(USA),
Carolyn Maher(USA),
Local Assistant Organizer: Mikio Miyazaki(Japan),
Liaison IPC Member: Gila Hanna.

Preparation

In particular, all the decisions (concerning the "call for contributions", the choice of papers for oral presentation and the program of the two sessions) were shared between the Chief Organizer and the Associate Organizers.

A "call for contributions" was circulated one year in advance through different international E-mail lists (both lists concerning specialists in the field "proof and proving in mathematics education", and general lists including a great deal of mathematics educators were used). The "call for contributions" document addressed a wide spectrum of topics and perspectives, according to current trends in mathematics education research (in particular, but not only, in the field of "proof and proving"):

The TSG 12 activities will encompass the following issues:
I. The importance of explanation, justification, and proof in mathematics education;
II. Conditions for building proofs in classrooms; and
III. Long-term building of mathematical ideas related to proof making.

These issues will be considered from the following points of view:
(a) Historical and epistemological, related to the nature of mathematical proof and its functions in mathematics in an historical perspective;
(b) Cognitive, concerning the processes of production of conjectures and construction of proofs;
(c) Social-cultural aspects for student construction of proofs;
(d) Educational, based on the analysis of students' thinking in approaching proof and proving, and implications for the design of curricula.

Selected contributions will introduce discussions on the different issues.
Keeping into account this general orientation, people interested in contributing to the debate preparing the activities of TSG 12 at ICME 9 were invited to write a four-page text in English, and submit it to the Chief Organizer. Prof. N. Balacheff kindly offered the possibility of hosting contributions to TSG 12 on the IMAG website on "proof": <http ://ww-cabri.imag. fr/Preuve>.

16 contributions were received in the period December 1999-may 2001; two of them

327

were not published on the website (because their content was far from the subject of TSG 12, and/or was not suitable for an international audience). The following 14 papers (presented by authors from 10 countries) were published on the website:

Bartolini Bussi, Maria G. (Italy): *Early Approach to Mathematical Ideas Related to Proof Making.*

Bolite Frant, J. & Rabello de Castro, M. (Brasil): *Developing Proofs in Geometry: Different Concepts Build upon Very Different Cognitive Mechanisms.*

De Villiers, M. (South Africa): *Understanding of Proof within the Context of Defining Quadrilaterals.*

Douek, N. (France): *Comparing Argumentation and Proof in a Mathematics Education Perspective.*

Gravina, M.A. (Brazil): *The Proof in Geometry: Essays in a Dynamical Environment.*

Orenier, D. (France): *Learning Proof and Modeling.. Inventory of Teaching Practice and New Problems.*

Harada, K. ; Gallou-Dumiel, E.; Nohda, N. (Japan and France): *The Role of Figures in Geometrical Proof-Problem Solving-Types of Students' Apprehensions of Figures in France and Japan.*

Healy, L. (UK and Brazil): *Connections between the Empirical and the Theoretical? Some Considerations of Students' Interactions with Examples in the Proving Process.*

Maher, C. A. and Kiczek, R. (USA): *Long Term Building of Mathematical Ideas Related to Proof Making.*

Olivero, F. (Italy): *Exploring, Constructing, Talking and Writing during the Proving Process within a Dynamic Geometry Environment: what Continuity(ies)?.*

Richard, P. R. (Spain): *Figurative Inference.*

Roulet, G. (Canada): *The Legacy of Piaget: Some Negative Consequences for Proof and Efforts to Address Them.*

Sekiguchi, Y. (Japan): *Mathematical Proof, Argumentation, and Classroom Communication: A Japanese Perspective.*

Winicki Landman, G. (Israel): *Making possible the Discussion of "Impossible in Mathematics".*

In general, all the issues of the "Call for contributions" were covered by the authors (particularly the second and the third issue); all the suggested points of view were considered, sometimes more than one in the same paper. The titles of the contributions represent well the wide spectrum of research and educational interests covered by the authors: from comparative studies to long term teaching experiments, from theoretical investigations concerning the relationships between proof, proving and other mathematical activities to deep investigations about students' behaviours and attitudes.

As remarked by the Chief Organizer in his introductory talk, we may consider the Set of contributions published in the website as representative of the last years research trends in the field of "proof and proving in mathematics education"; but this does not mean that contributions repeat already published results and orientations: many original elements even surface in the list of titles!

Choice of papers for oral presentation
It was not easy to make a choice of papers to be presented orally, in order to start the debate in the two TSG 12 sessions. Indeed all papers brought some new ideas, or interesting experimental data, or original interpretations concerning phenomena related to proof and proving in the classroom.

Contributions were chosen according to the following criteria:
- diversity of countries and research paradigms (in order to cover a wide spectrum of orientations);
- novelty (in relationship with preceding, already published contributions by the same authors);
- generality (contributions addressing general ideas were preferred) ;
- level of refinement (Clear contributions addressing final results were preferred to papers reporting initial steps of promising research work);
- and, obviously, engagement in taking part in the two sessions at ICME 9 (some authors did not get funds to take part in ICME 9).

As a result, a set of five contributions were chosen for oral presentation of 20'. Keeping into account the high quality of the other contributions, presenting authors were warmly invited to take into account, during their presentations, the content of the other published papers (when related to the topics dealt with in their presentation).

Participants
Forty-eight people from 15 countries attended the two sessions (almost all the participants of the first session attended the second session). Most of them were researchers in mathematics education. More than one half were researchers engaged in the field of "proof and proving in mathematics education" or in near fields (e.g., development of argumentation in mathematics education). According to data collected during the first Session, more than one half of the participants had read most contributions published in the Website. The relatively homogeneous composition of attending people, and their research interests in the field, allowed a strong involvement of participants in discussions; apparently, both presented and discussed issues were deeply and largely shared by the audience.

First session
Paolo Boero introduced the activities, then Nadia Douek and Yasuhiro Sekiguchi

presented their papers, making substantial links with other contributions published on the Website. The following discussion concerned: the relationships between argumentation and proof in relationship with the culture of the classroom (considered from two points of view: the cultural belonging of students, depending on their sociocultural environment; and the culture developed under the guidance of the teacher); the development of the specific "Culture of theorems" in different countries; some epistemological aspects of the relationships between argumentation, proof and proving, and their educational implications; the differences between "proving an assertive statement" and "proving the impossibility of".

Second session
Lulu Healy, Denis Grenier and Regina Kiczek presented their papers; again substantial links were made to other published contributions.
The following discussion concerned various issues related to the presented papers and other published contributions: in particular, the potential (and some, possible limits) of computer environments in promoting conjecturing and proving were analyzed; different theoretical frameworks were considered and compared, in order to analyze students' behaviours; possible distinctions were suggested between different phases of the activities concerning conjecturing and proving; modeling in different mathematical and extra mathematical fields was discussed as a possible source of productive conjecturing and proving activities.

Followup
At the end of the second session people discussed some possibilities of ensuring an appropriate follow-up for the TSG 12 activities; a traditional (or electronic) volume, including the thirteen contributions published on the website in the preparation phase, was considered the most suitable initiative. The authors should extend and improve their texts, particularly in order to keep into account the ideas coming from the other published contributions and (for those attending the two sessions ? 10 authors took part in them) from the TSG 12 oral presentations and discussions. A "peer review" process shall be organized, in order to mutually cooperate in improving the texts.

TSG 13: Mathematical Learning and Cognitive Processes

Chief Organizer: Fou-Lai Lin(China-Taiwan),
Associate Organizers: Hee-Chan Lew(Korea),
Kristina Reiss(Germany),
Local Assistant Organizer: Kayo Matsushita(Japan),
Liaison IPC Member: Peng Yee Lee.

*"What is at stake in mathematics education through particular content acquisition
is the construction of this (cognitive) architecture, because it creates future
abilities of students for further learning and for more comprehensive
understanding."(Duval, 2000)*

This building of structure is what we are trying to design when we talk about cognition and learning. Hart K. opened this study group with the above citation that describes the theme of TSG 13 properly. During the two sessions of TSG 13, eight speakers from the East and West countries are selected and invited to present their studies related to the above theme. The situations about students' learning of number operations, solving quadratic equations, concepts of place-value, concept of infinite, concept of definition, mental calculation, problem solving and mathematical induction have been analyzed.

Both formal and non-formal mathematics learning were discussed. Collectively, they have presented a variety of perspectives about mathematics learning. Indeed, some cognitive architectures have been built by those studies.

Based on her philosophy that failure helps nobody, it is a waste of life, if we match what is to be learned to what a child knows and if we tailor it so that the next step is understood with confidence the child will feel in control of her mathematics and not at its mercy." Hart K. provided a piece of example from her previous research to show that when there is a gap in children's knowledge they need to fill it and the filling is reasonable to them but in mathematics it may be incorrect. Thus, designing the cognitive architecture to match the mathematics to the child becomes essential in mathematics learning.

Yu-Wu, J.Y. used mathematical induction problems as contexts to address one aspect of reasoning difficulty students have in mathematics confusion between the validity of arguments and the truth of assertions. Yu-Wu showed that this confusion is a genuine difficulty for senior high students and it is closely related to their difficulty in conceptual understanding in mathematical induction. Students with intuitive and procedural knowledge of mathematical induction still faced the conceptual difficulty.

Based on the result of her teaching experiment, Yu-Wu suggested that teaching topics such as mathematical induction and proof by contradiction through daily life examples and activities, and offering connections which catches the conceptual difficulties could help students learning these proof methods conceptually.

Tsamir P. examined primary and secondary intuitions of secondary school prospective teachers of mathematics about actual infinity. Three main types of intuitions regarding infinity were analyzed: infinity as being a single magnitude, infinity as being different magnitudes and infinites as being incomparable. Tsamir then studied the impact of two types of courses on prospective teachers, intuitions about actual infinity. One type of set theory course was the traditional Cantorian theory, and the other was designed especially for them, taking into account students, intuitive tendency to over generalize from finite to infinite sets. Tsamir showed that the primary intuitions of prospective teachers before studying Cantorian set theory are similar to those found among young students. It also showed that participation in a course where prospective teachers were aware of their intuitive ideas, of the need for consistency and of its link to formal knowledge, contributed more to their intuitive grasp of actual infinity than participation in a traditional course.

Among many East Asia countries, under the pressure of their entrance examination, there is a well-known "double school phenomenon". Majority of students go to both formal school and non-formal school for their mathematics learning. Matsushita.K. distinguished Japanese formal school mathematics from non-formal school mathematics as inquiry math and Juku Math respectively. Very often both teachers and students have to face the conflict caused by the different culture of inquiry math and juku math everyday. Matsushita observed a teacher who acted like a dilemma manager in his class. This teacher intended to generate learning as an inquiry math by covering two kind of activities, one similar to juku learning and the other similar to inquiry learning. He designed a process in which figures and symbols manipulate both are used to transform the quadratic expression into a perfect square. This activity was quite new even to the students who had seen the formula in juku. And it needed very little expertise in algebraic or computational techniques-skills in which the juku students are good. So the non-juku students were not left behind. Thus the activity could blend the two cultures together and thereby reduce the conflict.

Bills, C. reviewed the literature on structures, modality and mechanisms of mental representations and considered particularly the role of language in the development and communication of these cognitive structures. He categorized the level of generality of the students, aged 8~9, responds to mental calculation tasks as "specific", "generic" and "general". Bills found that spontaneous expression of generality has a strong association with accuracy in mental calculation. The ability to give a correct answer and articulate a generalized procedure indicates an effective mental representation that is sufficiently explicit to be expressed.

Wilson, J. tested a theory about the structure of metacognition, in terms of metacognitive functions (Awareness, Evaluation and Regulation), in an empirical study of the use of student metacognition by grade 6 students in problem solving situations. She showed that the sequences of student metacognitive behavior are predictable regardless of school, class, sex and task.

Arshavsky N. showed that Dynamic Geometry Environment (DGE) can be used to create situations that present a cognitive conflict for students. In the classroom, students were shown a quadrilateral. The vertices of the quadrilateral were dragged around, and each time the movement stopped, the students were asked to characterize and define a figure they saw on the screen. They were also asked to justify any of their conclusion. But when 3 vertices of a quadrilateral become collinear or when two sides intersect each other, the two ways of students' classification produce different results. This situation presents a cognitive conflict for students. Such cognitive conflict can be a starting point for the discussion of the role of the definition in mathematics. DGEs create ambiguities that don't exist in static environment, and so raise the question of definition quite effectively.

Learning from each other is the most important aim for educators around the world to attend ICME. Cotter J.A. observed that in the U.S. half the children in fourth grade are still learning place value concept, whereas, the East Asia children develop this concepts years earlier. She identified several Asian practices that could greatly benefit U.S. and many other children. These are minimizing counting, visualizing quantities, explicit number naming, and carefully choosing manipulatives.

Further researches to build suitable cognitive architecture for students' mathematic learning are recommended during the follow up discussion after each presentation from the participants.

Contributions: (according to the order of presentation)
Hart K.M., *Matching The Mathematics to The Child.*
Yu-Wu,J.Y, *Reasoning Difficulty in Mathematical Induction: Confusion between Validity and Truth.*
Tsamir P., *Prospective Teachers' Primary and Secondary Intuitions of Actual Infinity.*
Matsushita K., *What Dose Juku Going to Do School Mathematics Learning?*
Bills,C., *Children Mental Representations for Mental Calculation.*
Wilson J., *Assessing Student Metacognitive Behavior During Mathematical Problem Solving.*

Arshavsky N., *Attention to Variance and Invariance in A Dynamic Geometry Environment*.

Cotter J.A., *Visualization and Explicit Number Naming as A Foundation for Children's Early Work in Mathematics*.

Reference

Duval, R. (2000) , Basic Issues for Research in Mathematics Education, in Nakahara T. & Koyama M. (eds.), *Proceedings of the 24th conference of the International Group for the Psychology of Mathematics Education*, V.1, pp.55-69.

TSG 14: Constructivism in Mathematics Education

Chief Organizers: Koeno Gravemeijer(Netherland),
Jeong-Ho Woo(Korea),
Associate Organizers: Masataka Koyama(Japan),
Ema Yackel(USA),
Local Assistant Organizer: Tetsuro Sasaki(Japan),
Liaison IPC Member: Tadao Nakahara.

General orientation

The label 'constructivism' is so widely used, that some elaboration was needed to clarify what we wanted 'Constructivism in Mathematics Education' to mean for this study group. To bring some order in the wide variety of forms of constructivism we discerned three 'constructivist theories', labeled as psychological, epistemological, and pedagogical. Constructivism as an epistemological theory is grounded in the claim that all knowledge is self constructed, and does not mirror an objective reality.

Constructivism as a psychological theory builds on the notion that acquiring knowledge asks for active construction by the learner. Constructivism as a pedagogy refers to the notion of intellectual autonomy; according to this pedagogy, the role of the teacher is to help the students elaborate and expand their own constructions. These three theories do not exclude nor imply each other. The objective of this theory study group was to focus on the implications of constructivism for instructional practice (including teacher education and instructional design). Within this framework, attention was asked for the interplay between social and psychological perspectives, and for the role of symbols and language within mathematics education.

Interactive forum

During the first session, an interactive forum was held with the title
"What does constructivism in mathematics education mean for instructional practice?"
The panel consisted of:
1. Jae-Hoon Yim, Chonnam National University, Korea;
2. Christine Keitel-Kreidt, Free University of Berlin, Germany;
3. Martin Simon, Penn State University, USA.
Discussant was David Clarke, University of Melbourne, Australia.

Jae-Hoon Yim posed the question what we have to conceive of as a "constructivist classroom". He identified a variety of instructional practices that are perceived as "constructivist" by practitioners but cannot bear the scrutiny of criticism. While acknowledging that constructivism can contribute to the teaching of mathematics by letting people focus more on the process knowledge construction, Yim identified as an important shortcoming, the lack of an explanatory theory of how learning and instruction might take place according to a constructivist pedagogy.

Christine Keitel-Kreidt reported data that suggest that pre-service teachers are sensitive to a tension between the classroom practice of negotiating mathematical meaning and the demonstrable success of mathematics to model "natural phenomena." Keitel-Kreidt's other contribution was to describe her use of constructivism and other theories of learning as possible frameworks for the analysis of classroom practice. Used in this way, gaps, shortcomings, misunderstandings and unrelated and conflicting aspects within the theories are revealed in reflective discussion by the pre-service teachers.

Martin Simon et al. took the issue that was brought to the table by Yim one step further by reporting on their efforts to articulate and explicate a theoretical framework for mathematics teaching. Within this framework, they try to specify mechanisms of students' conceptual leaning and the role of teachers in promoting that learning. In relation to this, they made an inventory of "constructivist" teaching strategies. They noted that students learn some things spontaneously, through relatively unstructured inquiry lessons, or as result of a cognitive conflict, but they argue that taken together these options offer a limited repertoire. They argued that it is essential to extend this repertoire with "organizing instruction to foster reflection on particular activity-effect relationships".

David Clarke started by his comments by noting that if we are to refer to the "constructivist classroom", this must refer to "a classroom in which constructivist pedagogy is enacted"; not to "a classroom in which knowledge is constructed". He argued that what was required was a clear statement of the characteristics and goals of constructivist pedagogy. According to him, such a statement was not provided in any of the three papers, but might take this form: A constructivist classroom elicits details of student constructions, uses these constructions to advance class discussion, and takes the scaffolding of progressive refinements of these constructions as the main teacher obligation.

According to Clarke, Yim identified a most important shortcoming of discussions of constructivist pedagogy or of instructional practice derived from constructivist learning theory: The lack of clear criteria by which instructional effectiveness might be evaluated from a constructivist perspective.

In reaction to Christine Keitel-Kreidt, Clarke noted that the tension that pre-service teachers experience coincides with the challenge of reconciling constructivist conceptions of the nature of knowledge, the process whereby knowledge develops, and the means by which we facilitate that process. He further acknowledged the potential usefulness of the way in which Keitel-Kreidt tried to foster reflective discussion by the pre-service teachers, but noted that the central question of the instructional entailments of constructivism remained unanswered.

Clarke endorsed the quest for a coherent theory of instruction aligned with a theory of learning by Simon et al., in which they stress that we should foster that students begin to observe regularities in the nature of their activity and the effects that it produces. He wondered, however, about the process whereby the learner's construal of those features of activity or effect as salient can progressively come to resemble the teacher's. In relation to this, he pointed to the danger of a dichotomization of teaching and learning as distinct bodies of practice. In his opinion, teaching and learning, as they occur in classrooms, should be conceived as aspects of a common body of situated practice and studied as such.

All in all, the forum provided the occasion for some lively and useful discussion that revealed the need for clear criteria by which instructional methods might be critically compared and evaluated within the framework of a constructivist pedagogy.

Paper Presentations
The second session was devoted to four paper presentations:
Michelle Stephan, Purdue University Calumet, *USA. Features of Argumentation that Support Students' Mathematization.*
Arthur Bakker, Freudenthal Institute, Utrecht University, The Netherlands, *Constructivism Facing School Reality; Looking through the Eyes of the Students.*
Ivanka van Dijk, Bert van Oers & Jan Terwel, Free University Amsterdam, The Netherlands, *Strategic Learning in Primary Mathematics Education: Effects of an Experimental Program in Modeling.*
Auxencia Limjap, De La Salle University, Manila, Philippines, *Social and Individual Aspects of Learning: Developing Frameworks for a Deeper Understanding of School Mathematics in the Philippines.*
The paper presentations addressed: the role of the teacher, instructional design, modeling, and language within the framework of a constructivist pedagogy.

Michelle Stephan analyzed the teacher's role in supporting learning from an argumentation perspective. In her conclusion, she pointed at the use of whole-class discussions to elicit progressively sophisticated explanations, and the teacher's role in providing symbolic records or tools that can provide the teacher in opportunities to initiate shifts in the argumentation.

Arthur Bakker discussed the design of an instructional sequence on data analysis.

Reflecting on a cyclic series of small teaching experiments and (re)design activities, he pointed to the importance of shuttling back and forth between an actor's point of view and an observer's point of view.

Invaka van Dijk et al. reported on an experimental approach that aimed at the construction and use of models by the students in guided co-construction, which was contrasted with an instructional setting where students were provided with ready-made models.

Auxencia Limjap discussed the capability of the Philippine mathematics education system to absorb the CGI philosophy of teaching. In relation to this, she pointed to the important role that language proficiency plays in the CGI approach, and argued against the current bilingual policy.

The papers are available on the website http://www.f1.uu.nl/ICME9/TSG14/

TSG 15: Mathematics Education for Students with Special Needs

Chief Organizer: Sudhakar C. Agarkar(India),
Associate Organizers: Petra Scherer(Germany),
Claude Comiti(France),
Local Associate Organizer: Tetsuro Uemura(Japan),
Liaison IPC Member: Peng Yee Lee.

Session 1: Low achievement and learning disabilities

The introductory presentation of the first session "Learning Disabled, Classroom practice and Teacher Education" given by Petra Scherer (University of Bielefeld,Germany) focused on the connection between mathematics education and special education. Two important directions concerning the learning of individuals should be taken into account. On the one hand the child's learning has to be analyzed and one has to ask for consequences for mathematics education. The other direction asks if and which conclusions can be drawn for the learning of low attainers from research in (regular) mathematics education. It seems that in the past special education ignored the development, the results of research in mathematics education and that pedagogical and psychological aspects had major priority. It was pointed out that further research concerning mathematics for students with special needs and empirical work with a close connection to the didactics of mathematics is necessary.

Claude Comiti (IUFM de Grenoble et Universite Jeseph Fourier, France) spoke about "Some Hypothesis about Conditions for Support for Low Achievers". In France, schools are provided with specific organizations which take responsibility for students with special needs. For example, during primary school, if deep learning troubles are prematurely detected, children are given the benefit of additional supports, such as psychologist's help, linguistic and logico-mathematical supports. Nevertheless, national assessments show that a lot of them do not have a mastery of basic skills, neither in French language nor in mathematics. First, an assessment of the principal difficulties encountered and an analysis of them in the light of recent didactical research was given. Secondly, some hypothesis about specific conditions for support organizations to low achieving children were proposed, as for instance a change in the teacher's view of low achievers which may lead to a better understanding of the individual thinking and learning.

Elisabeth Maser Optiz (Freiburg University, Switzerland) presented a study about "Mathematical Knowledge of Children with Special Needs at the Beginning of Their School Career". This research project of the Institute for Special Education of Freiburg University evaluated the mathematical knowledge of 162 children classified as learning disabled or retarded in development at the beginning of their school career. For this purpose a special test in the form of a game was constructed fitting to the needs of those children. The results of this study were presented and discussed with regard to the traditional concepts. The study showed that most of the children managed pre-numerical tasks and moreover the numerical knowledge was much more higher than actual approaches which can be characterized by a long period of practice in the pre-numerical zone and a step-by-step progression presuppose.

"A New Method for Addition with Teaching Tools" was presented in the form of a video-tape by *Seiji Mori* & *Mami Yamashina* (members of the AZUMINO Group, Tokyo, Japan). The group made up a teaching system named "Azumino plan". The characteristics of the teaching tools for this method of addition are based on the concept of "5-2 system" which regards 10 as two 5 and uses two boxes (of five cubes each) put lengthwise. By this device, children should easily recognize 0 to 5 and 6 to 10 and understand why the new unit ten become one. It was reported that the whole process facilitates children acquire the skills of calculation.

Julie Menne (Utrecht University, The Netherlands) illustrated a training programme for (re)productive practice up to 100 "Jumping Ahead". At the Freudenthal institute a developmental research was carried out on weak students at grade 2. Purpose of the project is to develop a support programme so that at the end of one year of practice all children Can do their arithmetic up to 100 in a flexible way. The presentation gave an explanation of this training programme using several examples with the empty number-line. The interest of practice and the required principles of practice for providing a lesson which is as efficient as possible were clarified (what to train and how to do it), thereby the given support to teachers and their experiences are taken into account.

Session 2: Education of special groups

Sudhakar Agarkar (Tata Institute of Fundamental Research, Mumbai, India) presented salient features of the programme undertaken at the Homi Bhabha Centre for Science Education for socially disadvantaged students. With reference to an ongoing "Quality Improvement Programme for Ashram Schools" he described the problems faced by tribal students in learning concepts in mathematics. He then went further to discuss how institutional developments, teacher preparation and enhancement of child-child interaction help to overcome these problems. It was reported that the programme implemented in 135 Ashram Schools of the state of Maharashtra in India has led to desirable changes in teacher pupil interaction with positive effect on the scholastic achievement of the students.

Tirupalavanam Ganesh (Arizona State University, USA) made a presentation on "Special Educationally Disadvantaged Students' Access to Powerful Learning

340

Technology in Mathematics: A Conflict of Internet in Schools". He discussed a research study at a federally funded school for at-risk children in an urban setting of a large city in the south west of United States. Although the school has a majority of students declared to be 'Limited English Proficient', English is the only medium of instruction for these students. He emphasized that for the special students 'language is the key for access to mathematics Learning and Technology' and brought out the need to take into account the role of language in designing and delivering mathematics instruction as well as technology.

"Arithmetic Performance of Students with Learning Disabilities" was the title of a joint presentation by *Rene S. Parmar* (St. John's University, USA) and *Wen Fan Yan* (Indiana University of Pennsylvania, USA). Both together discussed findings of the study that examined the arithmetic computation performance of students with learning disabilities between the ages of 9 and 14 years. As compared to the performance levels of normally achieving students at the same age, students with learning disabilities scored lower on all four operations and also failed to show growth patterns across the elementary years. Algorithmic errors were more common for the special groups while higher percentage of computation error were observed for normal groups. Based on this study they had put forth four important parameters that should influence curriculum decisions: a) time of introduction of a new topic, b) choice of algorithm, c) spiral verses intensified presentation and d) discussion of commutative properties.

Sinikka Huhtala (University of Helsinki, Finland) dealt with a study undertaken in an lnstittlte of Social and Health Care with nurses and nursing students. It was found that this group is weak in mathematical skills and has difficulties in drug calculation. She observed that students' own mathematics is formed of three core categories: Previous experiences as a learner in mathematics, emotions toward mathematics and the present encounter of mathematics. It was emphasized that in any remedial programme undertaken for nurses all these aspects need to be taken care of.

"Addressing the Communication Needs of Deaf Children in Mathematics Classroom" was the topic of a presentation by *Terezinha Nunes* (Oxford Brookes University, UK). She described a project undertaken to include the teaching of mathematical ideas learned informally by hearing children and to make drawings and diagrams to represent mathematical problems. The project was designed for the teachers dealing with deaf children to promote learning of intuitive ideas connected to four target concepts: Additive composition, Additive reasoning, Multiplicative reasoning and Fraction/Ratio. Problems were represented through drawings collected in booklets. The drawings and diagrams supported communication helped the teachers to follow pupils reasoning. Assessment of this intervention was found to make normal curriculum accessible even to deaf children.

Thus in TSG 15, different aspects concerning mathematics education for students with special needs were illustrated and made obvious to the wide field of special education.

Several presentations pointed out that the mathematical abilities are not independent from other competencies (e.g., linguistic ability play an important role). The discussions however created a positive environment that the problems of students with special needs are not insurmountable. There is a scope for cross country exchange of ideas to facilitate learning of mathematics by students with special needs.

TSG 16: Creativity in Mathematics Education and the Education of Gifted Students

Chief Organizers: Hartwig Meissner(Germany),
M. Kathleen Heid(USA),
Associate Organizers: William Higginson(Canada),
Mark Saul(USA),
Local Assistant Organizer: Hideyuki Kurihara(Japan),
Liaison IPC Member: Jerry Becker.

Session 1 on "Creativity" (Chair Hartwig Meissner and William Hgginson).

An international team of specialists had prepared this session to give state-of-the-art reviews as well as to let the participants experience and discuss 'Creative Activities." Gerald Goldin (New Jersey USA) and Norma C. Pres-meg (Illinois USA) started with a survey including theoretical, psychological, social, and affective components. The emphasis on creative environments also included perspectives on representation, affect, and creativity.

After this overview a collection of "creativity problems" was distributed to pairs of participants who selected one or two of them on which to work. Participants were focused less on correct solutions than on the creative processes that arose while solving these problems. On the basis of these experiences Regina Bruder, Friedhelm Kaepnick, and Marianne Nolte (all Germany) then reflected "Needs of the Learners." They concentrated on conditions necessary for creativity in pupils: it is necessary that pupils are creative, that they want to be creative, and that they are allowed to be creative. The presenters discussed individual and social components to keywords like motivation, curiosity, self-confidence, flexibility, engagement, humour, visualization, responsibility,... or fantasy, happiness, acceptance of self and others, satisfaction, success, and so on. Their case studies reported about children who can invent and modify problems, who can listen and argue, who can define goals, who can cooperate in teams, who are active, who discover and experience, who enjoy and have fun, who guess and test, and who can laugh at their own mistakes. They have analyzed problem-solving processes used in characteristic problems: Often open ended, fascinating, interesting, exciting, thrilling, important, provoking, challenging, and problems with surprising contexts and results.

William Higginson (Canada) then analyzed "The Role of the Teacher". To summarize, there are different conceptions:
· Creativity as 'novelty' ·the teacher attempts to introduce concepts in ways that are

'different', 'unusual' or 'innovative'.
• A "creative mathematics teacher" works hard at a "hands-on" approach to learning and makes extensive use of physical materials and models.
• Creativity fits well with a.problem-solving' emphasis, the use of computer software packages, modeling and Hofstadter's idea of "Variations on a Theme". The teacher attempts to structure the leaning environment so that students have maximal opportunity to follow their own interpretations.

In the last part of Session I, speakers presented a summary of projects, examples, and problems of "Creative Mathematics." There were short reports from "Creativity Conferences" in Germany (1999 in Muenster and in Jena) and - with many contributions from the floor - from existing projects and experiences. Session 1 ended with a vivid discussion in which the approximately 70 participants exchanged ideas and experiences.

Session 2 on "Creativity and the education of the gifted" (Chair M. Kathleen Heid and Mark Saul).

Invited papers presented during the second session focused on how mathematically gifted students might be engaged in creative thinking. Papers were: The Needs of Mathematically Gifted Learners: Raising the Challenge of Academic Tasks by Camel M. Diezmann James J. Waters, and Lyn English (Queensland University of Technology, Australia);.Teaching for Mathematical Creativity by Susan Edkiins (Illinois Mathematics and Science Academy, USA), Daniel J. Heath (Minnesota Academy of Mathematics and Science, USA), and Daniel J. Teague (North Carolina School for Science and Mathematics, USA); Environment is a Global Concept.. Latvian Expen'ence) by Liga Ramana and Agnis Andzans (The universify of Latvia, Riga, Latvia); and Creative Mathematics by Tony Gardiner (United Kingdom).

Camel Diezmann and Lyn English presented four research-based strategies for providing gifted students with opportunities for higher order thinking. First, teachers can use the strategy of "problematising a task", transforming routine problems so that they are problematic. Teachers can accomplish this in a variety of ways, including requiring that students' solutions be novel applications of specific mathematical knowledge or introducing additional constraints. Second, teachers can engage students in "mathematical investigations," problem situations in which students conduct research, collaborate with peers, explore multiple strategies, and engage in open-ended inquiry. Third, teachers can use "ends-in-view" problems with their students. In these problems, although students are clear about the desired endpoint, the existing conditions are ill-defined or poorly framed. Finally, teachers can engage students in "model-eliciting activities" (e.g., recognizing number structures, identifying rates of change, and generating notational systems).

During session 2, Daniel Teague and Susan Eddins engaged the audience in a thought-provoking discussion of the role of the teacher in fostering or inhibiting creativity in students. In their paper, co-authored with Daniel Heath, the authors pointed out three roles that teachers need to play in order to foster the development of creative thinking in high school students. First, teachers need to create an environment that supports students taking risks and that views failures as opportunities to learn. Second, teachers need to recognize and appreciate creativity (knowing what skills and understandings the student brings to the task) and understand the advice, intervention, and coaching that will help students in the early stages of their potentially creative efforts. Third, teachers must have a deep understanding of mathematics and a store of appropriate problems. They need to know problems that can elicit creative solutions. The paper included descriptions of the programs at their own schools and the ways in which those programs address creativity.

Liga Ramana and Agnis Andzans spoke about the Latvian experience with encouraging the development of talent in students. In their paper, they pointed out the importance of fostering the development of two kinds of creativity: the ability to apply given rules to uncommon situations and the ability to deviate form given rules. They discussed some of the ways that they created an environment for creativity within lessons: using multi-level textbooks, supplying a great number of non-standard problems, and engaging students in problem solving in mathematics classes as well as in other disciplines. Discussing ways to foster creativity in the environment external to lessons, they described mathematical olympiad competitions, characterized by their openness at early levels, their intense competitiveness at the later levels, and their prestigious nature throughout. Opportunities exist even for students in mainly rural areas with the correspondence schools and contests. Regular courses on problem solving are offered for teachers, and degree programs are offered at The University of Latvia in "Modern elementary mathematics."

As the final speaker in Session 2, Tony Gardiner provided his insights on the needs of mathematically talented students and how those needs might be addressed. He noted the necessity of providing for students at a variety of levels of talent. His paper raised and addressed the issue of the difficulty that panted materials have in conveying the problem-solving process, alluding to ways materials could be structured to help active readers produce complete solutions on their own without explicitly leading them to solutions.

Presentations by Distribution

The Topic Study Group was further enriched by "Presentations by Distribution":
Can Akkoc (Alabama School of Mathematics and Science, USA;

Shashi Prabha Arya (Maitreyi College, New Delhi India);

Mariko Giga (Department of Mathematics Nippon Medical School, Japan);

David Ginat (Tel-Aviv University Israel);

Okamori Hirokazu (Shitenouji International Buddhism University, Japan) ;

Ji Sung Lee (Pusan Electronic Technical High School, Korea) and Boo Yoon Him (College of Education Pusan National University, Korea);

Istvan Lenart (Department of Methodology and Mathematics Instruction, Budapest, Hungary);

Keiichi Onishi (Osaka Women's Junior College, Japan), Mikihru Terada and Hiroshi Kanaya (Seifu Senior High School, Japan), and Naoyuki Masuda (Kansaisouka Jr High School, Japan);

Assadollah Razavi (Iran);

Lindkl J. Sheffield (Northern Kentucky University, USA);

Daniel J. Teague and Dorothy Doyle (North Carolina School for Science and Mathematics, USA).

TSG 17: Mathematics Education and Equity

Chief Organizer: Robyn Zevenbergen(Australia),
Associate Organizers: Luis Ortiz-Franco(USA),
Ferdinatnd Fuveria(Philippines),
Maria-Jesus Leulmo(Spain),
Local Assistant Organizer: Miho Tomada(Japan),
Liaison IPC Member: Gilah Leder.

The Equity TSG worked around a number of presentations. The initial planning for the group involved requests being sent out via various email lists seeking submissions of papers for the group. Long abstracts were sought that provided an outline of the presentation content and methodology. The abstracts that were submitted were sent to the Chief Organizer and then to the Associate and Local Assitant Organizers for review. All papers were reviewed by at least three of the organizers and recommendations were made as to their status for this group. A key criteria for inclusion in the program was that the papers must address some aspect of equity. A total of seven papers were included in the program.

Chrik Day, (South Bank University, UK)
An Activity Theory approach to Equality of Opportunity in the Teaching and Dynamic Assessment of Mathematics
Reported on a project that sought practical ways to promote equality of opportunity based on an activity theory approach to the teaching and dynamic assessment of mathematics. The work was developed with the aim of investigating the form of the steps an educational program must go through to develop practical orienting concepts. It looked at procedures that might be necessary and sufficient for developing these concepts in children with a variety of different social backgrounds.

Renuka Vithal, (University of Durban- Westville, South Africa)
Differentiation, in Opposition and Operation with Equity in a Mathematics Classroom
Using research data from a specifically arranged classroom situation to explore these theoretical ideas through the practice of project work, a special relationship between differentiation and equity, as both needing each other but also antagonistic to each other, is described and explained through the notion of complementarity. With this theme of equity and differentiation it is possible to weave a thread from the very heart of mathematics teaching and leaning, through the community of a classroom, to the society of which it is a part.

Paola Valero (Royal Danish School of Educational Studies, Denmark)

Equity in the School Organization of Mathematics Education
This presentation places equity in mathematics education in the context of the organization and functioning of mathematics teaching and leaning in the complex structure of the school. This organization refers to the basic interaction of at least four groups of actors involved in mathematics education: the administrators, the group of mathematics teachers, teachers as individuals and students. Having in mind the interaction among these four actors, equity can be defined in terms of the opportunities that such a network of relationships offers in order to fulfill democratic schooling aims, professional development among teachers and a meaningful, social-oriented learning of mathematics. Based on portraits of schools in Colombia, Denmark and South Africa, the presentation will discuss how in that organizational structure opportunities or obstacles to equity in mathematics education emerge and consolidate.

Dave Baker (University/ of Brighton, UK)
Mathematics as Social: Schooled and Community/Home Numeracy Practices
This presentation was part of the Leverhulme Numeracy Research Programme (1997-2002) investigating Low Educational Achievement in Numeracy in the United Kingdom. The intentions of the overall programme are to contribute to: understanding of the critical points in progression in primary mathematics; knowledge of how classroom practices affect attainment; identifying training and intervention strategies; understanding teacher change; understanding the effects of social factors. The intentions of the research reported are to seek explanations for underachievement in numeracy that derive from understandings of mathematics as social from a broad perspective. In our research we want to understand why some children struggle with schooled numeracies yet engage readily and easily with home/community numeracy practices. The presentation will consider some of the conceptual and methodological issues that have arisen in the research. Fieldwork in reception classes (ages 4 to 5) in three schools from very different catchment areas will be used to throw further light on issues. Possible implications for both research and schooling will be raised.

Noraini idris (University of Malaya, Malaysia)
Gender Equity and Computing in Malaysian Mathematics Classrooms: A Case Study
This paper explored the issue of gender equity in the use and access of computers in Malaysian mathematics classroom. The researcher observed the class intensively and interviewed a selected number of students, the class teacher, a principal and computer teacher. A video camera was set up at the back corner of the classroom, to enable the camera to record the whole classroom activities.

Gilah Leder, (La Trobe University Australia) and Helen Forgasz, (Deakin

University, Australia)
Mathematics: Behind the Stereotypes

For many years mathematics has been regarded as a more appropriate field of study for males than for females. Traditional measures of students' attitudes to mathematics fail to tap new concerns. The construct, mathematics as a male domain, has been considered a critical explanation for females' under-representation in the most demanding mathematics subjects offered at school and higher education, and in related careers. The Fennema-Sherman Mathematics Attitude Scales [MAS] consist of nine subscales - Mathematics as a Male Domain [MD] among them - and have been widely used to measure and compare attitudes towards mathematics. It has recently been argued that the content of some of the MD items is anachronistic and that responses to others can no longer be reliably interpreted. Two versions of a new scale, loosely based on the MD, have been developed and trialed. In this paper the authors presented results which indicate (1) changes in perceptions about some aspects of the gendering of mathematics and (2) that ethnic/cultural backgrounds influence stereotyping of some dimensions of mathematics education. The overall findings contribute an important dimension to the contemporary debate on concerns about the educational disadvantage of boys.

Nuria Planas i Raig and Nuria Gorgorio i Sold, Universitat Autonoma de Barcelona (Spain)
Is Always Mathematics Participation in the Classroom a Democratic Practice?

In 1997, the starting of a collaborative research project, MUMA[i], centered on finding more appropriate ways to teach mathematics to minority students, has developed for the whole team a great concern on the central notion of participation. A number of key questions were central to the research: Are all participations in the mathematics classroom equally legitimized? To what extent do teachers' expectations, beliefs and values interfere in the participation process of the students? Why are minority students more silent than local students when a mathematical question is posed? Is it enough to move from episodes of teacher-talk to episodes of only-certain-students-talk? In general, what does it mean a democratic discourse in the mathematics classroom? The paper presented an approach grounded on a socio-cultural view of education and on critical pedagogy.

i) This is a project funded by Fundacio Propedagogic, a Catalan foundation devoted to education, and supported by Universitat Autonoma de Barcelona.

TSG 18: Mathematics Competitions in Mathematics Education

Chief Organizers: Titu Andreescu(USA/Romania),
Claudi Deschamps(France),
Associate Organizers: Maria Falk de Losada(Colombia),
Peter Talor(Australia),
Junda Zhang(China),
Local Assistant Organizer: Yoshiaki Ueno(Japan),
Liaison IPC Member: Jerry Becker.

TSG18 was accompanied by WFNMC sessions held in the evenings. There were between 75 and 85 participants in TSG 18 and WFNMC altogether. Below you will find the list of official talks and a remark about a central issue that emerged during the proceedings.

TSG 18 First Session
Topic: *Relations between maths competitions and mathematics education.*
Andjans, Agnis and Liga Ramana: *Internet and Mathematical Competitions: Latvian Experience.*
Leder, G. and Taylor, P.: *Hobbies and Careers of Young Mathematicians Today and Yesterday.*
Dowsey, John and Bruce Henry: *Some Unsolved Problems Inspired by the Mathematics Challenge for Young Australians.*
Pederson: *Effects of self-selection of entrants on group means in the Australian Mathematics Competition.*
Pollard, Graham, Peter Taylor and Warren Atkins: *Trends in Gender Comparisons over 13 Years of the Australian Mathematics Competition.*
TSG 18 Second Session
Topic: *Competitions training experiences.*
Andreescu, Titu: *A Presentation of the American Mathematics Competitions.*
Berinde, Vasile and Becheanu, Mircea: *On Mathematical Competitions in Romania: Tradition and Continuity Mathematical Topics relating to Competition Problems.*
Soifer, Alexander: *Squares in a Square: a Cycle of Problems.*
Bellot-Rosado, Francisco: *Generalization of a Contest Problem and Two Solutions.*
Bilchev, S. and Velikova, E.: *About a Group of Geometric Transformations.*
WFNMC First Session
Gardiner, Tony: *What Should be the Goals of Mathematics Competitions and Mathematics Enrichment?*
Bankov, Kiril: *Third Junior Balkan Mathematics Olympiad.*
WFNMC Second Session

Yoshigahara, Nob: *Sliding Puzzles.*

Kenderov, Peter and Bilchev, Svetoslav: *Mathematical Winter Competitions in Mathematics, Informatics and Mathematical Linguistics.*

WFNMC Third Session

Presentation of the Paul Erdös Awards to Francisco Bellot-Rosado (present), Janos Suranyi (present) and Istvan Riemann (not present).

WFNMC Fourth Session

Topic: *Forum of Future Directions*

Dunkley, Ron; Rejali, Ali; Kenderov, Peter and Losada, Maria.

Comment:

If I were to focus on one issue that came up during the TSG18 and WFNMC proceedings, it was that of getting more teachers actively involved in mathematics competitions. (Titu Andreescu, titu@amc.unl.edu)

TSG 19: Entrance Examinations and Public Examinations in

Mathematics Education

Chief Organizer: Shigeru Iitaka(Japan),
Associate Organizers: I.K.Bansal(India),
Sin Hitotumatu(Japan),
Local Assistant Organizer: Kazutaka Sato(Japan),
Liaison IPC Member: Pen Yee Lee.

The Topics Study Group 19 was organized in order to study mathematical education to discuss entrance examinations and public examinations. This attempt was the first one in the history of ICME. The TSG 19 activities encompass the following issues:

1. In some countries, motivation of students to study mathematics is to pass university entrance examinations. Is this good or bad? Would the motivation endure in the next century?

2. Nationwide entrance examinations are also important. Math problems presented there should be examined carefully.

3. Good problems in nationwide entrance examinations will be studied.

From 1999, the web site FORUM TSG 19 was open. Since then many information and materials were presented there. Discussions were often shown in the web. The TSG 19 met for two one-and-an-hour slots at ICME 9. The list of speakers and the their topics in the TSG 19 sessions on August 2 and 3 are as follows.

Jonghae Keum (Korea): *Mathematics Problems in College Entrance Examination and Mathematics Education in Korea.*
Yeap Ban Har (Singapore): *The Advanced Level Mathematics Examinations in Singapore.*
Ren Zizhao(China): *China's College Entrance Examination and Its Impacts on Teaching and Learning in Middle School.*
Max Stephens and Mack John Michael (Australia): *Transition from school to university in Australia.*
Akio Furukawa (Japan): Time for math exam is too short.
Judit Lukacs and Klara Tompa (Hungary): *Hungarian Mathematics examination reform.*
Svetoslav Jordanov Bilchev and Emila Angelova Velikova (Bulgaria): *The Advantages of MQ-MA Examinations.*
Jack Carter , Beverly Ferrucci and S.Yanagimoto (USA,USA,Japan): *A New Testing

Method for Examining Students' Mathematical Thinking Ability.

<u>Short presentations</u>
Masahiko Beppu (Japan): *On New Test.*
Sin Hitotumatu (Japan): *On Suken (Mathematical Certification).*
Takayasu Kuwata (Japan): *The Relationship between the Entrance Examinations and the Teaching of Mathematics.*
Shigeru Iitaka (Japan): Mathematical Problems in Japanese University Entrance Examinations in Japan.
<u>Presentation by Distribution</u>

Moreover, some mathematics problems of nationwide university entrance examinations (Korea, China, Japan) and advanced level mathematics examinations and final examinations of high schools were distributed among participants, who tried to solve them.

Concluding Remarks by Jonghae Keum
In some countries like Japan, Korea, China, and Singapore, to name a few, math is an important subject for students as they must study it hard to enter a college or at least a better college in their own countries. There are fierce competitions in the college entrance examination, and students are forced to do excessive amount of drills and practices. In school math, drills are very important and make pupils skillful on simple algorithmic problems. But I like to point out that too much drills might weaken the creativity and the thinking ability of students, and make them lose their interest in math. We must design the examination to be the one measuring students' reasoning process and thinking ability. As for good students, we have to design certain ways allowing them to learn some exciting new mathematics in certain advanced level, not simply repeating the same stuff over and over again not to make a stupid error in the examination. Finally, math examination should not be a speed test, where students' mathematical thinking abilities are easily ignored, and no thinking and just rushing is required.

TSG 20: Art and Mathematics Education

Chief Organizer: Vera W. de Spinadel(Argentina),
Associate Organizer: Keming Liu(China),
Local Assistant Organizer: Tadashi Nomachi(Japan),
Liaison IPC Member: Julianna Szendrei.

The main purpose of this topic group was to gather contributions from different countries and cultures, so as to have a great display of how Art interacts with Mathematics Education.

As every TSG, we have allotted two 90-minute time slots and we organized a very nice and successful picture and models exhibition that ran parallel to them. More than forty participants chose TSG 20 as their first choice when they registered.

The first session was devoted to Visual Arts and Cultural History. The invited speakers were the following:

1) Javier Barrallo Calonge and Marfa Francisca Blanco (Spain): "Mathematical Simulation of Gothic Structures". This lecture emphasized the importance of the development of a mathematical model to analyze the complexity of a gothic cathedral. This mathematical model was elaborated in four Stages: a) knowledge of the previous history of the Structure; b) physical analysis of the materials used in the construction as well as of the atmospheric factors that could have influenced on the structural behavior; c) monitory and control process and d) measurements in situ of existing tensions at different points of the building. This methodology was applied to many gothic cathedrals at the Northern part of Spain, proving that this approach is very appropriate to teach Mathematics to Architecture students, for example.

2) Liu Keming (China): "Mathematical issues in Chinese ancient painting and drawing". Painting theory and its practice contributed greatly to Chinese art theory. The features of mathematics issues in ancient Chinese painting art are: a) some drawing tools such as rulers, compasses, etc.; b) projection means such as central projection and parallel projection and c) different scales and proportions applied in the sharp-edge paintings so as to make them meet the demands of architectural plans. During the conference, the speaker showed 50 very interesting slides to illustrate his researches.

3) Muneki Shimono (Japan): "Creating works of Art by computer programming · Teaching of the cultural history of Mathematics". Oblique projection and Perspective are not included in the geometrical education of Japanese senior high school students. Therefore, they believe that a sketch is "an outline of looking". But

drawing methods have been acquired in the past and have been developed in the history of people's untiring drawing practice). The purpose of this research is to clarify how the teaching of the cultural history of mathematics changes and improves considerably the cognition state of the students.

The second session was devoted to Mathematical education and its relation with Art. The speakers were the following:

4) Julianna Szendrei (Hungary): "Art and Mathematics in primary teachers' training". Mathematics has always been a little-liked Subject among students who begin their work at primary teachers' training colleges in Hungary. Therefore, primary teachers to be must be educated in the sense of motivating their students. This motivation could be made using art pieces as starting points for introducing and/or applying mathematics concepts, procedures, thinking methods and problem solving strategies, in a non-artificial and illuminating manner, as connected with arithmetic, algebra, geometry, combinatorics, probability and mathematics history. The art pieces shown included paintings, graphics, architecture structures, applied art and folk art.

5) Marfa Victoria Ponza (Argentina): "Mathematics and dance". The lecturer began insisting on the thesis that the use of other different languages than the verbal one is a rich experience. Geometry, for example, is a very rich field for the body language that simultaneously replevies the ludic sense: to play with the body, to dance and to discover that Geometry is alive. For that purpose, she showed a beautiful video (15 minutes) that began with the point (basic element) and ended with the body (space), passing through the line, the plane and geometrical figures. The video was based on the book "Point and line on the plane" due to Vassili Kandinsky.

6) Vera W. de SpinadeT (Argentina): "Number theory and Art". I invented a fablerelated by a strange old man: the famous Golden Mean. This curious personage introduced himself as well as part of his relatives, all of them members of the Metallic Means Family: the Silver Mean, the Bronze Mean, the Copper Mean, the Nickel Mean, etc, all the members of this family enjoy common interesting mathematical properties that indicate the existence of a promisory bridge linking the most rational scientific approaches of modern technologies and the aesthetical emotion of a piece of Art.

Finally, we had some PbyD presentations including displays at the exhibition. For example, Liu Keming exhibited more than 20 pieces of fine Chinese calligraphy and paintings of ancient China, Muneki Shimono exposed some interesting pupil's work; Kumiko Adachi (Japan) showed how to cultivate and draw out the student's ability through a mathematical picture book and a hand-made family emblem using "origami" ; Marfa Agripina Sanz (Spain) presented an analysis of Cristo de la Luz Mosque through symmetry; Tadashi Nomachi exhibited polyhedra and their linear transformations. Among them the beautiful stellated octahedron (Nomachi's Stella Octangula I and II). Besides, Akio Matsuzaki (Japan) showed how to accomplish the integration of Mathematics and flower arrangement (KADO), focusing on modeling the process of recreating a work of art.

The conclusions of this group were the following

Being the approach quite multidisciplinar, we agreed that Art, in any of its many forms, has to be used as a main tool in teaching Mathematics to ANY student, not only to students engaged in artistic studies.

TSG 21: Ethnomathematics

Chief Organizer: Ubiratan D'Ambrosio(Brazil),
Associate Organizers: Abdulcarimo lsmael(Mozambique),
Andy Begg(New Zealand),
Gloria Gilmer(USA),
Local Assistant Organizer: Shin Watanabe(Japan),
Liaison IPC Member: Tania Campos.

The idea of ethnomathematics came as a broader view on how mathematics relates to the real world. Mathematics is an intellectual instrument created by the human species to describe the real world and to help in solving the problems posed in everyday life.

Like every living individual, humans look for survival. But differently than any other species, humans look also for explanations of facts and phenomena, which can be seen and felt, and thus develop new manners of getting from nature what is needed for survival and pleasure. How do these manners differ from other species? There are many answers, which include the capability of humans developing language, tools, art, music, humor and mathematics, and looking for intellectual enhancement.

Indeed, the human species is unique among all the animal species to create agriculture: it is the only one to develop a sense of past and future, that is, to measure time; and the only species that developed language. From prehistoric ages humans have been accumulating knowledge to respond to these drives and needs. Of course, the responses vary from region to region, from culture to culture. It is clear that people living in tropical forests have developed different ways of measuring the lands than those living in a prairie, thus they have different geo[land]- metries[measurement].

Those living near the Equator perceive days and nights elapsing in the same way during the all year, while those living above the tropics recognize how the seasons affect the duration of days and nights. Thus calendrical systems, and consequently means of production and its control and distribution, of organizing labor, and many other practices which occur in daily life, have been developed, since immemorial times, in different ways, related to the natural environment. This builds up into arithmetic, which is different from culture to culture.

In the sixteenth century, European nations, beginning with Portugal and Spain and soon followed by Holland, England and France, conquered practically the entire planet and established colonies all over the World. This brought new ways and means of production and of commerce, together with new ways of doing mathematics, as well as language, religion, medicine and so many other cultural expressions.

The end of the colonial era marked the renaissance of cultures that for centuries have been ignored, in many cases forbidden. As a consequence, we have seen in recent years an explosion of new forms of art, of health care, of religions and of costumes in general. Even languages that have forgotten, sometimes forbidden, are now heard and written. And ways of doing mathematics, largely forgotten, are now being recovered. But this opened the way for the recognition of different forms of mathematics, practiced by culturally differentiated groups such as workers, farmers, artisans and professionals of various fields.

Ethnomathematics is the result of the recognition of this broad range of mathematical ideas and practices.

In lCME-9, Topic Study Group 21 met twice, in a total of 3 hours, chaired by U. D'Ambrosio. About 100 participants attended the sessions. Although the time given to the TSG was very limited, it was possible to schedule 6 short presentations, giving a broad coverage of the several strands of ethnomathematics.

After welcoming the participants and a few opening remarks, the chair gave the word to Andy Begg, of the University of Waikato, New Zealand, who delivered a paper on "Ethnomathematics: why, and what else?" The paper presented a constructivist perspective, considering the implications of enactivism and other ways of thinking on ethnomathematics. The conclusion is that the influence should be broader- that different cultural groups may have different ways of knowing, that we may be asking the wrong questions, and that we might need to consider 'ethno-education'.

The next speaker, Ana Maria Petraitis Liblik, from Curitiba, Brazil, presented a paper on "Different cultures, different ways of understanding the world", in which she relates her experience in teaching geometry through some of the cultural expressions of children from immigrant families coming from several countries.

Then Cinzia Bonotto, from the University of Padova, ltaly, spoke on "How to connect school mathematics with student's out-of-school knowledge". She presented an explorative study for which special cultural artifacts have been used, i.e. supermarket receipts, to try to construct with 9-year old pupils (fourth class of primary school) a new mathematical knowledge, i.e., the algorithm for multiplication of decimal numbers. She also discussed estimation and approximation processes which have been introduced in the lectures.

Gelsa Knijnik, from Unisinos, Brazil, presented "Building connections between ethnomathematics and popular education in a Brazilian landless movement settlement". In her paper, Knijnik focuses on the repercussions of a pedagogical project centered in the productive activities of a community of settlers. These repercussions are seen in the relations involving 14 years old students, the mathematics teacher and land surveyors, which have the governmental duty of demarcation of properties in the settlement.

"Ethnomathematics: a fundamental of instructional methodology" is the title of the paper presented by Lawrence Shirley, from Towson State University, USA. The author claims that ethnomathematics is no longer an add-on, a frill, an enrichment topic. Rather it is at the heart of instructional methodology. Teachers see their diverse classrooms and must reach out to their entire class. Beyond boosting minority interests, it is necessary to prepare majority students to work in a diverse, multicultural world, with recognition that not only the majority has or can make contributions to mathematics. Teacher education programs have incorporated study of multicultural classrooms into the Pre-Service preparation of teachers. Teachers must learn special instructional skills to accommodate different backgrounds and different learning strategies.

Tadato Kotagiri, from the University of Ryukyus, Okinawa, Japan, presented the paper "Okinawan Ethnomathematics. Warazan and Suchuma". Warazan is a knotted system, which bears some resemblance with the quipus of the Incas. Suchuma is a hieroglyphic system that is similar to the hieroglyphics in the ancient times. Both were developed more recently, in the 17th, 18th and 19th centuries. In the course of the 20th century, when public school system was established in Okinawa, these everyday practices were gradually forgotten.

Ted L. Shockey, from the University of Wisconsin-Stevens Point, USA, spoke on "Ethnomathematics of a Professional Class: Thoracic Cardiovascular Surgeons", in which he looks into the ethnomathematics of a professional class, specifically a group of thoracic cardiovascular surgeons. The research was done by observing surgeons in their performance and inquiring about mathematics involved in their practices. Shockey recognized the participant's use of tools and language that was embedded with mathematical meaning, mental problem solving, and the use of experience and intuition that were beyond busy computation.

Ample discussion followed the presentations and there was the possibility of short unscheduled presentations. Shin Watanabe, from Tokai University, Japan, spoke on the culture of Japanese mathematics as compared with those of Europe and China. Dilip Kumar Sinha and Amal R. Bhaumik, from India, presented a case study on a kind of ethnomathematics that stems from a type of games prevalent in regional rural communities of India.

359

The session closed with a mutual commitment of the participants to keep the study group active. Next opportunity for the group to get together will be during the Second International Congress on Ethnomathematics, in Ouro Preto, Brazil, in 2002.

TSG 22: Topics in Mathematics Education in Asian Countries

Chief Organizers: Fr. Bienvenido F. Nebres(Philippines),
Dianzhou Zhang(China),
Associate Organizers: Susanti Linuwih(Indonesia),
Siriporn Thipkong(Thailand),
Linquan Wang(China),
Local Assistant Organizer: Kazuyoshi Okubo(Japan),
Liaison IPC Member: Mogen Niss.

Introduction

In the last few decades, many activities and initiatives in mathematics education have nourished in the Asian region. For instance, SEACME (the Southeast Asian Conference on Mathematics Education) for Southeast Asian countries has been going on since 1978 and the last one was the 9th(held in Manila, Philippines in May 1999). Other initiatives include EARCOME (the East Asian Regional Conference on Mathematics Education) for East Asian countries, and several regular activities in Australasia and Brunei. In this light, TSG 22 focused on the nature and trends in mathematics education in individual countries, within the two main geographical blocks, and in the region as a whole. A total of 12 papers were presented and discussed during the parallel sessions. In retrospect, three main themes emerged from these discussions: (1) reports on the activities and status of mathematics education in individual countries in Asia, (2) reflections on the major differences in mathematics education between East Asia and Southeast Asia, and (3) recommendations for greater cooperation among Asian countries, and the eventual emergence of a mathematics education that is distinctly Asian (vis-?-vis Western models of pedagogy and research).

National reports on mathematics education

Let us first focus on the past and current status of mathematics education in East Asia. In "A History of Exchanges Between Japan and China on Mathematics Education Research," Izujmi Nishitani introduced the history of exchanges between these two countries--through conferences, seminars, and congresses on general mathematics education and specific areas such as history, cultural history and informatics. In "New Directions in Mathematics Education in Japan," Kazuyoshi Okubo stressed a paradox-internationally, students' achievement is evaluated as high, but self-evaluation about achievement is low. He cited a report by the Ministry of Education which revealed that most students acquire adequate mathematical knowledge, but insufficient critical thinking skills and problem solving abilities.

How about Southeast Asia? In "A Perspective of School Mathematics in

Indonesia," Susanti Linuwih reported that teacher education is a main concern, and that innovative teaching methods are already being undertaken. In "Mathematics Education in Thailand," Siriporn Thipkong gave statistics on the student population, and expounded on the need for teacher training programs to enhance mathematics education.

East Asian versus Southeast Asian emphases on mathematics education

International studies have consistently shown that East Asian students excel in mathematics achievement tests, and several papers in TSG 22 touched on this. In "Mathematics Education and Culture: The `CHC' Leaner Phenomenon", Ngai-Ying Wong stressed that East Asian achievement has been attributed to the Confucian Heritage Culture (CHC) Learner phenomenon, but that several misconceptions of this exist, including equating Chinese culture with Confucianism and collectivism. He detailed the historical background of Confucian learning, and stressed that Confucius in fact valued individualized learning (a notion quite contradictory to collectivism).

However, East Asian countries are deeply concerned about the nature of their mathematics achievement--they admit that their students have grasped the fundamentals, but fear that they lack the creativity required for more in-depth understanding and problem solving. To this end, they have proposed reforms on various fronts. In "An Open Mathematics Lesson in Shanghai," Ida Ah Chee Mok delineated the use of open-ended problems and the adaptation of an open pedagogical approach inside the classroom. She analyzed the characteristics of such a method within a.framework of variation, based on a learning theory by Western researchers, who see learning as a way of experiencing. In "Reforms in the Mathematics Curriculum in the Primary School in China," Lu Jiang stressed the need for a reformulation of the goals of mathematics education to meet the requirements of the present age in China, characterized by a market economy, information technology, and globalization. He enumerated various reforms in the curriculum, which include deleting contents which are too impractical or out of date, focusing the attention of students on practice, emphasizing integration in the methods of mathematics teaching, and introducing the calculator.

However, in Southeast Asia, the emphases of mathematics education are quite different. Southeast Asian students (except Singapore, which actually shares most of the characteristics of East Asia) do not perform as well as their East Asian counterparts in international mathematics examinations. Students (and teachers) have not quite grasped the fundamentals well enough, thus much of the effort has gone into curriculum and textbook reform, and teacher training programs. In "Mathematics Education in Southeast Asia: Major Concerns and Challenges", Fr. Bienvenido Nebres, S.J. stressed these points time and again. Linuwih and

Thipkong mentioned this in their papers. In "Some Factors in Mathematics Leaning and Teaching: Observations in Lao People's Democratic Republic," Beth Southwell raised the question of whether students learn mathematics better if the context wherein it is situated is relevant to their lives.

Learning from one another

Asian models of mathematics education (whether East Asian and Southeast Asian) have been heavily influenced by the West. This has both advantages and disadvantages, as explored by several papers. In "Some Characteristics of Mathematics Education in East Asia," Dianzhou Zhang acknowledged the achievement of Chinese students in mathematics, which can be attributed to a serious examination culture, cultural and familial motivation to exert effort, a rich tradition of calculation, and a stress on constant practice. Yet he believes that mathematics education in East Asia lags behind the West, especially in terms of the classroom environment and mathematics education research, and recommends that a balance between the East and the West may be the best approach. In "Leaning from Overseas and Keeping Our Own Characteristics in Mathematics Education", Wang Linquan essentially made the same points. He cited the duality of reforms in the National Matriculation Exam, which has been simplified and where students are now offered the opportunity to choose the assessment subject they desire. He also stressed the reforms in the program of teaching mathematics, which includes not just the content, but also the methodology and intrinsic motivation of leaning mathematics. Another instance involves national standards of school mathematics, where China studied the experiences of the USA, the UK, Russia and Japan. He concluded by saying that Chinese educators are trying to learn from the experiences of other countries-at the same time adhering to the "good points" of their own system. This call for cooperation among different cultures was echoed by Lim Chap Sam in "Cultural Differences and Mathematics Learning in Malaysia". She acknowledged that while culture can be a dubious term that encompasses many things, from ideology to technology, the main issue is not that one culture or ethnic group may be fundamentally better at mathematics teaching, learning and achievement than another, but what and how we can lean from different cultural practices, beliefs and values to help us improve mathematics leaning in all cultures.

Finally, Fr. Nebres noted that while Western approaches may have worked for the West (primarily the US, with its decentralized school system and larger resources), they have not worked too well in Southeast Asia. He reiterated the need for Southeast Asia and East Asia to learn from one another, by reflecting from his own experience in a teacher training seminar conducted in the Ateneo de Manila High School, which helped teachers think about three issues, among others: (1) their way of teaching mathematics and other ways from which they can lean best practices, inspired by viewing the TIMSS videotapes of actual classroom teaching in the US,

Germany and Japan, (2) the mathematics content in the education of future teachers, stemming from a discussion of Liping Ma's Profound Understanding of Fundamental Mathematics, and (3) how teachers and actual classroom experience can become the key elements in an incremental process of curricular and teacher-training reform, inspired by the process of Japan's Lesson Study in Stigler and Hiebert's the Teaching Gap.

Towards an Asian model of mathematics education

Based on the papers above, the TSG 22 participants conducted a lively discussion, and decided to use their electronic website (http://m.mathsci.math.admu.edu.ph) as a forum for future discussion, with a particular eye towards the joint SEACME-EARCOME conference to be held in Singapore in 2002. They have agreed to continue the dialogue, and to learn best practices in pedagogy and research from one another. These processes will certainly be enriched by Western research, but the participants have decided to critically adapt only those methods which may work in the Asian setting. The ultimate goal is to work towards the emergence of a model that is distinctly Asian.

TSG 23: TIMSS and Comparative Studies in Mathematics Education

Chief Organizers: Berinderjeet Kaur(Singapore),
Liv Sissel Gronmo(Norway),
Associate Organizers: Michael Neubrand(Germany),
Sharleen Forbes(New Zealand),
Kyung Mee Park(Korea),
Local Assistant Organiser: Tohru Tomitake(Japan),
Liaison IPC Member: Gila Hanna.

This topic study group offered participants a unique opportunity to re-look at some of the general concerns of comparative research and of the Third International Mathematics and Science Study (TIMSS) in particular. A number of individual researchers and countries having had re-analyzed data from their own perspectives presented their findings during the two 90 minutes sessions. The presentations were grouped according to themes that resulted in very thought provoking discussions. During the first session the opening address by Michael Neubrand from Germany touched on the Components of TIMSS. Following which two themes (i) Cultural Factors and Mathematics Education and (ii) Attitudes and Mathematics Outcomes were addressed. Kyung Mee Park from Korea, Pauline Vos from The Netherlands and Hsiao · Li Chi from Taiwan presented their papers touching on Cultural Factors and Mathematics Education. Constantinos Papanastasiou from Cyprus and Liv Sissel Gronmo from Norway presented their papers on their respective perspectives on Attitudes and Mathematics Outcomes. Following all the presentations during the first session, participants engaged in a discussion making reference to the presentations and also offering their own perspectives on the two themes addressed. It was interesting to note that the participants of the session were very keen to lean from each other about the wealth of research data made available by TIMSS and the research findings of different countries.

During the second session the two themes addressed were (iii) Mathematics Instruction · Teachers' and Students' Perspectives and (iv) New Challenges in Mathematics Education. Johana Neubrand from Germany, Yoshinori Shimizu from Japan and Berinderjeet Kaur from Singapore presented their papers on the theme Mathematics Instruction. Following the three papers, fifteen minutes were spent on discussing the papers and addressing comments from the participants. The second half of this session was spent on New Challenges in Mathematics Education. Michael Neubrand from Germany and David Burghes from United Kingdom spoke on PISA and International Project on Mathematical Attainment (IPMA) respectively. These are two Comparative studies on Mathematics Education that were on-going in the year of the conference. Berinderjeet Kaur from Singapore summarized the presentations of the two sessions in her closing remarks at the end of the second session.

Brief descriptions of the presentations follow:

Korean Students' High Achievement in TIMSS and Analysis of Contributing Cultural Factors by Kyung - Mee Park (Hongik University, Korea). Park in her presentation drew the attention of the participants to some of the negative aspects of Korean students' achievement in TIMSS despite their ranking second in both the Populations 1 and 2 for Mathematics in TIMSS. She claimed that there were large differences in the achievement of students from large and small cities. Korean students also exhibited the largest gender differences in mathematics scores in TIMSS. Park emphasized the teaching practices of Korean mathematics teachers and classroom environments of Korean schools that disadvantaged Korean students in their learning of mathematics. *Dutch TIMSS Results and the RME Curriculum* by F.P. Vos & W.A.J.M. Kuiper (University of Twente, Netherlands). Vos, who presented on behalf of Kuiper and herself, in her presentation highlighted that the TIMSS achievement tests did not fully match the new Dutch curriculum "Realistic Mathematics Education" (RME) yet Dutch students performed well in TIMSS. They claimed that the new curriculum has established itself well and students' performances seem to have benefited from it. *Students' Perceptions in Taiwan and New Zealand Mathematics Classrooms* by Hsiao-Li Chi (Tai-Shan Junior High School, Taiwan). Chi in her presentation shared with the participants her study that compared the teaching practices and assessment practices of mathematics teachers in Taiwan and New Zealand mathematics classrooms. A significant finding of her study is "Taiwanese teachers were more strict and forced students to study".

The Effect of Attitudes on Mathematics Education by Constantinos Papanastasiou (University of Cyprus). Papanastasiou in his presentation revealed that the TIMSS Population 2 data for Cyprus, Hong Kong, Korea, Singapore and USA show that attitudes towards mathematics did not satisfactorily predict mathematics achievement scores among students in all five countries. In Cyprus majority of students had positive attitudes towards mathematics but their achievement did not follow the same pattern. The reverse was true for Korea. Singapore was an exception, with the highest percentage of students with positive attitudes and highest mean achievement, but attitudes was found not to be the reason.

Gender Differences among Norwegian Students in Achievement, Attitudes and Self-Concepts by Liv Sissel Gronmo (University of Oslo, Norway). Gronmo in her presentation highlighted that Norway exhibited the largest gender differences in achievement in mathematics literacy in Population 3, and also the largest gender differences in attitudes in Population 2. Among the Scandinavian countries generally rather large gender differences were reported in both achievement and attitudes. These findings were discussed in relation to the culture for doing mathematics in the Scandinavian countries, and the fact that the Scandinavian countries in general seem to stress equity for women as an important goal in society.

Characteristics of Problems in the Lessons of the TIMSS-Video-Study by Johanna Neubrand (University of Lueneburg, Germany). Neubrand in her presentation shared that Japanese, German and US lessons were distinct with respect to the structure of the lessons, and in particular with respect to the selection of the problems posed during seatwork for independent work. Of interest were the geometry problems posed in the three countries; each having their unique type.

Discussing Multiple Solutions to a Problem: A Japanese Perspective on the TIMSS Videotape Classroom Study by Yoshinori Shimizu (Tokyo Gakugei University, Japan). Shimizu in his presentation discussed the distinct features of Japanese mathematics lessons that are part of the TIMSS Videotape classroom study. He mentioned that a unique feature of these lessons was discussing multiple solutions to a mathematical problem in the class as a group. The discussion was teacher led but students were pushed to their limits by the questions teachers asked and the demands made by the mathematical tasks.

TIMSS - Students' and Teachers' Perspectives on Mathematics Instruction in Singapore Schools by Berinderjeet Kaur (National Institute of Education, Singapore). Kaur in her presentation shared the findings of the Teacher and Student Questionnaires for both Populations 1 and 2 in TMSS. She disclosed that students viewed mathematics lessons in Singapore as teacher centerd with teachers almost always explaining concepts, rules and definitions. Teachers saw lesson planning as an important aspect of their teaching and relied very much on the textbooks they were using. Teachers were also very serious about homework and monitored the progress of their students carefully.

International Project on Mathematical Attainment (IPMA) by David Burghes (University of Exeter, UK). Burghes in his presentation stressed that international comparative projects can be used to inform, influence and act as catalyst for change rather than emphasize meaningless "league tables". He outlined the aims and methodology of IPMA. The overall aim of IPMA is to share good practice in all aspects of primary (and kindergarten) mathematics teaching and learning and make both national and international recommendations for good practice in primary mathematics. The methodology, in general, involves testing the pupils, collecting data using pupil and teacher surveys, interviewing the pupils and teachers, and classroom observations of mathematics lessons. Brazil, China, Czech Republic, England, Finland, Holland, Hungary, Ireland, Japan, Poland, Russia, Singapore, South Africa, Ukraine, USA, and Vietnam are participating in the project. More information about the project and its progress is available from http://www.intermep.org.

Programme for International Student Assessment (PISA) by Michael Neubrand (University of Flensburg, Germany). Neubrand in his presentation clarified the definition of mathematics competence, highlighting mathematics literacy as a basis for assessing student achievement in mathematics used in PISA. He explained that PISA emphasized students' meta-cognitive skills in their learning process and had a Cross Cultural Competence (CCC) component that included students self regulation of leaning as well as their attitudes towards the subject. 32 countries are participating in the project, that concentrate on 15 year old students. 28 of the countries are members of OECD but the remaining 4 (Brazil, Latvia, China and Russia) are not. More information about the project and its progress is available from www.pisa.oecd.org and pisa@oecd.edu.ou.

Presentation by Distribution and Reports on Working

Groups

Presentation by Distribution at WGAs & TSGs

In consideration of the very limited time for oral contributions, and of the strong demand of many participants to present their results at WGAs & TSGs, presentation by distribution(PbyD) at WGAs & TSGs which was accepted and carried out by many COs except WGA 8, TSG 4, TSG 11, TSG 17 and TSG 18.

The paper which was distributed as PbyD was consisted of two sheets of A 4 size— both sides of the sheets was alright, which could be made the paper of 4 printed pages. And actual distribution of papers for PbyD was taken place in the room of the session or around its door, and as a rule at the following time point. As for WGA, at the end of the second time-slot WGA(2), and as for TSG, at the end of the first time-slot TSG(1).

PbyD was favorably reviewed.

Reports on Working Groups

A report-back session for WGAs was introduced in a two 45 minutes time slot as shown below on the last day, where the general audience could hear the activities and results of several WGAs different from their own but of concern to them.

Place	8:30-9:15	9:25-10:10
Convention hall	Unit 1(WGA 1,2)	Unit 5 (WGA 8,9,11)
Room 201	Unit 3(WGA 3,6)	Unit 4 (WGA 7,10)
Room 301	Unit 3(WGA 4,5)	Unit 6 (WGA 12,13)

ICMI Studies

Summary Report of the ICMI Study: The Teaching and Learning of Mathematics at University Level

Michele Artigue, Derek Holton (Chair)
and Urs Kirchgraber.

The current ICMI Study on university level mathematics was commissioned for several reasons. Among these were first, that universities world-wide are accepting a much larger and more diverse group of students than has been the case. Second, although university student numbers have increased significantly, there has not been a corresponding increase in the number of mathematics majors. Hence mathematics departments have to be more aware of their students' needs in order to retain the students they have and to attract future students. Finally, university mathematicians tend to teach as they were themselves taught. Hence this Study was commissioned to provide a forum for discussing, disseminating and interchanging, educational and pedagogical ideas between and among, mathematicians and mathematics educators.

The Discussion Document for this Study appeared in the ICMI Bulletin, No. 43, December 1997. As a result of the submissions stimulated by this Document, participants were invited to attend the Study conference that took place in Singapore in December 1998. This working conference included plenary sessions, submitted papers, panel discussions and working groups. The conference and the ideas and material developed at the conference forms the basis for the Study Volume which is to be published in 2001. This material has been complemented by extra work that has been assembled since the conference.

One publication related to this Study, which is not in the general pattern of ICMI Studies, was the publication in February 2000, of a special issue of the International Journal of Mathematics Education in Science and Technology (volume 31, number 1). Papers produced for this issue were expanded versions of papers given at the Singapore conference.

The Study Volume is divided into seven sections, an Introduction, and sections on Practice, Research, Mathematics and Other Disciplines, Technology, Assessment, and Teacher Education. In each of these sections general issues are discussed and particular examples of good practice are presented. So, for example, a general discussion of research in mathematics education at the tertiary level is given in the Research section. In addition specific examples are given of research into topics such as linear algebra and calculus. In addition some possibly unexpected issues are considered. In the Introduction there is an article on equity and Teacher Education

372

includes not just the education of primary and secondary teachers but also recent initiatives in England and France to provide teacher education at the tertiary level.

The Chair of the Study, Derek Holton,
Department of Mathematics and Statistics, University of Otago, Dunedin, New Zealand (email: dholton@maths.otago.ac.nz) can be contacted for matters relating to the Study. The Study Volume can be obtained from Kluwer Academic Publishers.
All three were members of the International Programme Committee for the Study.

The Role of History of Mathematics in the Teaching and Learning of Mathematics: Presentation of the ICMI Study and the Study Book

Jan Van Maanen

The presentation of the ICMI Study Book, History in Mathematics Eductation, The ICMI Study (Dordrecht: Kluwer 2000), edited by John Fauvel and Jan van Maanen, took place on Friday, 4 August. The session was chaired by Jan Van Maanen. Those six authors of chapters who attended ICME 9, presented their respective chapters. The chair gave an overview of the other chapters and a sketch of the four years project which led to the book.

The study in the years 1996-2000

The study, about "The role of the history of mathematics in the teaching and learning of mathematics" was ordered by the Executive Committee of the International Commission on Mathematical Instruction (ICMI) at ICME-8, in Seville 1996. Fauvel and Van Maanen were invited to co-chair the study. They started their work producing a discussion document (DD) with 12 main research questions. The DD was published Spring 1997 in various journals and newsletters. The complete text is extant in the Bulletin of the International Commission on Mathematical Instruction, vol. 42 (June 1997), a shortened version can be found in L'Enseignement Mathématique vol. 43 (1997), and in various other journals. French, Italian and Greek translations became available, as was a summary in Chinese. With the help of Jean-Luc Dorier, who took care of the local organization, the co-chairs invited 70 colleagues from 29 countries for a Study Conference, which took place in Luminy (France), a week in April 1999. The chapters of the Study Book were set up at this meeting. Most of the chapters were composed by teams of authors on the basis of texts that were submitted before the meeting, mainly essays in reply to topics from the DD. The teams were coached by 11 "convenors", a process which continued during the year after the conference. The final editing of the book was done by the co-chairs, and the book was produced by Kluwer in 2000. A provisional copy was available at ICME 9, the release is planned for Autumn 2000.

Originally the co-chairs had proposed to Kluwer a different title for the Study Book, i.e., "What Engine of Wit", which had to be given up in favor of the eventual title "History in Mathematics Education". The argument for the change is obvious: the proposed title is poetic and puzzling, but it is not informative for those who search information about the role of the history of mathematics in the teaching and learning of mathematics, certainly not when they do an electronical search using key-words. Yet "What Engine of Wit" stands perfectly for the spirit of the study, and therefore it features prominently in the introduction to the book. Henry Briggs spoke these words, when in 1616 he visited the inventor of the logarithm John Napier. Briggs was so impressed by the power of the logarithm that he traveled four hundred miles north to Scotland, in order to pay his respect to Napier, as he said when he was brought into Napier's room. An account by a witness reads: "Almost one quarter on an hour was spent each beholding the other with admiration, before one spoke: at last Mr. Briggs began: "My lord, I have undertaken this long Journey purposely to see your Person, and to know by what Engine of Wit or Ingenuity you came first to think of this most excellent Help to Astronomy, viz. the Logarithms; but, my Lord, being by you found out, I wonder nobody else found it out before, when now known it is so easy."

This quotation has many layers of significance, which are worked out in the 11 chapters of the Study Book. Learners of mathematics need an Engine of Wit, and teachers should provide clues which function as such. Especially the contribution of the history of mathematics as an Engine of Wit is studied in the book. For example, does it help someone who is learning the concept of logarithm, when the necessity for this tool (think about the astronomical calculations that Briggs was referring to) is felt, when the admiration is felt when tedious multiplications are transformed by the logarithm into easy-to-perform additions? Can the original thoughts of the inventors be used? What type of historical input is possible in the classroom, and for what mathematical subjects?

Presentation of some individual chapters

After this introduction six convenors (coordinators and main authors of chapters) spoke about their chapters. An overview of the other chapters was given by the chair. Florence Fasanelli (Ch. 1) discussed the political background that underlies the position of history in mathematics curricula worldwide.

In some countries the curriculum is very strict and dictates the programme up to the level of the individual lesson, in other countries the situation is much more liberal. Sometimes history is prescribed, e.g., in Skandinavian countries, but also when this is not the case there remain possibilities to integrate history. Jan van Maanen briefly reviewed Chapters 2 to 5 (coordinated by Grugnetti, Barbin, Schubring and Radford respectively).

Some theoretical and philosophical backgrounds are discussed there, as well as the role of history in the training of mathematics teachers, a chapter (Ch. 4) which reviews the situation in many countries and presents some longer cases from selected teacher training institutions.

Karen Dee Michalowicz presented the work of her team (Ch. 6) about history for groups with special needs (primary education, under-resourced students, adults returning to mathematics education, students from minority groups, gifted students). It appears that history raises enthusiasm by offering a change of perspective. The recognition that there are people behind mathematical findings appears to be most supportive for many of the students under discussion.

Chapter 7 was composed by Abraham Arcavi and Costas Tzanakis, both present at ICME 9. Tzanakis presented an analytical exposition of the ways in which history can be brought forward in the mathematics classroom. The scope of methods discussed is wide and included in full in this report, precisely in order to indicate how many possibilities teachers have with history: historical snippets, student research projects based on history texts, primary sources, worksheets, historical packages, taking advantage of errors and alternative conceptions and the like, historical problems, mechanical instruments, experimental mathematical activities, plays, films, outdoor experiences, the WWW.

Chapters 7 and 8 were written as a kind of twins, and Man-Keung Siu presented the chapter of his team (Ch. 8) accordingly. It concentrates on the various branches of school mathematics -arithmetic, algebra, geometry, trigonometry, probability theory and statistics-, and presents a series of concrete cases for these sub-disciplines, thus supplementing the theoretical presentation of Chapter 7.

After the break Niels Jahnke (Ch. 9) argued in favor of getting in touch with mathematicians and methods from the past by reading original mathematical documents. The chapter elaborates on a number of cases and summarizes a broad collection of useful primary sources.

History fits remarkably well with today's techniques of research and presentation, as Ryosuke Nagaoka, the convenor of Chapter 10, explained. Multimedial presentation, on CD-rom or through the Internet, is most suitable, since the various aspects of history can be highlighted and related. Also mathematical dramatisation and the value of the 'new' media in teaching are amply discussed in the chapter, and the available www-resources are evaluated.

The final chapter (Ch. 11), Jan van Maanen explains, was organized by John Fauvel, co-chair of the study. Fauvel was invited to chair this presentation, but is sadly missed at ICME 9 because of a stay in hospital. The chapter presents an annotated bibliography about history in mathematics education, with sections about publications in Chinese, Danish, Dutch, English, French, German and Italian, and with descriptions of the major books and special issues of journals, all in Fauvel's magnificent style of characterizing work of colleagues in very short but rich abstracts.

Conclusion

The chair concludes the presentation of the book with a summary of its assets:
- it gives a precise description of the situation with respect to the role of the history of mathematics in the teaching and learning of mathematics throughout the world;
- it discusses the philosophical and theoretical principles behind the integration of history in mathematics education;
- it presents examples of this integration in the classroom, both with negative and with positive outcome;
- it is accessible from various perspectives: for the teacher who wants to teach a specific subject, the teacher trainer, the curriculum developer, the librarian, the educational researcher.

Over all: history is present within mathematics teaching world-wide; there are many positive results but also problems still to be solved such as the level of knowledge of the teachers and the rigidity of the curriculum in many countries.

For further details one may consult: John Fauvel & Jan van Maanen, History in mathematics eduation, Dordrecht: Kluwer, 2000.
Address of the author: maanen@math.rug.nl (University of Groningen, NL)
This report was completed after the death, on 12 May 2001, of John Fauvel. John gave the inspiration to the project, many of the concepts and words in the book are his. May the book remind us of John, and of his longing for good and human mathematics education.

Affiliated Study Groups

History of Mathematics at ICME 9

Jan van Maanen
University of Groningen

Next to WGA 13, which dealt with History and Culture in Mathematics Education, and the regular lectures by Niels Jahnke (Germany: about Historical sources in the mathematics classroom: ideas and experiences), by Osamu Takenouchi (Japan: about Some characteristic features of Wasan, the Japanese traditional mathematics) and by Ewa Lakoma (Poland: about History of mathematics in educational research and mathematics teaching - a case of probability and statistics) the history of mathematics was represented in two sessions of the International Study Group on the relations between History and Pedagogy of Mathematics (HPM).

The following colleagues presented their work:
*Bjoern Smestad (Norway) on History of mathematics in Norwegian textbooks
*Peter Ransom (UK) on Teaching geometry through the use of old instruments
*Osamu Kota (Japan) on John Perry and mathematics education in Japan
*Yoichi Hirano, Katsihusa Kawamura and Shin Watanabe (Japan) on Mathematical exhibits at museums from viewpoints of mathematics education
*Nobuki Watanabe (Japan) on A practice of the cultural history of mathematics in elementary school.

The second HPM-session was concluded by the installation of HPM's new chair for the period 2000-2004, Fulvia Furinghetti (University of Genova, Italy).

International Organisation of Women and Mathematics Education

Jo Boaler

Newsletter Editors: Megan Clark and Sharleen Forbes

At ICME 9, the International Organisation for Women and Mathematics Education (IOWME) met for four different symposia gatherings at which women and men from 24 countries came together to consider issues of equity and social justice in mathematics education. Presenters from Australia, England, Germany, Greece, Hungary, Israel, India, Japan, Singapore, the USA, Wales, and the West Indies reported upon their research findings. The sessions were extremely well attended, with members from 24 countries joining in with the debates. The symposia, organised by Leone Burton, from the UK, the outgoing convenor of IOWME, provided an extremely important forum for members to consider patterns of mathematics achievement and participation of girls and boys, women and men, and students of different cultural and social class groups across the world. All of the previous IOWME meetings have resulted in a publication and the sessions in Japan will form the basis of a book: Which Way Social Justice in Mathematics Education? This will appear in 2003 in the series for which Leone Burton is the series editor, called International Perspectives on Mathematics Education, published by Greenwood.

At the Annual General Meeting, held on August 5, 2000, from 6 pm to 7 pm the outgoing convenor Leone Burton and the outgoing editor of the newsletter, Lesley Jones (both of the UK) were succeeded by myself as convenor and Megan Clark and Sharleen Forbes (both from New Zealand) as joint newsletter editors.

Priorities for the group for the next four years continue to be: careful attention to equity, including the under-representation and participation of girls and women; and increasing the participation of members in under-represented countries to the group. The new newsletter editors are welcoming articles written in languages other than English, and they plan to publish two Newsletters a year and circulate it to all the national co-ordinators (representing 42 countries). Thanks to the recent hard work of Leone Burton and Lesley Jones, as well as many others, IOWME is still a flourishing organization within ICMI. We are gradually increasing the membership of previously under-represented countries in the world. Other ideas for the next four years that I have shared with IOWME members through the newsletter are:

To consider a changed name that reflects our broad concern for equity, beyond issues of gender, such as the international organisation for equity in mathematics education (IOEME).

To consider the introduction of a constitution, as IOWME currently has a vast number of members. This will give the organisation an official structure within ICMI and help the smooth and fair election of future officials.

International activities that will allow members from different countries to work on substantive issues together and learn about each other's countries. For example, the national co-ordinator from India has suggested that the newsletter should include a regular problem solving section that invites girls to send in solutions, that we are currently exploring.

IOWME Newsletter Volume 14, No. 2. 2

Convenor of IOWME: Jo Boaler, Stanford University, CA, USA.
MOIFEM/IOWME Bulletin/Newsletter

Psychology of Mathematics Education at ICME 9

Gilah Leder

Introduction

The International Group for the Psychology of Mathematics Education (PME) celebrates its 25th anniversary in 2001. The group was established in 1976 at ICME-3 in Karlsruhe and is an affiliated subgroup of ICMI, the International Commission on Mathematics Instruction.

The major goals of the group are:

· to promote international contacts and the exchange of scientific information in the psychology of mathematics education;
· to promote and stimulate interdisciplinary research in the aforesaid area, with the cooperation of psychologists, mathematicians and teachers;
· to further a deeper insight into the psychological aspects of teaching and learning mathematics and the implications thereof.

Membership is open to those involved in active research consistent with the aims of PME. The organisation has about 700 members from some 50 different countries. The group's main activity is its yearly conference of four or five days.

PME sessions at ICME 9

Four sessions, each of 60 minutes, were available for "show casing" the work of PME. This offered an opportunity to describe activities in which members have been engaged as well as highlighting group products completed by PME members. The presenters, and the material they covered, are summarised in Table 1.

Table 1: Overview of PME presentations

Presenter/ Coordinator	Brief description of material covered.
Paolo Boero	Reported the results of a survey of PME community research on *proof*, based on material covered in PME Plenary Lectures, Research Reports and Research Fora over the past 8 years (i.e., since ICME-7)
Gerald A Goldin	Presented a developing perspective on the role of representation, particularly internal and external systems of representation, in mathematical learning and problem solving. This work evolved during several years of activity by the PME Working Group on Representations, and appears in two consecutive special issues of the Journal of Mathematical Behavior (v. 17, Nos. 1 and 2, 1998) edited by Goldin together with Claude Janvier.

Presenter/ Coordinator	Brief description of material covered.
Simon Goodchild	Previewed a book: 'Classroom research in mathematics education: a critical discussion of methods'. The book (then still in preparation) contains a collection of accounts of research activity by members of the PME *Classroom Research* discussion and project groups. Classroom research is presented from the perspective of active researchers who are concerned to demonstrate methodological congruence between theory, inquiry, context, and methods.
Kath Hart	Described how the research expertise of the PME community is used in a wider area. Examples were provided of the way in which members have helped to inform policy and curriculum in other countries.
Barbara Jaworski	Presented issues arising from a PME Working Group which addressed research into the professional 'inservice' development of mathematics teachers, and which led to the publication of a book 'Mathematics Teaching Development: Critical International Perspectives' (Jaworski, B., Wood, T. and Dawson, S. 1999; Falmer). These issues included the role of constructivist theory in mathematics teaching development; overcoming deficit models of improving teaching; teachers and educators working together in enquiry modes to enhance teaching and teacher education. The chapters in the book show a progression of development of mathematical learning and thinking from inservice courses, through school based inservice development to teachers acting as researchers in their own classrooms, and the learning of mathematics teacher educators. Research is seen as both a means of enquiry into teaching development and a basis itself for teaching development.
Nicolina Malara	Gave a detailed overview of research reported at PME conferences over the years 1990-1999 in Plenary Lectures, Research Reports and Research Fora on *the problems in teaching and learning algebra.*
Vânia Maria Santos-Wagner	Provided an overview of the activities of the PME project group on *Research on Mathematics Teacher Development.* An overview of the book with this focus and nearing completion was also provided.

This list of research activities and projects testifies to the research productivity and diversity of the members of PME.

Gilah Leder President PME June 2001

Report on WFNMC Meeting

Peter Taylor

A new executive, a number of awards, excellent lectures and some new directions resulted from the WFNMC meeting held in Tokyo/Makuhari, in conjunction with ICME 9.

New Executive

Peter Taylor was elected President after Ron Dunkley had made known his intention to stand down. Ron was elected as Chairman of the Awards Committee, while Maria de Losada (Colombia) was elected to the vacant Vice-President position. Bulgaria's Petar Kenderov assumes the Senior Vice-Presidency, together with the Chairmanship of the Program Committee.

At the end of the General Meeting Ron Dunkley was presented with a crystal decanter, engraved with the WFNMC logo, to honor his many years of service to WFNMC since it was founded at ICME-5 in Adelaide in 1984. He was an inaugural Vice-President, founded the international conferences of WFNMC with an outstanding conference at Waterloo (WFNMC1) in 1990, filled in the gap to become President in 1996 and saw through, at his own initiative, a Constitution, which was approved in 1996.

The full list of the new Executive and various subcommittee members can be found at the WFNMC web site www.amt.canberra.edu.au/wfnmc.html.

Erdös Award Presentations

Two mathematics educators, Francisco Bellot Rosado (Spain) and Janos Suranyi (Hungary), were presented with WFNMC Erdös Awards for outstanding contribution to mathematical enrichment both in their own countries and internationally. A third mathematics educator, Istvan Reiman (Hungary), later had his award presented in Budapest by the President.

Speakers' Program

A program of excellent lectures was presented in cooperation with the ICME organizers of TSG18. Highlight was possibly the Japanese speaker Nob Yoshigahara, a puzzle creator, who showed some ideas that might also be useful in the creation of mathematics problems.

Forum on Future Directions

The last session took the form of a forum on future directions of WFNMC. Now that WFNMC has an established Constitution, it is seeking to define its role more clearly in the next few years. It also intends to articulate the role and use of competitions in mathematics education. The forum took the form of addresses by four members from different continents, followed by open discussion.

The discussion was lively and useful. One of the main results was a decision to form a task group, led by Tony Gardiner (UK) and comprising a number of members who are school teachers, to consider and report on ways in which teachers may become more involved.

Presentation of Latvian Medals
This year is the 50th year of the Latvian Mathematical Society, which decided to commemorate the year by awarding Gold Medals to a number of mathematicians who had made international contributions to their field.

In the WFNMC programme at ICME 9 four such medals were presented by Agnis Andjans and Liga Ramana, on behalf of the Latvian Mathematical Society, to four members of WFNMC, Nikolay Konstantinov (Russia), Andy Liu (Canada), Jordan Tabov (Bulgaria) and Peter Taylor (Australia).

Peter Taylor
President of WFNMC, University of Canberra, Australia

The Forum of All Chinese Mathematics Educators at ICME 9

A Report on the Forum of All Chinese Math Educators at ICME 9*

FAN Lianghuo
ZHANG Dianzhou
and GU Lingyuan

Among a large variety of programs offered at the Ninth International Congress on Mathematical Education (ICME 9) held in Tokyo/Makuhari, Japan from July 31 to August 6, 2000, was the Forum of All Chinese Math Educators. The Forum, sub-titled "Festive and Academic Gathering of Chinese Descendants and Other Interested Parties", was the first of its kind in ICME's history.

The three coordinators, FAN Lianghuo, ZHANG Dianzhou, and GU Lingyuan, met twice in March and June 2000 in Shanghai to discuss and prepare for the event. It was decided that the main purpose of the Forum would be to study the characteristics of Chinese mathematics education from an international perspective and, through face-to-face discussions, to promote communications among Chinese mathematics educators as well as academic exchanges between Chinese and international mathematics educators. Chinese mathematics education was broadly interpreted for this purpose, more from a cultural and ethnical perspective.

The Forum was programmed as a special event of the congress and had two sessions. Both sessions were very successful given that they were well received. The first session was held from 18:15 to 19:15 on August 1 and attended by about 120 people, many more than expected. The second session was held on the following day from 18:15 to 19:30, a quarter of an hour longer than scheduled, and attracted an audience of about 140 people. The participants were from Mainland China, Hong Kong, Taiwan, Singapore, Malaysia, USA, Japan, Russia, etc.

Hiroshi FUJITA, the chair of the International Program Committee (IPC) for ICME 9 opened the Forum by giving a speech at the beginning of the first session. His warm welcome was followed by four invited speeches.

WONG Ngai-Ying from Hong Kong talked about his recent work and findings on how to understand the superior academic performance of Asian students in international comparisons. He argued that "Confucian Heritage Culture" might only explain part of the successful story, and it should not be overemphasized. He suggested that the quality rather than the quantity of problems that students work through in their learning of mathematics could be another key to understanding the issue.

Jinfa CAI from the U.S. introduced a study he recently undertook. The study compared Chinese and American students' performance on mathematics problem solving. He revealed that Chinese students performed better on some routine problems, but worse on some non-routine and open-ended problems. He also found that Chinese students displayed good skills in abstract thinking while American students showed good skills in intuitive thinking.

LIN Foulai from Taiwan introduced, among others, two important issues concerning the development of mathematics education in Taiwan. The first is about curriculum reform, and the second is about how to advance mathematics education research in Taiwan. He pointed out the importance of establishing a solid foundation that pays good attention to the local context and environment for further development. For this purpose, mathematics educators in Taiwan are currently making an effort to build up a large-scale database on the teaching and learning of mathematics in schools, and they hope to exchange ideas with and receive input from other mathematics educators.

REN Zizhao from Beijing introduced some recent development in the national college entrance mathematics examination, for which he is responsible, in Mainland China. He described two general directions in the current test reform. One is that the test increased emphasises on students' ability of using mathematics to solve problems and meanwhile reduced emphasises on their memorizing mathematical facts, formulas, and so on. The other is that the test placed more emphasises on application of mathematics.

The speakers in the second session included WANG Jianpan (China), LEE Peng Yee (Singapore), Zalman USISKIN (USA), YE Qixiao (China), Igor F. SHARYGIN (Russia), Yoshiko FUJITA (Japan), Jianhua LI (USA), and WANG Shengzhi (China). The topics were extensive and diverse.

Serving on the Executive Committee of ICMI, WANG Jianpan introduced the participants to some recent as well as forthcoming ICMI studies and activities. He also discussed some issues as well as recent reform initiatives concerning mathematics teacher education at university level in Mainland China, particularly at East China Normal University, where he is president.

LEE Peng Yee described some cultural traditions of Chinese people in South East Asia. He argued that, when studying Chinese mathematics education from the cultural perspective, one should note not only similarities but also differences between the cultural tradition of Chinese people in the homeland and that in South East Asia where Chinese immigrated a long time ago.

Zalman USISKIN shared with the audience his experience of visiting China for three times and attending 8 ICMEs over the last decades and his observations about the rapid changes of society, mathematics, and modern technology during this period of time, as well as their influence on mathematics education. He emphasized the importance of using the latest technology in mathematics education to enable future generations to benefit from recent advances in the subject of mathematics.

In his speech, YE Qixiao focused on one aspect of the university mathematics education reform in the last decade in Mainland China: the teaching of mathematical modeling and application. He indicated that there has been an annual large-scale contest in mathematical modeling at university level in Mainland China since the mid 1990s, which has had a positive influence on the university mathematics education and given mathematics educators useful experiences to learn from and reflect on.

In their short speeches, Igor F. SHARYGIN, member of the ICMI Executive Committee, expressed his wish to have more exchanges and sharing of experiences between Chinese and Russian mathematics educators, and Yoshiko FUJITA shared her experience of learning Chinese language and culture, as well as her good wishes for this festive gathering.

From his experience of working and studying in both China and the United States, Jianhua LI highlighted the need for Chinese mathematics education researchers to pay more attention to fundamental issues and to use, in their research, more well established research methodology developed in other countries.

WANG Shengzhi introduced two recent major developments in mathematics education in Mainland China. The first is related to national standards for mathematics curriculum. The preliminary version of the national standards for the stage of the 9-year compulsory education was recently released for the purpose of seeking feedback. The standards for the next three years' senior high school stage, is still being developed. The second development is about a large-scale and multi-level teacher training program in Mainland China which is currently being implemented and will involve 10,000 master teachers at the national level, 90,000 at the provincial level, and 900,000 at the city or regional level. He invited the audience to contribute comments and suggestions about the two initiatives.

ZHANG Dianzhou concluded the Forum by suggesting the establishment of a coordinating group for further communication and cooperation among mathematics educators in this area of research.

As a follow-up to the Forum, the transcribed records of the speeches, mainly in Chinese but some also in English, have been made available. These presentations can be obtained by contacting FAN Lianghuo. A website focusing on Chinese mathematics education and its comparison with international mathematics education is being established at the address "http://www.nie.edu.sg/chineseforum". In addition, the proceedings of the Forum is being planned for possible publication.

To conclude this brief report, we wish to express our gratitude to the IPC and its chair, Prof. Fujita, the speakers, the participants, and all the local organizers (including especially the NOC) and helpers who made the Forum possible and successful.

* An earlier version of this report was published in the ICMI Bulletin, Issue No. 49, December, 2000.

FAN, Lianghuo
National Institute of Education, Nanyang Technological University
ZHANG, Dianzhou
Department of Mathematics, East China Normal University
GU, Lingyuan
Shanghai Academy of Educational Sciences

Secretary's Closing Remarks

Bernard R. Hodgson
Universite Laval
Secretary of ICMI

Introduction

Ladies and gentlemen, dear colleagues and friends, participants to this 9th International Congress on Mathematical Education,

ICME 9 is now coming to an end and in my capacity as the Secretary of ICMI, it is my duty and honor to take charge of this last part of the closing session of the congress.

My first words are directed to all the Japanese colleagues who have made this extraordinary event possible and who have welcomed all of us here with their warm and friendly hospitality. The quality and smoothness of the organization of ICME 9 has been highly praised by many of the participants and on behalf of the whole ICMI community I would like to express our deepest appreciation and gratitude to all those who have devoted time and energy towards the success of this quadrennial gathering. The number of people involved in the various committees and sub-committees of the organizational structure of ICME 9 makes it impossible to mention them here, and many have worked anonymously to the majority of the congress participants. But they should all be assured that their dedication and efficiency have not remained unnoticed.

*(A statement in Japanese is read by the Secretary expressing
the gratitude of the congress participants to the National
Organizing Committee, its president, Professor Hiroshi Fujita,
and the many people who supported this congress.)*

The General Assembly of ICMI, which constitutes the formal body of the Commission, met earlier this week and I was asked to report here that the delegates then unanimously adopted a resolution of thanks to the National Organizing Committee of ICME 9 for the exceptional quality of the congress infrastructure and for the graciousness with which the participants were hosted in Tokyo/Makuhari.

Our Japanese hosts should also be thanked for the remarkable support provided to some of the congress participants. It has been stated in the Second Announcement of ICME 9 that a program of grants would be offered to participants from non-affluent countries. It was then indicated that the Grant Fund would be made of two components: first, 7% of the income from regular registration fees would be devoted to the fund; and second, a sum equivalent to approximately 3% of the total of the registrations fees would come from domestic donations. It has turned out that the donations received by the NOC was substantially more, so that this second part amounted to approximately 8% of the registration fees. These funds came essentially from individual private donations, the majority of these from persons not participating in ICME 9 but wishing to support mathematics education through ICME 9. Many of these donations were of the order of ¥1000, which indicates that the number of Japanese donators was quite high. All this allowed the organizers of ICME 9 to support 96 participants coming from 37 different countries through the Grant Fund.

I have a final information about ICME 9, this one concerning the future of this event so to say. A recent tradition has been established by the last two ICME congresses to the effect of having two publications resulting from the congress. In addition to the usual Proceedings of the congress, a second volume of so-called selected lectures has also been published, these being the full texts of most of the regular lectures presented at the congress. I was asked by the organizers of ICME 9 to inform you that at this stage they are not yet in a position to confirm that such a publication will take place, and if so in which form. However regular lecturers at this congress should been informed within the next two months whether they are expected to submit a full text for this second volume.

After one week of intensive and strenuous, if not hot, work, the more than 2000 participants to ICME 9 are now familiar with the spirit and functioning of the International Congresses on Mathematical Education and have experienced how stimulating and rewarding these professional meetings can be. Possibly many of us are also aware that this ninth congress, the first one to be held in Asia, belongs to a series of events going back more than 30 years ago and held in leap years, except for the very first one:

ICME-1	(1969) Lyon	(France)
ICME-2	(1972) Exeter	(United Kingdom)
ICME-3	(1976) Karlsruhe	(Germany)
ICME-4	(1980) Berkeley	(USA)
ICME-5	(1984) Adelaide	(Australia)
ICME-6	(1988) Budapest	(Hungary)
ICME-7	(1992) Quebec	(Canada)
ICME-8	(1996) Sevilla	(Spain)
ICME-9	(2000) Tokyo/Makuhari	(Japan)
ICME-10	(2004) Copenhagen	(Denmark)
ICME-11	(2008) ?	

Since ICME-5 in Adelaide, the overall format of the ICME congresses has been rather similar from one to the other to quite a large extent: in addition to a few plenary lectures, the core of the program is formed by a substantial set of so-called regular lectures together with interactive (more or less) small group activities in what were designated here as Working Groups for Action and Topic Study Groups. All this is complemented by activities of various types: short presentations, national presentations, reports on ICMI Studies, sessions of ICMI Affiliated Study Groups, etc. A very special ingredient of this ninth ICME was the International Round Table held on the opening day and which constituted a vivid existence proof of the feasibility, if not cheapness, of multisite international videoconferencing.

A new team of collaborators has already started the preparation of the next ICME and it would be important to provide them with your observations, concerns and proposals on both the structure and the content of the ICME congresses. You are thus invited to convey your comments and suggestions to me at your earliest convenience, by letter, fax or e-mail:

Prof. Bernard R. Hodgson
ICMI Secretary
Departement de mathématiques et de statistique
Universite Laval
Quebec   G1K 7P4   Canada
fax: +1 418 656 2817
e-mail: bhodgson@mat.ulaval.ca

What is ICMI?

The ICME congresses are held on behalf of and under the auspices of ICMI, the International Commission on Mathematical Instruction. But the ICMEs are not organized by the Commission itself, its direct role being the selection of a site and the appointment of an International Program Committee, including representatives of ICMI. The Commission has a long history going back to the beginning of this century, as it was first established at the International Congress of Mathematicians held in Rome in 1908 - the eleventh ICME congress will thus coincide with the centennial of the Commission. The first President of ICMI was Felix Klein and its first Secretary-General was Henri Fehr.

After an interruption of activity between the two World Wars, ICMI was reconstituted in 1952, at a time when the international mathematical community was being reorganized, as an official commission of the International Mathematical Union, IMU. Thus, the Terms of Reference of ICMI are established by the General

393

Assembly of IMU, which is also responsible for the election of the Executive Committee of the Commission. Furthermore, the far majority of the funding of ICMI comes from IMU. I should also add that via the International Mathematical Union, ICMI belongs to ICSU, the International Council of Scientific Union, whose president Professor Hiroyuki Yoshikawa, also president of the Science Council of Japan, greeted us during the opening ceremony of this congress. This affiliation implies that ICMI is to abide to the ICSU statutes, one of which establishes the principle of non-discrimination. This principle affirms the right and freedom of scientists to associate in international scientific activities regardless of citizenship, religion, political stance, ethnic origin, sex, and suchlike. But apart from observing general IMU and ICSU rules and principles, ICMI is fully autonomous in its work.

As in the case of IMU, the members of ICMI are not individuals but states, most of which, but not all, are also members of IMU. There are currently 80 members of ICMI, each them being requested to designate a National Representative to ICMI. Together with the Executive Committee members, these National Representatives form the General Assembly of ICMI, a body which met earlier this week. The current four-year term of the Executive Committee runs until the end of 2002.

ICMEs

I would like to review with you briefly the main activities undertaken by ICMI. The most extensive of these activities are doubtless the International Congresses on Mathematical Education, the tenth of which will be held in 2004. The following information is now familiar to most of you, but it is my pleasure to officially announce to this Assembly that the Executive Committee of ICMI has accepted the invitation received from the Danish ICMI Committee to hold ICME-10 in Copenhagen on July 4 to 11, 2004. This congress will be organized in close collaboration between the Nordic countries Denmark, Finland, Iceland, Norway and Sweden - such a cooperative model being a first in the history of ICMI. Professor Carl Winslow from Denmark, member of the Local Organizing Committee, Professor Anna Kristjansdottir from Iceland, member of the Nordic Contact Committee, and Professor Mogens Niss from Denmark, chair of the International Program Committee, will now present to you a Nordic invitation. (An invitation is presented by the Nordic countries to the mathematics education community to gather in Copenhagen in 2004.)

With ICME-10 already well on its way, it is now time to start thinking of the following congress, ICME-11, to be held in 2008, the year of the centennial of the Commission. The ICMI Executive Committee is thus launching to all its member states an official call for bids to host the eleventh ICME. As the task of organizing an international congress of the size of an ICME becomes increasingly immense, complicated and demanding, it is hoped that a formal decision about the site of

ICME-11 could be made not too late in 2003. We would thus like to propose the following schedule: declaration of intention of presenting a bid should reach the Secretary by September 1, 2001; formal bids should be presented to the Secretary by September 1, 2002. A written call for bids will be presented in the December 2000 issue of the ICMI Bulletin, which will also include indications about the kind of issues a bid should address. Those wishing to be informed of these guidelines sooner should contact me.

ICMI Studies

For more than 15 years, the Commission has conducted a series of so-called ICMI Studies devoted to crucial current themes or issues in mathematics education. The general aim of a Study is not to give any "ICMI-labeled" solution to any educational problem, to use the words of former ICMI President Jean-Pierre Kahane, but rather to provide an up-to-date presentation and analysis of the state-of-the-art concerning a given theme. It is not appropriate here to describe in details the functioning of a Study and I refer those interested to a short review paper which has appeared in a recent issue of the ICMI Bulletin:

> Bernard R. Hodgson, "The ICMI Studies: background information and projects", ICMI Bulletin No. 46 (June 1999) 32-36.

Information about all the Studies completed since the inception of the series can also be found there.

With the incoming of a new Executive Committee of ICMI last year, it was felt appropriate to renegotiate the terms of the contract with the publishing house of the ICMI Studies volumes, Kluwer Academic Publishers. I am pleased to inform you that the following conditions will now apply to personal orders for volumes of the New ICMI Studies Series made under ICMI patronage. Individuals buying a Study volume for personal use are entitled to a 60% reduction on the hardbound edition. In order for this reduction to be applied, orders will have to be made using a special order form to be printed in the ICMI Bulletin and posted on the ICMI website, or by quoting a special ICMI code. Details on the procedure will be given in the next issue of the ICMI Bulletin. These conditions apply to all volumes published in the Kluwer NISS Series. Although this might not solve all the difficulties related to the cost of the Studies volumes, it was felt that this represents a valuable agreement. All of you are invited to disseminate this information among your colleagues.

The near past

Since 1996, three Study volumes have been published in the so-called "New ICMI Studies Series" (NISS) published by Kluwer:

ICMI Study 8: *What is Research in Mathematics Education and What are its*

Results?
The Study Conference was held in College Park, USA, May 1994, and the Study Volume (two books) appeared in 1998 under the title: Mathematics Education as a Research Domain: A Search for Identity, eds: Anna Sierpinska and Jeremy Kilpatrick. (NISS 4);

ICMI Study 9: *Perspectives on the Teaching of Geometry for the 21st Century.*
The Study Conference was held in Catania, Italy, September 1995, and the Study Volume published in 1998 under the same title; eds: Carmelo Mammana and Vinicio Villani. (NISS 5)

ICMI Study 10: *The Role of the History of Mathematics in the Teaching and Learning of Mathematics.*
The Study Conference was held in Luminy, France, in April 1998 and the resulting volume, published under the title History in Mathematics Education: The ICMI Study (NISS 6) and edited by John Fauvel and Jan van Maanen, was launched at this congress.
One other Study Conference was held in addition to that of the History Study just mentioned:

ICMI Study 11: *Teaching and Learning of Mathematics at University Level.*
The Study Conference took place in Singapore in December 1998 and will result in two publications. The first is a special issue of the International Journal of Mathematical education in Science and Technology (iJMEST), Vol. 31 (1) January-February 2000, entirely devoted to selected papers from the Study Conference. Work on the Study Volume to appear in the NISS Series is currently under way and it is expected that this book will be published in 2001 (NISS 7).

The present
Two Studies have been launched in the recent past and are now in progress.

ICMI Study 12: The Discussion Document for the next study in the series, *The Future of the Teaching and Learning of Algebra,* has appeared in the *ICMI Bulletin* No. 48, June 2000, and elsewhere. The Study Conference will take place at the University of Melbourne, Australia, in December 2001 and contributions in order to be invited to participate should be submitted no later than January 31, 2001. More information about this Study can be obtained from the Chair of the International Program Committee, Professor Kaye Stacey from the University of Melbourne.

ICMI Study 13: The next Study has as a tentative title *Mathematics Education in*

Different Traditions: A Comparative Study in Asian and Western Countries. The two co-chairs for this Study are Professors Klaus-Dieter Graf, Freie Universitat Berlin, Germany, and Frederick K.S. Leung, the University of Hong Kong, and the IPC, appointed early in 2000, met twice during this congress. It is planned that the Discussion Document will appear in the next issue (December 2000) of the *ICMI Bulletin* and that the Study conference will be held in Hong Kong in October 2002. Contributions should be submitted by end of September 2001.

The near future
The Executive Committee of ICMI decided during its annual meeting held just prior to ICME 9 to mount two new Studies. The tentative titles for these Studies are Applications and modeling in mathematics education and Teacher education and development. The Program Committees for these Studies are now in the process of being appointed. More information about these two Studies (Discussion Documents, dates of submission and of conference) will be announced in forthcoming issues of the ICMI Bulletin. Potential interested participants are invited to contact the Secretary for further information.

The distant future
The following topics are now being considered as candidates for possible Studies (any comments about this should be addressed to a member of the Executive Committee):

> *The role of proofs and proving in mathematics education
> *Stochastics and probability in mathematics education
> *Information technology revisited (in reference to the first ICMI Study held in 1985)
> *Mathematics for and from the workplace

Affiliated Study Groups
Over the years, four international study groups have joined the Commission as so-called Affiliated Study Groups of ICMI. These groups are neither appointed by ICMI nor operating on behalf or under the control of ICMI. They stage activities of their own and they are also offered slots inside the programs of the ICMEs. The ICMI Affiliated Study Groups produce quadrennial reports presented to the General Assemblies of ICMI. The four ICMI Affiliated Study Groups, with their year of affiliation to ICMI, are:

HPM: The International Study Group on the Relations between the History and Pedagogy of Mathematics (1976)
PME: The International Group for the Psychology of Mathematics Education (1976)

IOWME: The International Organization of Women and Mathematics Education (1987)
WFNMC: The World Federation of National Mathematics Competitions (1994)
More information about these groups can be found in the ICMI Bulletin or on the ICMI website.

Other activities

The Commission "raison d'etre" is the be an international organization. In this context ICMI has tried to foster the development of mathematics education in various parts of the world by supporting - morally or financially, the latter unfortunately mainly in symbolic terms - regional conferences. Some four ICMI regional meetings were held during the last four years, in Vietnam (1996), Korea (1998), Philippines (1999) and France (2000). Two more are to come in the future, one to be held next month in Russia and another one in 2002 in Singapore. More information about these activities is also to be found in the ICMI Bulletin.

In collaboration with the editors of the journal L'Enseignement mathématique, the official organ of ICMI, the Executive Committee is organizing on the occasion of the centennial of the journal a symposium on the history of mathematics education in the last century. This symposium will be held in October 2000 in Geneva, the home of L'Enseignement mathématique since its inception.

The Solidarity Program and Fund

In 1992, at the 7th ICME held in Quebec, ICMI announced the establishment of a Solidarity Program in Mathematics Education, created under the impulsion of its President Miguel de Guzman. The overall objective of the Solidarity Program is to increase, in a variety of ways, the commitment and involvement of mathematics educators around the world in order to improve the situation of mathematics education, in particular in those parts of the world where the economic and socio-political contexts do not permit adequate and autonomous development. The first stage in this program of international assistance was the mounting of a Solidarity Fund based on contributions by individuals, organizations, etc. The Solidarity Fund has received over the years donations from various organizations and individuals, in particular from France and Korea during the last years. Two projects recently supported are taking place in Africa.

An ad hoc committee, chaired by Professor Colette Laborde (France) has been set up in 1999 by the Executive Committee of ICMI to review the functioning and the impact of the Solidarity Fund, after its eight years of existence, and to bring recommendations to the EC concerning its orientation and development. Comments and suggestions should be given to Professor Laborde or to myself.

ICMI Awards

I would like to conclude this survey of various aspects of the life of ICMI with preliminary information about a new initiative to be launched by ICMI. It has been frequently suggested in the past that the Commission should establish some ICMI sponsored awards aiming at recognizing exceptional contributions to mathematics education. An ad hoc committee of internationally renowned scholars was formed last year to bring recommendations to the Executive Committee of ICMI. These recommendations, which were received at the recent EC meeting, were positive and the EC is now working on defining some of the parameters for these awards. An hypothesis currently being considered is the establishment for the time being of two awards, one recognizing a major program of research on mathematics education during the past ten years, and the other for life-time achievement in mathematics education. Information about these awards will appear in a forthcoming issue of the ICMI Bulletin.

In this connection, and also because this has been frequently suggested to the Executive Committee independently of the project of awards, it now seems appropriate for ICMI to have a visual identification in the form of a logo. Suggestions of parameters for the selection of such a logo, as well as sketches of logos, are most welcome and should be forwarded to me as soon as possible.

Those interested in having more information about ICMI activities should contact me, or visit the ICMI website which has recently been relocated at:

http://www.mathunion.org/ICMI/

Conclusion

This brings us to the conclusion of this session. At this stage the Executive Committee of the Commission wishes to pay tribute to a Japanese friend and colleague who has played a preeminent role in organization of ICME 9. I am sure many of you have been involved over the years in the organization of scientific meetings of various sizes: a few hundred participants, maybe up to a thousand. But I do not know if many were involved in the organization of a gathering of more than two thousand people, especially in an international setting. Cumulating the roles of President of the National Organizing Committee and that of Chair of the International Program Committee is truly a daunting task. The Executive Committee of ICMI was especially impressed by the skill and graciousness with which Professor Hiroshi Fujita has lead these committees, in particular the IPC of ICME 9, a committee appointed by the Executive Committee of ICMI, where efficiency and judgment combined with sensibility for cultural nuances are so important. I now invite Fujita san to come back on the dais. Please join us in expressing our warmest thanks to our splendid colleague.

(Professor Hiroshi Fujita is greeted by ICMI President Hyman Bass, which offers him a book as a tangible sign of gratitude - the Collected Works of Seki Takakazu, a Japanese mathematician from the period of Newton.

The accompanying dedication card, signed by all the members of the ICMI Executive Committee, reads as follows:

"To Hiroshi Fujita:

On behalf of the ICMI community, we present to you this token of our appreciation and gratitude for your extraordinary and spirited dedication to the success of ICME 9. the Executive Committee of ICMI, August 6, 2000")

It is now my duty to declare the 9th International Congress on Mathematical Education, held from July 31 to August 6, 2000, officially closed.

I wish all of you a safe trip back home and I look forward to seeing you all again in Copenhagen in July 2004. Good bye! Au revoir! Sayonara!

List of Participants

ICME 9 Participants (by country)

Country	Participant	Accompanying	Total
Argentina	9	2	11
Australia	64	4	68
Austria	6	2	8
Belgium	6	2	8
Brazil	22	2	24
Brunei Darussalam	3	1	4
Bulgaria	5		5
Cameroon	1		1
Canada	17	5	22
Cayman Islands	1	1	2
Chile	2		2
China	84	1	85
China-Hong Kong	20	5	25
China-Taipei	17	4	21
Colombia	3		3
Cyprus	1		1
Czech Republic	4	1	5
Denmark	32	7	39
Egypt	2		2
Estonia	1		1
Fiji Islands	1		1
Finland	18	2	20
France	24	6	30
Germany	36	11	47
Greece	5		5
Hungary	6	1	7
Iceland	4	1	5
India	7		7
Indonesia	5	1	6
Iran	6		6
Ireland	4	2	6
Israel	31	13	44
Italy	10	1	11

Japan	958	47	1005
Korea	39	8	47
Kuwait	4	1	5
Latvia	2		2
Lebanon	2	1	3
Luxembourg	3		3
Malaysia	8		8
Mexico	10		10
Netherlands	28	4	32
New Caledonia	1		1
New Zealand	13	2	15
Norway	12	2	14
Papua New Guinea	1	1	2
Paraguay	1		1
Peru	6		6
Philippines	16		16
Poland	4		4
Portugal	12	5	17
Romania	2		2
Russia	8		8
Singapore	9	1	10
Slovakia	3		3
Slovenia	3		3
South Africa	11		11
Spain	25	4	29
Swaziland	1		1
Sweden	37	8	45
Switzerland	7	4	11
Thailand	10	2	12
Trinidad	1	1	2
Turkey	2		2
Uganda	1		1
UK	86	20	106
Ukraine	2		2
USA	223	53	276
Venezuela	1		1
Vietnam	1		1

Zimbabwe	2		2
	2012	239	2251

List of Participants

Name	Country	Name	Country
Nestor Edgardo Aguilera	Argentina	Tony Jones	Australia
Maria Eugenia Alvarez	Argentina	Clive Kanes	Australia
Juan Carlos Dalmasso	Argentina	Paulene Margaret Kibble	Australia
Lidia Ester Ibarra	Argentina	Barry Kissane	Australia
Norma Cristina	Argentina	Gilah Leder	Australia
Maria Victoria Ponza	Argentina	John Michael Mack	Australia
Vera W. de Spinadel	Argentina	Agnes Jean Macmillan	Australia
Roberto Torres	Argentina	John A. Malone	Australia
Maria Luisa Trejo	Argentina	Kevin Joseph	Australia
Warren James Atkins	Australia	David Georges Pederson	Australia
Lynda Maree Ball	Australia	Brian Richard Phillips	Australia
Dawn Bartlett	Australia	Graham Hilford Pollard	Australia
Jeff Baxter	Australia	Peter David Renshaw	Australia
Jennie Bickmore-Brand	Australia	Michael Anthony	Australia
Alan John Bishop	Australia	Margaret Anne	Australia
Sandra Christine Britton	Australia	Wee Tiong Seah	Australia
Tanya Christine Brooks	Australia	Malcolm Shield	Australia
Marjorie Chelsea Carss	Australia	Dianne Elizabeth	Australia
Michael Sean Cavanagh	Australia	Ron Smith	Australia
Wai-Man Raymond Chow	Australia	Beth Gwen Southwell	Australia
Barbara Anne Clarke	Australia	Len Sparrow	Australia
David John Clarke	Australia	Gt Springer	Australia
Philip Clarkson	Australia	Kaye Christine Stacey	Australia
M. A. (Ken) Clements	Australia	Max Walte Stephens	Australia
Lorraine Joy Davis	Australia	Gloria Ann Stillman	Australia
Carmel Diezmann	Australia	Andrei Storozhev	Australia
Brian A Doig	Australia	Peter Arnold Sullivan	Australia
John Dowsey	Australia	Peter James Taylor	Australia
Lyn Denise English	Australia	Jan Thomas	Australia
Gail Fitzsimons	Australia	Dave Tout	Australia
Peter L. Galbraith	Australia	Dubravka Viskic	Australia
Vincent Stephen Geiger	Australia	Jeni Margaret Wilson	Australia
Noel Geoghegan	Australia	Brian John Woolacott	Australia
Merrilyn Goos	Australia	Robyn Zevenbergen	Australia
Susie Groves	Australia	Willibald Dörfler	Austria
David H. Haimes	Australia	Karl Josef Fuchs	Austria

Pamela Marion	Australia	Robert Geretschläger	Austria
Jenny Henderson	Australia	Konrad Krainer	Austria
Fritz Schweiger	Austria	Enzo Carli	Canada
Ivan Cnop	Belgium	Peter Crippin	Canada
Dirk De Bock	Belgium	Ronald Garth Dunkley	Canada
Francine Grandsard	Belgium	Claude Gaulin	Canada
Guido Herweyers	Belgium	William Higginson	Canada
Jacques Navez	Belgium	Bernard R. Hodgson	Canada
Lieven Verschaffel	Belgium	André Ladouceur	Canada
Yuriko Yamamoto Baldin	Brazil	Andy Liu	Canada
Marilena Bittar	Brazil	Miroslav Lovric	Canada
Tania Campos	Brazil	Eric Muller	Canada
Jorge T. Da Rocha Falcao	Brazil	Cynthia Nicol	Canada
Ubiratan Dambrosio	Brazil	Graham Rankin	Canada
Rabello M. De Castro	Brazil	Nathalie Michelle	Canada
Lulu Healy	Brazil	Peter D. Taylor	Canada
Sonia B. Camargo Igliori	Brazil	Walter Whiteley	Canada
Gelsa Knijnik	Brazil	Desiree Ann	Cayman Islands
Monica M. Borges	Brazil	Quezada Veronica Diaz	Chile
Ana M. Petraitis Liblik	Brazil	Letelier Alvaro Poblete	Chile
Romulo Lins	Brazil	Feng Ji An	China
Antonio Jose Lopes	Brazil	Na Bao	China
M. C. S. de A. Maranhao	Brazil	Shen Cen	China
Edilson Roberto Pacheco	Brazil	Wei Chang	China
Joao Carlos Passoni	Brazil	Bailin Chen	China
Regina Maria Pavanello	Brazil	Shiyou Chen	China
Maria Graca Pereira	Brazil	Yong Chen	China
Maria Maynart Pereira	Brazil	Yunqin Chen	China
Elsa Midori Shimazaki	Brazil	Zhenhua Chen	China
Edmir Rebeiro Terra	Brazil	Guanghui Cheng	China
Edna Maura Zuffi	Brazil	Feng Chao Ding	China
Irene Martin Domingo	Brunei	Yuxiang Du	China
John Suffolk	Brunei	Liming Fan	China
Khoon-Yoong Wong	Brunei	Jiancheng Fang	China
Kiril Gueorguiev Bankov	Bulgaria	Siming Gui	China
Svetoslav Yordanov	Bulgaria	Ghoyan Han	China
Radost Stefanova	Bulgaria	Xitang Han	China
Petar Stoyanov Kenderov	Bulgaria	Jiyu He	China

Jordan Borissov Tabov	Bulgaria	Lhong Huang	China
Etienne Bebbe-Njoh	Cameroon	Xiang Huang	China
Ann Gladys Anderson	Canada	Yi Ming Jiang	China
Jim Glen Anderson	Canada	Caihua Jin	China
Chuanzhong Li	China	Yan Xia	China
Jianhua Li	China	Xinguo Xue	China
Shiqi Li	China	Changli Yang	China
Xing huai Li	China	Kunrong Yang	China
Yanlin Li	China	Qixiao Ye	China
Yuqing Li	China	Lingfeng Yi	China
Yuwen Li	China	Min Yu	China
Bin Liang	China	Qianyong Zhan	China
Wenying Liang	China	Dianzhou Zhang	China
Yulin Liao	China	Hai Zhang	China
Bailian Liu	China	Jin jun Zhang	China
Keming Liu	China	Jingbin Zhang	China
Jiang Lu	China	Miao Zhang	China
Shihu Lu	China	Shao Chun Zhang	China
Zhiding Luo	China	Shen Zhang	China
Deliang Ma	China	Gongming Zhao	China
Yunpeng Ma	China	Hong Yan Zhao	China
Jianhua Qi	China	Ling Yun Zhao	China
Zizhao Ren	China	Lian Zheng	China
Mingzho Shen	China	Xue Zheng	China
Zurao Shen	China	Zhipei Zheng	China
Chu Shi	China	Huaying Zhu	China
Yongsheng Shi	China	Chun Chun Litwin	China-HK
Lianju Sun	China	Yat Lai Cheng	China-HK
De Xiang Tang	China	Pak-Hong Cheung	China-HK
Ruifen Tang	China	Katherine On Ki Fok	China-HK
Wenzhong Tao	China	Chun-Ip Fung	China-HK
Jian-pan Wang	China	Tak-fong Agnes Fung	China-HK
Jidong Wang	China	Percy Lai-yin Kwok	China-HK
Jiyan Wang	China	Huk Yuen Law	China-HK
Junbang Wang	China	Chi-kit Leung	China-HK
Kunxin Wang	China	Frederick K. S. Leung	China-HK
Linquan Wang	China	Shuk-Kwan S. Leung	China-HK
Mao Xi Wang	China	Sze Ngar Li	China-HK

Nanzhang Wang	China	Shui Ping Lok	China-HK
Shang Zhi Wang	China	Ida Ah Chee Mok	China-HK
Shian Wang	China	Man Keung Siu	China-HK
Yueting Wang	China	Mei-yue Tang	China-HK
Xiaoping Wu	China	Sui Wah Betty Tse	China-HK
Dongxi Xia	China	Ka Ming Patrick Wong	China-HK
Qian Ting Wong	China-HK	Kristine Jess	Denmark
Ying Ngai Wong	China-HK	Carsten V. Jorgensen	Denmark
Ching-Kuch Chang	China-Taiwan	Poul Jungersen	Denmark
Ing-Er Chen	China-Taiwan	Leif Kragh	Denmark
Hsiao-li Chi	China-Taiwan	Merete D. Lundsgaard	Denmark
Yi-Chun Chi Chien	China-Taiwan	Arne Mogensen	Denmark
Jing Chung	China-Taiwan	Ellen S. Munkholm	Denmark
Hsin-Mei Edith Huang	China-Taiwan	Henrik J. Nielsen	Denmark
Yu-Fen Huang	China-Taiwan	Mogens Niss	Denmark
Brenda Lee	China-Taiwan	Jette Ovesen Nygaard	Denmark
Yuh Chyn Leu	China-Taiwan	Anne Winther Petersen	Denmark
Fou-Lai Lin	China-Taiwan	Pernille Pind	Denmark
Pi-Jen Lin	China-Taiwan	Elsebeth Roehl	Denmark
Po-Hung Liu	China-Taiwan	Mikael Skaanstroem	Denmark
Wei-Jiun Shiu	China-Taiwan	Jeppe Skott	Denmark
Hak Ping Tam	China-Taiwan	Allan Tarp	Denmark
Theresa Ning-Chun Tan	China-Taiwan	Paola Valero	Denmark
Wen-Huan Tsai	China-Taiwan	Tine Wedege	Denmark
Jya-Yi Wu Yu	China-Taiwan	Carl Winslow	Denmark
Maria M. B. de Meza	Colombia	Attia A. Ashour	Egypt
Maria Falk De Losada	Colombia	William Tawadros Ebeid	Egypt
Carlos Wilson L. Gomez	Colombia	Eno Tõisson	Estonia
C. A Papanastasiou	Cyprus	Fiona Walls	Fiji Islands
Alena Hospesova	Czech Republic	Eivor Bjorkqvist	Finland
Marie Kubinova	Czech Republic	Ole B Bjorkqvist	Finland
Ivan Meznik	Czech Republic	Markku Sakari Hannula	Finland
Jarmila Novotna	Czech Republic	Sinikka T. Huhtala	Finland
Helle Klitgaard Alrø	Denmark	Tapani Jussila	Finland
Charlotte Krog Andersen	Denmark	Tapio Olavi Keranto	Finland
Leif Karlo Andersen	Denmark	Liisa Kinnunen	Finland
Michael Wahl Andersen	Denmark	Sinikka M.I. Lindgren	Finland
Stig Andersen	Denmark	Juha Oikkonen	Finland

Morten Blomhoej	Denmark	Erkki Kalevi Pehkonen	Finland
Torben Christoffersen	Denmark	Anu Tuulikki Pietilä	Finland
Lisser Rye Ejersbo	Denmark	Harry Silfverberg	Finland
Karsten Enggaard	Denmark	Riitta Soro	Finland
Hans Christian Hansen	Denmark	Pertti Toivonen	Finland
Helle Lyngsted Jensen	Denmark	M. J. Uus-Leponiemi	Finland
Sven Toft Jensen	Denmark	Tuula Uus-Leponiemi	Finland
Tomas Højgaard Jensen	Denmark	Raija Terttu Yrjonsuuri	Finland
Yrjo Samuli Yrjonsuuri	Finland	Goetz Krummheuer	Germany
Andre Antibi	France	Gustav Adolf Lörcher	Germany
Michele Artigue	France	Hartwig Meissner	Germany
Remi Belloeil	France	Hans-Joachim Mittag	Germany
Jean Bichara	France	Regina Moller	Germany
Claude Comiti	France	Johanna E. Neubrand	Germany
E. Cousquer-Teissandier	France	Michael Neubrand	Germany
Beanadette Denys	France	Marianne Nolte	Germany
Claude Deschamps	France	Fríedhelm Padberg	Germany
Nadia Douek	France	Andrea Peter-Koop	Germany
Catherine Dufossé	France	Beate Maria Ruffer	Germany
Elisabeth Gallou-Dunlel	France	V. M. P. Santos-Wagner	Germany
Denise Grenier	France	Ruediger H. Schaefer	Germany
Corinne Hahn	France	Petra Scherer	Germany
Alain Kuzniak	France	Heinz Schumann	Germany
Colette Claudine Laborde	France	Heinz Steinbring	Germany
Jean-Marie F. Laborde	France	Rudolf Straesser	Germany
Jean-baptiste Lagrange	France	Rudolf Vom Hofe	Germany
Claire Margolinas	France	Hans-Georg Weigand	Germany
Michel Merle	France	Erich Ch. Wittmann	Germany
Ama Lobo Mesquita	France	Bernd Zimmermann	Germany
Catherine Sackur	France	D. G. Kontogiannis	Greece
Catherine Taveau	France	Stavros G. Papastavridis	Greece
Gerard Tronel	France	Haralambos Sakonidis	Greece
Luc Trouche	France	Constadinos Tzanakis	Greece
Oscar João Abdounur	Germany	Marianna Tzekaki	Greece
Rolf Biehler	Germany	András Ambrus	Hungary
W. Hans-Joachim Blum	Germany	Susan Agnes Bereusi	Hungary
Regina Bruder	Germany	István Hortobágyi	Hungary
Wolfram Eid	Germany	Janos Suranyi	Hungary

Marianne Franke	Germany	Julianna Szendrei	Hungary
Klaus-Dieter Graf	Germany	Klara Tompa	Hungary
Norbert Gruenwald	Germany	Kristin Bjarnadottir	Iceland
Hans Wolfgang Henn	Germany	Fridrik Diego	Iceland
Herbert Henning	Germany	Kristín Halla Jónsdóttir	Iceland
Hans Niels Jahnke	Germany	Anna Kristjansdottir	Iceland
Friedhelm Käpnick	Germany	Sudhakar C. Agarkar	India
Christine Keitel	Germany	Shashi Prabha Arya	India
Gerhard Käpnick	Germany	Amal Kanti Bhavmik	India
Günter Krauthausen	Germany	Madan Mohan Chel	India
Surja Kumari	India	Irit Peled	Israel
Asha Rani Singal	India	Ruth Shane	Israel
Dilip Kumar Sinha	India	Lea Spiro	Israel
Sadijah Cholis	Indonesia	Jonathan Stupp	Israel
Susanti Linuwih	Indonesia	Dina Tirosh	Israel
Marsigit	Indonesia	Pessia Tsamir	Israel
Soedjadi R	Indonesia	Shlomo Vinner	Israel
Didi Suryadi	Indonesia	Greisy Winicki Landnan	Israel
S. Bakhshalizadeh	Iran	Orit Zaslavsky	Israel
Soheila Gholam Azad	Iran	Ferdinando Arzarello	Italy
Zahra Gooya	Iran	Mario Barra	Italy
M. H. Pourkazemi	Iran	Luciana Bazzini	Italy
Ali Rejali	Iran	Paolo Boero	Italy
A. Shahvarani-Semnani	Iran	Cinzia Bonotto	Italy
Noel C. Colleran	Ireland	Fulvia Furinghetti	Italy
Jane Mary Horgan	Ireland	Nicolina A. Malara	Italy
John O'Donoghue	Ireland	Maria A. Mariotti	Italy
Richard Oliver Watson	Ireland	Federica Olivero	Italy
Dan Aharoni	Israel	Ornella Robutti	Italy
Amos Altshuler	Israel	Kumiko Adachi	Japan
Miriam Amit	Israel	Yuko Adachi	Japan
Abraham Arcavi	Israel	Hirohiko Aikawa	Japan
Phyllis August	Israel	Toshiyuki Akai	Japan
David Ben-Chaim	Israel	Osamu Akimatu	Japan
Hava Bloedy-Vinner	Israel	Miyo Akita	Japan
Naomi Chissick	Israel	Akiko Akiyama	Japan
Amos Ehrlich	Israel	Jin Akiyama	Japan
Ruhama Even	Israel	Masayuki Ando	Japan

David Ginat	Israel	Tetsuya Ando	Japan
Rina Hadass	Israel	Tsuyoshi Ando	Japan
Dina Hassidov	Israel	Masao Aoki	Japan
Bat-Shera Ieany	Israel	Chikara Aoyama	Japan
Bracha Kramarski	Israel	Kazuhiro Aoyama	Japan
Tamar Lapidot	Israel	Yuko Aoyama	Japan
Talma O Leviatan	Israel	Hitoshi Arai	Japan
Azriel Levy	Israel	Sachie Arai	Japan
Adiva Liberman	Israel	Koji Arashida	Japan
Giora Mann	Israel	Junya Arata	Japan
Ibby Mekhmandarov	Israel	Shigeru Ariga	Japan
John Oberman	Israel	Yasuho Arita	Japan
Teruko Asada	Japan	Shinichiro Furukawa	Japan
Yuji Asami	Japan	Mariko Giga	Japan
Kazuo Asano	Japan	Ko Ginbayashi	Japan
Kazuyuki Asanuma	Japan	Fumi Ginshima	Japan
Kenichi Asanuma	Japan	Tadashi Goda	Japan
Kazutoshi Aso	Japan	Mitsuharu Goto	Japan
Taku Azuma	Japan	George Gotoh	Japan
Kaori Baba	Japan	Kyoichi Gowa	Japan
Yutaka Baba	Japan	Kazuo Haga	Japan
Maximo Montana	Japan	Kenzo Hamada	Japan
Kenich Chino	Japan	Toshiaki Hamada	Japan
Kimiho Chino	Japan	Hisashi Hamano	Japan
Yasuo Doi	Japan	Katsuyuki Hanano	Japan
Shinya Ebara	Japan	Susumu Handa	Japan
Toshiaki Ebisawa	Japan	Akio Haneda	Japan
Hideyo Emori	Japan	Kouhei Harada	Japan
Tomoyuki Emori	Japan	Jun Haraguchi	Japan
Shin-ichi Esaki	Japan	Kaoru Hasegawa	Japan
Kazumasa Fujii	Japan	Katsuhisa Hasegawa	Japan
Shiro Fujii	Japan	Takako Hasegawa	Japan
Toshiakira Fujii	Japan	Takashi Hasegawa	Japan
Tomoe Fujimoto	Japan	Mitsugu Hashimoto	Japan
Yoshiaki Fujimoto	Japan	Yoshihiko Hashimoto	Japan
Masato Fujioka	Japan	Yoshihiro Hashimoto	Japan
Hiroshi Fujita	Japan	Yoshitaka Hashimoto	Japan
Taro Fujita	Japan	Yuichiro Hashimoto	Japan

Yasunori Fujita	Japan	Yumiko Hashimoto	Japan
Yoshiko Fujita	Japan	Satoshi Hasui	Japan
Shinichi Fujiu	Japan	Kazuyoshi Hata	Japan
Daiki Fujiwara	Japan	Yoshitaka Hatano	Japan
Hisashi Fukagawa	Japan	Hiroe Hatta	Japan
Hiroo Fukaishi	Japan	Masahiro Hatta	Japan
Mikio Fukase	Japan	Yukio Hattori	Japan
Seiichi Fukuda	Japan	Hajime Hayakawa	Japan
Yumi Fukuda	Japan	Ken Hayakawa	Japan
Nobuo Fukumori	Japan	Yoshinori Hayakawa	Japan
Yaeko Fukuoka	Japan	Tomohide Hayasaka	Japan
Toshiyuki Fukuzawa	Japan	Etsuo Hayashi	Japan
Shunsuke Funakoshi	Japan	Juichi Hayashi	Japan
Akio Furukawa	Japan	Kazumichi Hayashi	Japan
Kenichi Hayashida	Japan	Noemi Ichihara	Japan
Setsuko Hazama	Japan	Kimio Ichihashi	Japan
Kunio Hazumi	Japan	Naotaka Ichiyanagi	Japan
Teiichi Higuchi	Japan	Hirohisa Ieda	Japan
Keiko Hino	Japan	Kan Igarashi	Japan
Hiroaki Hirabayashi	Japan	Hiroshi Iguchi	Japan
Ichiei Hirabayashi	Japan	Shinji Iida	Japan
Hirotoshi Hirahata	Japan	Yasuo Iijima	Japan
Katsuaki Hirai	Japan	Yasuyuki Iijima	Japan
Katsuhiro Hirai	Japan	Kyoko Iitaka	Japan
Yasuhisa Hirai	Japan	Shigeru Iitaka	Japan
Kosaburo Hirakawa	Japan	Koichi Ikari	Japan
Fumiko Hiraki	Japan	Kuniko Ikari	Japan
Naoki Hiramatsu	Japan	Fumio Ikeda	Japan
Yoichi Hirano	Japan	Fumio Ikeda	Japan
Hajime Hirao	Japan	Itsuko Ikeda	Japan
Kenji Hiraoka	Japan	Takeshi Ikeda	Japan
Tadashi Hiraoka	Japan	Toshikazu Ikeda	Japan
Yosiko Hiraoka	Japan	Yoshito Ikeda	Japan
Haruo Hirata	Japan	Masahiko Ikedo	Japan
Mitutake Hirobe	Japan	Masaharu Ikeno	Japan
Tokufumi Hiroi	Japan	Keiko Ikuse	Japan
Takeo Hisamatsu	Japan	Kogen Imai	Japan
Katumi Hisanaga	Japan	Noriko Imai	Japan

Sin Hitotumatu	Japan	Toshihiro Imai	Japan
Mieko Hodumi	Japan	Takuya Imanari	Japan
Mitsuru Homma	Japan	Rei Inagaki	Japan
Toshihiro Homma	Japan	Jiro Inaida	Japan
Mitsuyuki Honma	Japan	Masahide Inoue	Japan
Tetsuro Hori	Japan	Reiko Inoue	Japan
Youko Horii	Japan	Yoshihiro Inoue	Japan
Mitsunobu Horio	Japan	Haruo Inui	Japan
Mituaki Hoshi	Japan	Takao Irite	Japan
Satoko Hoshi	Japan	Yoko Ishibashi	Japan
Hiroshi Hosokawa	Japan	Ichizo Ishida	Japan
Kazuhiro Hosoya	Japan	Junichi Ishida	Japan
Terumi Hotta	Japan	Naomi Ishida	Japan
Teruhiko Houshi	Japan	Tadayuki Ishida	Japan
Mi Hu	Japan	Haruo Ishigaki	Japan
Satoshi Ibaraki	Japan	Yukiro Ishiguro	Japan
Hiroshi Ishii	Japan	Hiroshi Kanaya	Japan
Masashi Ishikawa	Japan	Kyoji Kanda	Japan
Michio Ishikawa	Japan	Ririko Kaneda	Japan
Naoyuki Ishimura	Japan	Hiromi Kaneko	Japan
Masayuki Ishitani	Japan	Masafumi Kaneko	Japan
Michiya Ishizaki	Japan	Mitsuo Kanemitsu	Japan
Norio Ishizaki	Japan	Yoshimichi Kanemoto	Japan
Shigeko Ishizuka	Japan	Takashi Kaneta	Japan
Masami Isoda	Japan	Kaori Kanno	Japan
Yoshio Itagaki	Japan	Hiroko Kanoh	Japan
Hidetoshi Ito	Japan	Kenichi Kasai	Japan
Junichi Ito	Japan	Mitsuo Kasai	Japan
Katsuaki Ito	Japan	Hiroo Kashihara	Japan
Kosyo Ito	Japan	Mutsuhiko Kashimura	Japan
Michiho Ito	Japan	Kazuhisa Kasuga	Japan
Michitake Ito	Japan	Kazuo Katagiri	Japan
Toshihiko Ito	Japan	Shigeo Katagiri	Japan
Yoshihiko Ito	Japan	Kei Kataoka	Japan
Setsuro Itoh	Japan	Hiroshi Katayama	Japan
Yumiko Itoh	Japan	Hisae Kato	Japan
Kazuo Iwagoh	Japan	Hisakazu Kato	Japan
Jun Iwama	Japan	Naoki Kato	Japan

Hiroshi Iwasaki	Japan	Ryugo Kato	Japan
Hidetugu Iwata	Japan	Takeshi Kato	Japan
Kazuo Iwata	Japan	Yasuhiko Kato	Japan
Koji Iwata	Japan	Yasuo Katsumata	Japan
Kazuya Izumi	Japan	Yoshio Katsumi	Japan
Yasuhiko Izumi	Japan	Hiroaki Katsutani	Japan
Hitoshi Izumori	Japan	Hiyori Kawabata	Japan
Takashi Izushi	Japan	Tatsuya Kawada	Japan
Katuro Jimbo	Japan	Masayo Kawai	Japan
Katsuhisa Kagami	Japan	Toshio Kawai	Japan
Kazuya Kageyama	Japan	Masaharu Kawamoto	Japan
Toshiko Kaji	Japan	Anna Kawamura	Japan
Kyoko Kakihana	Japan	Junichiro Kawamura	Japan
Akeshi Kamae	Japan	Katsuhisa Kawamura	Japan
Hiroyasu Kamiya	Japan	Kazuhito Kawamura	Japan
Hideaki Kamiyama	Japan	Hideo Kawarada	Japan
Hirofumi Kanai	Japan	Michihiro Kawasaki	Japan
Shouichi Kanai	Japan	Tatsumi Kawasaki	Japan
Tetsuro Kawasaki	Japan	Tetsuya Kobayashi	Japan
Toshikazu Kawasaki	Japan	Tohru Kobayashi	Japan
Tatushi Kawashima	Japan	Yukio Kobayashi	Japan
Kiyoshi Kawazu	Japan	Takayuki Kodera	Japan
Masami Kayahara	Japan	Ichinose Kogi	Japan
Kenji Kazama	Japan	Koji Koike	Japan
Kimie Kazama	Japan	Shin-etsu Koizumi	Japan
Nobuaki Kazumi	Japan	Jun Kojima	Japan
Kimiyo Kido	Japan	Koichiro Kojima	Japan
Kiyoshi Kido	Japan	Makoto Kojima	Japan
Makoto Kikkawa	Japan	Makoto Komano	Japan
Fumitsugu Kikuchi	Japan	Hikosaburo Komatsu	Japan
Hisato Kikuchi	Japan	Makoto Komatsu	Japan
Miki Kikuchi	Japan	Hiroshi Komatsugawa	Japan
Tetsuya Kikuchi	Japan	Haruo Komiyama	Japan
Tsugio Kikuchi	Japan	Takako Komura	Japan
Hiroshi Kimura	Japan	Hitoshi Kondo	Japan
Rinako Kimura	Japan	Tadahiko Kondo	Japan
Suteo Kimura	Japan	Tomohiro Kondoh	Japan
Toshiko Kimura	Japan	Toshiji Kondoh	Japan

Yoshio Kimura	Japan	Yutaka Kori	Japan
Yuzo Kimura	Japan	Reiko Kosaka	Japan
Hisashi Kinoshita	Japan	Hiroaki Koseki	Japan
Tomohiro Kinoshita	Japan	Kiyoshi Koseki	Japan
Junichi Kishi	Japan	Toshihiko Koshiba	Japan
Tadayuki Kishimoto	Japan	Hideo Koshigoe	Japan
Makoto Kishine	Japan	Hiroaki Koshikawa	Japan
Shigeki Kitajima	Japan	Kaoru Kosuge	Japan
Tsutomu Kitami	Japan	Osamu Kota	Japan
Kazue Kitamura	Japan	Tadato Kotagiri	Japan
Masashi Kitamura	Japan	Suehiro Koura	Japan
Naomitsu Kitani	Japan	Masataka Koyama	Japan
Takahito Kitani	Japan	Takehito Koyama	Japan
Yoshitaka Kitazawa	Japan	Yoshihiro Kubo	Japan
Tamotsu Kiuchi	Japan	Hirono Kumagai	Japan
Asako Kobari	Japan	Koichi Kumagai	Japan
Ichiro Kobayashi	Japan	Keisaku Kumahara	Japan
Kimikazu Kobayashi	Japan	Hiroyuki Kumakura	Japan
Michimasa Kobayashi	Japan	Keiyu Kunimoto	Japan
Tetsuo Kobayashi	Japan	Susumu Kunimune	Japan
Takahiro Kunioka	Japan	Kaoru Matsuda	Japan
Taro Kunitsugu	Japan	Kenji Matsui	Japan
Harumi Kuno	Japan	Ryohei Matsui	Japan
Tetsuji Kuno	Japan	Yoshiyuki Matsui	Japan
Nobutada Kurai	Japan	Eiko Matsuki	Japan
Hirohumi Kuramitsu	Japan	Kiyoharu Matsumiya	Japan
Hideyuki Kurihara	Japan	Akira Matsumoto	Japan
Isamu Kurishima	Japan	Junichi Matsumoto	Japan
Toshiro Kuroda	Japan	Naoto Matsumoto	Japan
Yoshiyuki Kuroda	Japan	Seiichi Matsumoto	Japan
Norio Kurokawa	Japan	Shinichirou Matsumoto	Japan
Fumitoshi Kuroki	Japan	Yukio Matsumoto	Japan
Sadao Kurosaki	Japan	Toru Matsumura	Japan
Shunji Kurosawa	Japan	Yoshihito Matsumura	Japan
Masao Kuroyanagi	Japan	Noriya Matsunaga	Japan
Kouzi Kusanagi	Japan	Nanae Matsuo	Japan
Zennosuke Kusumoto	Japan	Yoshiki Matsuo	Japan
Takayasu Kuwata	Japan	Hidefusa Matsushita	Japan

Xinsheng Lu	Japan	Kayo Matsushita	Japan
Kenichi Machida	Japan	Hiroshi Matsuura	Japan
Satoshi Machida	Japan	Akio Matsuzaki	Japan
Shoichiro Machida	Japan	Masao Matsuzaki	Japan
Katsutoshi Maeda	Japan	Masao Matsuzawa	Japan
Mariko Maeda	Japan	Masao Mikami	Japan
Shigenobu Maeda	Japan	Saburo Minato	Japan
Hideyuki Majima	Japan	Eiji Mino	Japan
Naomichi Makinae	Japan	Yoshie Mitsuma	Japan
Masahiro Makino	Japan	Naomi Mitsutsuka	Japan
Tomohiko Makino	Japan	Shinichi Miura	Japan
Hideyo Makisita	Japan	Yoshio Miura	Japan
Yukiko Manabe	Japan	Tatsuro Miwa	Japan
Noriko Maruyama	Japan	Yushi Miwa	Japan
Norifumi Mashiko	Japan	Teruo Miyakawa	Japan
Hizuru Mashimo	Japan	Tomoko Miyama	Japan
Iekazu Masuda	Japan	Ichiro Miyamoto	Japan
Mikio Masuda	Japan	Yutaka Miyamoto	Japan
Naoyuki Masuda	Japan	Masamitsu Miyashita	Japan
Yoshiko Masuda	Japan	Satoshi Miyashita	Japan
Takayoshi Masujima	Japan	Kiichiro Miyata	Japan
Eri Matsuda	Japan	Mutsuo Miyauchi	Japan
Shinichi Miyawaki	Japan	Yukinori Muroi	Japan
Katsuji Miyazaki	Japan	Kazuhiko Murooka	Japan
Mikio Miyazaki	Japan	Toyoko Nagahara	Japan
Shinichi Miyazaki	Japan	Hirokazu Nagai	Japan
Yutaka Miyoshi	Japan	Hiroyuki Nagai	Japan
Tatsuya Mizoguchi	Japan	Hitomi Nagai	Japan
Hirobumi Mizuno	Japan	Keiko Nagai	Japan
Naohito Mizutani	Japan	Masahiro Nagai	Japan
Sadanori Mizutani	Japan	Satoshi Nagai	Japan
Isamu Mogi	Japan	Hajime Nagaki	Japan
Daisuke Mori	Japan	Toshiyuki Nagami	Japan
Hironobu Mori	Japan	Azuma Nagano	Japan
Kiyomi Mori	Japan	Ryosuke Nagaoka	Japan
Koichi Mori	Japan	Eizo Nagasaki	Japan
Masao Mori	Japan	Daisuke Nagasawa	Japan
Masatake Mori	Japan	Hiroko Nagasawa	Japan

415

Naganori Mori	Japan	Yumiko Nagasawa	Japan
Seiji Mori	Japan	Akiyuki Nagase	Japan
Shigefumi Mori	Japan	Kiyoshi Nagashima	Japan
Yuichi Mori	Japan	Junichiro Nagata	Japan
Kazumi Morikami	Japan	Michiko Nagata	Japan
Ikutaro Miyako	Japan	Tatsuo Naitou	Japan
Akira Morimoto	Japan	Michiaki Naka	Japan
Hiroko Morimoto	Japan	Norikazu Nakachi	Japan
Mitsuo Morimoto	Japan	Hiroyuki Nakagawa	Japan
Naoki Morimoto	Japan	Ritsuko Nakagawa	Japan
Seiichi Morimoto	Japan	Satoshi Nakagawa	Japan
Tuneo Morimura	Japan	Koji Nakagomi	Japan
Yasuhiko Morimura	Japan	Toshifumi Nakagoshi	Japan
Seiji Moriya	Japan	Katuyoshi Nakahara	Japan
Sumie Moro	Japan	Tadao Nakahara	Japan
Tatsuo Morozumi	Japan	Hirofumi Nakajima	Japan
Yoshiko Motoya	Japan	Toshinori Nakajima	Japan
Misako Motoyoshi	Japan	Yasuo Nakajima	Japan
Kazuo Mukoyama	Japan	Yuji Nakakomi	Japan
Haruo Murakami	Japan	Kenta Nakama	Japan
Masayoshi Murakami	Japan	Akira Nakamura	Japan
Minori Muramatsu	Japan	Jun Nakamura	Japan
Hidekatsu Murano	Japan	Kaori Nakamura	Japan
Masahide Murata	Japan	Takashi Nakamura	Japan
Wakiko Nakamura	Japan	Tsuyoshi Nomura	Japan
Yoshinori Nakamura	Japan	Yuriko Nomura	Japan
Zenichi Nakamura	Japan	Ronald D. Notestine	Japan
Chimaki Nakanishi	Japan	Akihiro Nozaki	Japan
Masaharu Nakanishi	Japan	Kazuhiko Nunokawa	Japan
Takashi Nakanishi	Japan	Keizo Ochi	Japan
Hiroshi Nakano	Japan	Toshio Odaka	Japan
Junji Nakano	Japan	Kazuo Oeda	Japan
Toshiyuki Nakano	Japan	Susumu Ogawa	Japan
Yojiro Nakano	Japan	Yuriko Ogawa	Japan
Hideo Nakasawa	Japan	Fumihiro Ogihara	Japan
Izumi Nakashima	Japan	Ryuzo Ogita	Japan
Mie Nakata	Japan	Yutaka Ohara	Japan
Makoto Nakatani	Japan	Keiichi Ohnishi	Japan

Haruyoshi Namatame	Japan	Hiromu Ohno	Japan
Yukihiko Namikawa	Japan	Katsuhiro Ohno	Japan
Shoichi Namiki	Japan	Toshimi Ohno	Japan
Masahiro Narita	Japan	Shigenori Ohsawa	Japan
Yasuo Narukawa	Japan	Minolu Ohta	Japan
Seiya Negami	Japan	Shinya Ohta	Japan
Hide Negishi	Japan	Hitoshi Ohtaki	Japan
Taeko Nemoto	Japan	Minoru Ohtani	Japan
Kazuto Niida	Japan	Yoshiko Oikawa	Japan
Hiroe Nikami	Japan	Mutsumi Ojima	Japan
Hiroyuki Ninomiya	Japan	Tsuneharu Okabe	Japan
Yasutoshi Nishida	Japan	Yasuyuki Okabe	Japan
Toshiyuki Nishimori	Japan	Haruhiko Okada	Japan
Toshihiko Nishimoto	Japan	Yoshio Okada	Japan
Keiichi Nishimura	Japan	Hirokazu Okamori	Japan
Shigeto Nishimura	Japan	Kazuo Okamoto	Japan
Kazuhiro Nishio	Japan	Koji Okamoto	Japan
Izumi Nishitani	Japan	Hideaki Okamura	Japan
Yoshiko Nishiwaki	Japan	Hiroshi Okayasu	Japan
Hiromasa Nishiyama	Japan	Hiroshi Okazaki	Japan
Yutaka Nishiyama	Japan	Masakazu Okazaki	Japan
Hitoshi Nishizawa	Japan	Kazuyoshi Okubo	Japan
Kenichi Noguchi	Japan	Toshiharu Okumiya	Japan
Ryuta Nohara	Japan	Akiko Okumura	Japan
Nobuhiko Nohda	Japan	Hiroshi Okuno	Japan
Tadashi Nomachi	Japan	Toshihiro Onishi	Japan
Tomoko Onose	Japan	Masahiko Sakamoto	Japan
Tsunemichi Oohashi	Japan	Yasuko Sakamoto	Japan
Yutaka Ooneda	Japan	Yuichi Sakanaka	Japan
Tomikatsu Orita	Japan	Satoru Sakanashi	Japan
Hironori Osawa	Japan	Sachi Sakashita	Japan
Ikuko Osawa	Japan	Senne Sakashita	Japan
Takayuki Osawa	Japan	Tosao Sakashita	Japan
Kazue Oshida	Japan	Hiroshi Sakata	Japan
Teruo Osumi	Japan	Toshiko Sakata	Japan
Kunio Ota	Japan	Takashi Sakazume	Japan
Katutosi Otagiri	Japan	Shinya Sakitani	Japan
Keiko Otagiri	Japan	Osamu Sakuma	Japan

Noboru Otake	Japan	Keiko Sakurai	Japan
Takayoshi Otani	Japan	Naoko Sakurai	Japan
Masazumi Otomo	Japan	Katsunori Sanada	Japan
Shunji Ouchi	Japan	Ayumi Sanji	Japan
Shigeyoshi Owa	Japan	Kazuto Saruya	Japan
Sumio Owa	Japan	Hiroyuki Sasa	Japan
Mitsuharu Oyama	Japan	Shozo Sasada	Japan
Tetsunori Oyama	Japan	Tetsuro Sasaki	Japan
Akihiko Ozawa	Japan	Hajime Sato	Japan
Kenichi Ozawa	Japan	Junko Sato	Japan
Sachiko Ryono	Japan	Katsuhiko Sato	Japan
Yutaka Saburi	Japan	Katsuzo Sato	Japan
Akihiko Saeki	Japan	Kayo Sato	Japan
Nanae Saeki	Japan	Kazutaka Sato	Japan
Minoru Saiba	Japan	Kosaku Sato	Japan
Makoto Saito	Japan	Shigeto Sato	Japan
Noboru Saito	Japan	Tamotsu Sato	Japan
Norikazu Saito	Japan	Toshihiro Sato	Japan
Shigechiyo Saito	Japan	Yoshitaka Sato	Japan
Shigeo Saito	Japan	Kennichi Satoh	Japan
Takasi Saito	Japan	Nobuaki Satou	Japan
Harumichi Saitou	Japan	Toshio Sawada	Japan
Chieko Sakai	Japan	Tetsuo Sawaki	Japan
Toshinori Sakai	Japan	Susumu Sayama	Japan
Yutaka Sakai	Japan	Sadanobu Seino	Japan
Makoto Sakakibara	Japan	Tatsuhiko Seino	Japan
Toshiaki Sakama	Japan	Kimio Seishi	Japan
Kenji Sakamoto	Japan	Takao Seiyama	Japan
Fumio Seki	Japan	Shigeshi Shirasaka	Japan
Yasuhiro Sekiguchi	Japan	Minako Shiroishi	Japan
Kaoru Sekino	Japan	Kiyoaki Shoda	Japan
Akio Senda	Japan	Minoru Shouda	Japan
Hanako Senuma	Japan	Rio Showder	Japan
Hye Sook Seo	Japan	Tatuo Simizu	Japan
Katsuaki Serizawa	Japan	Yoshinobu Soeda	Japan
Shirou Seyama	Japan	Izumi Soga	Japan
Masaaki Shiba	Japan	Miho Soma	Japan
Hiroki Shibano	Japan	Sumihiko Soma	Japan

Masanori K. Shibata	Japan	Hitohiro Someha	Japan
Toshio Shibata	Japan	Kazuhiko Souma	Japan
Hisashi Shibuya	Japan	Hiroshi Suda	Japan
Yoshio Shida	Japan	Katsuyuki Suenaga	Japan
Keiichi Shigematsu	Japan	Michihiro Suetake	Japan
Masato Shikama	Japan	Tatsunori Suga	Japan
Isao Shimada	Japan	Hiromi Sugaike	Japan
Kazuaki Shimada	Japan	Tsuyoshi Sugaoka	Japan
Keiko Shimada	Japan	Yukio Sugawara	Japan
Toshiro Shimada	Japan	Katsumi Sugaya	Japan
Kouji Shimasaki	Japan	Michio Sugie	Japan
Shinobu Shimazu	Japan	Michiko Sugioka	Japan
Fumie Shimba	Japan	Shiba Sugioka	Japan
Hiroshi Shimizu	Japan	Hiroyuki Sugita	Japan
Hiroyuki Shimizu	Japan	Makiko Sugiyama	Japan
Iwao Shimizu	Japan	Tomoyuki Sugiyama	Japan
Katsuhiko Shimizu	Japan	Yoshishige Sugiyama	Japan
Norihiro Shimizu	Japan	Toru Sunahara	Japan
Shizumi Shimizu	Japan	Siro Suwaki	Japan
Toshinori Shimizu	Japan	Akihiro Suzuki	Japan
Yoshinori Shimizu	Japan	Akira Suzuki	Japan
Hisao Shimomachi	Japan	Atsushi Suzuki	Japan
Osamu Shimomura	Japan	Hiromi Suzuki	Japan
Muneki Shimono	Japan	Jiro Suzuki	Japan
Mitsuru Shinanokozi	Japan	Junko Suzuki	Japan
Shingo Shinba	Japan	Kazumi Suzuki	Japan
Hiro Shiozawa	Japan	Kiyoo Suzuki	Japan
Iseko Shirai	Japan	Kyoko Suzuki	Japan
Kazuo Shiraishi	Japan	Makoto Suzuki	Japan
Kanetoshi Shirakawa	Japan	Masahiko Suzuki	Japan
Masayuki Suzuki	Japan	Yoshinori Takashima	Japan
Sakiko Suzuki	Japan	Toshio Takasu	Japan
Shin'ichi Suzuki	Japan	Setsuo Takato	Japan
Toshiki Suzuki	Japan	Kageki Takemura	Japan
Toshio Suzuki	Japan	Yoshiko Takenaka	Japan
Yoshihiko Suzuki	Japan	Osamu Takenouchi	Japan
Yoshio Suzuki	Japan	Toyoichi Takeuchi	Japan
Teruhiko Tabata	Japan	Yoshie Takeuchi	Japan

Kaori Tabeta	Japan	Koji Takezawa	Japan
Masato Tadokoro	Japan	Akira Takii	Japan
Kentaro Tago	Japan	Reiko Takimoto	Japan
Hiroko Taguchi	Japan	Masao Takiue	Japan
Kyoko Takada	Japan	Reiko Tamada	Japan
Noriko Takada	Japan	Osamu Tamaki	Japan
Shinobu Takada	Japan	Fumitaka Tamamura	Japan
Takashi Takada	Japan	Masahiko Tamura	Japan
Tashiyoshi Takada	Japan	Yoichi Tan	Japan
Hiroshi Takagi	Japan	Ayako Tanaka	Japan
Kazuhisa Takagi	Japan	Hirokazu Tanaka	Japan
Emiko Takahashi	Japan	Kenji Tanaka	Japan
Hiroaki Takahashi	Japan	Makiko Tanaka	Japan
Hitoshi Takahashi	Japan	Masakazu Tanaka	Japan
Hitoshi Takahashi	Japan	Masao Tanaka	Japan
Junko Takahashi	Japan	Masaru Tanaka	Japan
Koichi Takahashi	Japan	Seiyu Tanaka	Japan
Masaki Takahashi	Japan	Shigeru Tanaka	Japan
Nobuhiro Takahashi	Japan	Shotaro Tanaka	Japan
Shuichi Takahashi	Japan	Tsutomu Tanaka	Japan
Susumu Takahashi	Japan	Yoshihisa Tanaka	Japan
Takeo Takahashi	Japan	Tateo Taneki	Japan
Tomihiko Takahashi	Japan	Kenji Tani	Japan
Yoshihisa Takahashi	Japan	Mayumi Tani	Japan
Yoshio Takahashi	Japan	Yoshihiko Tazawa	Japan
Hiroshi Takahata	Japan	Akiko Tazima	Japan
Sayuri Takahira	Japan	Katsuro Tejima	Japan
Yukitaka Takama	Japan	Bunji Terada	Japan
Mahiko Takamura	Japan	Mikiharu Terada	Japan
Setsuko Takano	Japan	Atsuko Tezuka	Japan
Yoshiko Takano	Japan	Kazuyori Thunehiro	Japan
Hiroshi Takao	Japan	Hisao Todoroki	Japan
Sigeko Tohata	Japan	Kenji Ueno	Japan
Osamu Toki	Japan	Miho Ueno	Japan
Akira Tokinaga	Japan	Yasuhiro Ueno	Japan
Jun-ichi Tokuda	Japan	Yoshiaki Ueno	Japan
Shigeyuki Tokutake	Japan	Tsuneo Uetake	Japan
Naozou Tomioka	Japan	Masatsugu Uewaki	Japan

Koichi N. Tomita	Japan	Akiko Ujiie	Japan
Tohru Tomitake	Japan	Michihisa Ukon	Japan
Miho Tomoda	Japan	Kazumi Ukyou	Japan
Rie Tomoda	Japan	Hideyuki Umeda	Japan
Hiroshi Tomokawa	Japan	Yoshio Umeno	Japan
Humihiko Tomura	Japan	Hironobu Urabe	Japan
Makoto Tonegawa	Japan	Tohsuke Urabe	Japan
Norio Torigoe	Japan	Toshio Urata	Japan
Toshitaka Toyonari	Japan	Masataka Usui	Japan
Saburou Tsubakihara	Japan	Kenichi Uzuki	Japan
Akihito Tsuboi	Japan	Hiroshi Wada	Japan
Takehiro Tsubokawa	Japan	Masayo Wada	Japan
Kozo Tsubota	Japan	Shinya Wada	Japan
Toshimi Tsuchiya	Japan	Toshiko Wada	Japan
Ei Tsuda	Japan	Tosio Wada	Japan
Hiroko Tsuji	Japan	Katsutoshi Wakabayashi	Japan
Kumiko Tsukahara	Japan	Kazumi Wakazawa	Japan
Keiko Tsukamoto	Japan	Kimio Watanabe	Japan
Kuniki Tsukamoto	Japan	Michiko Watanabe	Japan
Katsumi Tsuno	Japan	Miho Watanabe	Japan
Ryou Tsunoi	Japan	Nobuki Watanabe	Japan
Yukio Tsurumi	Japan	Shin Watanabe	Japan
Shigeru Tsuyuki	Japan	Tad Watanabe	Japan
Toru Tundna	Japan	Yukio Watanabe	Japan
Hirokazu Uchida	Japan	Toshiaki Yabe	Japan
Masayuki Uchimura	Japan	Hiroshi Yadohisa	Japan
Hiroko Uchino	Japan	Akio Yajima	Japan
Hirohumi Uda	Japan	Atsushi Yamada	Japan
Atsumi Ueda	Japan	Norihiko Yamada	Japan
Masaya Ueda	Japan	Chisato Yamaguchi	Japan
Yoshinori Uede	Japan	Takeshi Yamaguchi	Japan
Wataru Uegaki	Japan	Tetsu Yamaguchi	Japan
Mutsunori Uehara	Japan	Tomoko Yamaguchi	Japan
Tetsuro Uemura	Japan	Minatsu Yamaji	Japan
Yasuo Yamamori	Japan	Hajime Yoshida	Japan
Hideki Yamamoto	Japan	Hiroyuki Yoshida	Japan
Hiroyuki Yamamoto	Japan	Kaori Yoshida	Japan
Keigo Yamamoto	Japan	Machiko Yoshida	Japan

Shinya Yamamoto	Japan	Minoru Yoshida	Japan
Shuichi Yamamoto	Japan	Takeshi Yoshida	Japan
Tamae Yamamoto	Japan	Yuji Yoshihashi	Japan
Tooru Yamamoto	Japan	Shigeo Yoshikawa	Japan
Yuji Yamamura	Japan	Yukio Yoshikawa	Japan
Kazuhito Yamanaka	Japan	Takaharu Yoshimachi	Japan
Toyoko Yamanoshita	Japan	Isao Yoshimura	Japan
Hiroshi Yamasaki	Japan	Satoru Yoshimura	Japan
Mami Yamashina	Japan	Akio Yoshioka	Japan
Shiko Yamashina	Japan	Akira Yoshioka	Japan
Akira Yamashita	Japan	Nozomi Yoshisako	Japan
Hajime Yamashita	Japan	Mitsuo Yoshizawa	Japan
Mariko Yamauchi	Japan	Yoshiaki Yuikawa	Japan
Hiroyasu Yamazaki	Japan	Kyung Yoon Chang	Korea
Koji Yamazaki	Japan	Young Han Choe	Korea
Yuko Yamazaki	Japan	Sang Sook Choi-Koh	Korea
Hiroko Yanaba	Japan	Jong-Suk Chu	Korea
Ayako Yanagihashi	Japan	Inki Han	Korea
Akira Yanagimoto	Japan	Sunwook Hwang	Korea
Ikkyu Yanagimoto	Japan	Doo-Young Jeong	Korea
Shigekazu Yanagimoto	Japan	Mee-Kwang Kang	Korea
Tomoko Yanagimoto	Japan	Yun Soo Kang	Korea
Hiroshi Yanai	Japan	Jonghae Keum	Korea
Michiko Yanai	Japan	Boo Yoon Kim	Korea
Takehiko Yanase	Japan	Hwa Soo Kim	Korea
Kazuyuki Yano	Japan	Nam Hee Kim	Korea
Shinichi Yasutomi	Japan	Sung Sook Kim	Korea
Yasuhiro Yoko	Japan	Yangwoon Kim	Korea
Kiyoshi Yokochi	Japan	Yong Dae Kim	Korea
Takeo Yokonuma	Japan	Young Kuk Kim	Korea
Katsuhiko Yokosawa	Japan	HooKyoung Ko	Korea
Atsuki Yokota	Japan	Minho Koh	Korea
Atsuko Yokoyama	Japan	Kwang Jo Koo	Korea
Hinoto Yonemitsu	Japan	Oh Nam Kwon	Korea
Akihiro Yoshida	Japan	Byung-Soo Lee	Korea
Eiko Yoshida	Japan	Jisung Lee	Korea
Kang Sup Lee	Korea	Gomez Rosalba Lopez	Mexico
Kwang Bok Lee	Korea	Teresa de Jesus Navarro	Mexico

Heechan Lew	Korea	Teresa Rojano	Mexico
Gwisoo Na	Korea	Carlos Rondero	Mexico
Baehun Park	Korea	Maria Trigueros	Mexico
Han Shick Park	Korea	Arthur Bakker	Netherlands
Kyung Mee Park	Korea	Nina Boswinkel	Netherlands
Younghoon Park	Korea	Maarten Dolk	Netherlands
Young Yzk Rhim	Korea	Koeno P. E. Gravemeijer	Netherlands
Kyeong Hah Roh	Korea	Kees Hoogland	Netherlands
Hyunyong Shin	Korea	Sieb Kemme	Netherlands
Youngjun Song	Korea	Martin Kindt	Netherlands
Byun Uyl-Hyo	Korea	Wim Kleijne	Netherlands
Kyu-Han Yang	Korea	Douwe Kok	Netherlands
Jae-Hoon Yim	Korea	Marjolein Kool	Netherlands
Ok Young Yoon	Korea	Michel Lokhorst	Netherlands
Abdulkhudhur A. Ali	Kuwait	Jan Van Maanen	Netherlands
Husain Ali Alkandary	Kuwait	Wim Matthijsse	Netherlands
Hassan N. Almohanna	Kuwait	Marja Meeder	Netherlands
Ali Abdulla Alsarraf	Kuwait	Julie Menne	Netherlands
Agnis Andzans	Latvia	Frans Moerlands	Netherlands
Liga Ramana	Latvia	Henk N. Schuring	Netherlands
Murad Eid Jurdak	Lebanon	Harm Jan Smid	Netherlands
Iman Mohammed Osta	Lebanon	Lambrecht Spijkerboer	Netherlands
Robert Dieschbourg	Luxembourg	Donald Staal	Netherlands
Marie Monique Klopp	Luxembourg	Heuvel-Panhuizen Marja	Netherlands
Rene Michel Klopp	Luxembourg	Ivanka Van Dijk	Netherlands
Rosihan M. Ali	Malaysia	Jan Vandenbrink	Netherlands
Munirah Ghazali	Malaysia	Henk Vanderkooij	Netherlands
Noraini Idris	Malaysia	Heleen B. Verhage	Netherlands
Siew-Eng Lee	Malaysia	Anders Vink	Netherlands
Chap Sam Lim	Malaysia	Pauline Vos	Netherlands
Mohd Sahar Sauian	Malaysia	Pieter Van Der Zwaart	Netherlands
Afza Shafie	Malaysia	Maurice Starck	New Caledonia
Wan F. W. Ahmad	Malaysia	Anne Carolyn Abbott	New Zealand
Silvia Alatorre	Mexico	Glenda J Anthony	New Zealand
P. E. Balderas-Canas	Mexico	Bill Barton	New Zealand
Ricardo Cantoral	Mexico	Andrew J. C. Begg	New Zealand
Crisologo Dolores	Mexico	C. P. P. Chamdimba	New Zealand
Rosa Maria Farfan	Mexico	Megan June Clark	New Zealand

Roger Harvey	New Zealand	Soledad Asuncion Ulep	Philippines
Derek Allan Holton	New Zealand	Luz Dara Igos Valconcha	Philippines
Anne-Marie Hutton	New Zealand	Catherine P. Vistro-Yu	Philippines
Sergiy Klymchuk	New Zealand	Ewa Lakoma	Poland
Dennis F. McKenzie	New Zealand	Dabrowski M	Poland
Tamsin Jillian Meaney	New Zealand	Zbigniew Semadeni	Poland
Peter John Watson	New Zealand	Zawadowski Wackek	Poland
Anne Berit Fuglestad	Norway	Maria Cristina Almeida	Portugal
Liv Sissel Gronmo	Norway	Carolina F. Carvalho	Portugal
Ingvill Merete Holden	Norway	M. A.P-Silva Cesar	Portugal
Einar Jahr	Norway	António M. Domingos	Portugal
Marit Johnsen-Høines	Norway	Elsa Maria Fernandes	Portugal
Nora Linden	Norway	Elisa M. V. G. Figueira	Portugal
Johan Nygaard	Norway	Leonor Filipe	Portugal
Bo Rosen	Norway	Ana Lopes	Portugal
Bjørg Kristin Selvik	Norway	José Manuel Matos	Portugal
Bjorn Smestad	Norway	Joao P. Ponte	Portugal
Harald Solbakken	Norway	Maria Lurdes Serrazina	Portugal
Rolf Venheim	Norway	Pedro Figueira Torres	Portugal
Neela Sukthankar	PNG	Vasile Berinde	Romania
Emi Hisaoka	Paraguay	Florence Mihaela Singer	Romania
Julia Armas	Peru	Nikolai P. Dolbilin	Russia
Irma L. Barandiaran	Peru	Valery A Gusev	Russia
Gina M. Mantero	Peru	Oleg A. Ivanov	Russia
Muzante Mauro Enrique	Peru	Alexander P. Karp	Russia
Victoria Otarola	Peru	Nikolai N. Konstantinov	Russia
Luis Palomares	Peru	Serguey N. Pozdnyakov	Russia
Herminia J. Autajay	Philippines	Ildar S. Safuanov	Russia
Edna Gabriel Callanta	Philippines	Igor F. Sharygin	Russia
Justina M. Evangelista	Philippines	Huei Wuan Ee	Singapore
Rene Payad Felix	Philippines	Lianghuo Fan	Singapore
Florenda Lota Gallos	Philippines	Berinderjeet Kaur	Singapore
Kathy Aquino Josue	Philippines	Tiong-Kah Kong	Singapore
Lydia Mejia Landrito	Philippines	Peng Yee Lee	Singapore
Auxencia Alarcon Limjap	Philippines	Suat Khoh Lim-Teo	Singapore
Charita A Luna	Philippines	Swee Fong Ng	Singapore
Reginaldo Marcelo	Philippines	Ban Har Yeap	Singapore
Bienvenido Florendo	Philippines	Yeen Peng Yen	Singapore

Erlina Rosales Ronda	Philippines	Mária Berová	Slovakia
Reamar Eileen Rimando	Philippines	Tibor Marcinek	Slovakia
Edita Partova	Slovakia	Moses V. Zungu	Swaziland
Vlasta M. Kokol-Voljc	Slovenia	Bengt Ahlander	Sweden
Dushan Pagon	Slovenia	Lilian Irene Ahlm	Sweden
Milena Strnad	Slovenia	Lena Brita Alm	Sweden
Jill B. Adler	South Africa	Gunilla L. Bengtsson	Sweden
Iben Maj Christiansen	South Africa	Agneta M. Beskow	Sweden
Michael David De Villiers	South Africa	Maria Bjerneby Hall	Sweden
Cyril Julie	South Africa	Lars-Eric Arne Bjork	Sweden
Hanlie JC Murray	South Africa	Lisa A. C. E. Björklund	Sweden
Lynette Marilyn Rossouw	South Africa	Gerd Brandell	Sweden
Mokgoko Petrus Sebela	South Africa	Tor Per Evert Englund	Sweden
Mamokgethi Setati	South Africa	Lil Engstròn	Sweden
Jonathan Swanepoel	South Africa	Gert Gabrielsson	Sweden
Cornelis F. Vermeulen	South Africa	Barbro Grevholm	Sweden
Renuka Vithal	South Africa	Owe K. Kågesten	Sweden
Pedreira Mengotti Alicia	Spain	Katarina I. Kjellström	Sweden
Claudi Alsina	Spain	Inger Marie Larsson	Sweden
Javier Barrallo	Spain	Kerstin Larsson	Sweden
Francisco Bellot-Rosado	Spain	Anita Lindberg	Sweden
MaFrancisca Blanco	Spain	Lisbeth Monica Lindberg	Sweden
Carmen Burgues	Spain	Thomas Lingefjärd	Sweden
Vicente Cara	Spain	Leif Maerker	Sweden
Josefina Dexeus	Spain	Ebbe Möllehed	Sweden
Lourdes Figueiras	Spain	Lars Mouwitz	Sweden
Joaquin Giménez	Spain	Roland Enk Munther	Sweden
Carlos Gomez Bermudez	Spain	Ingemar Nilsson	Sweden
Nieves Gonzalez Alvarez	Spain	Gull-Maj Nordin	Sweden
Nuria Gorgorio	Spain	Gunilla Olofsson	Sweden
Chacon Inigo Jose Maria	Spain	Kristina Olstorpe	Sweden
Maria-Jesus Luelmo	Spain	Roland Olstorpe	Sweden
G. C. Mo Isolina	Spain	Sofia Olstorpe	Sweden
Olga Moro	Spain	Torulf Bo Palm	Sweden
Salvador Naya	Spain	Astrid B. Pettersson	Sweden
Raig Nuria Planas	Spain	Ingegerd M. Sellander	Sweden
Matilde Rios Fachal	Spain	Carl-Axel Sjöblom	Sweden
Maria del Carmen Rodr	Spain	Inger Slettenmark	Sweden

Sixto Romero	Spain	Håkan Svensson	Sweden
Jose Varela	Spain	Kyril Tintarev	Sweden
Hormes Antonio Viloria	Spain	Aldo Dalla Piazza	Switzerland
Jose R. Vizmanos	Spain	Serge Hazanov	Switzerland
Urs Kirchgraber	Switzerland	Lynn Churchman	UK
Margit Kopp	Switzerland	Diana Cicely Coben	UK
Elisabeth Moser Opitz	Switzerland	Fiona Jane Crooks	UK
Anthony Peiris	Switzerland	David Crowe	UK
John Barry Smith	Switzerland	Christopher James Day	UK
Saitong Amornwichet	Thailand	Colin Dixon	UK
Sakorn Boondao	Thailand	Bryan Robert Dye	UK
Maitree Inprasitha	Thailand	Julie-Ann S. Edwards	UK
Yuda Keratirags	Thailand	John Fauvel	UK
Supattra Pativisan	Thailand	Ruth Forrester	UK
Luddawan Pensupha	Thailand	Anthony David Gardiner	UK
Paramee Reankittiwat	Thailand	Simon Goodchild	UK
Siriporn Thipkong	Thailand	Jeffrey Alan Goodwin	UK
Suwattana Utairat	Thailand	C. W. K. Greiffenhagen	UK
Somchit	Thailand	Howard Groves	UK
Margaret Ann Bernard	Trinidad	Rosemary Anne Hafeez	UK
Sirinoglu Nuriye	Turkey	Christopher Haines	UK
Behiye Ubuz	Turkey	Kathleen Mary Hart	UK
George Larry Ekol	Uganda	Jeremy Hodgen	UK
Stephen John Abbott	UK	Rosalyn Margaret Hyde	UK
Jack Abramsky	UK	Susie Grayne Jameson	UK
Michael Askew	UK	Barbara Jaworski	UK
Dave Alan Baker	UK	Keith Jones	UK
Robert Hugh Barbour	UK	Lesley Gail Jones	UK
Gill Beeney	UK	Ramesh B. Kapadia	UK
Roger Beeney	UK	Susan Kelly	UK
Tamara Bibby	UK	Joseph Kyle	UK
Chris Bills	UK	Pamela Leon	UK
Elizabeth Janet Bills	UK	Stephen Lerman	UK
Craig Bishop	UK	John Ling	UK
Albert Brian Bolt	UK	Thomas Gunn Macintyre	UK
Rute Elizabete Borba	UK	Irene Fraser Mackay	UK
Mark Boylan	UK	Diana Mackie	UK
Richard Thomas Bridges	UK	Norrie Mckay	UK

Margaret Brown	UK	David Miller	UK
Roger G. Brown	UK	Josephine Miller	UK
David Noel Burghes	UK	Peter John Mitchell	UK
Hugh Burkhardt	UK	Heather Jane Morris	UK
Leone Burton	UK	James Robert Nicholson	UK
Douglas Cairns	UK	Nobuyoshi Nishizaka	UK
Naomi Norman	UK	Jerry Page Becker	USA
Terezinma Nunes	UK	Rick Billstein	USA
Nicholas Gerald O'Neil	UK	Roger Isaac Blanco	USA
Christopher Peter Ormell	UK	Carol Joyce Blumberg	USA
David Panther	UK	Jo Boaler	USA
Joyce Porteous	UK	Bruce Kevin Boehne	USA
Jenny S. Ramsden	UK	Alexander Bogomolny	USA
Peter Howard Ransom	UK	Raouf Boules	USA
William P. Richardson	UK	Jacqueline Kim Bowman	USA
Jim Ridgway	UK	Sadie Chavis Bragg	USA
Susan Elisabeth Sanders	UK	Mary Lynn Breyfogle	USA
Paul Scruton	UK	Sue Brown	USA
Jane Seaton	UK	Gail F Burrill	USA
Sue Shilton	UK	Jack Burrill	USA
P. Sivasubramaniam	UK	Jinfa Cai	USA
Jane Smith	UK	Patricia F. Campbell	USA
Valerie Ann Snowden	UK	David W Carraher	USA
Caroline Mary Starkey	UK	Robert Lee Carson	USA
Susan Anne Starkings	UK	Phyllis Victoria Caruth	USA
Ian Thompson	UK	Betty Jean Causey-Lee	USA
Geoff David Wake	UK	Ozlem Cezikturk	USA
Akiko Watanabe	UK	Ping-Tung Chang	USA
Jenni Anne Way	UK	Phyllis Zweig Chinn	USA
Dylan Wiliam	UK	Ann M. Chisko	USA
Derek Woodrow	UK	Lily E. Christ	USA
Ruslan Nicholas Motoryn	Ukraine	Marta Civil	USA
Tatyana A. Oleinik	Ukraine	Debra Susan Coggins	USA
Sergei Abramovich	USA	Paul Seth Cohen	USA
Mangho Ahuja	USA	Cynthia Larson Connell	USA
Angela Giglio Andrews	USA	Joan Alice Cotter	USA
Nina P. Arshavsky	USA	Lucille Croom	USA
James Clark Ashby	USA	Frances Rena Curcio	USA

Dorothy Ann Assad	USA	Beatriz Silva D'Ambrosio	USA
Ayoub Barsoum Ayoub	USA	Mark Davis	USA
Patricia Baggett	USA	Marsha J Davis	USA
Robert Nelson Baker	USA	Yolanda De La Cruz	USA
Deborah L. Ball	USA	Franklin D. Demana	USA
Hyman Bass	USA	Edwin Milton Dickey	USA
Carole Ann Bauer	USA	Mary Downton	USA
Susan Ruth Beal	USA	Ed Dubinsky	USA
Penelope H. Dunham	USA	Inchul Jung	USA
Susan K. Eddins	USA	Leslie Kahn	USA
John James Edgell, Jr.	USA	Lakshmi Kambampati	USA
Laurie D Edwards	USA	Constance Kazuko Kamii	USA
Wade Elliss, Jr.	USA	Gail Kaplan	USA
Mohamed Ahmed Eltom	USA	James J. Kaput	USA
Florence D. Fasanelli	USA	Karen Jo Kaul	USA
Shelley Kim Ferguson	USA	John Kenelly	USA
Joan E. Ferrini-Mundy	USA	Rebecca Jean Kessler	USA
Tom Ferrio	USA	Michael Kie Kestner	USA
William Finzer	USA	Regina D. Kiczek	USA
Linda Fisher	USA	Catherine Ann King	USA
Judith M Flowers	USA	Kate M. Kline	USA
Jan E Ford	USA	Hari P. Koirala	USA
Catherine T. Fosnot	USA	Roberta Koss	USA
T. G. Ganesh	USA	Stephen Alan Krevisky	USA
Maureen M. Gavin	USA	Jean Krusi	USA
Accamma George	USA	Carole B. LaCampagne	USA
Alice J. Gill	USA	Carol Ruth Langbort	USA
Lynda Bette Ginsburg	USA	Edward D. Laughbaum	USA
Paul E. Goldenberg	USA	Beth Ellen Lazerick	USA
Gerald A. Goldin	USA	Xiaodan Leng	USA
Cristina Gomez	USA	Bobbie Jean Leonard	USA
Jacqueline E. Goodloe	USA	William Leonard	USA
Daniel L. Goroff	USA	Inwon Hwang Leu	USA
Raymond P. Guzman	USA	Rachel Levy	USA
Duane Habecker	USA	Jianhua Li	USA
Brenda Hines Hammond	USA	Xuhui Li	USA
Delwyn L. Harnisch	USA	Sally Irene Lipsey	USA
Eric Woodson Hart	USA	Madeleine J. Long	USA

Larry L. Hatfield	USA	Martha H. Lowther	USA
Shandy Hauk	USA	Lynn Greene Mack	USA
M. Kathleen Heid	USA	Alison L. Mall	USA
Whit Hickman	USA	Michelle Manes	USA
Marie Hoover	USA	Myrna Manly	USA
Jackie F. Hurd	USA	Paul Richard Manning	USA
Nicholas Jackiw	USA	Pat Scott Mara	USA
Bill Jacob	USA	Jody Anne Martin	USA
Graham Alfred Jones	USA	Marilyn Elaine Mays	USA
Thomas William Judson	USA	Edward McClew	USA
Wilbur Mellema	USA	Lawrence Hoyt Shirley	USA
Denjse S. Mewborn	USA	Tod Shockey	USA
Karen Dee Michalowicz	USA	Martin Simon	USA
Carol Wickham Midgett	USA	Sara Brame Skinner	USA
Mary J. Mitchell	USA	Alexander Soifer	USA
Judith E. Mumme	USA	Megan Elizabeth Staples	USA
Catherine M. Murphy	USA	Lynn Arthur Steen	USA
Teri Jo Murphy	USA	Michelle Stephan	USA
Kenji Naito	USA	Michael Steuer	USA
Judy Summers O'Neal	USA	Lee V. Stiff	USA
Luis Ortiz-Franco	USA	Frances Stillman	USA
Warren Page	USA	Wei Sun	USA
Rene Parmar	USA	Carl T. Swanson	USA
Deborah S. Patonai	USA	Akihiko Takahashi	USA
Anne C. Patterson	USA	Daniel J. Teague	USA
Barbara Johnson Pence	USA	Denisse R. Thompson	USA
Blake E. Peterson	USA	DeAlwis Tilak	USA
A. Duane Porter	USA	Marie Pia Turini	USA
Bob Pospick	USA	Jerry Uhl	USA
Norma C. Presmeg	USA	Karen Usiskin	USA
Jack Price	USA	Zalman Usiskin	USA
Nancy J. Priselac	USA	Laura Ranae Van Zoest	USA
Carol Hotelling Qutub	USA	Joan Josephine Vas	USA
Chris Larson Rasmussen	USA	Carlos E. Vasco	USA
Steven Rasmussen	USA	Marjie Vittum-Jones	USA
Diane Resek	USA	Charlyn W. Walker	USA
K. Safford-Ramus	USA	William Thomas Ward	USA
Mark E. Saul	USA	Erik Michael Waterkotte	USA

Subhash C. Saxena	USA	Elizabeth P. Waycaster	USA
Richard Schaar	USA	Norman Lott Webb	USA
Milo Schield	USA	Matthew Weiss	USA
Deborah Schifter	USA	Lucy West	USA
Analucia D. Schliemann	USA	Dottie Whitlow	USA
Roberta Y. Schorr	USA	Nancy C. Whitman	USA
James Edward Schultz	USA	Ann McLeod Williams	USA
Nanette Marie Seago	USA	Beverly A. Williams	USA
Annie Selden	USA	Juana A. Wilson	USA
John Selden	USA	Patricia Simmons Wilson	USA
J. Michael Shaughnessy	USA	Mary Jean Winter	USA
Linda Jensen Sheffield	USA	Joseph M. Wisenbaker	USA
Tamae Wong	USA		
Susan S. Wood	USA		
Debra J. Woods	USA		
De Ting Wu	USA		
L. Eileen T. Wu	USA		
Erna Beth Yackel	USA		
Sharon K. Yamamoto	USA		
Rose Mary Zbiek	USA		
LingLing Zhang	USA		
Paul Zorn	USA		
Hugo Enrique Parra	Venezuela		
Mui Huynh	Vietnam		
Indira Chacko	Zimbabwe		
David K. Jani Mtetwa	Zimbabwe		